Invisible Nation

Invisible Nation

HOW THE KURDS' QUEST FOR STATEHOOD IS SHAPING IRAQ AND THE MIDDLE EAST

Quil Lawrence

Walker & Company
OCN173240096
New York

Published by Walker Publishing Company, Inc., New York
Distributed to the trade by Macmillan

All papers used by Walker & Company are natural, recyclable products
made from wood grown in well-managed forests.
The manufacturing processes conform to the environmental regulations
of the country of origin.

LIBRARY OF CONGRESS CATALOGING-IN-PUBLICATION DATA

Lawrence, Quil.
Invisible nation : how the Kurds' quest for statehood is shaping Iraq
and the Middle East / Quil Lawrence.—1st U.S. ed.
p.   cm.
Includes bibliographical references and index.
ISBN 978-0-8027-1611-8 (alk. paper)
1. Kurds—Iraq—Politics and government—21st century. 2. Kurds—
Politics and government—21st century. 3. Iraq—Politics and
government—2003– 4. Middle East—Politics and government—21st
century. I. Title.

DS70.8.K8L39 2008
956.700491567—dc22

2008000142

Visit Walker & Company's Web site at www.walkerbooks.com

First U.S. edition 2008

1   3   5   7   9   10   8   6   4   2

Designed by Rachel Reiss

Typeset by Westchester Book Group
Printed in the United States of America by Quebecor World Fairfield

For Faiz and Marla

Contents

Black Sea

RUSSIA

Caucasus Mountains

GEORGIA
⊗Tbilisi

⊗Ankara

ARMENIA
Yerevan⊗

AZERBAIJAN

⊗Baku

TURKEY

Caspian
Sea

•Diyarbakir

KURDISTAN

Mediterranean Sea

•Mosul   •Erbil

•Tehran

SYRIA

•Kirkuk   •Sulimaniya

Zagros Mountains

LEBANON
Beirut⊗
        ⊗Damascus

Tigris

IRAN

ISRAEL
Tel Aviv•

⊗Baghdad

IRAQ

Karbala•

⊗Amman

Najaf•

Kut•

Euphrates •Nasr

JORDAN

Nasiriya•

Basra•

Um Qasr•

SAUDI ARABIA

Bussia•

⊗Kuwait City

0 Miles   100   200   300

KUWAIT

Red
Sea

0 Kilometers   300

Persian Gulf

© 2008 Jeffrey L. Ward

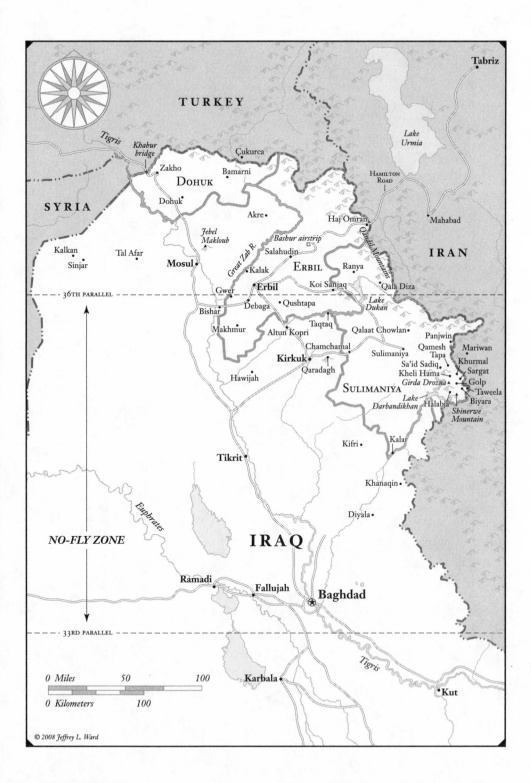

Acronyms

AKP	Justice and Development Party (Turkey)
CPA	Coalition Provisional Authority
GOI	Government of Iraq (pre–April 2003)
IMK	Islamic Movement of Kurdistan
INA	Iraqi National Accord
INC	Iraqi National Congress
ITF	Iraqi Turcoman Front
KDP	Kurdistan Democratic Party
KDPI	Kurdistan Democratic Party of Iran
KIU	Kurdistan Islamic Union
KRG	Kurdistan Regional Government
MKO	Mujahideen-e-Khalq Organization
OPC	Operation Provide Comfort
ORHA	Office of Reconstruction and Humanitarian Assistance
PKK	Kurdish Workers' Party
PUK	Patriotic Union of Kurdistan
SCIRI	Supreme Council for the Islamic Revolution in Iraq (since 2007 the Supreme Islamic Iraqi Council)

Cast of Characters

KURDS

Salah al-Din al-Ayubi ("Saladin")   United the Muslim world under his Ayubbid Caliphate in 1174 and conquered Jerusalem.

Sheikh Mahmoud Barzinji   Led two Kurdish rebellions against the British, in 1919 and 1922.

Sheikh Ahmed Barzani   Led the first uprisings in the Barzan areas of Kurdistan in 1932.

Kurdistan Democratic Party (KDP)

Mulla Mustafa Barzani   Led Kurdish rebellions from 1943 to 1975; founded the KDP in 1946.

Masoud Barzani   Mulla Mustafa's son; took over the KDP in 1975 and became the first president of the Kurdistan Regional Government (KRG) in 2005.

Nechirvan Idris Barzani   Masoud's nephew; first prime minister of the Kurdistan Regional Government.

Masrour Barzani   Masoud's son and chief of KDP security.

Sami Abd-al-Rahman   KDP commander who ran as an independent in the 1992 elections.

Hoshyar Zebari   KDP foreign envoy and Iraqi foreign minister 2003–present.

Fadhil Mirani   KDP liaison to General Jay Garner in 1991.

General Babakir Zebari   Head of the KDP military and later chief of the Iraqi Armed Forces.

Muhammad Ihsan   KDP operative with CIA coup attempts in the 1990s, and later KRG human rights minister.

Patriotic Union of Kurdistan (PUK)

Mam Jalal Talabani   Formed the PUK in 1975. Iraqi president 2005–present.

Ibrahim Ahmad   Kurdish intellectual and cofounder of the PUK.

Hero Ahmad Talabani   Ahmad's daughter, Talabani's wife, and Iraq's first lady 2005–present.

Bafel Talabani   Mam Jalal's son and PUK counterterrorism chief.

Qubad Talabani   Mam Jalal's son; PUK representative in Washington and then KRG representative to the United States.

Kosrat Rasul   PUK military leader and later vice president of the KRG.

Nawshirwan Mustafa   Cofounder of the PUK and deputy to Talabani; split in 2006 to form his own party.

Barham Salih   PUK representative in Washington and later deputy prime minister of Iraq.

"Mam" Rostam (Rostam Hamid Rahim)   PUK pesh merga leader in Kirkuk.

Ramadan Rashid   PUK underground resistance leader in Kirkuk.

Islamists

Sheikh Othman Abdulaziz and Ali Abdulaziz   Brothers from Halabja who founded the Islamic Movement of Kurdistan (IMK).

Ali Bapir   Leader of Komala Islami (Islamic Group), which splintered from the IMK in 2000.

Mullah Krekar (Najmaldin Faraj Ahmad)   Spiritual leader of Ansar al-Islam and a Kurd who fought in Afghanistan.

"Abu Wa'el"   An Iraqi Arab who allegedly tried to make contacts with Ansar al-Islam for Saddam Hussein's security services.

Independents

Mahmoud Othman   KDP leader with Mulla Mustafa Barzani; later independent Kurdish member of the Iraqi parliament.

Najmaldin Karim Mulla Mustafa Barzani's personal physician; later president of the Washington Kurdish Institute

Hussein Sinjari PUK liaison to General Jay Garner in 1991, then pro-democracy advocate.

OTHER IRAQIS

Ahmed Chalabi Secular Iraqi Arab exile and leader of the Iraqi National Congress (INC).

Abd Aziz al-Hakim Shi'ite Arab leader of the Supreme Council for the Islamic Revolution in Iraq (SCIRI).

Adel Abdul-Mahdi Member of SCIRI and Iraqi vice president 2005–present.

Ibrahim al-Ja'fari Head of the Shi'ite party Da'wa Islamiya (Islamic Call) and prime minister of Iraq in 2005.

Nuri al-Maliki Da'wa member and prime minister of Iraq 2006–present.

Ayad Allawi Secular Shi'ite, former Ba'athist, and founder of the Iraqi National Accord (INA); Iraqi prime minister from June 2003 to April 2004.

Sharif Ali bin al-Hussein Head of the Constitutional Monarchy Movement.

TURKS

Abdullah Öcalan ("Apo") Leader of the Kurdistan Workers' Party (PKK) 1974–present; imprisoned in Turkey since 1999.

Turgut Özal President of Turkey 1989–1993.

Abdullah Gül Turkish foreign minister 2003–7; elected president of Turkey in August 2007.

Recep Tayyip Erdoğan Prime minister of Turkey 2003–7.

Deniz Bölükbaşı Turkish diplomat and negotiator with the U.S. military in 2003.

General Yaşar Büyükanıt Chief of General Staff, Turkish Armed Forces 2006–present.

Murat Karayilan PKK military commander.

AMERICANS

Henry Kissinger Secretary of state and national security advisor to President Richard Nixon and President Gerald Ford.

Brent Scowcroft Kissinger's assistant and later national security advisor to presidents Ford and George H. W. Bush.

Peter Galbraith Democratic Senate staffer and later ambassador in the Clinton administration and occasional consultant to the KRG.

Bob Baer and Warren Marik CIA agents based in Kurdistan in the mid-1990s.

Lieutenant. General Jay Garner (ret.) Commander in Iraq of Operation Provide Comfort in 1991, and later director of the Office of Reconstruction and Humanitarian Assistance in Iraq (ORHA) April–May 2003.

Morton Abramowitz Ambassador to Turkey 1989–91.

Marc Grossman Ambassador to Turkey 1994–7; undersecretary of state for political affairs, 2001–5.

Tony Lake National security advisor to President Bill Clinton 1993–7.

George Tenet Director of Central Intelligence 1997–2004.

Bob Deutsch U.S. State Department advisor on Iraq 1995–7; deputy ambassador to Turkey 2002–5; deputy senior advisor on Iraq 2006–present.

Paul Wolfowitz Deputy secretary of defense 2001–5.

Douglas Feith Undersecretary of defense for policy planning 2001–5.

L. Paul Bremer America's postinvasion presidential envoy and director of the Coalition Provisional Authority May 2003–June 2004.

General David Petraeus Led the 101st Airborne Division in Mosul 2003–4; supervised the training of Iraqi security forces in Baghdad 2004–5; commanding general of U.S. forces in Iraq 2007–present.

John D. Negroponte U.S. ambassador to Iraq July 2004–February 2005.

James Jeffrey Deputy to Negroponte.

Zalmay Khalilzad White House envoy to the Iraqi opposition 2002–3, ambassador to Iraq 2005–6.

Ryan Crocker U.S. ambassador to Iraq 2006–present.

The Prodigal Republic (Mr. Talabani Goes to Washington)

ON SEPTEMBER 13, 2005, JALAL TALABANI, the first democratically elected president of Iraq, walked beside President George W. Bush past an honor guard into the East Room of the White House. Talabani might have marveled that when he had started his struggle against the government of Iraq, Harry Truman strode these same halls. Now the septuagenarian Kurdish guerrilla, in a tailored suit and silk tie, came to represent Baghdad in Washington and at the U.N. General Assembly. Bush introduced him to the assembled press corps, and Mr. Talabani delivered the first of two messages he carried to the White House.

"Thank you. Thank you, Mr. President, for your kind remarks. It is honor for me to stand here today as a representative of free Iraq. In the name of the Iraqi people, I say to you, Mr. President, and to the glorious American people, thank you, thank you, thank you," Talabani said in his near-perfect English.

The two men could not be more different. Fit and trim, Bush kept a constant laddish grin, displaying the sheer confidence that had carried him through his entire presidency. Talabani, laboring under the weight he had gained since he stopped running around mountains, wore a more bemused smile under his white mustache. Bush was born in 1946, the same year a teenage Talabani joined a student underground resistance against

Iraq's monarchy. By the time Bush went away to boarding school, Talabani was an important lieutenant in the guerrilla war against Baghdad that
would consume the next four decades of his life. Improbably, both men
were presidents now and they needed each other badly. Talabani wanted
to make sure that America would finish the job it started in Iraq, after two
years of bumbling occupation. Bush desperately wanted someone from
Iraq to do what Talabani had just done—thank him and assure him that
the Iraq invasion was not a historic blunder.

Talabani gave his gratitude without guile; the people who supported
his presidency truly felt indebted to America. Not Arab Iraqis, whose affection for the United States by that time had disintegrated along with
their own sense of security in cities like Baghdad, Mosul, and Basra.
Rather, Talabani spoke sincerely on behalf of the millions of Kurds in the
north of Iraq, for whom America still seemed a friend and a liberator. The
Kurds had turned out in great numbers on Iraq's Election Day and supported the American agenda as a block. And Talabani's second message
went directly to them, without President Bush even noticing.

Used to fielding questions in four languages, Talabani called on a journalist from Al Arabiya satellite news. After the exchange in Arabic, Bush
quipped, "I'm not sure if I agree or not." The Washington correspondents laughed. They thought it even funnier a few moments later when
Bush yielded the last question to his guest. Talabani picked an older-
looking reporter from the Voice of America and then feigned mild surprise when the question came not in English or Arabic, but Kurdish.
Talabani begged President Bush's indulgence.

"Yes, answer his question—perfect," Bush said with mock exasperation,
oblivious to the history being made. He let Talabani finish and without waiting for a translation, said, "On that cheery note, the press conference is over."

Bush ushered Talabani back out of the hall, between two tall rows of
flags, American and Iraqi. But Kurds all over the world were cheering.
The reporter, an old friend of Talabani's, had asked a question about the
United Nations, but that didn't matter. After a century of struggle, a head
of state had spoken Kurdish in the White House. Jalal Talabani had
planted the flag of Kurdistan in Washington, D.C.

SADDAM HUSSEIN'S REGIME ended for most on April 9, 2003, when American soldiers used a tank retriever to pull down his likeness in Baghdad's

Firdus Square. For millions of ethnic Kurds in northern Iraq, the regime ended the following day, when they pulled down a similar statue in the northern city of Kirkuk. The difference was that the Kurds pulled down the statue by themselves, without an American soldier in sight. From that day on, the history of Iraq and of its northern Kurdish zone diverged like alternate realities—one a sort of dream, the other a nightmare. Americans now sit transfixed by their entanglement in the horrible civil war unfolding in Arab Iraq, but they scarcely notice that Iraqi Kurdistan is slowly realizing all of America's stated goals for the region.

The Kurds are the largest ethnic group on earth that has no homeland. When European powers shared out the Ottoman Empire after World War I, they promised but never delivered a state to the millions of Kurds living around the borders of Turkey, Iran, Iraq, and Syria. Today they might number more than twenty-five million, but a precise figure is impossible to calculate, because none of the four countries wants to fully recognize them. About four and a half million live inside what is now Iraq, which has been the cruelest host, the only country that ever subjected them to outright ethnic cleansing. Kurds are predominantly Sunni Muslims, although nationalism has generally overshadowed currents of religious fundamentalism—after all, their oppressors, the Arabs, the Persians, and the Turks, have always been Muslims as well.

As Iraq and the region brace for a monumental conflict between Shi'ite and Sunni Muslims, the Kurds have no natural side. During the dark days of Saddam Hussein, the Sunni Arab world never lifted a finger to protect them as co-religionists. The Shi'ites in Iran sheltered them at times, but always with a clear self-interest. Through a history that dates back to biblical times, Kurds have survived by compromising with greater powers, but it's no secret that they've always desired a country of their own. Several of their greatest leaders in the twentieth century turned to America, the land of freedom and self-determination, to aid them in reaching that goal. Each time American promises fell victim to political expediency, leaving the Kurds holding the bag. America's sad record of betraying the Kurds changed, however, through two accidents, made by two presidents named Bush.

The first accidental liberator of Kurdistan was President George H. W. Bush. At the outset of his 1991 Gulf War, Bush had no intention of becoming the protector of the Kurds—or the Iraqis, for that matter. Bush desperately wanted to keep the 1991 Gulf War short and neat. After restoring Kuwait's monarchy, he tried to put the Iraq djinn back in the bottle, but his rhetoric about freedom and a new world order sent a different message. Believing the American army was at their back, the Kurds and Shi'ite Arabs rose against the dictator. Fearful of empowering Iran and destabilizing the region, Bush told his half-million troops to remain behind their line in the sand. Once Saddam realized—to his amazement—that he had survived, he embarked on his last great wave of atrocities, slaughtering the rebels in the thousands.

Bush and his team of realists might have ignored the killings, but their own propaganda about human rights snared them. After declaiming to the world that Saddam had once "gassed his own people"—the Kurds—Bush couldn't abandon them completely. Along with France and Britain, the United States sponsored a tiny safe haven in northern Iraq, where a no-fly zone kept the Kurds safe from Saddam. It was the bare minimum, but enough. Bush had prepared the fertile ground, and the seed of modern Kurdistan sprouted.

The Kurdish safe haven was supposed to serve Washington's Iraq containment strategy, a launching pad for the harassment of Saddam Hussein. But there was an unintended consequence: one of the most successful nation-building projects in American history. The Kurds held elections, set up their own social services, and started educating their children in Kurdish, not Arabic. They banned the Iraqi flag and the currency with Saddam's face on it. It wasn't always pretty, but for the next dozen years Kurdish leaders stumbled their way toward political maturity. America's policy amounted to benign neglect, doing little more than patrolling at thirty-five thousand feet, but when the Kurds expanded their tiny safe zone across all of the ethnic Kurdish north, the American air support effectively expanded with them. Though the Kurds constantly pressured for more assistance, the laissez-faire approach may have served them in the long run, keeping them from developing a culture of dependency on Washington.

By early 2003, the Kurds had pushed the limits of shadow statehood as far as they could, living off blackmarket oil smuggling and whatever Saddam allowed the U.N. Oil-for-Food program to let through. Some aid organizations set up shop, but no foreign company considered investing in a country that might not be there in the morning. After half a generation in limbo, their fate wasn't clear until another accidental nation builder came along. President George W. Bush set out to finish the job his father had started, and again, unwittingly, he succeeded at a different task. The destruction of Saddam Hussein's regime and the collapse that followed left Kurdistan as the only fully functioning part of Iraq. The Kurds will never willingly go back—America has played midwife to a Kurdish homeland that cannot be unmade, save by catastrophe. That catastrophe could begin with American departure.

I MADE MY first trips to Iraq and Iraqi Kurdistan in the spring of 2000 as a freelance journalist, and have returned over the past eight years for the BBC. Despite many other assignments in the interim, I have been unable to turn away from either of the two histories unfolding in Iraq. Like anyone who knew Iraq under Saddam, I wished for the kind people I met to find freedom and happiness after he fell. Certainly I never dreamed that life could get worse than it had been under such a dictator. The joyful chaos of Iraq's liberation quickly wore away under the relentless daily defeats of civility and humanity. My trips there became a catalog of car bombs, simmering hatreds, and endless American missteps. At the scene of massacres, survivors cursed whatever evil force was determined to prod Iraqis into a fratricidal civil war, and then like players in a Greek tragedy, they rushed to fulfill that prophecy. Believers in the new Iraq felt their optimism crushed and their hearts broken—it would be dishonest not to count myself in their number.

With each disaster that befell Iraq, the Kurds took a step forward. On the day Iraq's army was abolished in May 2003, Kurdish leader Masoud Barzani, son of the Kurds' greatest rebel leader, attended a graduation ceremony for Kurdish military cadets. In the rest of Iraq the abolition of the army meant hundreds of thousands of angry, insulted, unemployed men on the streets. For Kurdistan it meant that their sixty thousand irregulars now ranked as the second largest military force inside the country (smaller than the U.S. military presence, but bigger than the British army contingent inside the coalition). As death squads terrorized Arab Iraqis into silent complicity, Kurdish civilians flooded their security forces with telephone tips about any suspicious activity. As the count of American soldiers killed in action approached four thousand, not a single one of them had been killed inside the Kurds' three provinces. Construction cranes sprouted across the skylines of Kurdish cities. Cement factories worked at capacity—they also filled the south's endless need for ugly concrete blast walls to surround government ministries and homes. Kurdistan inaugurated its own parliament, selected a cabinet, and ratified a regional constitution. New exploration for petroleum in the north began before Baghdad had even restored prewar levels of oil production.

Iraq's war started killing journalists and aid workers, and like most other outfits, the BBC limited its reporters' mobility. The golden year of reporting Iraq, when I could drive to Fallujah in my own car, ended in early 2004. From that point on, the only way to safely travel was to make the compromise of embedding with U.S. troops. When the roads became too dangerous to drive from the south, the Kurds opened up daily flights to Baghdad as well as Amman, Istanbul, and Frankfurt. As the Iraqi government went back to its arcane visa rules, the Kurdish officials simply stamped my American passport with a smile. At their airport as well as their border crossing from Turkey, the Kurds put up a banner reading "Welcome to Kurdistan." The second or third time I crossed under it, I realized that while my colleagues and I were chronicling the destruction of Iraq, we were witnessing the creation of Kurdistan.

Kurdistan has everything the Bush administration promised for Iraq. It's a Muslim state that is pro-democracy, pro-America, and even pro-Israel. So in a dearth of good news, why isn't the United States crowing about this one great achievement in Iraq? Because Kurdistan's success could be cataclysmic. Like no event since the 1948 creation of Israel, a declared Kurdish state within the borders of Iraq will unite the entire region in opposition, from the Black Sea to the Persian Gulf. National liberation is a zero-sum game, and Syria and Iran have already seen unprecedented disturbances by their own Kurdish populations, inspired by the freedom Kurds now enjoy inside Iraq. Most important, Turkey, America's NATO ally, has fought a bloody war against Kurdish separatists for decades. The Turks see an independent Kurdistan in Iraq as an existential threat and have promised to intervene if Kurdistan grows too strong. The Iraqi Kurds understand this better than anyone, and have been willing so far to limit themselves to virtual statehood. No force within Iraq can stop them at the moment, and the forces outside have been kept at bay by the presence of the American army.

When the Kurds offered their troops to aid the invading coalition in 2003, they thought for sure their luck had changed. After decades of betting on losers, it seemed the Kurds had finally hit the jackpot. But as Iraq's war becomes a regional conflagration, there's room for doubt. Iraq's Shi'ite Arab parties accept aid and influence from Iran. The Sunni Arabs can count on the same from the wealthy Gulf kingdoms. After their collaboration with Americans has marked them as traitors to other Iraqis, and as apostates to Islamic extremists, the Kurds now fear the United States is feeling in the dark for an exit.

Iraq may yet recover its footing and Baghdad take its rightful place as a peaceful, vibrant, and opulent Middle Eastern capital. If it does, the Kurds might enjoy an autonomous zone inside Iraq, contributing their diversity to Iraq's mosaic and enjoying the country's vast wealth of oil, land, and rivers. I hope for this outcome, because it would cost so many fewer lives than the other possibilities. Far more likely, the madness in Iraq will continue and the Kurdish zone will be pulled into the fray or overreach as battle lines are drawn. And then America will have to decide if its prodigal republic is worth saving. Some realists may see Kurdistan as the perfect location for a residual U.S. force in the region to stare down Iran and keep a hand in Iraq. Kurdistan is the only place in the region still welcoming the idea of an American base. True believers in promoting democracy may see Kurdistan as the best place in the region to nurture the seed of representative government. Kurdistan could then become an albatross around Washington's neck: the country it helped create and must defend.

More probably, political realists coming into Washington to clean up the mess will look at the Kurds the way the world powers always have, as a small, expendable player in their great game. I have never heard a moral argument against the Kurds' right to a homeland, but it's hard to imagine America is willing or able to embark on another moral crusade in Iraq, one with even less regional support than the invasion. Betraying the Kurds will likely be just part of the ugly price of escaping from Iraq, but the ramifications of throwing away America's most natural ally in the region may be far greater than in the past.

This book draws on eight years of reporting on Iraq and the Kurds, as well as on the politicians in Washington whose decisions carry such heavy consequences so far away. It's inevitable that my perspective has been skewed by the many months of hospitality offered to me by Kurds, but this book is not intended to push their agenda. Rather, I hope it can help explain the vital role the Kurds play in the drama unfolding in this new, volatile Middle East. More than anywhere this understanding is needed in America—the country that accidentally enabled Kurdistan's creation and could just as carelessly cast it to the winds.

CHAPTER ONE

The Stolen Sheath

I am a bare dagger!
My Motherland is a stolen sheath.
Don't think I am bloodthirsty.
Go; find fault with the one
Who unsheathed me.

"THE DAGGER," BY KURDISH
POET ABDULLAH PASHEW

KURDISTAN WOULD SURELY BE A POWERFUL and recognizable country to-day had its most famous son not been stolen away by a higher calling.

In the first half of the twelfth century, in the Mesopotamian city of Tikrit, the greatest Muslim warrior in recorded history was born to a family of soldiers. He would live to unite the lands of Islam and drive the Christian crusaders out of Jerusalem, and reign over his empire with tolerance and generosity. In keeping with their luckless history, no one seems to remember that Saladin was a Kurd.

Salah al-Din al-Ayubi, "Saladin," followed in the footsteps of his uncle to become a soldier, then as now, an esteemed profession among Kurds.[1] Through a combination of bravery on the battlefield and a genius for picking his battles, Saladin established the Ayubbid Caliphate in 1171 and ruled Egypt, Syria, and parts of Iraq. His conquest ended the divisions inside the Muslim kingdom, which had allowed the crusader army to enter and brutally sack Jerusalem eighty years earlier. Knowing his enemy well, he taunted the Christian Knights' chivalry until they foolishly marched through a night without water and met his mujahideen* at the battle of Hattin in 1187. Saladin burned the parched fields around the infidels and then attacked once the sun rose hot behind his charging cavalry. But Saladin also bested many of the knights when it came to their own sense of honor and chivalry. Jews, Christians, and Armenians living in Jerusalem remember his conquest for its fair-minded generosity, a stark contrast from the carnage inflicted by the crusaders upon anyone who wouldn't accept their faith.

Saladin stepped into the realm of romantic legend when the Christians tried to take back the Holy Land in the third Crusade, led by England's King Richard the Lionheart. Facing the undisputed greatest fighter of the age, Saladin again managed to stretch Richard's forces out until they found the countryside around Jerusalem barren of fuel or forage, the wells poisoned. In no condition to do battle, Richard's crusaders retreated fitfully. In the last battle of the crusader withdrawal, Saladin watched from a hillside as the Christian king fought off a vastly superior force, personally dispatching dozens of foes. When Richard somehow became unhorsed, Saladin couldn't bear to see his noble opponent simply trampled down. The sultan sent two of his own best horses down and made them a gift to the king in the middle of the battle. Richard and his men were treated with generosity in defeat, and Saladin signed a treaty allowing Christians the right of pilgrimage.

Within a century of his death in 1193, even the West had canonized Saladin; Dante wrote him a place with the saintly pagans in Limbo. Of all those afforded a spot in Christian heaven's waiting room, Saladin was the only Muslim—and of course, the only Kurd.

Modern Kurds are both possessive of their ancient hero and emphatically disdainful. On one of my first visits to the city named for him, Salahudin in northern Iraq, I assumed the identity of the statue in the center of town. Trying to impress my host, I asked about the Kurds' hero. He saw right through my pandering and informed me that the statue was not Saladin, but a more recent Kurdish poet.

---

* It's hard not to note the near synonymy of the words "crusade" and "jihad." In their home contexts, both words mean a personal moral struggle or a military campaign. Both "crusaders" and "mujahideen" have at different times in history found religious justification to perpetrate mass murder.

"We do not like Saladin," he said coldly.

Saladin never proclaimed himself a Kurd. He fought for Islam and did no special favors to the Kurds in his kingdom, even when he was the most powerful man on earth. His best fighters often hailed from his homeland, and he trusted Kurdish warriors to lead troops and sometimes police his Turkish and Arab troops from looting too much after victory, though tensions existed between the races even then.[2] Saladin could have made the Kurds a famous empire like the Persians or Ottomans, but instead he fought for God, leaving his people invisible.

My host said that he admired Saladin simply for being successful and didn't think it fair to blame the ancient conqueror for the Kurds' modern-day condition. Saladin makes an important figure in today's clash-of-civilizations debate. Mainstream Muslims celebrate the conqueror as the best example of enlightened Islamic rule. Al-Qa'ida supporters also claim Saladin as a hero for driving out nonbelievers and establishing a caliphate, and also for his most barbaric act: beheading all the knights he captured from the orders of the Templars and Hospitalers (Saladin called them incurable cults that would endlessly make war in the Holy Land). The same so-called jihad Web sites declare that the modern-day Kurds are nothing more than American and Zionist tools.

Saladin's unified front, from Cairo to Gaza to Jerusalem, Damascus, and Baghdad, is still the envy of Arab leaders, and over the centuries many have tried to claim his mantle. The most galling appropriator of Saladin was the Kurds' twentieth-century nemesis, Saddam Hussein. Also born in Tikrit, Saddam tried to convince the Arab world that he was the next Saladin, returning to repel the Western hordes, as well as the Persians.

Still, Kurds are loath to give up such a local boy made good. Each time Saladin surfaces in a novel, video game, or Hollywood movie, the Kurdish Web sites light up with passionate lectures on his Kurdishness.* When *Time* chose Saladin as one of its "people of the millennium" in 1999, Kurdish nationalists beamed with pride. But they grit their teeth each time they rise to claim Saladin, bracing for the inevitable response: "What's a Kurd?"

---

* A British paper appreciated Ridley Scott's 2005 film *Kingdom of Heaven* for its accurate, even overly generous, portrayal of the Muslim caliph. The reviewer gushed that Saladin was "played by that wonderful Syrian actor Ghassan Massoud—and thank God the Arabs in the film are played by Arabs."

Kurds are physically fairer than Arabs, and many have angular features and some have blue eyes. But it's not always possible to tell them apart from Arabs, Turks, or Persians by appearance. Numerous stories of smuggling and escape involve Kurds not realizing that they are in a taxi full of other Kurds until they hear a few words in their native tongue. It may be easiest to say a Kurd is any native speaker of Kurdish (further complicated by the fact that there are at least four distinct dialects). Kurds are mostly Sunni Muslims, with a small Shi'ite minority, as well as a number of Jewish Kurds who now live in Israel, but they celebrate some Zoroastrian holidays like their springtime new year, Newroz. Religious minorities have a long history in Kurdish land, and early records after Muslim conquest gave the impression that Kurds weren't following Islam to the letter. Tribal loyalty has often trumped religion, and tribal sheikhs have often doubled as religious leaders.[3] This may explain a saying in the region that the "Kurds are only Muslims when compared to infidels." Women are rarely veiled, and it's not a taboo for a woman to receive a visitor in her home without her husband or father there. Kurdistan has several storied female leaders, and in the more liberal city of Sulimaniya there is even a unit of women soldiers that saw combat in the 1990s.*

KURDISH ORIGINS ARE unclear. Most of their creation myths involve a lost tribe being driven into the mountains, either fleeing from a child-eating giant or from King Solomon's harem after being sired there by djinns.[4] Many historians trace the Kurds back to the Medes, an Indo-European people who established an empire around the sixth century B.C. This links the Kurds with the magi who attended Jesus's birth, and some Christian missionaries travel to northern Iraq with a bilingual booklet called *The Kurds in the Bible*, which they claim is used for English instruction.[5] Early notices of the Kurds included mostly complaints that traveling through Kurdistan was dangerous because of local brigandry—and this from such authorities on the subject as the Mongol emperors. In several ancient

---

* From a personal perspective, the mellow attitude about religion has always made Kurdistan an easier place for Western visitors, with little fear of making a mortally offensive breach of etiquette. On my first day in the Kurdish city of Sulimaniya, whiskey was served with lunch, and it was not only for my (delighted) consumption.

languages of the region, *Kurd* is close to the word meaning "strong" or "warlike."[6] Over the centuries the Kurds have seemed to excel at rebellion, highway robbery, and general unruliness.

For several thousand years the Kurds have inhabited the area that now encompasses southeastern Turkey, northwest Iran, northern Iraq, and the eastern tip of Syria. Iraqi Kurdistan includes the provinces of Dohuk, Erbil, and Sulimaniya, each with an eponymous capital city. Maps of this "Greater Kurdistan" sell like hotcakes in the bazaars of northern Iraq, showing a territory spanning from Armenia to the Mediterranean. In fact, the Kurds could hardly be called a nation during the centuries leading up to the Ottoman Empire, though many prominent Kurdish chieftains rose and fell, often soldiers in the pay of passing conquerors. Kurdistan is most noticeable through the 1500s as the battlefield between the Turks and Persians. But nobody much cared to exactly define the borders of Kurdistan until oil was discovered in the Ottoman province of Mosul, and by that time the Europeans were making the maps.

The turn of the twentieth century found Kurdistan in disarray after famines and massacres. In its last throes, the Ottoman Empire employed Kurdish soldiers as cannon fodder against the Russian army. The same Kurdish tribesmen were instruments of the Turkish genocide against the Armenians in 1915, in which a million men, women, and children were slaughtered.* The Kurds hardly escaped the terror of the times, though, losing perhaps eight hundred thousand people to World War I and its repercussions.[7] A famine in 1917 is reported to have killed 70 percent of the city of Sulimaniya.[8] As the Kurds reeled from their ill-use by greater powers, the French and British were taking a carving knife to the Middle East—their spoils after winning the Great War. The British claimed Mesopotamia, then the bottom two thirds of what is now Iraq. Upon consideration they took the top third as well—then the Ottoman province of Mosul—for its strategic foothills. Their decision seemed all the wiser when the oil fields in the city of Kirkuk began to produce enough black gold to make the entire new country rich.[9]

The Kurds, puzzled to find themselves in a country called Iraq, pinned their hopes on the president of the United States, in what would become

---

* *Genocide* is a small word to describe so much suffering, and this brief treatment given to the Kurds' involvement in the attempt to eliminate the Armenians is in no way meant to minimize it.

a regrettable habit. Woodrow Wilson declared a new age of self-determination; his fourteen points for world peace became a holy document for the Kurds. In 1920 their promised independence was delivered in the French city of Sèvres, which, later historians pointed out wryly, was known for fine china that is particularly easy to break.[10] The Allies forced the Treaty of Sèvres on the Ottoman Empire, explicitly giving the Kurds the right to form a country and include with it the Kurds from Mosul province. The Treaty of Sèvres was the first time the Kurds had seen their names in print on an international document, and to this day it remains something like a Dead Sea scroll for Kurdish nationalists.

But the treaty was stillborn. A visionary Turkish soldier by the name of Mustapha Kemal, later known as Atatürk, was determined to claw together a country from the remnants of the Ottoman Empire. Though a secularist, Atatürk clung to the Muslim identity of Turkey to defend it against the clear Christian threats in the region, Greece and Armenia, and he also saw any ethnic division as detrimental to Turkey. Atatürk knew that Europe was ruined and bankrupt from the war and had no stomach to fight for the romantic notions of self-determination in the Treaty of Sèvres, which had been signed by a puppet government in Istanbul. The Treaty of Lausanne superseded it in 1923, establishing modern Turkey and leaving Kurdistan divided and invisible.[11] The Turkish state continued without mentioning the Kurds for most of the century, claiming that the millions of people in the southeast were "mountain Turks who have forgotten their language."*

The British, meanwhile, were trying to get a handle on the new country they'd created: Iraq. Then as now, the country was around 60 percent Shi'ite Arabs, 20 percent Sunni Arabs, and 15 to 20 percent Sunni Arab Kurds, with minority ethnic Turcomans, Chaldo Assyrians, and Yazidis filling in a 5 percent margin. Winston Churchill, in charge of the Middle East, didn't seem opposed to the idea of Kurdish independence. The deputy head of the British Colonial Office, Arnold Wilson, described the Kurds in Mosul province as a troublesome bunch "numbering half a million and [who] will never accept an Arab ruler."[12] But his boss, Sir Percy

---

* Kurds love to tell the story of how the Turks protested to Egyptian Gamal Abdel Nasser when he began broadcasting some nationalist radio programs in Kurdish. Flirting with the Kurdish nationalists, Nasser responded that since there were no Kurds in Turkey, this shouldn't offend them.

Cox, and the famous British Arabist Gertrude Bell wanted to keep the Kurdish territory in Iraq to help offset the Shi'ite Arab majority. The Kurds gave them no reason to think it would be easy—four British officers were murdered in Kurdistan during a few months in 1919.[13]

The most powerful man in Kurdistan at the time was a wild-eyed sheikh named Mahmoud Barzinji, who is seen in a few photographs at the front of other tribal leaders with a curved dagger, a turban, and a walrus mustache. The British tried putting the fox in charge of the henhouse by appointing him as their governor for the Kurdish north in December 1918, but he was no Saladin.[14] Sheikh Mahmoud began stacking the local administration with his family members, and within months he declared himself the king of Kurdistan, seizing the British treasury in Sulimaniya and raising his own flag. He intercepted British couriers and cut telegraph lines. A British political officer caught wind of the rebellion and managed to flee south with the news.[15] The British description of Mahmoud was entirely pejorative—he was said to be an animal, a thief, a cruel and unpredictable tyrant. But Arnold Wilson, upon meeting the sheikh in Sulimaniya, described a man who quoted President Woodrow Wilson's fourteen points verbatim and wore a Kurdish copy of the Treaty of Sèvres, with pages from the Koran, like a talisman wrapped around his arm.[16]

As the British marched north to put down the rebellion, they met surprisingly stiff resistance. Sheikh Mahmoud first turned the British back at Tasluja Pass—one of the same mountain walls that would keep the Iraqi army at bay later in the century. His early victory made Mahmoud overconfident, and the British 18th Division scaled the cliffs of Bazyan and surrounded him. He was sentenced to death, but then spared, since he had not executed his captured British officers. They exiled him to India instead.[17]

The British occupation of Iraq can begin to sound uncomfortably familiar to an American one in the twenty-first century, with Kurdistan substituted as the troublesome Anbar province of Ramadi and Fallujah. The British tried once again to co-opt the locals and brought Sheikh Mahmoud back in 1922. Within months he had declared himself king again.[18] This time the British put him down with Sikh troops transported to the area by plane. This was a military innovation at the time,[19] and not the only one the British discovered between their world wars.

"I am strongly in favor of using poisoned gas against uncivilised tribes [to] spread a lively terror," was the judgment of Winston Churchill at the

time. Gas was used to quell Arab rebellions in the south, and aerial bombardment employed against the Kurds in the north.* When the British
had imposed King Faisal as the ruler of Iraq in 1921, the Kurdish city of
Sulimaniya boycotted the referendum on his rule, and the city of Kirkuk
was the only significant no-vote across the country.[20] Sheikh Mahmoud
was only one of many Kurdish troublemakers, and his people demonstrated that they weren't quite ready to get behind a unified nationalist
struggle. After a brief exile in Persia, Sheikh Mahmoud submitted to the
British government in Iraq and slipped quietly back into his homeland in
1927. His uprisings were over, but the greatest of all the Kurdish rebels
was just learning his trade.

No GUERRILLA COMMANDER of the twentieth century—not Ernesto
"Che" Guevara, not Afghanistan's Ahmed Shah Masoud, not Sudan's
Dr. John Garang—fought more wars over more years than Mulla Mustafa
Barzani. He may also hold the dubious record for the number of countries he took aid from over the decades: the Soviets, the government in
Baghdad, the shah of Iran, the Israelis, the Jordanians, the British, and finally the Americans. Born in 1903, Barzani had a career that spanned
seven decades. He founded the Kurdistan Democratic Party (KDP) in
August 1946, which now flies its flag (and never the Iraqi one) all over the
Kurdish region of Iraq. Barzani did not aim to be the king of Kurdistan—
in fact he seemed originally motivated by a natural desire to protect his
tribe and his own small mountain region. But Barzani would grow to be-

---

* This may have been the first carpet bombing of civilians, predating the German
  Luftwaffe's 1937 bombardment of Guernica in the Spanish civil war. The full
  context of Churchill's memo is a bit more forgivable: "*I do not understand this
  squeamishness about the use of gas. We have definitely adopted the position at the Peace
  Conference of arguing in favour of the retention of gas as a permanent method of warfare. It is sheer affectation to lacerate a man with the poisonous fragment of a bursting
  shell and to boggle at making his eyes water by means of lachrymatory gas. I am strongly
  in favour of using poisoned gas against uncivilised tribes. The moral effect should be so
  good that the loss of life should be reduced to a minimum. It is not necessary to use only
  the most deadly gasses: gasses can be used which cause great inconvenience and would
  spread a lively terror and yet would leave no serious permanent effects on most of those
  affected.*" Winston S. Churchill, War Office departmental minute, May 12, 1919
  (Churchill papers: 16/16).

come the Kurds' first modern revolutionary, playing the cold war game pragmatically in the hope of gaining at least a measure of recognition for the invisible millions of Kurds. As important, he planted the seeds of the Kurds' national army, which would only triumph years after his death.

Barzani was stout and short, and even in old photographs it's easy to see the intense, piercing eyes that persuaded thousands of men to follow him into the mountains, usually against devastating odds. He was famous for his physical strength even into his seventies, and like Fidel Castro and Ahmed Shah Masoud, he easily seduced Western journalists into romantic press coverage. When he died in exile in 1979, even the Israeli Mossad held a fawning memorial service.[21]

Though it sounds like the stuff of Greek myth, Barzani could actually claim he was weaned in prison. Before he was three years old, his entire family was jailed in Mosul by the Ottomans. His grandfather, his father, and one older brother were hanged for different rebellions.[22] Mulla Mustafa got his own first taste of combat in his teens, leading several hundred men in Sheikh Mahmoud's first rebellion in 1919.[23] The name Barzani later became a curse in the mouth of Saddam Hussein, who rounded up and executed eight thousand Barzani tribesmen in the 1980s.

The first Barzani rebellion in the early 1930s was led not by Mulla Mustafa, but his older brother Sheikh Ahmad of Barzan. While "Mulla" was a family name and had no religious significance, Sheikh Ahmad was a cleric, though it's not entirely clear he was preaching Islam. Rumors spread that he was encouraging his parishioners to drink wine, eat pork, and have a good free-loving time. Ahmad also reportedly instructed them to pray not southwest to Mecca, but north to the village of Barzan. This did not go down with King Faisal, Iraq's British-sponsored Arab monarch in Baghdad.[24] The Iraqi government, with Royal Air Force backing, set out to punish the entire Barzan region, and in 1932 exiled the two Barzani brothers to various other cities.[25] In 1943 Mulla Mustafa Barzani escaped from exile and found his home destroyed and his people starving on the moutainside. His appeals for aid to Baghdad were refused, and Mulla Mustafa Barzani went back to war.[26]

This time Mulla Mustafa fought for more than just his starving tribesmen. Barzani demanded that Baghdad create an autonomous Kurdish region in the north, encompassing the same areas the Iraq Kurds control today. He asked for Kurdish to be made an official language and for a share of the cabinet in Baghdad. As World War II raged, both the Allied and Soviet propaganda pushed freedom and self-determination, and Barzani—audacious or naïve—thought he somehow had British support against Baghdad. His rebellion failed, not least because one of his biggest Kurdish allies, the Zebari tribe, defected to the Arab side in 1945.[27] Pro-government Kurds would tip the balance one way or another in many battles to come.*

Barzani again found himself on the run, and he took three thousand followers into Iran, where the Soviet Union had promised to sponsor a homeland for Kurds. The 1946 Mahabad Republic, based in the Iranian province of the same name, remains at this writing the only declared Kurdish state in history.[28] The attempt at building a Kurdish homeland was led by Iranian Kurd Qazi Muhamad, who had founded the Kurdistan Democratic Party of Iran (KDPI). He and Barzani didn't get along perfectly, but Qazi Muhamad had no choice but to accept Mulla Mustafa as an equal; Barzani was already a legend among the Kurds on both sides of the border, and his pesh merga troops were the best Kurdish fighters of the day.† What undid the Mahabad Republic first is not clear—the internal divisions or the fact that the Soviets withdrew their support in the spring of 1946, under pressure as the other former Allied powers lined up behind the shah of Iran, Mohamad Reza Pahlavi, who had taken the throne from his father in 1941.[29]

The shah was thus free to crack down on the Kurds with his newly created secret police (later the infamous SAVAK). By the next year the Mahabad Republic was a smoking ruin and hundreds of KDPI were hanging from gallows, including Qazi Muhamad. Iraqi Kurdish leaders were sent back to Baghdad, where many of them also swung, charged with treason for creating a Kurdish state even across the border in Iran.[30] Barzani

---

* These Kurdish soldiers fighting for Baghdad became known as *jahsh*, which means "baby donkeys" in Kurdish but is close to the Arabic word for "army," *jaysh*.

† *Pesh merga* is often translated as "those who face death," but the word "pesh" means "forward," so the title implies not just facing death but fearlessly running at it with a dagger in your teeth. Having been a pesh merga is a crucial part of Kurdish manhood. I'm not sure I've ever met a male Kurd over thirty who didn't claim to have been a pesh merga at some point, from urbane intellectuals to peasant farmers.

narrowly escaped back to Iraqi Kurdistan, where he gathered several hundred followers for a freezing exodus through the mountains, on foot, to Soviet Azerbaijan.[31] They fought their way through the mountains, clashing often with the Turkish and Iranian armies, and finally reached the Soviet Union after fifty-two days. What would become an eleven-year exile in the USSR earned Barzani the nickname "the Red Mullah."

Barzani's flight to the Soviet Union made sense, and not only because he had nowhere else to go. The Russians had taken an interest in Central Asian minorities, including the Kurds, from the early days of the century. By the 1930s Russian scholars had developed a Cyrillic alphabet for the Kurdish language and held "kurdology" conferences, perhaps seeing the Kurds as a card to play in the region's great game.[32] During the Mahabad period, the Soviets sent encouragement in the form of Kurdish-language radio broadcasts. Kurds hoped the USSR would be the great power that would finally hear their cries. But Barzani's Soviet exile seemed to disabuse him of any socialist leanings he had. He and his men did take advantage of the opportunity for some of their first formal education, mostly as craftsmen, and Barzani himself learned Russian at the language academy in Moscow, though he dismissed rumors that the Soviets gave him military training.[33]

When Abd-al-Karim Qassim staged a military coup in Baghdad in 1958, he gave Barzani the green light to return. The KDP had been in contact with the Iraqi free officers (modeled after Gamal Abdel Nasser's Egyptian free officers), and they thought Qassim might offer their first chance at being equal citizens in Iraq.[34] Barzani's return to Kurdistan was somewhere between a homecoming and a second coming. His status had assumed godlike proportions, and the Kurds hung on his every word, ready to fight or make peace at "General" Barzani's command.

As Iraq's prime minister, Qassim was interested in using the Kurds to balance the power of Arab nationalists, and it wasn't long before he was practicing the age-old method of co-opting a tribal leader—by giving Barzani a stipend and a government car.[35] Kurds were favored for a time under Qassim, and Barzani's men served the government, even helping Baghdad put down a rebellion in 1959, which included some dirty work against Qassim's Ba'athist and nationalist rivals in the city of Mosul, something the Ba'athists would not soon forget.[36]

Barzani's time with the Baghdad government didn't bring out the best in him, as with many mountain fighters who get citified. Critics said that Barzani wasn't pushing Kurdish issues hard enough and that he still let tribal divisions get in the way of his people's aspirations.[37] Qassim's affections soon drifted, and he began to also patronize Barzani's *jahsh* rivals, the Surchi and Karki tribes. In 1961 the divided loyalties became too much for the general, and he raised his men in rebellion again.

At the time, the American press had no sympathy for the "Red Mullah," whom they considered a Russian tool (and mistakenly thought to be a religious radical). A rather partial account of the rebellion ran in *Time* magazine's May 4, 1962, issue:

> The revolt could not be dismissed as merely another example of Kurdish cussedness. The rebels have moved steadily south out of the Zagros Mountains to within 70 miles of Baghdad, now have a quasi hold on sizable parts of Iraq . . . Buffeted within and without, Qassim's regime is in danger of collapse . . . Leading the rebellious Kurds is veteran pro-Communist Mustafa Barzani, a onetime mullah—religious teacher—and military boss of a Red-supported puppet republic of Kurdistan just after the war . . . Barzani began last summer by leading his hotheads in raids on isolated Iraqi police outposts.

Indeed, Qassim was overthrown in 1963 by the same Ba'athists and Nasserites the Kurds had helped him suppress in Mosul. At the same time the seeds of Kurdistan's most important schism sprouted. Despite what America thought, Barzani was no more red than he was yellow. But the Kurds were not immune to the socialist revolutionary current around the globe. The real reds in the KDP started a push to modernize the KDP from its tribal roots, led by a young Barzani protégé who would become his greatest rival, Mam Jalal Talabani.

Talabani was born in 1933 near the town of Koi Sanjaq, and his family had a natural sphere of influence in the southern part of Iraqi Kurdistan, the area around Sulimaniya and Kirkuk. While "Mam"—"uncle" in Kurdish—is a common honorific, Talabani bore the title even when he joined the Kurdish resistance at age thirteen. Before his son was born,

Talabani's father had had a dream in which his late uncle Jalal gave him an apple, and so he named the boy "Uncle Jalal."*

Talabani studied law in Baghdad, and while he was as much a worshipper of General Barzani as many others, he also followed the more intellectual leanings of the KDP's secretary general, Ibrahim Ahmad. Along with Ahmad, Talabani represented the Kurdish intelligentsia who had been discussing and writing about Kurdish rights in cafés in the capital.[38] Talabani cut a dashing figure in those days, with broad shoulders, and a hearty grin under a bushy mustache. He was a clear favorite of Barzani's and translated for the general, but on a trip to Baghdad representing the KDP in February 1964, Talabani went far beyond what Barzani saw as his mandate. Seizing a chance to broaden the Kurds' support, Talabani extended his trip to Algeria and Egypt, where he had a high-profile meeting with Arab nationalist Gamal Abdel Nasser. Barzani disagreed with the purpose of Talabani's trip and also took umbrage at the youngster's unauthorized actions.[39]

Before the end of that year, Talabani and Ahmad challenged Barzani publicly and even held a rival KDP conference. Barzani never forgave the affront, considering most of the KDP politicians as slick, vain city dwellers who let men like him do the real fighting. Over the next ten years their split would undermine all progress, and the Kurds' enemies found it easy to pit the factions against each other.[40]

Luckily for the Kurds, divisions and distractions hobbled Baghdad as well, which on several occasions pulled the Iraq army back from the brink of what looked like certain defeat for the Kurdish resistance. Outside powers had begun to take a more active interest as well, and by the late 1960s Israel and Iran were plying Barzani with weapons and cash. The Kurds had found their new calling: to tie down several divisions of the Iraqi army with constant harassment at the behest of foreign powers. Iraq sent no significant troops to fight Israel in the 1967 Six Days War, mostly because Barzani stepped up his attacks on government positions in a coordinated effort. Aid flowed to him through Iran, but with an ugly price: Barzani pledged to shut his border to Iran's Kurds, allowing the shah to mop them up.[41]

The Ba'athist coup in 1968 began thirty-five years of brutal continuity

---

* Even Talabani's wife calls him "Mam." After he had become president of Iraq in 2005, I asked if he would rather be called "President Talabani." Keeping with Mulla Mustafa's famous disdain for fancy titles, he said, "No, call me by my name, Mam Jalal." Then he told me the story of his uncle.

in Baghdad. Talabani and Ahmad initially welcomed the Ba'athists as the first regime to extend a hand of friendship to the Kurds—the same wishful thinking Barzani had felt toward Qassim ten years earlier.* This time Talabani had the stipend from Baghdad, an office, and his own Kurdish newspaper.[42] On March 11, 1970, the reunited KDP signed an autonomy agreement with Saddam Hussein, who was already controlling the Ba'athist government from the vice president's office. The deal gave the Kurds everything they wanted—Kurdish as an official language, guaranteed places in government, land redistribution, and the return of Kurds displaced by war.[43] The Kurds would soon learn that treaties with Saddam Hussein weren't worth the paper they were printed on, and worse, their deal with Baghdad angered the shah of Iran, who would bide his time before taking his revenge.

BARZANI LATER SAID that he suspected the Ba'athist regime wasn't sincere, but felt he could not refuse to sign on to such generous terms. His suspicions soon took human form—in the infamous incident of the exploding imams.

Though Barzani had emerged as the clear leader of the clan and the Kurds, despite the fact that he wasn't a real "mullah," he always respected his more spiritually inclined older brother, Sheikh Ahmad Barzani. Mulla Mustafa always deferred ceremonially to Sheikh Ahmad,† and an up-and-coming Saddam Hussein exploited the weakness in September 1971.

Baghdad was officially at peace with Kurdistan at the time, and the group of Shi' ite and Sunni clerics didn't suspect foul play when Saddam's functionaries asked them to travel to Kurdistan and sound out Barzani's views toward his Arab countrymen. So interested was the regime in Barzani's every word that they asked the imams to allow themselves to be wired for sound. In fact the Ba'athists rigged them up like roman candles before their scheduled meeting at the Kurdish leader's headquarters. Luckily, Iraqi hospitality mandated that copious amounts of tea be served

---

* The Ba'ath Party was founded in 1947 by a Syrian Christian named Michel Aflaq. Saddam Hussein's version grew so perverted that it is probably better termed Saddamism than Ba'athism.

† Critics claim it was also Sheikh Ahmad Barzani who encouraged Mulla Mustafa's faith in America.

during the meeting. While the tea boy leaned in front of Barzani and his lieutenant Mahmoud Othman, one of the clerics thought it would be a good moment to hit what he thought was the Record button on the secret "tape deck" hidden inside his robes.

"When Barzani started talking, the man sitting across from us—he exploded!" recalled Mahmoud Othman.

Othman, a medical doctor, gave Barzani a once-over and saw no major injuries—the tea boy had saved their lives at the cost of his own. Four of the clerics were dead, and in the confusion, Barzani's pesh merga rushed in and shot the rest of the visitors, thinking they were complicit. When Othman and Barzani stepped outside, they discovered the real assassins—the clerics' government drivers, who threw a hand grenade at them.[44] It fell short, killing one pesh merga and wounding a dozen—still Barzani escaped harm. Othman tried to get the Kurdish soldiers to take the attackers alive.

"We told the pesh merga to capture them, but they were so furious when they saw Barzani with blood on his face, they just—everybody was killed," Othman remembered.

Naturally, Barzani no longer felt bound by the treaty with Saddam—all the more after two other assassination attempts against him and his family, including a gift box of fairy-tale poisoned apples. The general reengaged in discussions with Saddam's mortal enemies, the shah of Iran and Israel, which helped draw the cold war battle lines when Saddam finally decided to negotiate with the Soviets after several years of flirtation. In April 1972, Iraq signed a friendship treaty with the Soviet Union and started collecting Russian tanks and planes. The treaty gave Barzani more leverage with Iran, but he knew the neighborhood too well to trust it. He felt there was only one country on earth that would give its word and keep it.

"We do not trust the Shah," Barzani told the *Washington Post* in 1973. "I trust America. America is too great a power to betray a small people like the Kurds."[45]

CHAPTER TWO

Betrayal and Holocaust

THE AVERAGE AMERICAN TEENAGER MAY not have any idea who Henry Kissinger is, but a Kurdish high school student ruefully spat out his name during a schoolyard poll in the chilly February of 2003. The war drums were beating in Washington, and the gaggle of teenagers couldn't wait for the American soldiers to come and take away Saddam Hussein, whom they could safely mock from inside the Kurdish area. At first they stuck to the approved language, which they had learned by heart.

"Our dream really is to make one Kurdistan," said a student named Mustafa, whose deadly serious stare was somewhat mitigated by his peach-fuzz mustache. He continued with the standard disclaimer: "But at this time for us it's better to be a part of Iraq."

It took only a little troublemaking to get them going. Were they Iraqis or Kurds? No one waited their turn to shout that they were Kurds first, and Iraqis—well, maybe not even second. A sixteen-year-old girl from Halabja said she had never met her older brother, who died when the Iraqi army gassed the city in 1988. Then another young man spoke up in broken English.

"In fact there's something. I am sorry to say that we never forget Great Britain had canceled Kurds from their country," he said as if he were addressing the United Nations. "And I want to say that I am Kurd and not Iraqi."

Bringing up the 1920s is always fair play in the Middle East, even if you were born in 1989. But this was a new century. Did they trust America? The answer boiled down to one name: Kissinger.

"BARZANI WAS DRIVEN by the single-mindedness without which few independence struggles would ever be undertaken . . . Heroes, we were learning, are more pleasant to read about than to deal with; the very qualities that inspire their courage also meld their inflexibility," Secretary of State Henry Kissinger wrote in one volume of his memoirs, *Years of Renewal*.

It's not entirely clear what Kissinger wanted General Barzani to be flexible about in 1972, when his appeals for aid began arriving in Washington. The Kurdish rebel respected the covert action code of "plausible deniability," sending his requests through third parties like King Hussein of Jordan or the Israelis so the Americans could disclaim any involvement.

Since the assassination attempts, which he could only assume were official Baghdad policy, Barzani had opened the door to Iran again. Saddam Hussein, even as vice president, had started the saber rattling that would characterize his regime for the next thirty years, taking up the cause of Iran's small Arab minority in the Khuzestan province along the Shatt al-Arab River, the short confluence of the Tigris and Euphrates that links Iraq to the Persian Gulf. For his part, the shah was hardly innocent of provocations. Seeing that Iraq was fairly weak and had few allies, Iran reopened a dispute with Baghdad over the exact location of the Shatt al-Arab border. To create some bargaining chips, the shah encouraged the Kurds to be troublesome—never a difficult task.[1]

As a master of cold war politics, the shah expressed his worry to Nixon that the Kurds could go either way if they weren't supported—from being a handy thorn in Iraq's paw to being a Soviet ally. When the Soviet premier visited Baghdad in the spring of 1972, it was natural that Nixon visit the shah in Tehran. At the time, Iran was America's anchor in the Middle East, and U.S. policy was described as "give the Shah whatever he wants."* On this visit the shah got his choice of American jet fighters—F-14s or F-15s—and a promise of support for the Iraqi Kurds, who were regularly attacking Saddam's positions along the fringes of Iraqi Kurdistan, doing wonders at keeping Baghdad preoccupied.[2]

The guns and ammunition neatly came secondhand from the two largest recipients of American military aid in the world, Iran and Israel (bulwarks against Soviet allies Iraq and Egypt). Eventually the Kurds would get millions' worth of Soviet hardware captured from Egypt by the Israelis in 1973 and funneled through Iran.[3] Despite contributions from Britain as well, the covert program was still tiny next to the blood and treasure being spilled in Vietnam. Brent Scowcroft, Kissinger's deputy at the time, remembers American support for the Kurds as strictly an appendage of U.S.-Iran policy.

"The Kurds were derivative. The shah was a good ally. And he was having this problem with Iraq. We were emotionally supporting the Kurds, but it wasn't a big deal," said Scowcroft.[4] Yet while American support of Barzani's struggle may not have seemed much back in Foggy Bottom, to Kurdistan it felt like a covenant with God. The Voice of America broadcasts began describing Barzani's men as freedom fighters.

"Even kids younger than me knew the names Nixon and Kissinger, and we loved them," writes Hiner Saleem in his memoir of childhood in Kurdistan. "Radio Moscow called us vulgar rebels acting against Saddam Hussein, that champion of Socialism. But my father wasn't worried; America and Henry Kissinger were on our side."[5]

For a year or two the Kurds felt strong. The dissidents within the KDP reunited under Barzani and continued to distract a huge portion of the Iraqi army, to the delight of the shah and Israel's Golda Meir. But Barzani made it clear that he saw the American involvement as a guarantee that Iran wouldn't pull the rug out.[6] The general told a delegation of visiting journalists that he wanted Kurdistan to become the fifty-first state, and even mentioned that American companies could do a great job exploiting the oil in Kirkuk, so long as Washington's long arm would keep them safe. "We are ready to act according to U.S. policy if the U.S. will protect us from the wolves," Barzani said.[7]

---

* April 16, 1970, memo from Kissinger to Nixon, declassified in 2006. Kissinger added, "The Shah of Iran is an island of stability in an otherwise unstable area" and "the Shah's foreign policy, while increasingly flexible, is openly based on a special relationship with the U.S. From our viewpoint, he is a good friend."

Barzani had a fair amount of experience playing and being played in the cold war's great game, so he should have seen the low blow coming. What he did not anticipate was the way Kissinger and the shah kept reeling him in when they knew the Kurds were done for. The tide began to turn in Baghdad's favor in 1974, and the shah made overtures to Saddam. He offered to cut off aid for the Kurds if Saddam would accept the definition of the southern border as the deepest point of the Shatt al-Arab waterway. Saddam tried his own way first, offering Barzani a truce and another autonomy agreement on March 11, 1974, exactly four years since their previous deal. Not knowing it was his last chance, Barzani stonewalled the Iraqi leader and sent Washington an absolute pipe-dream request for a massive increase in covert aid. "If you give us arms to match those (Iraqi) arms we will fight. Otherwise we will make peace. We don't want to be massacred," Barzani wrote.[8]

Kissinger knew that the shah was negotiating with Iraq by February 1975.[9] Still, he gave Barzani no hints, writing him a gushing letter on February 20, restating his admiration for Barzani and his cause and inviting the Kurd to send an emissary to Washington. Meanwhile, the shah met with Saddam Hussein at an OPEC summit in Algiers, and they struck a deal that included "strict border security"—a euphemism for handing the Kurds to Saddam on a platter.[10] Somehow Kissinger maintains that on March 6 "the Shah stunned us with the announcement that he had reached a deal with Saddam."[11]

The shah waited five days to let Barzani know that he was in free fall, so the betrayal could land on the same bitter date that the shah had been holding his grudge over: March 11, five years after Barzani's autonomy agreement with Baghdad. The Iranian portal for aid closed within hours, and suddenly the Kurds had no acess to the outside and only bolt-action rifles to face Saddam's Soviet tanks.[12] News of the catastrophe spread by radio across Kurdistan. As Hiner Saleem recalls, "A long letter by General Barzani addressed to Kissinger, begging him to keep his promise, was read over our radio, but Kissinger abandoned us to our fate."[13]

Barzani's twenty-five-year-old physician, Najmaldin Karim, had been a member of the KDP since he was fourteen, and worshipped Barzani. He recalls watching his idol wrestle with the decision between the humiliation of defeat or extermination if he kept fighting. "I think Barzani would have stayed and continued the resistance if he had been fifteen years younger," said Karim.

Despair washed over Kurdistan like a dust storm. Initially, Karim said, the pesh merga vowed to fight on, sending their families into exile. By March 18, Barzani saw the writing on the wall and called on his followers to survive any way they could, focusing on getting as many of his loyal cadres as possible out of Iraq. About one hundred thousand crossed into Iran, where the shah at least accepted his recent allies as refugees. Others surrendered to Saddam's army. Some fighters committed suicide, and legendary commanders were seen weeping as they abandoned the struggle.[14]

Even decades later, Barzani's son Masoud would refuse to meet with Kissinger when offered the chance. Despite the defeat, Masoud could never criticize his father, whose face still looks down from the walls of every KDP office. "The doubts we had with the Iranians were clear," Masoud said. "He himself admitted we should have stayed more dubious. But he didn't think the Americans would cheat us."

At the time, others in Barzani's family did speak harshly about him, focusing on the general's failure to take Saddam Hussein's final autonomy offer. Some even suggested that Barzani's own authoritarian nature had prevented him from making a compromise that would have saved him and his people. Barzani could say only that he would have acted differently without the American imprimatur.[15] This was cold comfort, especially to the pesh merga families that couldn't escape with Barzani's to Iran.

Barzani was seventy-five years old, and he knew that his last chance of leading his people to independence had ended. He may also have had a warrior's premonition that his death was near. That summer Barzani called Dr. Karim to him in Tehran because of a lump he could feel under his collarbone. Karim immediately suspected it was lung cancer and asked Barzani to have an X-ray. But the general had one last trick up his sleeve. He insisted that no one diagnose him until he left Iran for the United States, believing that if he started treatment in Tehran he would be doomed to die there.

Kissinger and the shah had opposed Barzani coming to the States out of fear that he would go public about their double cross,[16] but there was already a bit of a fan base for the Kurdish rebel in Washington, especially among followers of Democratic senator Henry "Scoop" Jackson (who inspired neocons like Paul Wolfowitz, Elliot Abrams, and Douglas J. Feith, who would end up in the Bush administration in 2000) and with newspapermen like William Safire and Jim Hoagland. The KDP representative in the U.S. capitol used the threat of going public to get Barzani a visa and permission to leave Iran. Dr. Karim as well as Barzani's sons, Masoud and

Idris, flew with him to New York, where a CIA contingent met them at the gate and escorted Barzani to the Mayo Clinic in Minnesota. Barzani would thereafter spend the rest of his days in a quiet Washington, D.C., suburb.[17] Before the cancer killed him in 1979, Barzani had the consolation of seeing Kissinger (and his close associate President Gerald Ford) voted out of office, and the shah overthrown.

To be fair, Kissinger's explanation for what he calls "the tragedy of the Kurds" holds some water. At the moment in history when he would have been asking Congress for a massive increase in covert aid for the Kurds, President Nixon had just been forced to resign and the enormity of defeat in Vietnam was dawning on America. Congress opposed the initial aid to the Kurds and then turned around and castigated Kissinger for cutting off the program. Without the shah to help, there was no easy way to get aid to the landlocked Kurds. Still, a report compiled by Senator Otis Pike, leaked to the media in 1976, found that both the United States and Iran had acted with calculated disregard for the fate of the Kurds, hoping to benefit from a perpetual cycle of violence in which the Kurds never got their autonomy and Saddam never quite wiped them out.

Brent Scowcroft remembered it with refreshing simplicity: "In 1975, quite suddenly the shah made a deal with Iraq. And so he had no further interest in fomenting trouble up there in Kurdistan. As a matter of fact he had a disinterest, because there are a lot of Kurds up there in Iran. So then he wanted us to stop supporting them, and then we had no practical way to support them. We ended our support. It was just small potatoes. It wasn't really an issue at the time that I recall."

In Iraqi Kurdistan a wave of ethnic cleansing, torture, and executions began. It would ebb and flow for fifteen years.

IN THE 1970s Saddam Hussein had not yet made his reputation as one of the twentieth century's cruelest men. Arabists in the West thought Saddam seemed like a promising young socialist, a modernizer who might help Iraq's people benefit from their oil, fertile land, and great water resources. The Kurdish rebels and intelligentsia who fled to Europe after Barzani's defeat found little sympathy. The left didn't want to hear Saddam criticized; the right didn't want to upset a country with such huge oil reserves. Seeing the attention lavished upon the Palestinian Liberation Organization, some of the younger Kurds flirted with the idea of using hijacking, hostage taking, and bombs to get attention for their cause. The leadership, from General Barzani on down, rejected such methods, though they lamented that the Kurds were unknown because they killed only their own enemies. The exiles suffered the indignity of having to explain not their demands, but more basic questions ("what is a Kurd?"), while Saddam Hussein's Iraq flourished.[18] The Iraqi dinar was worth more than two dollars, and the Iraqi Central Bank had plans to be economically on par with southern Europe by the mid-eighties.[19]

With the Islamic revolution of Ayatollah Ruhollah Khomeini in Iran, Saddam suddenly looked even better to America. Granted, he was taking guns from Russia, but he wasn't an Islamic fundamentalist, and he didn't inaugurate his regime by taking fifty-two Americans hostage for a year. Saddam kept his purges within the family. In July 1979, the same year that Tehran fell, Saddam formally seized power, after years of ruling from behind the scenes. Setting the tone, Saddam held a meeting of the Ba'ath Party leaders, calling out sixty-eight names of supposed traitors, who were hauled sobbing from the auditorium. He executed twenty-two of them. In an early sign of his penchant for documenting his own atrocities, Saddam had the meeting videotaped.[20]

The Kurds, however, became aware of whom they were dealing with from the moment of Barzani's departure in 1975. Their war with Baghdad had already killed thousands, but with defeat the violence only increased. The government in Baghdad cleared a buffer along Iraqi Kurdistan's external borders sometimes eighteen miles (thirty kilometers) deep. It became a free-fire zone, and Iraqi soldiers were ordered to summarily execute any man, woman, or child found inside it. By 1978 more than one thousand villages had been razed, including Barzani's battered hometown. Thousands of his kinsmen were transported to the flat desert of southern Iraq, and their journey was only beginning.[21]

Saddam Hussein now revealed his true genius—the art of pitting Iraqis against one another. He cleaved the province of Kirkuk, then Iraq's main oil producer, into two new provinces: Ta'mim and Salahudin.* By splicing the Kurdish areas onto other provinces, Saddam ensured the ethnic balance

---

* *Ta'mim* means "nationalization," and referred to Iraq's assumption of state control over the oil industry in 1972. Salahudin, of course, was named after Saddam's misappropriated Kurdish hero, Saladin.

of Kirkuk would tip against the Kurds. Kurds left in the city were no longer allowed to own property and many went through a humiliating process of declaring themselves Arabs in order to get jobs or buy houses. Small Kurdish villages now found themselves tacked onto Sunni Arab provinces with capitals like Baquba and Tikrit. Massive deportations of Kurds would soon follow, and the regime imported poor Shi'ite Arabs from the south to replace them. Even years after Saddam's ouster, his ethnic and religious gerrymandering left Kirkuk like a Gordian knot tied with razor wire.

The Kurds spent several years tangled in their own internal divisions after the defeat of General Barzani in 1975. Jalal Talabani, from exile in Damascus, wasted no time in announcing the formation of a new party, the Patriotic Union of Kurdistan (PUK). Talabani framed his party as a modern leftist movement, particularly stressing that it would not be a family-run business.[22] General Barzani's sons, Masoud and Idris, took over the KDP and immediately condemned the PUK as a usurper of the Kurdish revolution. As the PUK announced a renewed guerrilla campaign against Baghdad, it would be fighting the KDP as well.[23]

Barzani's longtime lieutenant, Mahmoud Othman, also formed his own party, the Kurdistan Socialist Party, which tried to act as a mediator between the KDP and PUK. Talabani sent a letter to the ailing Kurdish hero in Washington, appealing for unity. But the letter was carried by Ibrahim Ahmad, the original urban Kurdish intellectual (and by then, Talabani's father-in-law). Ahmad was perhaps the only Kurdish leader Barzani liked even less than he liked Talabani. Even from his sickbed, General Barzani rejected this and other attempts to bring the movements together, fueling the critics in Kurdistan who claimed that Barzani held his own success above that of his people.[24]

The rivalry still might have been manageable, but a few incidents left bad blood that would linger for years. Two well-loved commanders, Ali Askari and Khaled Said, who had joined Talabani, were making peace overtures to their old comrades in the KDP, Masoud and Idris Barzani, arguing that the personal hatred between the Talabani and Barzani families should be put aside in favor of fighting Baghdad. Possibly by mistake, the KDP ambushed them on their way to Turkey in 1978 and both men were captured. In an unusually cold-blooded decision for the intra-Kurdish conflict, KDP commander Sami Abd-al-Rahman had them executed.[25] The wound wouldn't properly heal for some twenty-five years, and it helped outside powers to divide and neutralize the Kurds.

The Kurds' bickering neutralized them as a threat to Baghdad, but it was only one of the reasons Saddam Hussein thought the moment was ripe to attack Iran in September 1980. He had an armory full of shiny new Soviet tanks and the biggest ground force in the region. Iran was internationally isolated, poorly armed, and dealing with postrevolution chaos. Saddam hoped to win a quick war, take his concessions, and prove Iraq's regional dominance. Thus he embarked on what would become a long career of hideous miscalculations. In Iran, Ayatollah Khomeini saw the war as a convenient outside threat to galvanize the revolution and wipe out his internal rivals. The eight-year war brought horrific death to as many as one million people, and didn't win an inch of dirt for either side.[26]

Two years into the war, the Iraqi opposition was an alphabet soup of angry acronyms and no great threat to anyone. Nineteen groups from across the Iraqi spectrum met in Tripoli and signed an accord against Saddam during February 1983; the agreement didn't last the return journey.[27] The Kurds had stopped shooting one another, but they were still drawing battle lines. The KDP was taking Iranian money and in return helping the Iranians suppress their own Kurdish rebels, the Kurdistan Democratic Party of Iran (KDPI). Reaching out to his enemy's enemy, Talabani's PUK was friendly with the KDPI, and completing the circle, the KDPI had facilitated a cease-fire between the PUK and Baghdad.[28]

While Saddam strung Talabani along in negotiations, KDP scouts helped Iran seize the Iraqi border town of Haj Omran in July 1983. It was the most direct assistance to his enemy so far, and Saddam could not let it go unpunished. He took revenge on the thousands of civilians from Barzan who were still under his control. The villagers captured in 1975 had been transported first to the south and later to a camp in Qushtapa, between Mosul and the Kurdish city of Erbil. Shortly after the Haj Omran operation, Iraqi soldiers raided the camp and rounded up eight thousand males, young and old. Saddam paraded the doomed souls through Baghdad, and then they were gone. Not even their remains could be found until twenty years later.

Saddam Hussein took full credit for their deaths on national television, explaining to his people, "They betrayed the country . . . and we meted out a stern punishment to them and they went to hell."[29] With this mass murder, Saddam turned a corner and began slouching toward his final solution for Kurdistan. A few other circumstances conspired to box in the

Kurds. Turkey's Kurdish rebels, the Kurdish Workers' Party (PKK), were ramping up their guerrilla war against Ankara, making the Turks ever more paranoid about the notion of Kurdish autonomy anywhere. The PUK never found out if its negotiations with Baghdad had been in good faith; when the deal looked ready, Turkish leaders quashed it, threatening to shut down their end of Iraq's main oil pipeline if Saddam made peace with Talabani.[30] As their options were disappearing, and the war with Iran dragged on, the Kurds got a hideous preview of what lay in store.

Ayatollah Khomeini was using his country's larger population as a force equalizer—boys as young at twelve were being brainwashed in school and handed plastic "keys to paradise" to remind them of their heavenly reward if they died on the Iraqi front. The Islamic republic invented the "human wave" attack, where these young untrained recruits became human shields and minesweepers, and the gruesome tactic began to grind down Iraq's superior army.

Saddam was not to be outdone. He began firing mustard gas shells at the Iranian troops and experimenting with other methods of delivering chemical weapons. At the same time, to his delight, the Iranian successes on the battlefield inflamed sectarian tension in the Gulf. Iran's Shi'ite government scared the Sunni Arab regimes, and so concerned their allies in Europe and America. Until then the U.S. policy in the Iran-Iraq war had been a neutral "pox on both their houses,"[31] but fear that Iran might actually win convinced the United States to back Baghdad. The Reagan administration sent Donald Rumsfeld as its special envoy to Iraq; his mission was to revive diplomatic relations that had been shut down since the 1967 Arab-Israeli war. Rumsfeld, a veteran Republican operative, met twice with Saddam Hussein and Foreign Minister Tariq Aziz in December 1983 and March 1984. Economic support started flowing toward Iraq.* The detailed notes of Rumsfeld's meetings with the Iraqi dictator show no mention of chemical weapons, even though

---

* Twenty years later, as the second Bush administration prepared to invade Iraq, Secretary of Defense Rumsfeld must have expected questions about his Baghdad trips. For a while the American media seemed too polite to mention it (just as they never harped on Bob Dole's happy photographs with Saddam when Dole ran for president in 1996). It appears the first public question Rumsfeld got about his past contact with Saddam was from Senator Robert Byrd, a Democrat from West Virginia, in a congressional hearing on September 20, 2002. Rumsfeld put

his second meeting with Saddam occurred after the U.S. State Department had issued a bland condemnation of Iraq's use of mustard gas.[32] Back in 1984 that protocol sent Saddam a clear message: no one was going to make a fuss as long as he could stop the mullahs from Iran. The Kurds heard the message too.

Talabani's break with Baghdad was cemented in 1985, when progovernment jahsh attacked the village of Kalkan in the middle of the night, killing Talabani's half brother Sheikh Hama Salih and two of Salih's daughters as they slept. With their habitual bad timing, all the Kurdish parties finally managed to unify and come in on Iran's side in 1986, just as Iran started losing.* By the next year, Tehran was clearly exhausted from a war that had come to involve the entire international community by the proxy of Saddam Hussein. But Iranian troops still had freedom of movement throughout the Kurdish region, where the Iraqi government had no control outside the major city centers. Saddam's guns slowly swiveled from the Iranians to Kurdish fighters in league with Iran, to the entire troublesome Kurdish people. The Iraqi regime had already leveled another two hundred villages in an attempt to limit the Kurdish fighters' ability to move freely. Looking for a more permanent solution, Baghdad inaugurated a new campaign called Anfal. The word means "spoils" and comes from a verse in the Koran regarding the legality of plunder in war. Saddam would redefine the word forever, and raze the Kurdish hopes of statehood down to the roots.

"FROM NOW ON the term 'al-Anfal' must forever and for every Arab carry the new meaning that the Iraqi Ba'ath gave to it: the officially sanctioned mass-murder in 1988 of at least 100,000 non-combatant Kurds,"

---

the trip in context, saying that America's main concerns in 1983 were Syrian ties to the bombing of the marine barracks in Beirut, and the Iran-Iraq war. The following day, CNN's Jamie McIntyre asked Rumsfeld about it, and Rumsfeld added an extra detail. "In that visit, I cautioned him about the use of chemical weapons, as a matter of fact, and discussed a host of other things," he said. A Pentagon spokesman later clarified that Rumsfeld must have mentioned chemical weapons not to Saddam but to Tariq Aziz.

* One of the negotiators who brought the PUK into the fold for Iran was a young hardliner by the name of Mahmoud Ahmadinejad, according to a PUK official.

wrote Iraqi dissident Kanan Makiya in his exposé of Saddam, *Cruelty and Silence: War, Tyranny, Uprising, and the Arab World*.

On the ground the calamity crept up on the Kurds softly. In March 1987 Dr. Fayek Mahmoud Golpi, a pesh merga medic, had set up a battlefield aid station in the abandoned village of Peeka, in the jagged mountains south of the city of Sulimaniya. Golpi had been up for days treating bullet and shrapnel wounds—pesh merga have no combat medics; men are expected to grit their teeth and walk to the rear when they get hit. He was catching a rare bit of sleep when a well-known commander woke him, bearing a soldier with strange symptoms. The wounded man, short of breath, explained that an artillery shell had landed near him but didn't make a loud explosion, instead letting off a sickly sweet smell.

"I wasn't surprised. First I told him to take off his clothes, and we burned them. Then I took him to bathe," Golpi said. He had been dreading this moment. A few years earlier he had met a deserter from the southern front of the Iran-Iraq war who had described the horror of chemical warfare. The man had shared some of the Iraqi army training on how to deal with mustard wounds. Golpi therefore knew that the gas was still in the soldier's clothes and still burning him. He treated the man for infection and burns on his eyes and skin. Golpi was soon to become an expert in the makeshift treatment of chemical wounds.

"With mustard there's no antidote. You treat the symptoms, and they increase with time. Still today there are many Kurds affected by mustard gas, and in the cold and dusty weather they spit blood," Golpi said. Nerve gas, he explained, by comparison was more likely to kill instantly, but if the victim survived, he was usually all right.

As Golpi and the pesh merga retreated north into higher mountain cover, he saw more and more Kurds wounded or killed by mustard gas, especially civilians who had no idea what the strange smell of rotten apples or onions signified. Some children were intrigued by the silent bombs and went close to investigate—these made the most horrifying cases. Golpi recalls watching a young shepherd's son die over twenty-four hours, his entire body burned black after he picked up a piece of a mustard gas shell.

So began the Anfal campaign, the world's first chemical assault against noncombatants. The gas attacks, however, were only one prong of the offensive that would eventually put Saddam Hussein in the dock for genocide. Saddam was never known to be a religious man until it served his purpose, but the part of the Koranic verse that probably appealed to him was the exaggerated language regarding what can be done to infidels. "Strike them on their necks, and smite over their fingers and toes . . . This is [the torment], so taste it; and surely, for the disbelievers is the torment of the fire" (Surat al-Anfal 8:12–14).

Saddam initiated the Anfal campaign in early 1987 and named its chief executioner: his cousin Ali Hassan al-Majid, soon to earn the nickname "Ali Chemical." Majid had risen from the position of bodyguard and police sergeant to become one of Iraq's cruelest men amid stiff competition. Majid's brutality served as one of Saddam's most feared threats—unleashing his cousin on an enemy or perceived traitor was the ultimate punishment. Majid set up his office in the city of Kirkuk in March 1987, and the slaughter began.*

Majid's powers inside the Kurdish region were near absolute; he controlled all of the Ba'ath Party's main security mechanisms. To protect his boss, Majid made the decisions himself and shielded Saddam from much direct involvement, a fact that would complicate the genocide charges against the Iraqi dictator years later. First Majid declared new sections of Kurdistan as prohibited zones, including about a thousand villages. Any man, woman, child, or farm animal inside the zone was to be exterminated. He prohibited farming and forbade all foodstuffs from entering the areas. Majid ordered his troops to use artillery, helicopters, and airplanes, telling them to maximize casualties any way they could.

Some roads became killing zones as well—every car was emptied and its passengers executed. In the summer of 1987, some five hundred villages were destroyed by bulldozer, their inhabitants taken away to government camps.[33] Again the Ba'athist obsession with record keeping makes it easy to trace the path of the destruction. Majid's voice can even be heard on taped phone conversations, disregarding any negotiation with the Kurdish leaders.

"Jalal Talabani asked me to open a special channel of communication with him," Majid says on one tape. "That evening I went to Sulimaniya

---

* This information, including audiotapes of Ali Hassan al-Majid, comes from a trove of documents (about eighteen tons of them) discovered by the PUK in 1991 and turned over to the U.S. Senate—that is, given to staffer Peter Galbraith, who managed to get them flown out of northern Iraq. A team from Human Rights Watch helped analyze them and did extensive follow-up interviews in Iraqi Kurdistan.

and hit them with the special ammunition. That was my answer. We continued the deportations."

Talabani's troops had just begun a major offensive driving south through the valley below Lake Dukan. As Dr. Golpi implied, they were aware that chemicals might be used against them, but that didn't help much. Some commanders had gas masks and atropine (a nerve-gas antidote) acquired from Iran, but at the beginning the Kurds had only a few desperate countermeasures. "You're supposed to move up to higher ground so the chemicals will sink below you, and start fires to burn up the chemicals," one pesh merga leader recalled. But then he added with a disturbing laugh, "You have to remember to do this while you're being gassed."[34]

Saddam's troops carried out the Anfal campaign in eight distinct stages over the course of two years, each phase centered on the destruction of a Kurdish stronghold, primarily those of Jalal Talabani's PUK, which was the most powerful at the time. Attacks on the PUK's bases were punctuated by the annihilation of almost any form of life around them, leaving the guerrillas nowhere to shelter or resupply. It was the antiguerrilla tactic of "draining the water from the fish" taken to an extreme the world had never seen. Civilians fled across the snowy mountains to Iran and Turkey, many of them dying of exposure on the way. These countries hardly welcomed them, but the Kurds were so desperate that a mere rifle pointed at them by a border guard was easily preferable. Many other civilians fled south while the Iraqi army and its jahsh allies used something of a sweeping motion across Kurdistan's fertile valleys, herding the population toward internment camps.

Witnesses at Saddam's genocide trial in 2006 described the camps; many still didn't dare show their faces and spoke from behind a curtain. One woman told how her entire family was imprisoned, including her grandmother, who died quickly under the harsh conditions. She described how a pregnant prisoner gave birth in a toilet while the guards watched and did nothing. The witness recalled how an infamous warden named Ja'afar al-Hillawi used to grab female prisoners by their breasts.

"He grabbed a beautiful young woman from Koi Sanjaq," the witness recalled. "He caught her and told her, 'You are mine.' She spat in his face. He tore her clothes and raped her in front of her parents. Then he shot her. She remained alive for several minutes and then died."

Those thought to be active members of the pesh merga were more deliberately tortured to death, beaten with electric cables, burned by cooking stoves placed under bare wire bedframes, left under a slow drip of ice water on their foreheads. One prisoner described watching three suspected guer-rillas hanging by their hands from a post in a courtyard. The jailers then tied tanks of cooking gas to their scrotums. On a signal the heavy tanks were dropped, ripping off the men's testicles. They died within half an hour.[35]

Though the Ba'athists never constructed killing factories like the Nazis, they did implement a systematic approach to execution. Only a handful of people who saw it lived to tell the tale. A young boy named Taimour Abdullah Ahmad, twelve years old at the time, was thought for years to be the only survivor of Anfal's execution squads.* He was picked up by jahsh along with his father, mother, and three younger sisters on April 13, 1988, from the village of Kulajo. The soldiers told them they were going to be safe.

"Unfortunately, they lied to us," Taimour recalled. "They took us straight to jail, the military base close to the Iranian border, which is called Foratu. We stayed there for about ten days and a lot of kids, a lot of children died because there wasn't any water, there wasn't any food."

The Iraqis moved Taimour and his family to a second prison in the city of Kirkuk. Taimour watched as his father, along with all the other grown men, was stripped, manacled, and taken away in a freight truck, never to be seen again. A month later the trucks returned and loaded up the women and children. The journey took all day, and some children suffo-cated along the way. In the back of the trucks, some previous passengers had scrawled final, furtive messages in Kurdish about a journey to the Saudi or Kuwaiti border. Near dusk, they reached an empty desert where bulldozers were already digging trenches for them. Taimour had managed to slip his blindfold slightly and could see as the exhausted Kurds were pushed into pits. The soldiers then began emptying their rifles, shooting into the trenches from each end. Few put up any resistance as the bullets hit them. His mother and sisters were killed. A round hit Taimour in the

---

* Taimour's story was told to dozens of journalists and researchers over the years—he was kept safe in northern Iraq but used quite extensively by the PUK for propaganda against Saddam Hussein. Since he was seen as the sole survivor, it was a necessary evil for him to be exploited this way, though more than one interviewer came away just wishing the boy could be left in peace. In 1997 the Iraqi government had supposedly put a bounty on Taimour's head, and he was granted asylum in the United States. Human Rights Watch researchers eventu-ally found five other survivors of the pits.

shoulder, and then he scampered up the side of the pit toward one of the executioners.

"Please don't shoot us. I mean, we haven't done anything. We didn't do anything," he said. It's doubtful that the Arab soldier spoke any Kurdish, but for a moment Taimour thought he saw tears in the soldier's eyes. Then the Iraqi at the other end of the pit saw them, and Taimour was pushed back down. He was hit in the lower back by another bullet and lay down among the dead. When the bulldozers started to bury the Kurds in the pit, some of them still alive, Taimour made his break. He tried to convince a young girl to run with him, but she was petrified with fear. Taimour ran to the nearest empty trench and made himself a hole in the earth, where, having lost blood, he passed out for a while.

Taimour awoke when the bulldozers began to fill his trench with bodies. He scrambled out of the pit and away into the night. Taimour remembers feeling his breath coming though the hole in his shoulder. After walking a few hours he came upon a bedouin family who gave him shelter. The bedouins hid him until relatives in Kurdistan could be safely informed that he was alive. Taimour was smuggled back to the north in 1990 and hidden until the Kurds took control of the area. Only then did his story start trickling to the outside.[36]

DURING ANFAL THE Iraqi regime trusted the international community to be as silent as it had been when Saddam began gassing Iran. If they needed proof positive of the world's indifference, they got it in Halabja, a religiously conservative city on the eastern edge of Iraqi Kurdistan. Halabja was not part of Anfal, bureaucratically defined as the campaign against the Kurdish countryside. The PUK took control of the mountainside city on March 15, 1988, with clear assistance from the Iranian Revolutionary Guards. That put the Iranians within striking distance of the important reservoir at Darbandikhan Dam. As before, such direct cooperation with the enemy brought out the worst of Saddam's wrath.

A city of about sixty thousand, Halabja had already been ravaged by the war. Iraqi attacks on nearby villages had driven thousands down from the surrounding mountains into the city for shelter. The Iraqis had then bulldozed parts of the city as a punishment for supporting the rebels. On the day of the gas attack, March 16, many civilians were hiding out in cellars, taking cover from a conventional artillery bombardment that morning. It was the worst place for them to be when the planes started to drop chemicals, which are heavier than air and sink into the lowest ground. The invisible onslaught continued for several hours without pause. Those who reached the city after the attack found hundreds of bodies asphyxiated in their basement bomb shelters. Survivors described an initial wave of burns that spread to anything they touched—probably napalm and phosphorus. Then they spoke of the same sickly sweet smell. By then most Kurds knew what that meant, but could do nothing. Dr. Golpi's mother, older brother, and several nieces and nephews died in the attack. The Iranian Revolutionary Guards in the city slowly walked out as darkness fell, wearing their gas masks.[37]

Many victims spent their final hours stumbling about the streets laughing hysterically—one of the more macabre symptoms of nerve gas. In what became an iconic image, a man named Omar was found dead on top of a swaddled child he was shielding with his body, to no avail. Survivors made for the hills, but still the gas they had inhaled ate away at them, killing hundreds as they fled. As many as five thousand people died that day, and Halabja's soil was still deemed potentially toxic almost twenty years later.[38] Exiles from the area began to hear reports about the attack on Iranian radio, and the government in Tehran sent a team of reporters to document the massacre.* But Baghdad had no fear of the publicity.

"I will kill them all with chemical weapons!" Ali Hassan al-Majid said in a taped phone call. "Who is going to say anything? The international community? Fuck them! The international community and those who listen to them." And Majid wasn't wrong. In Washington, Barzani's old physician, Dr. Najmaldin Karim, desperately tried to draw attention to what was happening. Karim had stayed on in America and studied neurosurgery—as a resident he had even met President Reagan in the hospital after the president was shot and had told Reagan about the Kurds. But when he began pushing the information about Anfal, he found only deaf ears in Washinton. Even though the Pentagon was giving Saddam satellite targeting information to help against Iran, the White House viewed the gassing of the

---

* Kaveh Golestan, a photographer and later a BBC cameraman, was among the last survivors of those who had covered the attack on Halabja. He said that some of the Iranian reporters had handled clothing inside the town and later died of cancer, perhaps from exposure to residual mustard gas. Kaveh himself was killed by a land mine during the 2003 invasion.

Kurds as an internal Iraqi issue. A Defense Intelligence Agency report even suggested, conveniently, that it might have been Iran, and not America's ally, that had done the gassing in Halabja.* As in 1975, Washington was cynically hoping for a costly stalemate.[39]

Peter Galbraith, a staffer for Senator Claiborne Pell, had been traveling in Iraq during 1987 and practically stumbled on the empty villages of Anfal. The experience affected Galbraith deeply, and when he returned to Washington, he reported on what he saw as an unfolding genocide against the Kurds. Maine senator George Mitchell passed a nonbinding condemnation.[40] But the world was still interested in keeping on Saddam's good side. The war with Iran was drawing to a close, and corporations in the United States and Europe were blinded by their interest in reconstruction contracts with the oil-rich dictator in Baghdad.

Jalal Talabani traveled first to London and then to Washington in June 1988 carrying a big white book listing three thousand villages destroyed in Anfal. Dr. Karim hosted him in the United States. Talabani was a quick study of the new international media game, but could not at first shake his hard-line leftist days. Karim recalled that during his first interviews in London after Halabja, Talabani would still talk about having contacted "Comrade Gorbachev and our comrades in China." By the time he reached America, Talabani had tailored his message, yet he still found nothing but closed doors. Defeating Iran ranked first, pleasing Turkey second, and the Kurds didn't even make the list of Washington priorities. "We got nothing official. We had one meeting outside the [State Department] building, and they almost murdered the official who authorized it," Karim recalled.

The Anfal campaign killed as many as one hundred thousand people and displaced twice that number. For a population of only a few million Iraqi Kurds, it was a holocaust. The pretense that it was just part of the war with Iran soon fell away. The chemical bombings continued after that

---

* A CIA analyst at the time, Stephen C. Pelletiere continues to promote that theory, based mostly on the fact that many of the dead in Halabja had blue lips, which could be evidence of a blood agent that Iraq did not possess at the time. Washington had a motive to push this story, at least until Saddam became an enemy in 1991, but Pelletiere seems to believe it sincerely and still pops up occasionally to claim that Iran gassed its own allies to death in 1988. Whenever he does, as in a January 2003 *New York Times* op-ed, a dozen or so experts are obliged to debunk him.

war ended officially on August 20, 1988, when the eighth and final phase of Anfal hit the Barzani heartland from August 25 through 29. With practiced efficiency Saddam's troops killed several thousand more Kurds, mostly KDP families, and then smashed through the mountain valley, burning the bodies of the dead and demolishing another seventy-seven villages.[41]

When the attacks continued after the truce with Iran, Peter Galbraith and a few others tried to act but found that American interests wouldn't allow it. Iran had to be contained, and Turkey mollified. Saddam had even made new friends—Midwestern farmers and rice growers started to love him after the increased trade negotiated by Reagan. As Galbraith and Senator Pell tried to push a "Prevention of Genocide Act of 1988" through Congress, a rice lobbyist wept on the phone, accusing Galbraith of genocide against American farmers.[42] The bill, loaded with sanctions, failed. Congress just didn't care to agonize over a distant war between two unsavory regimes, and most Americans had no idea that a people called the Kurds were being slaughtered in the cross fire. That would remain the case, but only until the next time the United States let the Kurds down, in 1991.

CHAPTER THREE

Shame and Comfort

BEFORE DAWN ON AUGUST 2, 1990, Saddam Hussein's army rolled into Kuwait, crossed the empty waste between the border and the capital, and sacked Kuwait City. By the middle of the day the Kuwaiti army vanished like a mirage and the royal family fled. U.S. Defense Secretary Dick Cheney canceled his trip to a conference in Aspen, Colorado, and began looking at America's scant military resources in the Gulf. Secretary of State James Baker, meeting with his Soviet counterpart in Siberia, urgently requested that Moscow stop any arms shipments it had en route to Baghdad.[1] The Gulf War had begun, and in a London café, Hoshyar Zebari held up a newspaper and shouted with joy.

"It's over! We're through!" Zebari said to a friend, who had no idea what the Kurdish exile was talking about.[2]

Zebari had relocated from Kurdistan to Europe in 1988 to represent the Kurdistan Front—what remained of it after Anfal. The devastating campaign left the rebels demoralized and weak, and Zebari decided the next wave of Kurdistan resistance would not be fought on the battlefield. Though he had done time as a guerrilla fighter, Zebari had also studied abroad and finished a master's degree in sociology. By the time he became known as a spokesman for the Kurds, he looked more suited to a professor's tweed jacket than a rifle and bandolier, but that was part of Zebari's message.

"With 1988 we were really devastated. After Saddam had used chemical weapons, no matter how brave, how gallant a pesh merga you are, this really changed the dynamics of armed struggle. We needed to look for other ways. There was a heavy emphasis on internationalizing," Zebari said.

Zebari began to cultivate journalists, activists, and politicians in Europe and America. He had direct access to a rare thing—human intelligence from inside Iraq. And he had his own compelling story to offer. Born in the town of Akre in 1953, he had been imprisoned and tortured by the regime as a teenager. The charge was trumped up; his real offense was his family. Before Zebari was born, his older sister had married General Mulla Mustafa Barzani, uniting two important Kurdish clans. That made Barzani's sons Zebari's nephews, though Zebari was a decade younger than Masoud Barzani, who would step up to lead the KDP after his father's death in 1979. While Zebari was abroad, Saddam's security services went after his family. Two of his brothers died in car "accidents," and another was killed with thallium (used in rat poison), both favorite methods of the secret police.

Zebari set up Kurdistan Front offices in Rome and Berlin and finally decided by 1990 that London should be the hub of his foreign operations. There was only one problem: he had been doing all his European travel on fake Syrian and Iranian passports and had no visa to the U.K. He flew from Tehran to Vienna on his Iranian passport and there booked a flight on British Airways to London. Zebari put on his most expensive suit and waited until the final call to board the plane. Rushing through the gate, waving his first-class ticket, he was not questioned. When he arrived at Heathrow, he asked the immigration officials for asylum. Looking over the press clippings in which Zebari had denounced Saddam and been sentenced to death, they told him it wouldn't be a problem.

The front had been focused on Saddam's atrocities throughout the 1980s and did some "naming and shaming" of German, French, British, and American companies they accused of supplying Iraq with precursor chemicals and technology for weapons of mass destruction. Zebari arranged conferences where Jalal Talabani and Masoud Barzani would speak about the Anfal to anyone who would listen. Danielle Mitterrand, wife of the French president, became a champion of their cause. Both leaders began predicting far and wide that Saddam was keeping too large an army to remain peaceful and that he was dangerously in debt to the

Gulf States after the war with Iran. In early 1990, Jalal Talabani told an incredulous audience at Chatham House in London that Saddam would probably invade Kuwait.

"They said, 'Oh no, Mr. Talabani, you shouldn't exaggerate. It's not good for your reputation,'" Talabani recalled.

On the day of the invasion, Zebari took his office assistant over to the Kuwaiti embassy in London and found a crowd of Kuwaiti tourists who had gathered in a panic seeking information from home. After a while a Kuwaiti diplomat ventured out to inform his citizens that there may have been some military maneuvers on the border, nothing to be concerned about. "They shouted at him, 'Don't you watch television? Our country is finished. Saddam's at the Saudi border,'" said Zebari.

In the dawn of the twenty-four-hour news cycle, the Kurdistan Front office in London played the media buzz for all it was worth. Equipped with a fax machine, Zebari made himself the kind of source journalists love, providing the networks and newspapers with information and analysis and fluently discussing the careers of people like Ali Hassan al-Majid, whom Saddam had installed as the governor of Kuwait (as he had for Kurdistan during the Anfal campaign). The Kurds already had a cadre of columnists and reporters on their side—William Safire and Jim Hoagland among their champions in Washington, D.C. Dr. Najmaldin Karim bought a cell phone for his car—one of the early, briefcase-size models—and it rang off the hook. Those who had called them Cassandras now called up for advice. But acres of newsprint could not protect the Kurds remaining inside Iraq. Saddam's vice president, Izzat al-Douri, warned them not to take advantage of the moment, and he left nothing to the imagination. "If you have forgotten Halabja, I would like to remind you that we are ready to repeat the operation," said al-Douri.[3]

As the U.S. air war against Iraq began in January 1991, the Kurds remained invisible in the West, with back-door-only diplomatic recognition. A junior British diplomat met Zebari at a London restaurant; a few American policy makers would call him on the sly for advice. Senator Claiborne Pell, at the instigation of his aide Peter Galbraith, invited a Kurdish delegation to Washington that February. Jalal Talabani stayed with Najmaldin Karim in his home in Silver Spring, Maryland. Karim had to push for some additional arrangements when Zebari sheepishly confessed he still didn't have a legal travel document (the Home Office in London sped up his request for a passport). Madame Mitterrand joined the delegation, raising its profile. Talabani and Zebari gave impassioned speeches to the U.S. Congress, but they couldn't get through to the Bush administration. The Kurds pushed Mitterrand to make a plea during her meeting with Barbara Bush, but it went nowhere.

Still, as the American troops massed on the Iraqi border, the Kurdish delegation in Washington was upbeat—conversely hoping that Saddam would be as defiant as possible, requiring the Americans to really crush him. Zebari had become something of a newsaholic, and he glowed with each opportunity to denounce Saddam on radio or television. By mid-February the Iraqi army was surrendering in the tens of thousands, and Zebari proclaimed at a Washington press conference, "The battle for Kuwait is over. But the battle for Baghdad has just started!"

Zebari wasn't crazy; he had just made the mistake of listening to President George H. W. Bush. The morning of February 15, in a speech from the old executive building, Bush went off-script, and according to his memoir, "impulsively added" the following: "There's another way for the bloodshed to stop, and that is for the Iraqi military and the Iraqi people to take matters into their own hands and force Saddam Hussein, the dictator, to step aside."[4]

Bush wrote that he was anxious to see what his remarks might do, and he told the press a few days later that if Saddam were overthrown, he "wouldn't weep for him."

If there was any deliberate message in the president's remarks, it was not geared toward the Iraqi people, said Robert Gates, who was then Bush's CIA chief. "Our hope had been that at the end of the war the defeat would have been so humiliating that the army would have overthrown Saddam. So when President Bush called on the Iraq people to do this themselves, what he really meant was the Iraqi military."[5]

It was the beginning of what would be called the "one bullet" policy. Washington wanted a kindler, gentler Sunni Arab general to blow off Saddam's head and then put Iraq and its oil back on line for the world. But Bush failed to clarify that nuance, and his remarks were rebroadcast on the BBC, the Voice of America, and the CIA's propaganda transmissions to Iraq. Regular Kurds and Shi'ite Arabs heard it as a clarion call to rebellion. Conspiracy theories in the Middle East already pushed the idea that the all-powerful United States had tricked Saddam into invading Kuwait.*

A trip to the U.S. State Department curbed Zebari's exuberance. The highest-ranking "friend of the Kurds" inside the administration was Richard Schifter, the assistant secretary of state for humanitarian affairs. He had met Mulla Mustafa Barzani in Washington and stayed in contact with Najmaldin Karim. Dr. Karim would feed Schifter intelligence tips from Kurdish agents inside the Iraqi army, and it made the American look well informed inside the State Department. In gratitude and out of genuine sympathy, Schifter agreed to receive the Kurdistan Front delegation at the State Department on February 28. It turned out to be the day of the cease-fire with Saddam. "I felt so good," said Zebari, "We were going to the State Department! My goodness, I felt so happy."

He and Sami Abd-al-Rahman gave their names at the main lobby and the receptionist called Schifter's office. No answer. The secretary tried again. Thirty minutes passed, and then forty-five. The receptionist finally informed Zebari that he had no appointment, but that someone would come down to see him. Two well-dressed junior staffers from Schifter's office appeared and offered to have coffee with the Kurds. Not inside the building though.

"I said, 'Sami, really, this is bad. This is humiliating, degrading,'" said Zebari. "He said, no, let's at least go and tell them what we want." At a coffee shop around the corner, he smoked a cigarette while Abd-al-Rahman talked with the two staffers. Zebari made a point of grabbing the check.

After the cease-fire only one person in the Bush administration expressed any interest in meeting with Iraq's opposition: the young undersecretary for policy planning at the Defense Department, an Afghan American named Zalmay Khalilzad. The Kurdistan Front representatives had been making the rounds of the policy think tanks in Washington and New York, and Columbia University professor Bernard Lewis had seen what he described as some "smart Iraqis" speak at the Council on Foreign

---

* That theory didn't seem quite as crazy with the revelation that Saddam had sought approval from the U.S. ambassador to Baghdad, April Glaspie. When he asked Glaspie what America thought about his dispute with Kuwait, the ambassador replied that it was a local matter. Then she took a vacation and got out of the heat. Saddam may well have thought he had been given a green light.

Relations. He contacted "Zal" Khalilzad and suggested a meeting. The "smart Iraqis" were Ahmed Chalabi, Hoshyar Zebari, and Barham Salih (arguably the three men most responsible, albeit with different motivations, for persuading the United States to intervene and invade Iraq in 2003). Zalmay Khalilzad—who would play a key role in the second Bush administration's planning to invade Iraq and eventually take the lead as U.S. ambassador to Baghdad—in 1991 put through a request to meet with the Iraqi opposition. It was shot down.

"I asked my Middle East–region colleague and he said I couldn't meet with them because our policy was not to meet with the Iraqi opposition. I was startled. Here we had been at war with the regime and we couldn't see the opponents of the regime," he remembered.[6] Months passed before Khalilzad was finally able to meet Zebari and Salih, but once he did, the men formed a friendship that would serve them for the next fifteen years as they became major players in the Iraq game.

Turkish sensitivities had made the Kurds radioactive in Washington. President Turgut Özal sacrificed more than most of the Gulf War coalition members when he came on board with the United States, against Turkish public sentiment. As the Turks feared, their country lost a huge amount of trade with oil-rich Iraq when the war began (twelve years would pass before it formally opened again). For decades the Turks had resisted the notion that their country had any ethnic minorities, but the 1990s also marked an uptick in violence with the Kurdish separatist PKK. Ankara bristled at any mention of Kurds or Iraqi resistance, and they had a legitimate fear that over the long-term, pan-Kurdish nationalism had designs on southeastern Turkey as part of the reunification of "Greater Kurdistan." But Özal spoke more openly about the Kurds than any other president in Turkish history. He even implied that he had some Kurdish ancestry. With Iraq looking unstable, the American ambassador to Turkey, Morton Abramowitz, thought it was time to start making contact with the Kurds.

"Washington said, 'No way, too offensive to the Turks,'" Abramowitz recalled. "At the same time, unbeknownst to us, Özal was having secret meetings with the Kurdish leaders. So we were being much holier than the pope."[7]

All the diplomatic double-talk set alarm bells ringing back in Kurdistan. Its people wanted to believe the United States would support them, but the Kurds had been left holding the bag before. Kurdistan Front leaders prepared what they called the "plan of probabilities." They war-gamed an American victory that removed Saddam, as well as a victory that left him in power. They considered a Kurdish rebellion with American support and an insurrection without American assistance, with or without the pro-government Kurdish jahsh. Rebel radio began broadcasting calls for national unity, encouraging the Iraqi army not to fight and declaring an amnesty for any jahsh who came over to the Kurdish side. They di-vided the Kurdish region into administrative districts, with pesh merga commanders assigned to each. Before the leadership could agree on a di-rect course of action, however, Kurdish civilians made their own decision.

The Shi'ites were already taking the cities in the south, shooting up pictures of Saddam and toppling his statues along the Shatt al-Arab River. The Kurds followed suit, led by the desperate residents of Saddam's relo-cation camps and thousands of Kurdish deserters from the Iraqi army. On March 5, in the foothill city of Ranya, a mob attacked the Ba'ath Party headquarters and killed three dozen staff. A similar pattern spread across the north, focusing on the three branches of Saddam's security services and the Ba'ath Party offices. On March 7 the traditionally insubordinate city of Sulimaniya reached a tipping point after days of demonstrations. A mob that included women and children sacked the "red" building that housed the secret police. It massacred Saddam's security agents and dis-covered a torture chamber as well as a room full of discarded women's and girls' clothing—the rape room. Hundreds of agents died as they tried to fight what was now a popular uprising backed by urban cells of pesh merga.[8]

On March 11 the Kurdish leadership finally caught up with its people, and the city of Erbil fell in just three hours, with greater coordination than before. Long experience had taught Masoud Barzani that it paid to keep a back channel of communication with the leaders of the Iraqi divi-sions occupying Kurdistan. As the uprising surged, the conscript Iraqi army simply faded away, many of them taking shelter in Kurdish homes.[9] Kurds in Qushtapa—the camp where Saddam had put thousands of Barzani widows and children after killing their men—rose up and occu-pied the nearby headquarters of the Iraqi Fifth Corps, seizing weapons. The hard-core Republican Guards were far to the south guarding Bagh-dad and putting down the Shi'ite rebellion. With a few exceptions, the jahsh—perhaps a hundred thousand of them—came over to what they thought was the winning side, redeeming their tribes among the Kurds.

The balance tipped, and cities fell in a quick chain reaction—Chamchamal and Tuz Khurmatu, Kifri and Kalar along the southern fringe of the Kurdish provinces, Dohuk and Zakho near the Turkish and Syrian borders.

The Kurdish leadership tried to control the mission of the intifada and the message it sent to the outside world. Pesh merga forces had orders not to stay in the cities, instead withdrawing to the safety of the mountains after they had tipped the scales. The Kurds wanted to preserve their fighting strength but deny Turkey any excuse to claim that northern Iraq had separated. Their carefully chosen slogan was "Democracy for Iraq, Autonomy for Kurdistan"—quite a contrast to the Shi'ite rebels in the south who were crying for Iranian-style theocracy.

That didn't prevent the Kurds from going after the big prize: Kirkuk. Only a three-hour-drive from Baghdad, Kirkuk has enough oil to build a Middle Eastern emirate. With Jalal Talabani still hesitating in Damascus, his lieutenants Kosrat Rasul and Nawshirwan Mustafa made it to the city by March 20—the eve of the Kurdish New Year, Newroz. Another member of the front, Hussein Sinjari, recalled sharing a celebratory bottle of whiskey with the the pesh merga leaders on the first night of Kurdish rule in the oil-rich city. A flamboyant, jacket-and-tie-wearing intellectual, Sinjari remembered looting the city alongside the Kurdish soldiers: "What do you expect? We are Kurds. Are we Swiss? We looted all of the government buildings. When we left, the Iraqi government looted all the Kurdish homes."

Kirkuk was as far as the rebellion went—in fact it was already too far. America's mission was accomplished as soon as the Iraqi army quit Kuwait City and went fleeing back across their own border. The Bush administration had its heart set on a quick and clear victory in Kuwait, and the president several times spoke of using this war to erase the quagmire of Vietnam from America's psyche. Even the cease-fire was announced with an almost compulsive neatness: when Bush addressed the nation on the evening of February 27, he said hostilities wouldn't end until midnight, making the ground war exactly one hundred hours long.[10] Supporting the Kurdish and Shi'ite insurrections appeared much less tidy and Washington wanted no part of it. Amazed to find himself still alive and still in power, Saddam soon realized he had a green light to take care of business. The Republican Guard dispatched the rebellions in the south and then turned their attention to Kirkuk.

The Bush administration put the word out, with the Gulf War coalition as well, that the uprisings in Iraq were not to be encouraged. As the intifada faltered, Hoshyar Zebari found himself making a secret trip to Riyadh, courtesy of Prince Turki al-Faisal, the Saudi spy master, who wanted to make sure the rebels' goals fit Saudi interests. Zebari found himself locked in a room with Ayad Allawi, a dissident Ba'athist exile, and Ibrahim al-Ja'fari, the leader of the Shi'ite party al-Da'wa Islamiya (Islamic Call). Turki told them to come up with a political program for regime change in Iraq that the Saudis could get behind, and in exchange he would push it in Washington. But two days later the mood changed— Turki suddenly had no time to meet with the opposition. Languishing in his hotel room, Zebari chain-smoked as he watched the news that the Iraqi army had begun turning back the rebellion.

"I'm leaving tomorrow," Zebari told Turki's deputy. "I don't need your airplane ticket; I can buy one for myself. My people are being massacred and I'm sitting here doing nothing. That is the message. Tell your boss."

Prince Turki responded as Zebari packed his bags. There were complications, he explained, expressing his regrets and asking that kind regards be sent to brother Masoud Barzani. Zebari found out later that the complications had arrived in the form of President Bush's national security advisor, Brent Scowcroft, Kissinger's former deputy, on his own secret trip to Riyadh. He let the Saudis know that no one was to support an insurrection in Iraq.

The Kurds held Kirkuk for three chaotic days until they realized they had been set up for a fall. The Iraqi army that General Colin Powell had bragged he would "cut off and kill" remained intact. There was no coalition air support, no American secret agent coming to help them force Saddam to "step aside." If thoughts of a military coup had tempted the Iraqi army immediately after Saddam's decision to invade Kuwait, the uprisings scared them straight.[11] Iraq's internal schisms were laid bare: Shi'ites in the south carried placards of Ayatollah Khomeini, terrifying Washington almost as much as it scared the Iraqi elite. Saddam's Sunni Arab generals were petrified that the country was coming apart and their reign of privilege with it. They closed ranks behind Saddam, the only leader they thought could keep the country intact.

The Iraqi regime got an unwitting boost from an unexpected quarter—General Norman Schwarzkopf. On March 3, when the American general had dictated his terms of surrender to Iraqi defense minister

Sultan Hashim Ahmed, the Iraqi general had only one request: Iraq wanted to use its helicopters. Ahmed claimed they were for reconstruction of Iraq's bombed-out infrastructure, though he asked a second question: Would it be alright if the helicopters were armed? Schwarzkopf realized too late what he was authorizing.

"In the following weeks, we discovered what the son of a bitch had really had in mind: using helicopter gunships to suppress rebellions in Basrah and other cities. By that time it was up to the White House to decide how much the United States wanted to intervene in the internal politics of Iraq," he wrote in his memoirs.[12]

The Iraqi opposition, still drunk with dreams of regime change, had convened in Beirut in mid-March. Shi'ite and Kurdish leaders met and coordinated for the first time, but mostly they watched in wonder at the rebellions breaking out spontaneously as they sat in Beirut trying to plan one. Telling the rest of the representatives that he would see them in Baghdad, Jalal Talabani moved east across Syria and headed for the Iraqi Kurdish city of Zakho to make his triumphant return.[13] Syrian red tape caused some delays, and by the time he crossed the border, the uprising looked shaky. Zebari, still concentrating on winning the propaganda war, sent Talabani an urgent message about what to smuggle across the border: "Don't bring weapons—bring journalists!"

Talabani arrived in Zakho with an entourage of loyal pesh merga and combat paparrazi, ferried across a Tigris River swollen from late-winter snow. On March 27, with crowds cheering him, he announced that he and other members of the opposition would soon select a provisional government. Then the other boot dropped. After the adoring crowds in Zakho, Talabani moved to the city of Dohuk, arriving just in time to watch the entire city pack its bags and flee. The Iraqis were coming with tanks and cannons and helicopters. Two days later Talabani was appealing to the world for military help and food aid. As the population fled, his rebels scrambled back into their mountains along the Iranian border.

Columns of tanks descended on the city of Kirkuk, crushing rebels and civilians alike. Small Iraqi helicopters drew out the pesh merga's few anti-aircraft rounds. Once they had flushed out the rebels, the Iraqis swooped in to incinerate them with rocket fire from larger Russian-made Hind gunships, terrifying not only for their firepower but also because Saddam had used them to spray gas in the past.[14] The dominoes fell back in the other direction: on March 31, Iraqi troops retook Erbil; on April 2, they were in

Sulimaniya and heading for northern cities like Dohuk. Only three years after Anfal and the gassing of Halabja, the Kurds expected no mercy for man, woman, or child. The entire Kurdish population of Iraq seemed to reach the same conclusion: better anywhere but here. A million crossed into Iran, which opened its borders, and half a million started to bottle-neck on the frontier with Turkey.

Tank shells, helicopter machine guns, and phosphorus bombs killed tens of thousands of Kurds and Turcomans in and around Kirkuk, and that was just the direct violence. The winter lingered into April that year, and cold began to prey on the weakest as they walked, many barefoot, through the snowy mountain passes along the borders. Families became separated in the thick hordes of civilians; many of the old and sick were simply abandoned.

"The whole of Kurdistan was flowing up the road," said BBC reporter Jim Muir, who crossed into Iraq with Talabani. "They used any kind of vehicle you can imagine—things like bulldozers with a scoop full of children. People [were] fleeing from hospitals—with IV drip feeds hanging off and people in beds rolling along—because someone said they'd smelled poison gas."[15]

This time no black cars came to spirit away the leadership and their families. Sami Abd-al-Rahman's father died in the exodus, one among thousands of people too weak to continue the journey. Talabani made his headquarters in the shell of a schoolhouse in the village of Mawat, in the mountains above Qalaat Chowlan. At one point he and his wife, Hero, found themselves deserted in their retreat by all but a handful of guards. They stood their ground and looked ready to fight to the death—the kind of battlefield leadership that makes or breaks guerrilla action. Enough pesh merga were shamed or inspired into going back to stand with their leader, and they fought the Iraqis to a standstill.[16] Masoud Barzani, fifteen years younger than Talabani, moved around a bit more. His KDP force, less depleted from the 1980s, harassed Saddam's advancing army and covered the civilians' retreat. With only 150 troops, Barzani's pesh merga stopped a tank column advancing on the Kore mountain pass above Salahudin. Remembering his father's death in exile, Barzani pleaded with Kurds to stay inside Iraq and not become landless like the Palestinians and Armenians.

While Iran opened its borders, Turkey, by contrast, had no interest in letting half a million politically excitable Kurds into the already volatile southeast (a hot zone because of fighting with the PKK). The Turks let a tiny number cross the border each day and beat the others back with rifle butts. Hundreds of thousands of Kurds began to make ragged shelters in the mountains—at night their meager campfires lit up the hillsides. These were not the fabled Kurds of the rugged mountains but city dwellers from Dohuk, with no idea how to survive in the elements.

WASHINGTON'S FIRST ALARM was sounded at the embassy in Ankara on Easter Sunday, March 31.

"I remember clearly one night sitting at home and Ambassador Abramowitz called me," said Marc Grossman, then the deputy ambassador. "He had heard from Peter Galbraith, who had just swum across some river and said that hundreds of thousands of Kurds were fleeing the north and pushing up the mountains."

Jalal Talabani had invited Galbraith to northern Iraq to enjoy the great victory over Saddam Hussein. Instead, for the second time in five years, the Senate staffer was witness to the mass murder of Kurdish civilians. He hadn't actually swum the Tigris River across to Syria, but the boatman who ferried Galbraith did get shot on his next crossing.[17] His call to Abramowitz set the U.S. embassy in motion toward the southeast border, a region the Turkish government had under a state of emergency because of the PKK insurrection. Abramowitz called Turkish president Özal, who was already pondering what he saw as the horns of the problem: how to feed half a million freezing Kurds, and how to keep them from taking over southeastern Turkey. A previous posting to Cambodia made Abramowitz an expert on refugees. He and Grossman took an unusually proactive stance for diplomats. They called up their entire staff and started doling out embassy car keys, fax machines, and packets of five thousand dollars in cash. Each car had Turkish and American staff with instructions to drive as far to the south and east as they could and start sending back reports from the ground.[18]

Video footage of the Iraqi counterattack shot by Peter Galbraith aired on ABC's *Nightline* on April 1. Galbraith, despite his Senate position, became one of the loudest voices calling for a humanitarian intervention. Picking his target well, Hoshyar Zebari orchestrated a small, Britishly polite demonstration outside the house of recently unseated prime minister Margaret Thatcher, complete with a little girl in Kurdish garb to hand

Mrs. Thatcher a bouquet of flowers and a petition. On April 3, Thatcher obliged, giving her successor, John Major, an earful.

"The Kurds don't need talk, they need practical action. It should not be beyond the wit of man to get planes there with tents, food and warm blankets. It is not a question of standing on legal niceties. We should go now," she said.[19] But Major stuck to the coalition party line: the dying Kurds were an internal Iraqi affair. When asked by a reporter if the coalition hadn't egged them on, Major famously responded, "I don't recall asking the Kurds to mount this particular insurrection. There is a civil war going on . . . We hope very much that the military in Iraq will remove Saddam Hussein."

The White House and the Pentagon clung to the idea that it had been a good quick war and it was over. President Bush betrayed what would later reveal itself to be an unfortunate family habit of answering questions about wars from the golf course. After that he went fishing in Florida. The media sunk their hooks in. William Safire lamented in the *New York Times* that Bush had blown all the credibility gained by pushing Saddam out of Kuwait.

"He threw away our newfound pride . . . as a superpower that stands for the right and will not let defenseless allies be pushed around. It seems we defend the rich and sell out the poor . . . If a whole people can be decimated while the President of the U.S. goes fishing, no nation will put faith in American security guarantees," Safire wrote on April 4.

But at week's end Secretary of State James Baker had a road-near-Damascus conversion. Ambassador Abramowitz convinced the secretary of state that his visit to Ankara should include a flight out to see the magnitude of the crisis on the border. Baker, along with his director of policy planning, Dennis Ross, choppered in to the mountainside camp at Çukurca. As Baker stepped down from the helicopter, thousands of desperate men, women, and children swarmed around him begging for food. He stayed for about twelve minutes. The international media's initial reaction was to deride Baker for showing up in his Texas cowboy boots for a photo op and leaving so quickly. Morton Abramowitz would later call it the most effective twelve minutes spent in the history of refugee work.

Until the moment he landed, Baker had been arguing with Ross that the United States needed to keep Iraq from splitting apart above all other concerns. Ross felt that America had a moral obligation to help the people who had been encouraged to rebel. Ross coordinated with his counterpart in the Pentagon, Paul Wolfowitz, and they even came up with joint talking points to convince their bosses, Cheney and Baker, to do something. But the trip to the border did it all. Indeed, Baker later described the scene of the exodus in biblical terms. On the plane back from Incirlik air base Baker called President Bush and told him the U.S. policy needed to change. The American generals, who had been celebrating the end of their nice neat war, got a call from Washington telling them to prepare to airlift food within thirty-six hours.

"That was the beginning of the de facto state of what I call the law of unintended consequences," said Abramowitz. Nobody involved suspected this was anything but a humanitarian mission. Years later Abramowitz realized they had accidentally created Kurdistan.*

THE KURDISTAN FRONT had scraped together as many Kurds who spoke European languages as they could find to help the press broadcast their struggle to the outside world. But as the revolt collapsed, there was hardly anyone to interpret for. Most of the journalists who came in with Talabani had followed the Kurdish exodus up to the Turkish border, both to cover the humanitarian crisis and to get out from under Saddam's rockets.[20] The BBC's Jim Muir stayed behind and was led about the mountains mostly on foot by Hussein Sinjari, who combined a perfect knowledge of the rebel trails with an entertainingly snobbish critique of his backward Kurdish countrymen. The Kurds treated the reporter as a VIP, but that still meant scrounging rice and beans and maybe a few dates to eat.

Muir inadvertently became the British envoy to the Kurds through his live broadcasts. While traveling with Barzani, Muir would shout his reports across the Kurdistan Front's radio to Damascus, where they would be recorded and relayed to the BBC office. Talabani possessed a satellite phone—perhaps the only one in all of Iraq at the time—and Muir bor-

---

* It's easy to forget that humanitarian intervention, which followed later in Somalia and Kosovo, began only in 1991, and changed the way the international community viewed crises like Rwanda and Sudan. Now it was possible to ask why the United Nations authorized intervention in northern Iraq and not in Darfur, for example.

rowed it for two-way chats with the news anchor in London. On one of his calls he heard the anchor discussing a proposal by John Major to establish a safe haven in the north of Iraq. The British prime minister, after his tongue-lashing from Thatcher, had joined with the French in pushing for intervention.[21] Soon after, Muir did a battlefield interview with Masoud Barzani, who loved the safe haven idea. John Major, in turn, heard Barzani's endorsement on the BBC.

Along the Iraqi border in Turkey, the U.S. military and diplomats came around to the same thought. The team on the ground for what would be called Operation Provide Comfort eventually comprised soldiers and civilians from a dozen nations, including many nongovernmental organizations (NGOs).[22] The U.S. Special Forces, surprising themselves as much as anyone, discovered that their training in dealing with indigenous militias made them perfect for refugee work. They arranged for aerial drops of food and water to landing zones in the mountains. The death toll of one hundred people every day slowed down, but the refugees still had nowhere to go. The coalition designed a vast refugee city on the edge of the Iraq border that some worried would be a new Gaza Strip inside Turkey. But then a novel idea came from Fred Cuny, a disaster specialist from Texas whom Abramowitz had brought in on contract. Cuny surveyed the refugees and discovered that most of the Kurds who had fled in this direction were urbanites from the city of Dohuk. The aid worker approached the soldiers and diplomats with a modest proposal.

"You gotta invade Dohuk," Cuny told Marc Grossman. "And if you do that, people will go home."

Almost simultaneously the Kurds were being snubbed again back in Washington. Hoshyar Zebari, Barham Salih, and Mahmoud Othman were finally invited to meet with Ambassador David Mack, a deputy assistant secretary for Near Eastern Affairs, with explicit assurances that they would make it past the lobby this time. But the meeting didn't please them much more than the one at the coffee shop had. Mack told the Kurds that the United States would send them neither a single dollar nor a single American soldier to help them inside Iraq.[23] Zebari protested that the American soldiers were already on the ground in Turkey and should at least coordinate with the local Kurdish leadership, but Mack was silent. He then handed them a short statement of U.S. policy that had clearly been written in advance of the meeting: no contact with local leaders (it didn't even say "Kurdish"), no political aspect to the humanitarian mission, and a firm commitment to the territorial integrity of Iraq. The State Department had a clear idea that it didn't want to go creating any new countries.

"That, you could have sent us by fax," said Zebari.

But events back in Iraq knocked Zebari off his moral high horse. Kurdish leader Jalal Talabani had just been seen on television, worldwide, kissing Saddam Hussein on both cheeks.

THE KURDISTAN FRONT had decided to cover all of its bases. While the situation for civilians on the borders was stabilizing, the pesh merga could barely cling to their mountains against Saddam's attacks. With Washington still pretending not to know them, the Kurds felt a truce with Baghdad was their only chance. The Iraqi dictator was still shaky, looking for a deal himself that might quiet down at least one of his trouble spots. The parties selected Talabani to meet with Saddam, along with Sami Abd-al-Rahman and Masoud's nephew Nechirvan Idris Barzani.

"Saddam Hussein in a meeting is very polite, very calm," said Jalal Talabani. "He kissed us and he said, 'You are good strugglers, brave men. We thought we defeated you, we thought you'd never come back, and now you are on the ground. I'm now recognizing your rights.'" Talabani, quite literally, wasn't ready for prime time in the age of twenty-four-hour news. Kisses are a normal greeting between Middle Eastern men, but the image cut the legs out from under the Kurdistan Front.

In Washington, the Kurdish demand for guarantees was met with a glib State Department asking, "Why not wait and see what you get from Baghdad?" Talabani came back to Kurdistan dead-set against any more negotiations with Baghdad, not only because it looked bad, but also because he knew Saddam's promises were worthless. The Kurdistan Front outvoted him, believing that contact with Saddam could at least buy time. Masoud Barzani headed the next delegation to Baghdad. He didn't kiss Saddam when he got there, but remembering his father's betrayal, he didn't trust the United States much more than the Iraqi dictator. In fact neither the Americans nor the Iraqis were offering the Kurds much. They had hoped to force conditions on Saddam, but instead they found him defiant and not even willing to settle on the terms negotiated way back in 1970. Saddam all but told the Kurdish delegation that he was weak, and he knew that any concession he made would be like blood in the water to his enemies inside and out.[24]

By APRIL 16 the United States finally came on board with Britain and France, agreeing to reenter Iraq and create a safe haven for the Kurds. Besides the further shame inaction would shower upon them in world opinion, the coalition decided it would rather inflict the refugee crisis back on Saddam than on Özal in Turkey, whose efforts to keep out the Kurds were technically *refoulement*—the refusal to shelter refugees, proscribed by international law. But the operation itself was something never before authorized by the international community: humanitarian intervention against the will of a sovereign state.

By that time, the military on the ground were glad to oblige. Operation Provide Comfort was a feel-good mission—more than Desert Storm, soldiers felt like they were doing an unambiguous good deed, and they certainly saved the lives of thousands. Many of the U.S. soldiers had never seen such naked desperation. When the choppers landed on the hilltops to deliver food, Kurdish mothers threw their babies on board. Combat doctors back in Incirlik found themselves running a nursery.

"They were coming back with tears in their eyes," said General Anthony Zinni, who coordinated the effort from the Turkish border. Zinni admits it was hard not to become a partisan—the Kurds' determination to survive impressed the American soldiers, who saw them as real freedom fighters. Still, Zinni wondered as he prepared to move his forces across the border into Iraq, when they would be leaving. "When we put the security zone in place—where's the exit? Nobody could see an end state," he recalled.

U.S. soldiers and British marines entered the Iraqi city of Zakho unopposed on April 20. President Bush had already extended the no-fly rule to include helicopters, and warned Iraq not to undertake any military action north of the 36th parallel.[25] The French military set up a system of way stations to encourage refugees along the road; at each stop they would dispense just enough food and gasoline to get the Kurds to the next stop.

With only a few days to prepare, Major General Jay Garner got orders that he should fly to Incirlik air base and subsequently oversee the

reinvasion of Iraq on the ground.* Like most of the U.S. military personnel involved, Garner immediately asked, "What's a Kurd?" He left his
base in Germany with an overnight bag and didn't return for several
months. Garner set up his headquarters in an empty Iraqi army base in
the north of Zakho. Baghdad seemed eager to test the Americans' resolve
and sent three hundred secret police up to Zakho to intimidate the locals.
They set the tone by declaring the town's central well off-limits and threw
a grenade into a crowd of civilians there, killing several. After numerous
tense standoffs between the Americans and Iraqis, Garner pressured his
Iraqi liaison, who pulled out all but fifty policemen. Kurdish civilians or
pesh merga got the rest to leave by throwing their own grenade into the
police station.[26]

By the end of May the coalition effectively recaptured the city of Dohuk
on behalf of the Kurds. Humanitarian organizations took over the lion's
share of the relief work, coordinated by the United Nations High Commission for Refugees. They were strange bedfellows. The military viewed
the civilians as save-the-whales, "Kumbaya" dreamers; the postconflict aid
workers felt uneasy alongside the practitioners of war. But the military
needed the NGOs' expertise, and the NGOs needed the army's helicopters
and incredible resources. Soon the aid workers figured out that it was more
sustainable to employ Turkish truckers to bring in local food, instead of
dropping meals-ready-to-eat by helicopter (thousands of which had been
sifted through to remove the pork-based meals). Fred Cuny managed to
scrounge combine harvesters and get the Kurdish wheat harvest in, and
then sell it to none other than the Iraqi government, winning a bet with a
delighted General Garner.[27] For their part, the soldiers provided the aid
workers some security against the Iraqi army and all-important transporta-
tion in and about a region somewhere between peace and conflict.

---

* When Garner got a similar order in 2003, he must have felt a wicked sense of
déjà vu. In 1991 Garner came into the operation with no background—he
scrambled to find any books written about the Kurds. He found only one book,
penned by the aforementioned Stephen C. Pelletiere, who had theorized that
the Iranians were responsible for the gassing at Halabja. Years later, while Garner was lecturing at the Army War College, a member of the audience asked
him if he had read any books about the Kurds before his time there. He mentioned the one title, and the questioner indentified himself as Stephen Pelletiere. Garner asked him, "Where the hell were you in 1991?"

Operation Provide Comfort ranks among the most successful humanitarian missions in history according to the U.N. High Commission for Refugees. Inside several months, the majority of half a million refugees returned to northern Iraq and resumed their lives; in turn this inspired many of the million Iraqi Kurds in Iran to come home. Coalition troops, numbering about twenty-three thousand at their peak, only ever occupied the tiny northwest corner of Iraq, making a box around Zakho, Dohuk, and Akre. The no-fly zone, enforced by British, French, and American jets based in Turkey, extended along the 36th parallel. But the exact parameters didn't matter; it was their symbolic power that kept the Iraqi army out. Saddam wasn't yet sure he was going to survive, and he picked no fights with the Americans, keeping his helicopters out of the north. Two Kurdish cities showed the nature of the unspoken standoff: Sulimaniya lay south of the 36th parallel, but Saddam didn't assert his claim to it right away, knowing that resistance would be fierce. Kirkuk, on the other hand, also south of the no-fly zone, was a red line for the Iraqis and the Turks, and the Kurds knew better than to try to bait Americans into protecting them there. Oil-rich Kirkuk would never be part of the Kurdish safe zone.[28]

By June the acute humanitarian crisis and the immediate threat to Turkey had passed. Now even the U.S. government realized the absurdity of creating a Kurdish safe haven but refusing to communicate with the Kurdish leaders. General John Shalikashvili asked Jay Garner to set up a meeting with Barzani and Talabani, to which General Garner replied that he would have to find them first. Garner already had daily informal contact with representatives from the parties, but the leaders had remained aloof. The flamboyant Hussein Sinjari represented Talabani, while Barzani sent Fadhil Mirani, a longtime KDP member who had learned English in Nashville, Tennessee, where he had a car dealership.

Garner met his bipartisan Kurdish entourage at a landing zone in the far northeast near the Iranian border, where they agreed to take him to their leaders. He flew in with two Black Hawk transport helicopters and two Apache attack helicopters, as well as jet fighters overhead. The Kurds were strapped but tried to roll out the red carpet—Sinjari and Mirani had rustled up a looted Mercedes and BMW without even bothering to detach the Iraqi government plates. Mirani poked Garner in the ribs and said, "Damn, do you know what I could get for these back in Nashville?"

Talabani and Barzani gave Garner a warm Kurdish welcome with what food and drink they could scrounge and told him how grateful they were to America. They must have known that Garner was there to deliver the bad news—that the coalition troops were leaving as soon as they could. The Kurds desperately wanted the soldiers to stay, still fearing that Saddam would return at any moment. They politely nodded at Garner's assurances that help would be just across the border, in Turkey (what would be called Operation Poised Hammer). At some point Talabani noticed that Garner wasn't touching his drink.

"What's the matter, General, you don't like goat's milk?" Talabani asked. Garner allowed that he'd never liked milk and mused that it maybe explained why he turned out so small (though he was as big as Masoud, who was sitting at his left). Garner asked for water instead. "Then he got that sly little grin he gets," said Garner. Talabani put his hand on the general's knee and said, "You don't drink Scotch, do you?" Two pesh merga appeared with a tray of Johnnie Walker Black. The meeting stretched through the afternoon.

"Jim Jones, Bill Hackett, Talabani, and myself—Barzani didn't drink— we sat there and we drank Scotch and began cutting the deal to get us out of northern Iraq," remembered Garner.

Before they left, Talabani asked Garner if he wanted them to call back to his base to let them know to expect him. On what phone, the general asked. Talabani showed Garner a room full of high-tech communications equipment that rivaled that of OPC headquarters. "Who in the hell do you talk to on this?" Garner asked. Talabani bragged that he spoke with John Major twice a day. Garner left the meeting thinking, "No wonder he's better informed than me."

Four days later, on July 3, General Shalikashvili flew in to meet with the Kurdish leaders and made a bargain: the bulk of the coalition would move out to Turkey, but they would leave behind a small contingent of Special Forces in Zakho under the command of Colonel Dick Naab.[29] By mid-July, the last of the main force was pulling out, despite thousands of Kurdish civilians who showed up to protest their departure in Zakho.

Over the summer Barzani visited Baghdad, considering a deal. Hoshyar Zebari opposed it, and Talabani kept leaving the country whenever it looked like he might be required to meet with Barzani about the negotiations. As summer turned to autumn, the Kurds grew bolder. Skirmishes spread far south of the tiny safe haven around Dohuk. Unrest centered, as usual, in the city of Sulimaniya, thirty miles south of the 36th parallel.

At the end of October, Baghdad suddenly switched tactics and pulled out of the three northern Kurdish provinces, expanding the safe haven by default. With characteristic hubris, Saddam told the Kurds that they'd never survive without him and informed the legion of Kurdish civil servants that they had to relocate to Iraqi government territory or lose their salaries. But the Kurds stayed. Doctors, teachers, and traffic cops all went without their paychecks for months. The U.N. had slapped a total embargo on Iraq, and Saddam was now laying siege to Kurdistan even within that blockade. But the Kurds realized something that perhaps only their closest enemies understood: they had a country now.

"The decision in 1991, it made it like an incubator," said Nawshirwan Mustafa, for many years the deputy head of the PUK. "But imagine for a person who has been against the central government all their life—for fifteen years or thirty years they live in caves or mountains. They were against law and order, wanted to destroy the state. Suddenly they become the master of the land? They should change from freedom fighters to statesman? It's not easy."[30]

Washington unwittingly had become the midwife to a de facto Kurdish state, something it certainly never desired. Despite the conspiracy theories flying about the region, especially in Turkey, no one in the U.S. government suspected at the time that America had permanently altered Iraq; rather, they thought they'd managed a very clean exit. In retrospect, then CIA chief Robert Gates explained it: "Never mistake for malice that which is easily explained by stupidity or incompetence."[31]

Marc Grossman, who would later become ambassador to Turkey and a major figure in the second Bush administration, recalls a brief conversation with General Jim Jamerson, on a hillside overlooking the Khabur bridge connecting Turkey to Iraq. Jamerson wondered how long it would be before the U.N. took over the whole operation.

"We thought it would probably take thirty days," said Grossman.

The United States kept patrolling the safe haven in Iraqi Kurdistan for twelve more years. American jets overhead protected the Kurds from their exterior enemies—Iraq, Turkey, and Iran. But who would protect the Kurds from one another?

CHAPTER FOUR

Burning Down the House

Qubad Talabani, the younger of Mam Jalal Talabani's two sons, grew up mostly in the care of his grandfather, Ibrahim Ahmad, in the comfortable anonymity of London, south of the Thames. Born in 1977, Qubad arrived just in time for his father to slip back into Iraq to launch the PUK's rebellion—a war that would continue for twenty-five more years, sometimes fighting the Iraqi regime, sometimes fighting other Kurds. His mother, Hero, returned to Iraq to fight at her husband's side when Qubad turned two, and his brother, Bafel, six. Other than the odd meetings at their grandfather's house—full of rebels, coup plotters, and the occasional spy—Qubad tried to live the life of a normal young Londoner. But he couldn't escape the infernal question, "What's a Kurd?" On the playground, in the classroom, as a teenager mingling at a pub, Qubad resigned himself to a twenty-minute explanation before every conversation of who, what, and where were the Kurds.

The question still followed him years later when Qubad Talabani moved to the United States to assist and apprentice with Barham Salih, by then the PUK representative in Washington. Qubad's twenties had brought some political awakening, lots of creative border crossings, and a few close calls with guerrilla warfare. He had stopped trying to masquerade as a regular young man. On a hiking trip in New York with his American fiancée's family he couldn't help but ask, "So you do this for fun?"

His future father-in-law asked, wasn't he having fun? "Yeah," Qubad replied, "but the last time I did this there were people with guns chasing me and I had just burned my own house down."

Qubad had started going "home" to Kurdistan in the early 1990s, when the Kurds suddenly found themselves with a de facto country to run. In August 1996, as his summer holidays ended, he prepared to return to England to complete a degree in engineering. At the end of the month he set out toward Erbil to register with his university via the only working fax machine in the province. His father's pesh merga turned him back; the PUK and KDP were fighting, and he was advised to wait. In a few days, they said, the PUK would have Masoud Barzani on the run, if not completely wiped out. The following day, however, Talabani's men were running away. As a matter of family honor, they doused their family house in gasoline and torched it rather than have their enemy take shelter there. As the house went up in smoke, Qubad followed his father's war party into the peaks and crags along the Iranian border.[1]

FREE KURDISTAN, on the other hand, didn't from the start resemble a burning building, astounding all predictions.

Since the 1980s the Kurdistan Front had used the rhetoric of democracy in all its international public relations. In May 1992 it actually held an election, which Masoud Barzani's KDP expected to win in a walk. His family name was still the rallying cry for the Kurdish struggle, and his troops had been much stronger during the intifada. What's more, the jahsh tribes, counting for hundreds of thousands of votes, had pitched in with Barzani—perhaps because his more traditional style suited them better than the PUK's modern image, perhaps for protection.[2] Many of the jahsh had taken Saddam's silver during the Anfal campaign, apprehending, if not personally executing, thousands of mostly PUK supporters. While Talabani didn't challenge the amnesty given to them before the intifada, he unsuccessfully opposed giving the jahsh tribes voting rights in the elections.[3] Some tribes and clans sat on the fence and enjoyed a cheap bidding war between the parties with promises of patronage and actual cash paid, though economic hardship kept the sums low.[4]

Budding democracy in Kurdistan was not well received in the

neighborhood, and sent the Turks into a fit. Long before anyone in Washington considered that the safe haven had become its own country, conspiracy-minded Turks had seen through it as an American plot for Kurdish independence, expansion, and the destruction of Kemal Atatürk's dream. It fed such fantasies when a few of the American airdrops of food and water ended up in the hands of Turkey's Kurdish Workers' Party (PKK) rebels, one load falling directly to the PKK on the Turkish side of the border.[5] The United States exhibited its usual schizophrenia. The Turks demanded that America renew its permission to fly out of Incirlik every six months, a constant source of stress that would dog the U.S.-Turkish relationship for the next dozen years. As the United States fought to protect the Kurdish safe haven, it resisted the idea of promoting democracy there for the same old reasons: Turkish sensitivities and a fear of dismembering Iraq. The State Department put out an order well in advance that staff should be nowhere near Kurdistan on Election Day.

With just a week to go before the election, the Kurds hit a snag. The "indelible" ink they'd imported from Germany washed right off the fingers it was supposed to mark after people voted. They needed new ink, and it had to be expedited through Turkey. The request ran up a chain of U.S. officials, who realized they could make or break the Kurds' first democratic exercise. "Do we really want to just shrug our shoulders?" one diplomat asked Marc Grossman, in Ankara. The U.S. embassy wrestled with the Turks, and at the last moment, with resistance from Washington, finally got the Kurds their ink.

It was a real election, with a runoff planned if no candidate won a majority in the first round. Kurdish leaders actually hit the campaign trail and vied for influence; Sami Abd-al-Rahman, Mahmoud Othman, Jalal Talabani, and Masoud Barzani all spoke in public rallies, as did the Islamist candidate from Halabja, Othman Abdulaziz. The vote should have settled disputes and allowed the Kurdistan Front to move forward. However, Barzani won with only 45 percent of the vote, not by the vast margin he and his supporters had predicted. The PUK placed a surprisingly close second, with 43.6 percent, and succeeded in outflanking Barzani with more aggressive language about Kurdish rights, and a pledge not to negotiate with Saddam.[6] Though Talabani was older, he appeared more modern and internationalist than Barzani. Observers on hand said the elections were fairly clean—for Kurdistan. "I think everybody cheated," said Mahmoud Othman. "We don't know who cheated better."

Othman and Abd-al-Rahman certainly expected to do better, and had their parties won a larger share, it might have defused some of the tension that ensued. The Kurdistan Front stipulated the high threshold of 7 percent for a party to get any seats at all, and none of the minority parties qualified. A heated dispute led to a fifty-fifty power-sharing agreement in the parliament between the KDP and PUK, with five seats added for the minority Christian Assyrian Kurds, making an unwieldy parliament of 105 seats—6 of them held by women. The Kurdistan Front handed out ministries: one each for the Iraqi Communist Party, the Assyrian Democratic Movement, and the Kurdistan Toilers' Party, and the rest divided up between the PUK and KDP. Each KDP minister had a PUK deputy and vice versa; each menial job handed to a KDP loyalist had to be matched with a PUK patron. Othman, Abd-al-Rahman, and the Islamist party sat out.

The runoff election between Barzani and Talabani was postponed indefinitely after tensions flared and never faded. Kurdistan was neatly divided into two spheres of influence: Barzani's northwest against Talabani's southeast. Almost immediately influential Kurds—from military commanders to tribal leaders to poets to doctors—started lining up on one side or another, though Mahmoud Othman notably remained neutral. Barzani opened channels to the Turks, while Talabani tacitly supported the PKK. Any ideological differences were dwarfed by a pure battle of personalities.

"If you read the program of both parties at that time, or even now, and remove the title, you can't tell which is KDP and which is PUK," said Othman, who soon afterward resumed life as an exile back in London.

Even without the battle lines drawn, Kurdistan was free but desperate. For decades the least developed part of Iraq, it now went without the meager aid Baghdad had given. The region produced little but tobacco and grain and had served as a virtual colony to Baghdad.[7] The price of heating oil increased two hundred times over the previous subsidized rate,[8] and people started hacking down the remaining forests for lumber and charcoal. Most families found themselves selling off their heirlooms. The government lived off customs revenue from borders with Iran and the more lucrative Khabur bridge crossing to Turkey. At the same time, nongovernmental organizations started setting up shop. Their number was small, but given the poverty of the countryside, their cash made a difference. The NGOs also had the curious habit of hiring local Kurds based solely on their talents without regard to clan or family connections. The United Nations did the same, planting the seeds of a meritocracy. However, not all the people setting up shop were as nongovernmental as they seemed. Some time during 1992, Ahmed Chalabi arrived.*

IN MAY 1991, still believing that Saddam would fall under his own weight, President George H. W. Bush signed a "finding," authorizing the CIA to take a shot at removing the Iraqi dictator. By the end of that year the White House had authorized forty million dollars to that end, including an anti-Saddam propaganda campaign directed internationally by John Rendon, a cloak-and-dagger PR specialist.[9] Bringing the Iraqi opposition together has often been compared to herding cats. By the summer of 1991 the agency discovered a fiercely intelligent Iraqi exile they thought could lash the different groups together, the ex-banker Ahmed Chalabi. A secular Shi'ite Arab who had left Baghdad as a child, Chalabi formed the Iraqi National Congress (INC), based in London. By the fall of 1992, Chalabi moved to Iraqi Kurdistan and hung out his shingle as a rebel. His association with the CIA didn't come out right away, and was better concealed by the fact that Chalabi started bucking the CIA's direction almost from the outset.

The Kurdish parties already knew Chalabi from opposition conferences in Beirut and Vienna, where they made a marriage of convenience. Chalabi needed the Kurds for their boots on the ground, and eventually, their liberated territory; it allowed him to operate from inside Iraq and not be taken as an armchair revolutionary. What's more, Chalabi's domineering personality soon pared down the INC's membership. The religious Shi'ite factions, based in Tehran, didn't like the INC's Western support. Also halfway out the door was the Iraqi National Accord (INA), a group of ex-Ba'athists and military officers close to England's MI6. Chalabi needed the Kurds to give the impression that the INC was more than his cabal. The Kurds had a similar opinion of Chalabi from the

---

* Opinions vary about Ahmed Chalabi: exile, banker, MIT doctorate, patriot, hustler, spin doctor, scoffer at all things inferior, and probably the single person most culpable for selling the ideas that brought the American invasion in 2003. Peter Galbraith notes that Chalabi had no reason to be more loyal to American interests in Iraq than to his own interest in pulling down Saddam.

outset—he was their token Arab so they could convince the United States that their program was pan-Iraqi and not just Kurdish.[10] When Chalabi arrived in Iraqi Kurdistan, however, he found that everything, including his INC, got caught up in the competition between Barzani and Talabani.

Chalabi landed in Iraq with fewer than a hundred people, including the pesh merga assigned to him by Masoud Barzani. The INC intelligence chief, Arras Habib Karim, came from an old KDP family of Fayli Kurds and was able to converse with the locals in their own language.* The Kurdistan Regional Government based itself in Erbil, but Barzani quartered the INC in an abandoned hotel up the hill in Salahudin, a KDP stronghold. It's hard to say whether Barzani brought them close so he could show off his influence over the INC or if he just wanted to keep tabs on Chalabi.[11] The INC paid off the squatters living in the hotel, gutted it, refurnished it in fine style, and hired a small army of employees, presumably with CIA money. Chalabi then set out to rally recruits for the coming war with Saddam. Another war came instead.

With all of Kurdistan fighting over crumbs, the revenue coming in at the Khabur bridge from Turkey suddenly looked like a king's treasury, and it became the focus of a cold war between the KDP and PUK. Ostensibly, the elections had unified the pesh merga, but minor disputes led each side to charge the other with misusing Kurdistan's army.[12] Before that war turned hot, both parties did some settling with smaller factions. Most important, the PUK began what would become a long feud with the Islamic Movement of Kurdistan (IMK), which Iran was strengthening along the border from Darbandikhan all the way up to Ranya.

Four years of senseless civil war in Kurdistan began on May 1, 1994, in a tiff between a KDP landlord and a couple of PUK shop owners. In the city of Qala Diza, a tribal leader named Ali Haso Mirkan laid claim to a stretch of land given to him by the Iraqi government in 1973, which then took the land back from him in 1980 to put up government buildings. The government offices were sacked in the 1991 uprising, and the original owners of the land reclaimed it and put up some shops. Mirkan's son was a KDP security guard; KDP officials apparently gave him a new deed

---

* The Fayli Kurds are doubly unlucky—landless as Kurds and oppressed as Shi'ites in Saddam's Iraq. Saddam deported tens of thousands of them from Baghdad in the late 1970s and '80s, sending them to Iran, often with nothing but the change in their pockets.

for the property. The PUK sent a team to negotiate on behalf of the shopkeepers, and it's unclear who turned the parley into an ambush. Both Mirkan and a PUK official were killed along with many of their men, but each party's leader claimed no involvement.[13] Talabani was in France at the time meeting with President Mitterrand. As usual in the Middle East, this appeared less of an alibi than a conspiracy—KDP supporters theorized that Talabani had planned his absence so he could come back and negotiate once his troops had seized power.

PUK and KDP areas suddenly separated like oil in water. Talabani's troops took the towns of Ranya, Sulimaniya, and Koi Sanjaq. In most cases the KDP supporters were allowed to withdraw peacefully. Many were bused to the eastern city of Halabja, where the KDP formed a quick alliance with the Islamic Movement of Kurdistan. In the northern cities of Zakho and Dohuk, Barzani ordered all PUK pesh merga to evacuate. Many of the smaller commanders fell prey to ambushes on the roads— Talabani wasn't in the country to control his coalition, and Barzani apparently didn't stop his men from engaging in tit-for-tat violence. PUK prime minister Kosrat Rasul* met with Barzani to negotiate but claimed he could not control the actions of another PUK commander, Jabar Farman, who had amassed two thousand pesh merga and was threatening KDP headquarters. By the time Talabani returned to Erbil, flown in by a Turkish helicopter, full-fledged war raged in Kurdistan. The Turkish help probably wasn't aimed at ending the war so much as ensuring that neither side really won. A similar message from Iran warned the PUK not to wipe out Barzani's headquarters.[14]

The oasis of free Iraq now began to self-destruct, just as Saddam Hussein had predicted. The schism ended any serious efforts to threaten Baghdad, but at the same time it gave Ahmed Chalabi's INC a much more practical raison d'être. The INC, along with the Iraqi Communist Party, offered to play peacemaker and started setting up white-flag checkpoints between the warring Kurdish factions. Chalabi's stock went way up with local Kurds, and in Washington as well. By mid-July peace negotiations convened in Paris with Madame Mitterrand's loan of the president's summerhouse. Najmaldin Karim flew in from Washington along with other notable neutrals. The PUK sent Nawshirwan Mustafa, Talabani's deputy,

---

* Even this early, each party had its own prime minister; essentially two full governments existed, such as they were.

and the KDP sent Sami Abd-al-Rahman, who had allied himself with Barzani. On July 16 they signed an agreement, including provisions for the drafting of a constitution, holding the long-delayed runoff election, and sharing revenue from the bridge to Turkey. Peace lasted about four months.[15] By December 1994 the PUK laid siege to Erbil, surrounding the KDP's remnants in the Sheraton Hotel* just south of the old citadel. On January 15, 1995, after the INC helped get most of the KDP staff out, the PUK attacked the few dozen fighters who refused to leave the Sheraton. Erbil belonged to Jalal Talabani, and the bullet marks stayed on the side of the hotel for a decade.

It was an odd war. The joint parliament continued to operate until March 1995, when it finally stopped the charade, but people tried to go on with other aspects of life as usual. Although the war was always between the parties, not the people, civilians inevitably got caught in the fray. A drive from Sulimaniya to Erbil required passing through some two dozen checkpoints, each one an opportunity to meet a soldier in a foul mood. Beatings of civilians, even women, were common. Males of military age always felt targeted, and the battle lines split up families—men would be forced to confine themselves to one party's territory and their wives would have to travel across the line every few weeks for money and a brief conjugal visit. Soldiers suspiciously read any letters being sent between the cities. The enemy to the south was all but forgotten.

"I have been stopped and harassed by both PUK and KDP numerous times, and every time they accused me of being from the other side. They never stopped me and said, 'You are a Ba'athist,'" said one Kurd from Halabja.[16]

Amnesty International issued a report in 1995 deploring human rights abuses by all the parties, including practices of torture that could have been learned directly from Saddam: the use of electricity, sexual torture, and beating with hoses and cables. Even the minor parties involved ran secret prisons, but the KDP and PUK had the largest, and their internal security organizations also ran detention centers off the books, where they held alleged operatives from other parties as well as Iraqis from the

---

* In Iraq, "Sheraton" is a label applied to the biggest hotels. The largest hotel in Baghdad is called the Ishtar Sheraton, though it hasn't had any formal ties to the hotel chain for years. The same applied to the building in Erbil that the PUK shot up in 1995; when they rebuilt it in 2004, they called it "Sheraton" again.

south. Amnesty International condemned the use of heavy artillery inside cities and the mutilation and execution of prisoners.[17] Both Barzani and Talabani promised to address the issues and then went right on making their idiotic war.

U.N. personnel and NGO workers routinely traveled across the KDP-PUK front lines, though some organizations employed bodyguards from the neutral Surchi tribe that controlled pivotal points along the Hamilton Road (the highway between Erbil and Rawanduz built by British engineer A. M. Hamilton in 1932, still one of the best roads in Kurdistan).

"I was afraid the U.N. was going to get jerked out of here," recalled Stafford Clarry, who worked with the United Nations throughout the conflict. He remembers driving up to the front lines with impunity to berate the Kurdish leaders. "We are not here to protect you from Saddam in order for you to fight in peace amongst yourselves," Clarry recalled telling Jalal Talabani.

Naturally Washington, now the Clinton administration, began to sour on the Kurdish freedom fighters who seemed more interested in killing each other than hurting Saddam. Barham Salih, who had moved to the States as the Kurdistan Front representative, now reverted to his roots as the PUK's man. Still, he took no pleasure in trying to spin a positive side of the feud back in Kurdistan. "Dr. Barham" became a friend to many of the Middle East watchers in Washington and had soon perfected the art of the Beltway backyard barbecue, where much real political work gets accomplished. Just as he was getting his game on, the people he represented were acting horribly.

"Washington was probably among the best years of my life," Salih said. "And it was probably an impossible mission—explaining the complexities of Kurdish and Iraqi politics to Americans, and worse, explaining American politics and decisions to Iraqis and Kurds."

Salih soon rivaled his partner in London, the KDP's Hoshyar Zebari, for media savvy and government access. With the growing civil strife, the two men could no longer be partners. "The civil war was the most embarrassing time. I was never a hard-liner, anti-KDP—the same applies to my friend Hoshyar," said Salih, "but war pushed you into these trenches, and you have to take the other side on. Both of us recognized that it was stupid."

Skepticism grew at the State Department and the White House that this Kurdish safe haven would ever amount to a significant thorn in the side of Saddam Hussein. But Bush's "finding" was still in force, and the wheels in motion. About two years after Chalabi set up the INC shop, the CIA had sent two agents out to support and keep tabs on him. Both men, Bob Baer and Warren Marik, had done serious time in the Middle East and Afghanistan. Along with other agents, they rotated into a station house just up the road from the INC headquarters in Salahudin. Cowboys at heart, they saw their goal as bringing down Saddam, even as Washington started to question the wisdom of the idea.

Kurdistan was a good place to cultivate potential coup plotters. One of the first visitors to the station house was an Iraqi general named Wafiq al-Samarra'i, the former head of Saddam's military intelligence, Istikhbarat. Warren Marik recognized the Iraqi from his own service in Baghdad when the CIA was helping Saddam during the Iran-Iraq war. Samarra'i had met Masoud Barzani during one of the Kurdistan Front's negotiating trips to Baghdad, and the Kurdish leader had witnessed one of Saddam Hussein's sons-in-law dressing down the general publicly.[18] Samarra'i had kept in contact with Barzani, who helped smuggle him north. He met with Bob Baer in Zakho in fall 1994, just as the CIA had entered Kurdistan to begin setting up their operation. Samarra'i claimed to represent a network of key military officers—mostly his own family from the Sunni Arab city of Samara. He plotted to cause a disturbance in Baghdad that would spook Saddam and send him running for his fortified hometown, 'Awjah, near Tikrit. Once Saddam had bolted, Samarra'i would enlist a brigade and two divisions in on his plot, and a commander from the nearby armory school would commandeer a dozen tanks and corner Saddam. With the dictator stuck in his hometown, Samarra'i would declare a military government, friendly to the United States.[19]

Baer sent what details he could gather back to CIA headquarters in Langley, Virginia, where it received an unexcited response. This noncommittal feedback clearly jangled the coup plotters' nerves, but before long the plan was caught up in the Kurdish dispute. Ahmed Chalabi and Jalal Talabani proposed to join in the plot and start an uprising on the same day as the diversion, attacking the Iraqi Fifth Corps along the lines protecting Mosul and Kirkuk. They told Baer they would be able to humiliate Saddam by taking some of his territory away—perhaps even returning Kirkuk to Kurdish control and helping Samarra'i gain power. There was another motive. Both Chalabi and Talabani were short on cash.

Chalabi had competition for his spot as the CIA's man in the Iraqi opposition. In London the Iraqi National Accord, the group of former military officers led by Ayad Allawi, were gathering sources for their own putsch, with much more confident support from the CIA and Britain's MI6. Chalabi aimed to beat them to the punch, but his resources were few. The United States had promised funding for the INC as a mediation force between the warring Kurds, and then never decided which agency should pay.[20] Chalabi began borrowing money from merchants in Kurdistan, buying things in the bazaar on credit and hinting that all would be reimbursed when he and Uncle Sam took down Saddam.

Talabani's troubles related to money in a different way—his rival was making too much. Since the clashes began, whatever money the KDP had shared from the Khabur bridge stopped completely, just when the border crossing had become a gold mine. Tankers smuggling oil in breach of the U.N. sanctions on Iraq were crowding the road to the Turkish border. From the outset, America turned a blind eye to the black market trade, for it did a little bit to placate the Turks and did something to fund the Kurdish region. The trade also made enormous amounts of money for Saddam's regime, being one of his few ways of directly selling oil for cash. The KDP made far less money taxing the trucks as they went through to Turkey, but it gave them a clear advantage over the PUK. Masoud Barzani's nephew Nechirvan was rumored to control the business on the Kurdish side at Zakho, charging tolls that went straight into the KDP's coffers. Clearly a fair bit of the money also kept the party leadership healthy and well-heeled. American aid workers at the border started calling Nechirvan "the best dressed man in Kurdistan."[21]

Talabani decided in February 1995 that he didn't need to choose between attacking Saddam or attacking the KDP—he could do both at once. By attacking the Fifth Corps of the Iraqi army, he would rally Kurdish support and shame Masoud Barzani as either a follower behind the PUK and INC attack, a coward for sitting out, or a blackguard for attacking Talabani while he was fighting the good fight against Saddam.[22] This was all to occur with the American military backup that Bob Baer hadn't explicitly said was coming.

Reality fell like a thousand-pound bomb on March 3, the day before the planned offensive and coup. Somewhere on the rocky road from Salahudin to the CIA in Langley to 1600 Pennsylvania Avenue, a message had fallen through the cracks—the message about the entire conspiracy. To this day the missing link hasn't owned up, but Bill Clinton's national security advisor Tony Lake discovered the existence of the plot within a day of the zero hour. To add insult to insanity, Lake found out through a National Security Agency program eavesdropping not on the Kurds but on the Iraqis. Saddam was in on the CIA's plot before the White House was. The Iranians were also privy, possibly invited by Chalabi, and massed troops on the border.[23] Lake sent an urgent cable to Baer in northern Iraq, telling him to carry it to the INC and the Kurds. It read: "The action you have planned for this weekend has been totally compromised. We believe there is a high risk of failure. Any decision to proceed will be on your own."[24]

"On your own" apparently described Jalal Talabani's offensive, Ahmed Chalabi's INC, and the previous several months of Bob Baer's operation. Baer dutifully delivered the bad news on the morning of March 3. He discovered that the KDP already knew; Hoshyar Zebari had been checking with his own contacts in Washington and had told Barzani that Baer was blowing smoke.[25] Chalabi and Talabani decided to move ahead anyway.

"This 'Bob' came in the morning and said no, the White House decided that you must not move," Talabani recalls. "Bob said the Americans aren't coming, we don't want you to lose, they will crush you. We didn't listen to the advice from Tony Lake. We said, 'We will go.'"

Lake says his advice came purely from a desire to avert disaster. The military was finding out about the plan just as late, and had no resources to scramble even if they had wanted to. "I am still very confused about what happened," Lake says. "At the last minute we look into it, and it's clear to everybody—the CIA, Defense, State—that there was no chance. It was infiltrated by Iran *and* Iraq, a potential Bay of Pigs."

Regardless of what the putsch might have been with everyone reading from the same music, it didn't become the massacre Washington predicted. The pesh merga fought well; from Erbil, PUK commanders Omar Fattah and Kosrat Rasul made it as far as Altun Kopri—halfway to Kirkuk. Talabani himself got to Karahangir, the ridge overlooking Kirkuk. He suffered few casualties and captured thousands of Iraqi soldiers—most of them underfed conscripts who gave up at the first chance. Talabani claims that several more Iraqi officers were ready to surrender their men but that he halted when he heard that U.S. Secretary of Defense William Perry had announced the United States did not support the attacks.[26]

Wafiq al-Samarra'i's coup was stillborn. Clearly aware that something was afoot, Saddam never bolted toward 'Awjah and kept his entire army on alert. As Samarra'i set out to rally his conspirators, he found himself under arrest—by the KDP, who also stopped every INC member they could find and put them under house arrest until the window for action had passed.[27] Chalabi finally got the hint and moved his operation from Barzani's stronghold down the hill to Erbil—it seemed that Barzani didn't trust the INC and their American pals, or he simply wanted to thwart the PUK. Samarra'i left Iraq and wound up fuming with the other exiles in London. Back in Langley the CIA wondered if the coup was ever more than an attempt by Chalabi and Talabani to draw them into a war with Saddam. Jalal Talabani at least got some of what he wanted—an angry Masoud Barzani looking cowardly and the sight of rockets exploding over Kirkuk.

Two weeks later another neighbor reared its head. In "hot pursuit" of rebels from the Kurdish Workers' Party (PKK), the Turkish army thundered across the border into Iraqi Kurdistan with their biggest incursion yet: about thirty-five thousand troops backed by Turkey's tanks, helicopters, and American-built F-16s. Talabani had been allowing the PKK to move freely in his territory, while as with everything, Barzani was on the opposite side, fighting the PKK and earning Turkey's favor. Whether the PKK inspired the Turkish incursion, or Saddam requested it, or Barzani encouraged it is not clear. In any case, it was enough to force Talabani to pull back from the front lines near Kirkuk and protect his base. The Turks withdrew after about two months.[28]

For his part, Bob Baer returned to Washington, where he had been told that Tony Lake wanted his head on a pike. Who blew the coup remains a contentious debate. Baer eventually wrote a bestselling book, *See No Evil*, in which he blamed Lake for the mess and implied that the national security advisor had unleashed the FBI on him, starting an investigation for the attempted murder of a foreign head of state. (Warren Marik refers to the NSC head as "Bunny Lake," after an old Otto Preminger film in which a woman claims her daughter is missing but the daughter might not exist.) Lake pleads ignorance, and Baer himself seems to have softened his opinion, admitting that the plan must have seemed "nutty" to anyone who found out about it the way Lake did.*

Amid the absurdity, the United States had lost something very real. Despite all the double-dealing going on in Kurdistan, it was still the most logical place for America to cultivate human intelligence sources inside Saddam's Iraq. To anyone with a real chance of taking out Saddam, the message was clear. "The U.S. ends up looking like one hand isn't talking to the other," says Kenneth Pollack, a CIA alumnus who was Lake's director for Near East on the NSC. "It makes the Kurds wonder about what kind of a circus we're running."

Not long after Chalabi and Talabani's foray to the south, someone back in the greater Washington area leaked word of Chalabi's CIA sponsorships. Mark Parris, on the National Security Council, went to London to read Chalabi the riot act, and Chalabi's first honeymoon with Washington was over. The Clinton administration started to think of the INC as bad for business, and of Jalal Talabani as a dangerous wild card. One more low blow would come to make the trifecta.

Throughout the fall of 1995 the State Department's unofficial Kurdish desk, led by the senior officer for Iraq and Iran, Bob Deutsch, had tried to get Barzani and Talabani to end their rivalry. The KDP and PUK sent delegations to an American-sponsored peace conference in Drogheda, Ireland. But the two sides weren't ready to cut a deal, each wanting to hold a position of advantage. Talabani had even taunted Barzani that he was never going to see Erbil again, except through binoculars from the hilltop at Salahudin.[29] When the negotiators met with Deutsch, they found the United States wasn't bringing much to the table other than free advice, according to Nawshirwan Mustafa, the PUK delegate.

"I said, okay, we withdraw from Erbil, but if you guarantee that KDP doesn't attack and occupy Erbil; it remains neutral," said Nawshirwan Mustafa. "[Deutsch] said he can't guarantee it. I said, can you send retired

---

* Lake provided me with an e-mail forwarded to him on April 1, 2003, from Ron Kessler, who was corresponding with Baer for a book about the CIA. In the e-mail Baer wrote, "As for Lake, as I understand it, he was never told about the Samarra'i plan . . . or at least not until after March 5. No wonder he thought it was nutty." Baer can't be too upset these days after George Clooney played him in *Syriana*. Baer didn't respond to repeated requests to be interviewed for this book.

U.S. soldiers to keep the peace? We'll pay their salaries. He didn't agree. I said, we will withdraw from Erbil, but you guarantee that customs revenue from Khabur comes to the central bank. He said, I can't give you guarantee. I said, okay. I will stay in Erbil."

To the Kurds, America seemed uninterested and unwilling to spend a penny on a real peacekeeping effort. The two million dollars promised at Drogheda for a neutral Kurdish peacekeeping force never materialized— perhaps lost in President Clinton's mêlée with the new Republican-controlled Congress. To Washington, the Kurds seemed hopelessly uncooperative and ungrateful for all the political capital it took to keep Operation Provide Comfort running through Turkey.*

The CIA had one last arrow in its quiver: Ayad Allawi's Iraqi National Accord. Theirs was to be a "textbook" coup, with plotters inside Saddam's palace and a quick decapitation of the Iraqi regime. The Clinton administration was betting on Allawi's group of former military officers, and apparently so was Barzani. The KDP sent a young Kurd from Zakho, Muhammad Ihsan, to work with the coup plotters at the CIA station in Amman, Jordan. Ihsan recalls making several hair-raising trips to Baghdad to plant specially concealed Inmarsat satellite phones—at the time the most advanced and compact device, which was about the size of a laptop. Ihsan helped smooth the way for many Iraqi officers to slip into Kurdistan and sometimes in and out of the country from there. The INA managed to recruit people inside Saddam's military, his air-defense systems, and even his elite Republican Guard. But a nearly perfect coup plot was not enough to take down Saddam.[30] "I was in Amman when I heard," said Ihsan. One of their men had been taken at the lonely desert border on the road to Baghdad, probably picked up by Baghdad's dreaded secret police, the Mukhabarat. "I had the feeling that we were fucked and we were going to lose a lot of our friends."

Saddam didn't tip his hand for several months, letting the whole network reveal itself. In June 1996 he rounded up more than one hundred members of the conspiracy—all very well placed, and all discovered.

---

* Also American personnel had been lost in the effort. In April 1994 the small contingent of U.S. Special Forces led by Colonel Dick Naab had been pulled out after an incident of "friendly fire" in which an American F-15 shot down two American Black Hawk helicopters, killing twenty-five State Department and military personnel, Turkish officials, and Kurdish guards.

Then the Mukhabarat chiefs couldn't resist; they picked up one of the satellite phones, called the CIA in Amman, and told them to go home.[31] Baghdad sent an emissary to try to convince one of the prominent former Iraqi Army officers, Muhammad Abdullah Shahwani, to return to Iraq. The regime had collected both of his sons among the conspirators, and Saddam had offered to spare their lives if Shahwani would cooperate. It was folly, and Shahwani knew it; his sons were as good as dead, and not a quick death. The CIA agents took Shahwani with them as they packed up and fled back to America.[32]

"It convinced people in the U.S. government of something we were already suspecting, which was that any coup that we know about, Saddam knows about," said Ken Pollack. "And anyone [in Iraq] who was thinking about joining us looked at it and said, if I get in bed with these guys, I'm going to end up dead."

PERHAPS THE OLD warriors realized the endgame had begun, because both the KPD and PUK started a race to the bottom of dishonorable deals. In the summer of 1996 the KDP took issue with the Surchi tribe, which controlled a blind canyon along the crucial Hamilton Road. Barzani accused the tribe's leader, Hussein Agha Surchi, of breaking his neutrality by letting his son radio information to the PUK. The KDP staged a predawn raid on Hussein Agha's home, flattening his family compound and killing the sixty-five-year-old man, who reportedly died with his boots on and a warm gun in his hand. The KDP claimed that the dozens of Surchis killed in the raid had resisted arrest, but that didn't explain the destruction of their homes and the sale of their considerable business assets.[33] After that the tribes got the message and stayed out of the conflict.

For his part, Talabani cozied up to Iran, to the great consternation of the White House. Earlier in the conflict, Tehran had aided Barzani and the Kurdish Islamists in Halabja. The United States routinely scolded the Kurdish leaders for talking with the Islamic republic, but also understood that the Kurds needed to placate the Iranians inside what they considered their sphere of influence. After the Drogheda conference, Tehran quickly assembled its own repeat performance, with the same KDP and PUK delegations reaching the same unenforced deal. In the summer of 1996, though, Iran wanted something from Jalal Talabani.

The Kurdistan Democratic Party of Iran (KDPI) had been keeping a

base of exiled militants near Talabani's hometown of Koi Sanjaq since
1992.[34] But the KDPI had abused its welcome, staging a raid across the
border against an Iranian military base. Tehran pressured Talabani, and
he made them a deal. On July 27, thousands of Iranian revolutionary
guards with heavy artillery crossed into Iraqi Kurdistan, passing through
Sulimaniya to Koi Sanjaq. They shelled and rocketed the camp from the
hills above, leaving it a smoking ruin. Typical of deals with Jalal Talabani,
however, there was some fine print: he warned the KDPI in advance that
Iranian soldiers were coming, and when they hit the camp, most of the
families had evacuated.[35]

Talabani disputes to this day what he got in return. He and all the PUK
leaders claim that any weapons and ammunition from Iran came at
gouged, black market prices. But suddenly, Talabani began wiping up the
KDP, probably using Iranian territory to skirt around Barzani's battle
lines. The PUK leader launched an all-out offensive down the Hamilton
Road quite deliberately on August 16—the fiftieth anniversary of the
KDP's founding, and Masoud Barzani's fiftieth birthday. Barzani claims
the assault had Iranian artillery and air support; in any case it sent his men
fleeing to Salahudin.[36] Barzani sent out pleas in all directions warning
about Iranian incursions, and he pushed for the Clinton administration to
tell both Iran and Baghdad not to interfere in the north. His only response from Washington was another invitation, this time from Assistant
Secretary of State Robert Pelletreau, to meet for the next stage of peace
talks. The State Department started negotiations with KDP and PUK
members in London, completely detatched from reality. The elimination
of the Surchis, the bombing of the KDPI, then the offensive on Barzani's
birthday—all made for a summer of mayhem on the ground in Kurdistan.
Somehow, Washington failed to notice. Barzani then did the unthinkable.
Telling his people he had no other option in the face of the PUK's aggression, Barzani welcomed forty thousand of Saddam Hussein's troops
into Erbil on August 31 to help him.

In a region fabled for broken deals and rented loyalties, Barzani's invitation to Saddam Hussein may go down as the most shocking bargain
since God wagered with Satan that the devil couldn't break Job. While
back in 1966 Talabani had also fought with Baghdad against other
Kurds, that was before the era of Anfal and Halabja, poison gas and
mass graves. Most appalling to Barzani's own supporters must have
been seeing the Iraqi army roll through Qushtapa, where Saddam had

collected some eight thousand members of Barzani's clan for execution in 1983.

The Americans were the least prepared. "We had no clue. We felt absolutely blindsided by it," said Ken Pollack, "I know that the KDP says that they warned us. Whatever signals they were sending were too esoteric."

In London, the peace talks had been proceeding at their normal slow pace, and the State Department's Bob Deutsch pushed for an agreement on how the Americans and British might monitor a cease-fire. On August 31, Hoshyar Zebari had just called for a recess until the next morning so he could consult with Barzani back in Kurdistan. "We broke because we weren't making any progress," Deutsch recalls. "I went back to the hotel and immediately the phones started lighting up as we got information about Erbil."

When Zebari showed up the next morning to negotiate, the Americans were sure he had been playing dumb and sent him home. In fact the deal with the devil had probably been in the offing since at least July. State Department officials knew that Nechirvan Barzani had been making trips to Baghdad. The KDP had been sporting some new artillery and vehicles[37] and Saddam's tanks had been in motion weeks in advance. Rumors of KDP collaboration with Baghdad had spread around Kurdistan all summer, and Ahmed Chalabi's INC and Talabani's PUK both pushed the theory to the CIA station, which dutifully reported it back to Washington.* On August 31, as the offensive raged, Iraqi foreign minister Tariq Aziz took some delight in revealing that Barzani had requested Saddam's intervention nine days earlier in a letter in which he addressed the Iraqi dictator as "Your Excellency"—Barzani's version of kissing Saddam, and then some.[38] The KDP sat through the entire London conference knowing that the Americans were about to look very foolish.

IN A BACKHANDED compliment to Chalabi's INC, the Iraqi army hit them first, at Qushtapa on the way to Erbil. Helicopters and tanks overwhelmed the few hundred INC volunteers before dawn, and by daylight Iraqi sol-

---

* Again, the U.S. government's right hand didn't know what its left had done. A part of the State Department issued a démarche to Baghdad not to attack Erbil on August 28, but somehow Clinton administration high officials never realized that Saddam was about to attack Erbil, never prepared any military assets, and didn't warn Americans on the ground.

diers were rounding up Chalabi's recruits for execution. Ninety-six died the morning of August 31, and many more disappeared into Saddam's interrogation chambers. The INC's Arras Habib Karim made a frantic call to London, reporting that dozens of their operatives were in Saddam's hands, and that he himself had narrowly escaped from Erbil. Chalabi immediately made arrangements to fly back to Iraq.[39]

Erbil's streets trembled as hundreds of Iraqi tanks rolled into the city from four directions. The majority of the PUK forces retreated east toward the mountain-pass town of Degala, but the PUK's Erbil native Kosrat Rasul held on with a brigade of pesh merga, holed up in the parliament building as Iraqi helicopters made the windows shake. Rasul waited until nightfall and finally retreated. He lost about three hundred men as he fought his way out of the city around eleven P.M.[40]

"We knew Saddam would attack," Talabani said. "The Americans told us, 'Don't worry. If Saddam attacks, we will hit them.' We were depending on this. Otherwise we'd have used another tactic. If we knew America would not be helping us, we would have been coming out and saving hundreds of our forces. If the American airplanes came, we could have attacked the Iraqi army and gotten their tanks! But they didn't do it. We were obliged to retreat from Erbil in a very bad condition."

It quickly dawned on the nineteen-year-old Qubad Talabani that he wasn't going to reach England in time for school, though his summer vacation was clearly finished. The morning of the attack he awoke to the sound of his father pacing in the garden and shouting into a satellite phone. With his fluent English, Qubad found himself pressed into service as his father's satellite phone operator. He fielded calls from the press and spoke with the State Department's Robert Pelletreau several times, waiting for word about American air strikes. In their final conversation, Pelletreau told Qubad he was heading into an NSC meeting and would call back in two hours. That was the last word from him.

After the rout in Erbil the pesh merga prepared to make their stand at Degala, then fell back to Koi Sanjaq. Qubad Talabani remembers an angry and despairing call from Barham Salih. He told Salih to keep hope, maybe the line would hold at Koi Sanjaq. But Salih's information in Washington was better than what the PUK could see on the ground. "What are you talking about? Koi fell twenty minutes ago," Salih said over the scratchy line.

Koi's mountains protect a clear alley to Sulimaniya, and when they fell, the PUK's spirit crumbled. "In that part of the world, when your morale is gone, it's over," said Qubad. "You don't have technology—it's just pure balls that gets you through these battles." His father knew that as well. At some point during the day, Mam Jalal quietly took his son into the study and closed the door. There was very bad news. "Look, your mother . . . we're not sure where she is," Qubad recalled his father saying. "You have to be strong. People are going to look to you to judge the mood. However you may be feeling inside, you've got to put on a brave face."

Hero Talabani, the daughter of Kurdish intellectual Ibrahim Ahmad—who led the schism with the KDP in the 1950s—had been a late convert to the Kurdish resistance. As a student, Hero had no interest in politics, despite her father's prominence. After she married Talabani, she couldn't help but get involved, and in the 1970s she chose to stay with him in the mountains, sending her two sons back to her father's care. Hero is a slender woman, unassuming but intense. She was one of the few female members of the Kurdish parliament in 1992, and she also helped create the PUK's company of female pesh merga, which saw combat in the civil war, and helped found the Kurdish branch of the NGO Save the Children. On the same day Qubad had been told not to go to Erbil to fax in his university registration, his mother responded to a request from the NGO's office there—they needed her to bring in the payroll. War zones are always cash-only, so Hero Talabani put the forty-five thousand dollars in her suitcase and made what she had hoped would be a quick overnight trip to the Kurdish capital.

Like many other Kurdish leaders, Jalal Talabani had claimed a house in Erbil after the uprising; the Talibanis' house had belonged to Iraqi vice president Izzat al-Douri. When Hero got to the house, on the north edge of town, a repairman surprised her by knocking at her door. "Why are you here?" she asked suspiciously. "No one is supposed to know I'm in town."

"I didn't know you were back," the man replied. "I just had to tell somebody. I came on the road from Kirkuk, and it was full of Iraqi tanks."

Hero drove to the parliament building and found Kosrat Rasul gathering reports from all around the city. Kosrat expected an attack the next morning—August 31—and advised her to get out of town. One of the PUK's senior politicos, Omar Fattah, went with her back to the house, where they called Talabani by satellite phone. He asked his wife to leave. Moments later Kosrat called her on the satellite phone to make sure she had already left, and she put him off. Fattah tried to persuade her, and Kosrat even sent pesh merga to the house to plead, but she wouldn't go.

"I didn't do it. I don't like to run away. It's very bad for the morale of the pesh merga," she said.

When the attack began, it was like nothing she had ever seen. "From the roof we saw a line that was all fire—the Iraqi artillery. I lived for many years in the mountains, but this shelling was something else," said Hero. "You couldn't hear one or two—it was mixed together like bursts from a Kalashnikov. I informed my husband. I think I phoned Barham [Salih] also, in the U.S. that it had started."

By the following day the PUK line fragmented, and Hero's small group found the Talibanis' house on the front line of advancing KDP and Iraqi troops. As artillery shells started landing nearby, Hero's convoy pulled out. But the conspicuous group of cars started drawing fire. One of her bodyguards shouted over the din that it was time to run—a good decision, as the closest pursuers seemed more interested in looting Talabani's Oldsmobile, with the satellite phone in the back, than in actually catching the PUK first lady. They sprinted some distance in the clear before someone spotted them and started lighting up the ground with bullets. Hero's guards grabbed her by each arm and ran. "I cannot run like them," she said. "I was like a cartoon—running but my legs were not on the ground."

They sprinted across an open lot with bullets flying, but miraculously, no one was hit. In the safety of an alleyway the small group looked for a house to hide in, but several civilians held up a Koran and begged them not to enter. Finally they started jumping over the garden walls behind successive houses, stopping when they reached a high wall, and huddling down in a corner. Hero grabbed the chance to smoke the cigarette she had been dying for.

"We've got to write to the director of *Rambo* and apologize," she told Fattah. "I've always said no one could be shot at like they do in those movies and have nothing happen. Now we've just done it."

The next hours robbed her of her sense of humor. While scaling the next wall, Hero fell, hitting her head and landing on her back with a crash. They found an empty house where she could lie down to recover, and Hero asked her soldiers to find her some local clothes—she was wearing jeans and a striped T-shirt, which were now quite dirty and out of place to begin with in conservative Erbil. They holed up for the night and changed houses the next day. Hero started losing her own morale. One of the men in the group was a relative stranger and was acting frightened.

Fearing he would give them away, Fattah sent the man looking for a new, safe location, and when he left, the group deserted him and moved. The next afternoon they commandeered a car and tried to drive out of the city amid the looters and Iraqi tanks.

Hero hid a Browning pistol under her borrowed dress, but they passed the checkpoints without being recognized. The car broke down just past the last KDP checkpoint on the road to Degala, and miraculously an empty taxi materialized. When she caught up with the retreating PUK army, Hero says, Kosrat Rasul's men nearly pulled her arms out with joy.[41]

NEWS OF THE Iraqi incursion came to the U.S. embassy in Ankara by an urgent call from the CIA's six-man team in Erbil—they needed to get out fast. Marc Grossman, now the ambassador to Turkey, talked to the Turks about letting the men cross the border. But the number trying to escape mushroomed. Iraqi troops, with KDP help, were rounding up all the opposition groups based in Erbil—the Turcomans, the Shi'ites, the Islamists, and especially the INC and anyone who had been working with Americans.[42] An additional thirty-nine INC men had been executed in Erbil and scores more fought to the death.[43] Then Grossman got another call from northern Iraq, informing him that at least six hundred people were running for Zakho, fearing that Saddam had marked them for death for associating with foreigners. Back in London, Bob Deutsch feared the worst.

"Get all of the Americans out of there tonight," Deutsch remembered advising the administration. "We didn't know what deal Barzani had cut with Saddam," he said, "Obviously in retrospect the deal was that he would give him the INC people. But it could just as easily have been a deal that said 'we'll give him the Americans.'"

Grossman talked to the Turkish foreign ministry again and this time he chartered a plane to fly out to Diyarbakir.[44] In Erbil the KDP admitted that Iraqi Mukhabarat agents had probably infiltrated the city, and panic ensued. Grossman found himself reprising his efforts from 1991; fortunately he knew the logistics of southeastern Turkey inside and out. Embassy officials sent buses to the border and loaded up exactly the number of people for whom they had seats on each flight from Diyarbakir. At first it was just the Americans and their associates, but over the following days a mini-exodus began, and about seven thousand people fled toward the Turkish border. When they reached Zakho, Julia Taft, from the aid coalition InterAction (and later a member of the Clinton State Department), lobbied hard to get them all out. Someone back in Washington had a guilty conscience, because suddenly the United States began airlifting seven thousand Iraqi Kurds. Rather than process them all in Turkey, Washington ordered U.S. Air Force planes to take the Kurds to a secure, if bizarre, location: the U.S. territory of Guam. The FBI and Immigration and Naturalization Service processed the refugees there. Eventually most of them ended up in places like Nashville, Tennessee, and Harrisonburg, Virginia.[45]

Meanwhile the PUK arranged for its own extrication. Talabani had been putting out an announcement internationally that his wife had been captured, in the hopes that it would give her some protection if she did fall into KDP or Iraqi hands. When Hero appeared, four days after the assault began, the PUK leadership abandoned any defense of Sulimaniya and made for the familiar refuge of Iran. The KDP later charged that this was a case of theatrics and that Talabani was trying to appeal for international intervention. In any case, the momentum, all important in irregular warfare, had left the PUK and they needed a safe distance to regroup. Talabani made preparations to abandon his headquarters at Qalaat Chowlan, above the city.

Still more Londoner than Kurdistani, Qubad Talabani accepted his father's surreal notion that the house needed to be burned to the ground before enemies could loot it. Still, the smell of smoke shocked him a bit as he finished his breakfast. Following the smell he discovered to his horror that an overzealous pesh merga with two cans of gasoline had started the fire—in the computer room. Worse yet, he hadn't removed the computers first. Qubad rushed in to save the equipement and yelled at the soldier, who hadn't realized that a laptop—rare and expensive in Kurdistan—should be treated any differently than the desks or chairs being thrown on the fire. As the Talabanis joined a massive convoy leaving Sulimaniya, some munitions started cooking off somewhere in the compound, giving the PUK a startling send-off.

The Iraqi army had apparently made a bargain with the KDP that they would only stay in Erbil for a few days, and they honored it, redeploying to Qushtapa—probably less out of respect for Barzani than from fear that Washington might eventually make up its mind to do something. Still, the KDP had taken Erbil, never to relinquish it. Continuing to level the charge that Talabani was using Iranian revolutionary guards, Barzani followed the PUK's collapsing line all the way up to the mountains near Qala

Diza. Talabani had slipped across the border to Iran and then reentered Iraqi Kurdistan near the mountaintop town of Zele. The snowy peaks became a combat zone. There Talabani discovered he was sharing Zele with an old friend—Ahmed Chalabi, and the remnants of the INC.

"That was for us an indication of this guy's bravery," Qubad recalled. "Anyone else would have gone back to Mayfair, counted his losses, and gotten on with life. But he stuck around and lived the life of a pesh merga. Whatever anyone can say about Ahmed Chalabi, I will never doubt his bravery."

Jalal Talabani also recontacted Washington, and heard Robert Pelletreau advise him not to fight, to stay put and depend on Washington to sort out a cease-fire. From his perspective on the mountainside, with Barzani's troops vowing to finish him off, Talabani told Pelletreau he was through listening, and instead he intended to take back his cities. Remarkably, the PUK started a counteroffensive in October and turned the tide completely. Smashing through the KDP's overextended forces, Talabani regained all of his lost territory by the end of the month and prepared to attack Erbil. Before he could strike, warnings came screaming in from Washington, Tehran, and Baghdad that he shouldn't enter the city. Talabani stood down.[46]

The Clinton administration had ignored the Kurdish issue as long as it could, hoping to coast through the presidential election without dealing with Iraq. Inaction finally started to cost them. At a White House principals meeting the day after Saddam's incursion into the north, the National Security Council pondered their limited military options. Clinton's advisors feared any help they gave would mean supporting Talabani against Barzani, and at the moment they could hardly decide whom they liked least.[47]

"The northern no-fly zone was a bluff from day one," said Bruce Riedel, then a senior Pentagon official on the Near East desk. "And when Saddam called it, that was dramatically illustrated."

The Turks felt reluctant enough about lending their base at Incirlik for even symbolic flights over Iraq, and they let Washington know that *real* attacks were out of the question. The next closest planes could be launched from Saudi Arabia, a long, risky flight away, and all of it over Iraqi territory. Because Saddam had pulled back so quickly, U.S. forces would have bombed his tanks south of the no-fly zone. It would have meant a major escalation of a conflict the Clinton administration mostly wanted to disappear.[48] Instead the United States used the incident as an excuse to do something it really wanted. Washington declared that the southern no-fly zone that had been in place since 1991 would now extend up to the 33rd parallel, just south of Baghdad. Then, in a move that stymied the Kurds, the United States retaliated against Saddam's incursion in the north not by hitting the army that had attacked Kurdistan, but by destroying Iraq's air-defense systems in the south. Still, some inside the administration protested that the response made America look impotent.[49] Taking out Iraq's antiaircraft batteries seemed a great idea for the jets patrolling over Iraq, but what good was a no-fly zone if Saddam was allowed to roll tanks instead of flying helicopters?

To this day Masoud Barzani and his entire party maintain they did what they had to do to survive, having called for help everywhere else they could, in response to an outside threat. "The 31st of August was not against the PUK," said Barzani. "It was against the Iranian intervention. It's one point within the larger process."

Nonetheless, from outside, the events of 1996 dumbfounded even sympathetic observers. August 31 seemed to prove once and for all that Barzani hated Talabani more than he hated Saddam Hussein. But considering what happened to his father with the American betrayal in 1975, Barzani probably trusted the Americans less than he trusted Saddam to honor a bargain and come to his aid. Similarly, the PUK will always deny it got significant military aid from Iran. Talabani at least admits that Iran helped after August 31, 1996, and in doing so gives some rhetorical cover for his rival. "Churchill cooperated with Stalin," said Talabani. "This is something ordinary. It's not a catholic marriage. There are short- and there are long-term deals."

It should be said that at the time of writing, neither leader easily talks about the events of the Kurdish civil war, though grudges remain within their military commands. Qubad Talabani, looking back at the whole mess from his Washington office, ruefully listed the missed opportunities, ending with a sigh: "God, if we would not have done that . . . I would say we would be independent today."

Indeed, the Kurdish leadership looked hell-bent on destroying their chances for freedom and killing the Kurdish state in the womb. If anything positive came from the conflict, it was the conclusive proof that neither side could eliminate the other. Or, as several frustrated Kurds remarked to American visitors, "You had your civil war, and now we've had ours."

CHAPTER FIVE

Carnival in Limbo

AFTER THE DISASTROUS SUMMER OF 1996, Washington had fired all its guns with nothing to show for it. Saddam looked coup-proof, and the Kurdish safe haven wasn't safe from threats inside or out. Both Clinton on the campaign trail and Robert Pelletreau in congressional hearings had protested that the civil war in Kurdistan was an internal problem, and implied that the Bush administration had left them this mess. But Kurdistan remained America's only window into Saddam's secret world. Pelletreau invited Barzani and Talabani to Ankara, where serious negotiations began in late October 1996. Both leaders signed an agreement that finally had some money behind it—the United States put up three million dollars in cash and four million more in vehicles and equipment from the Pentagon to fund a four-hundred-strong Peace Monitoring Force (PMF). To placate the Turks, three hundred of the force were ethnic Turcomans, Iraq's Turkik minority.[1] The peace held, more or less, until the following spring, when the Turks and the Kurdish Workers' Party (PKK) helped crack it.

Turkey's Kurdish rebels followed their leader Abdullah Öcalan with a fanaticism that eclipsed any of their stated ideology. Öcalan's PKK was far more violent than the Iraqi Kurdish parties as it fought a decades-long war against the Turkish government in which neither side respected civilians. Both the PKK and Talabani's PUK were founded in the mid-1970s with a leftist tone, and PKK fighters had always been more closely aligned with Talabani's PUK than with Barzani's KDP. But the real conflict between Barzani and the PKK was territorial. The PKK had bases in Barzani's backyard—in the northwestern Badinan region of Iraqi Kurdistan—and competed with the KDP for influence and real estate. As the only group in the region advocating outright independence for all four Kurdish regions, the PKK occasionally picked up recruits from among Iraqi Kurds, especially when one of the other parties pulled a particularly cynical move. If Barzani disliked the PKK, it was a good enough reason for Talabani to like them. This was hardly an even trade—the aid of the PKK in exchange for the enmity of the Turks. In May 1997 the Turkish army stormed into Kurdistan again—this time with about fifty thousand troops, tanks, choppers, and jet fighters. Turkey claimed to have killed some thirteen hundred militants, not distinguishing Öcalan's men from Talabani's.[2] The PUK slung insults at Masoud Barzani for calling in outside help once again; again he in turn blamed the PUK's alliance with Öcalan for provoking the Turks.

The political partition of the north began to solidify, and by the beginning of 1997 the PUK erected its own government in Sulimaniya to rival the KDP government in Erbil. Both claimed to be governing the entire Kurdish region. Every civil institution had a mirror on the other side—Erbil banned the Sulimaniya newspapers and vice versa. The desperate poverty eased a bit, especially on the KDP side of the border. When Saddam had pulled out in 1996, without official announcement, the internal blockade of Kurdistan had ended, most directly for Erbil. Spies certainly infiltrated from Baghdad, but trade came too, and for average Kurds that looked like a fair bargain—some of them hadn't eaten meat or even chicken for five years. Black market fuel prices came back down to a reasonable level.[3]

Around the same time, the economic embargo on Iraq had softened. In 1995 the U.N. had adopted resolution 986, which came to be known as "Oil-for-Food." The economic blockade imposed on Iraq after the invasion of Kuwait would continue, but Saddam Hussein would be allowed to sell two billion dollars' worth of oil every six months in exchange for food and other nonmilitary products. The Iraqi government, the U.N., and the United States wrangled over the details for some time, so the first shipments of oil didn't flow out of Iraq until the eve of 1997.[4] The United States primarily wanted to take away one of Saddam's propaganda tools: the sympathy he was winning because of economic hardship under the sanctions. It also took away some steam from the growing number of countries in favor of opening up to Iraq—like Russia, China, and France (the French had unceremoniously pulled their jets out of the no-fly-zone patrols in 1994). Twenty-five percent of the revenues went from a U.N. escrow account to Kuwait as war reparations, and another 3 percent covered the U.N.'s operating expenses, including the weapons inspection program. Because of the U.N.'s respect for Iraq's soveignty, Saddam still exercised influence on how quickly aid went north, but some Oil-for-Food supplies started flowing to Kurdistan. Still, both Erbil and Sulimaniya were capitals at war, and with tens of thousands of fighters to support, teachers and doctors went for months without pay.

"It was very dreary," said one State Department official who visited Kurdistan in 1997. "They wanted us to see the pesh merga everywhere. Resources were going to mounting machine guns in pickup trucks. Not much was going to public service."

There is an old Kurdish proverb that fighting is better than idleness, but Barzani and Talabani started showing signs of battle fatigue. This coincided with the Clinton administration finally taking an interest, and even allowing the State Department to create a position for a de facto Kurdistan desk officer. The State Department believed the Kurdish leaders sincerely wanted peace but needed an outside power to help them with appearances. On the ground, the war had embittered commanders from both parties. Barzani's nephew Nechirvan earned a reputation as a hardliner, while the PUK's Kosrat Rasul, his body already a road map of battle scars, also pushed hard to keep fighting. As a native of Erbil, Kosrat thought defeating the KDP was the only way he would get back to his hometown with any sort of dignity, and he led many of the offensives from the front.[5] With Turkish air support, the KDP erased any PUK gains, and the two parties found themselves back at the cease-fire line at Degala. With so much bad blood, Barzani and Talabani welcomed the American imprimatur that they could claim was forcing their hands. In the summer of 1998, Assistant Secretary of State David Welch made the trek to Kurdistan and invited both leaders to the United States.

In the first week of September, Barzani arrived and made the rounds of high-level meetings, including those with Secretary of State Madeleine Albright and Clinton's new national security advisor, Sandy Berger. The White House saw Barzani as more resistant and wanted the extra time to work on him; they had done a similar job on Talabani the previous year, bringing him to Washington to insist he shut off support for the PKK.[6]

By the second week in September both leaders had arrived; the PUK set up at the Marriott Key Bridge hotel, while the KDP was at the Four Seasons, across the bridge in Georgetown. As the White House strong-armed, internal Kurdish diplomacy also played a role. Najmaldin Karim shuttled back and forth over the river urging the two leaders to shake hands. On September 17, after many all-night negotiating sessions, the Kurds signed the Washington Agreement, witnessed in writing by David Welch.[7] After a White House ceremony with Madeleine Albright, the two leaders went home to a cold peace. The deal permanently stopped the shooting but left the main issues unresolved. The PUK still accused the KDP of pulling down a million dollars each day at the Khabur bridge border; the KDP still protested that Talabani was collaborating with the PKK. The two sides held on to their prisoners from the civil war. From Washington's perspective the deal was a good one—the Kurds had promised not to invite nor provoke any more outside interference. Northern Iraq had a long way to go, but at least it wasn't hemorrhaging. And in the view of the Clinton administration, someday it might come in handy.

OUT OF ONE shivering newborn pseudo-state, the Kurds cleaved two totally separate provinces. This I discovered in January 2000, when I went looking for something that doesn't exist: a visa to an invisible country.

I was a freelance reporter, with only a few years' experience. I spoke some Arabic and had traveled in the Middle East, but my journalism experience came from Latin America. In 1999, while I was living in Bogotá, Colombia, I had read about the capture of the Kurdish rebel Abdullah Öcalan. U.S. intelligence helped nab Öcalan in Kenya, and he was turned over to Ankara, where everyone expected him to swing. Press reports of Kurds in Turkey and Europe immolating themselves in protest shocked and fascinated me. When I left Bogotá in 1999, I decided to make a trip to Kurdistan, but as a freelance journalist with almost no budget, getting there took some acrobatics.[8]

I first visited the PUK office near Union Station in Washington, with the smoothest Kurd in America, Barham Salih. Already the dean of the Iraqi opposition in D.C., Salih had been the first name mentioned to me by former ambassadors to the region. Warm, charismatic, and composed to a fault, "Dr. Barham" spoke flawless English with an accent that sounded British-becoming-American. He eloquently ran down the PUK's positions

for me and promised that I would see the great things happening in Sulimaniya. Taking notes at his elbow stood a young man in a tailored suit with
a neat goatee, who introduced himself as Qubad Talabani. They pledged to
do everything they could to make my trip to Kurdistan a smooth one and
listed off the sort of colorful projects going on that they knew would make
great newspaper copy. Then they told me the catch. From Tehran they
could make arrangements to get me across the border, but no one in the
PUK could lift a finger for me unless I got an Iranian visa, a long shot at the
time. I smiled, they smiled, and I went looking for the KDP office.

The KDP ran a river crossing from a tiny stretch of Syrian border near
Zakho. Many journalists had entered through there, as had foreign NGO
staff, often carrying tens of thousands of dollars in cash for their Erbil
offices. Washington's KDP representative also had a familiar surname.
Farhad Barzani had come to Washington as a young man and had taken
care of his ailing grandfather Mulla Mustafa Barzani. When I met him in
the KDP's Washington office, he gave me his version of how to get into
Kurdistan. First I was to get a Syrian tourist visa, and under no conditions
let them know I was a journalist. Once in Damascus I would contact the
KDP office, and they would get permission from the Syrian secret police
for me to unofficially cross the Tigris into Iraq near Zakho. I could stay in
Kurdistan, but only as long as my tourist visa allowed, and return pretending that I had never left Syria. A few weeks later I got the Syrian
tourist visa through some minor economies with the truth. I gave Farhad
all of my travel details, but I never heard from him. After many calls to his
office, I gave up on that route.⁹

With the American presidential elections coming that fall, Al Gore had
written a strong letter of support to the Kurds, promising to defend their
safe haven; but they found George W. Bush a more attractive suitor. Bush
himself showed no awareness that Kurds existed. (He had recently been
sucker punched when a journalist asked him to name the leaders of Taiwan, India, Pakistan and Chechnya—Bush ventured that the president of
Taiwan might be named Lee.) Rather, it was Bush's entourage that had the
Kurds daydreaming, chief among them, Paul Wolfowitz.

Wolfowitz had been thinking Iraq since the Ford administration. He
theorized that it was fertile ground for democracy in the Middle East, a
model he hoped could be more stable than the Arab dictatorships America
relied on for energy security. Wolfowitz and his fellow neoconservatives
had been uneasy with the way cold political realists had kept the 1991

Gulf War so limited in scope, but the Clinton presidency really boiled them. Fresh off the cold war victory that left America supreme, they had to fidget through eight years of languid restraint of U.S. power. As Clinton's presidency drew to a close, a group of congressional hawks and neo-conservatives pounded him on Iraq. In January 1998 a group called the Project for a New American Century sent Clinton a letter demanding a stronger Iraq policy. Nine of the signatories were destined to become prominent members of the Bush administration, including Wolfowitz, Donald Rumsfeld, and Zalmay Khalilzad.* In October 1998 Congress pushed through the Iraq Liberation Act, stating that it was U.S. policy to change the regime in Baghdad. It authorized Congress to spend ninety-eight million dollars on the Iraqi opposition, and the Kurds could have qualified for some of that money. Still, Clinton's cabinet advised him that containing Saddam was the only practical option.

Wolfowitz disagreed, of course. In January 2000, while president of Johns Hopkins' School of Advanced International Studies, he pushed for aggressive action, like turning the no-fly zones into "no-go" zones for Saddam's army. Kurdistan, he said, was already outside Saddam's control and the south of Iraq could be as well. The only Iraqi group willing to endorse this plan was Ahmed Chalabi's Iraqi National Congress, and it wasn't clear how sincerely the INC endorsed it—some Sunni members feared this plan would lead to an irreversible partition.[10] The INC's main theater had moved to Washington, D.C., as it tried to get at some of that ninety-eight million dollars. The State Department and CIA felt they had already been burned by Chalabi and wanted nothing to do with him, but the exile found a welcome at the door of many Iraq hawks. Chalabi egged on their ideas for action. The Kurdish parties were lukewarm to Wolfowitz's plan, but anyhow, it didn't seem more than musings at the time.†

---

* Also signing were Dick Armitage, John Bolton, Elliot Abrams, Robert Zoellick, Paula Dobriansky, and Peter Rodman. The other nine names included important advisors to the Pentagon like Richard Perle, William Kristol, Robert Kagan, Francis Fukuyama, and James Woolsey.

† Candidate Bush had shown little interest in foreign affairs beyond the Mexican border and had declared an aversion to nation-building. In his meetings with Bush, Wolfowitz said he admired the way the Texas governor would always bring the conversation back to basic themes the American people could understand when the discussion sank too far into details. Wolfowitz liked the idea of a president who didn't second-guess the experts in his cabinet. He even spoke

I asked Wolfowitz, among others, for suggestions on how to get into Iraqi Kurdistan, and he immediately suggested Barham Salih. When I told him that route was dry, he suggested I go through Turkey.[11] I called a few foreign correspondents based in Istanbul, and they told me the Turks had shut the border completely for journalists. If I wanted to go in that way, I'd have to take the huge risk of hiring a smuggler to stuff me under a load of grain. Visions of the Turkish prison in *Midnight Express* filled my mind, and I discarded the Turkish route. Only the front door remained: Baghdad.

A few journalists had recently traveled to the north from the Iraqi capital, getting permission through the United Nations. Resolution 986, Oil-for-Food, greatly reduced the general suffering around Iraq, but it was no substitute for a real economy. Before long the Oil-for-Food program became as much a rallying cry as the total blockade it replaced.* In the process of keeping out matériel that could be used for weapons, many important medicines and pieces of sanitation equipment were blocked. A U.N. study reportedly blamed the blockade for the premature deaths of half a million children by 1995—and Madeleine Albright infamously said she thought keeping Saddam under control was worth it.[12] That sent the anti-sanctions crowd into a tizzy, and helped me get into Iraq.

On my own I had no better luck getting a visa to Iraq than I had gaining access through either of the Kurdish groups. The old Iraqi embassy at the edge of Dupont Circle in Washington looked deserted from the outside. Someone had purposefully wound the flag so it wasn't visible, and last year's leaves still covered the driveway. Inside, a man who looked like he had been napping on the couch in the lobby took my application. My calls to the Iraqi mission to the U.N. implied that this was the correct procedure, but of course no word ever came, and I started to think that I would never get in. Finally I found out that Voices in the Wilderness, an

---

fondly of handing cue cards to President Reagan on a visit to the Philippines when it looked like Reagan wouldn't remember Ferdinand Marcos's name for the meeting.

* Years later the Oil-for-Food program became a huge scandal, and it might have ruined more careers had it not been overshadowed so quickly by the mismanagement of the U.S. occupation in Iraq. It's no surprise that the program allowed Saddam Hussein to steal millions—he was able to punish any would-be whistle-blowers inside the U.N. office by simply denying a visa to anyone who pointed out the corruption.

anti-sanctions activist group, was planning a trip. They told me they would love to have a freelance reporter along. The group, while quite sincere, also served the Iraqi government's purposes, and as such had no trouble getting visas. They put me on their list and my visa magically appeared, but when I reached Baghdad in March 2000, I discovered that the authorities wouldn't allow me to leave the group. I found myself driving about Baghdad and the south, on an official tour of the horrors of sanctions. While in Baghdad, I made contact with an Iraqi fixer of sorts, gave him five hundred dollars, and asked him to arrange a second visa for me. I reluctantly left Iraq with the anti-sanctions convoy, holed up at a hostel in Amman for ten days while the money worked, and then, finally, returned to Baghdad to make my way north to Kurdistan.

By way of comparison the trip south was valuable. The pain sanctions caused was plain to see, but it was nothing next to the overwhelming feeling of fear and hopelessness inspired by the portraits of Saddam Hussein on every corner. Iraq was blessed with all the resources in the world as it slid into decay. Seeing the richness of the country, in oil, water, land, and talented people, made both Saddam's rule and the U.N. embargo seem all the more senseless.

At the U.N.'s Baghdad headquarters, the old Canal Hotel on the east side of the city, George Somerwill, the spokesman for the Office of the Humanitarian Coordinator in Iraq (UNOCHI), was about to break in his third boss. The previous two had resigned to protest what sanctions had done to Iraq. Somerwill gave a rational explanation of what was happening: the amount of food permissible for Iraqis under Oil-for-Food was fine for a healthy population but not enough for a population that was also facing disease because of poor sanitation and lack of medical supplies.

But the anti-sanctions argument had one big hole in it—Kurdistan. The same U.N. studies that concluded sanctions were killing Iraq's children and un-developing the country also determined that in the north things had improved. The explanation was clear but impossible to say out loud in Baghdad: Saddam was robbing the program blind in his part of the country.[13] ("What the hell did they expect him to do?" one U.N. official asked me.) Baghdad also used the ration-card system to keep tabs on the population. In the Kurdish north, where the United Nations distributed food with a semblance of fairness, health and welfare had improved.

Somerwill had some numbers to counter that argument. The Kurds received (or were supposed to receive) 13 percent of the resources from

Oil-for-Food—commensurate with their share of Iraq's population. But the 13 percent came right off the top. After that, the punitive measures were taken out of Saddam's share—for war reparations and U.N. operating expenses. Therefore, according to Somerwill, 87 percent of Iraq's population living outside the three Kurdish provinces was living on only about half the oil proceeds. He also pointed out that NGOs were able to operate in the north and were filling in big gaps in areas such as literacy and civil society. The Oil-for-Food program in the north had a small cash component as well, allowing the purchase of cement and grain in an attempt to protect the local economy. Of course, all of the resolution 986 supplies going north had to come through Baghdad, and the Kurds had complained repeatedly to the U.N. that the program was wild with corruption and meddling by the regime. It made for an interesting discussion, but Somerwill caught on that what I really wanted was to get to Kurdistan. I needed a letter of permission from his office "to observe the implementation of the 986 program" in the north. He signed a form quickly, and I was on my way; it was April 1, 2000.

The Iraqi Information Ministry still wanted its pound of flesh. In addition to the visa fees, legal and informal, the ministry charged all visiting journalists a daily rate simply for being in the country, and they added charges for carrying any high-tech equipment like a satellite phone (though I hadn't paid this fee when I traveled with the anti-sanctions group Voices in the Wilderness). As a freelancer without much gear, I argued their rates down a bit, but it still came out to about two hundred dollars a day for me just to be in Iraq. I had to pay the official translator—or "minder," as everyone called them, because they reported all interviews and interactions back to the ministry. In addition, for my trip north they had an official driver for me to hire, a grizzled, graying man I'll call Abu Soran. He was one of the few Kurds working for the ministry and would translate from Kurdish for my minder, Ali, who looked much younger, with his wispy mustache and baby face. The two made an odd couple. Ali's manicured hand was limp when I shook it and he drew me in to kiss both his cheeks. Abu Soran had a handshake like a bridge troll.

Making friends with the people who are reporting your every move back to a sinister instrument of a brutal regime is a funny business, and I was new at it. Some of the minders had better reputations than others, and Ali was said to be harmless. I got a slightly worse feel from Abu Soran. I paid the ministry officials in advance. They took my letter from the

U.N. and wished me a nice trip. There is no April Fool's Day in Iraq, but the ministry official never gave back the letter, which soon became a problem.

So BEGAN MY first trip to Kurdistan, driving north from Saddam's Baghdad in an orange and white taxicab, accompanied by two low-grade Ba'athist spies. We left the sprawl of the capital and took the direct route through Baquba, stopping for lunch at a truck stop in Kirkuk, still outside Kurdish control. As we approached Erbil province, the foothills of the Zagros Mountains rose into view. The naked rocks looked like teeth, and for a moment I thought the Kurds had somehow built a ridge spanning the horizon to hold the Arab army off from the south. Over the rise we left the last Iraqi checkpoint and slowly rolled up to the ragtag Kurdish militiamen guarding their own border. When I couldn't produce the letter from the U.N., they promptly arrested us and took us to Erbil.

Getting arrested by KDP militiamen made Ali and Abu Soran rather nervous. I didn't feel worried—I was fairly certain the Kurds had nothing against journalists. The soldiers, armed with knockoff AK-47 assault rifles, asked me to get in their car, and a few of the men got in the cab with Ali and Abu Soran. Ali had never been to the north of Iraq and regarded the Kurds with fascination and a bit of fear—all his life Kurdistan had represented rebellion and anarchy. Abu Soran, a native of Koi Sanjaq, could have been worried about his occupation as a spy for Baghdad or simply about being originally from the PUK side of Kurdistan. They took us to a nondescript building in the center of Erbil and served us tea in a waiting room. The KDP security officer called the U.N. to ask if I my story was true, and then we waited for a call back. He took me into a thin-walled office and sat me down.

"Your friends—they are Mukhabarat?" he asked me in Arabic. I assumed the men were still right outside the door, so I tried to have it both ways.

"I don't know," I said, vigorously nodding my head yes.

The Kurdish officer smiled. When the U.N. called him back a short while later, he told us to enjoy our stay in Kurdistan.

People have lived in Erbil for perhaps eight thousand years—it is in the running with Damascus for the world's oldest continuously inhabited city—but that doesn't make it a particularly beautiful town. It has none of

Kurdistan's stunning mountains to frame it, no lazy riverfront like Mosul or Baghdad. At the city center a citadel rises up on a plateau towering about a hundred feet over the city.* Some Kurds live there today and claim they descend from the founders of the city. Unfortunately the rest of Erbil's architecture is Ba'athist industrial—great hulks of concrete and glass that soak up too much heat in the summer and seem immune to it in the wintertime. I've been told that the name comes from *arbah 'ila*—Arabic for "four idols." In Kurdish the city is called Hawler—"temple of the sun" in that language. On my first visit it could have been called the temple of Barzani: the KDP had put up a portrait of Mulla Mustafa for every portrait of Saddam they had taken down in 1991.

Abu Soran drove us to the U.N. compound, where I had arranged to stay in a guesthouse, and at that point my two minders checked out. They were both afraid to come with me on my KDP tour of the city and preferred to sit back at the U.N. guesthouse watching satellite television, with many racy channels unavailable in Baghdad. It was part of so many open deceptions going on. The Mukhabarat office back in Baghdad knew that once we got north, their spies wouldn't dare move about Kurdistan. They would bring back a little information about Kurdistan, a little information about me, but mostly everyone would get their cut of the cash.

Also feigning blindness were the U.N. staffers. They were allowed to talk to me because I had come from Baghdad with official (if mislaid) permission. But the U.N. agreement with the government of Iraq forbade any dealings with illegal visitors. They had to act as if other journalists didn't exist—most of the small number who made it into Kurdistan by unofficial routes. The same ban extended to the NGO workers who snuck in from Syria. The invisible treatment didn't endear the United Nations to the Kurds, but no matter how much the U.N. tried to pretend this was Iraq, the difference was unmistakable.

Emerald green pastures carpeted the landscape around Erbil—reminding me more of Ireland than Iraq. There wasn't an Arab headdress in sight, and men in the marketplace looked right at home in their traditional baggy trousers gathered at the waist with a wide cummerbund. The haggling there involved Iraqi dinars, but the old bills from before Saddam started printing his face on all of Iraq's money. In Baghdad a shopping bag

---

* UNESCO took on a project to restore the citadel in 2005.

full of "Saddam dinars" was needed to buy the same volume of groceries that could be had for a handful in Erbil. In the north the exchange rate was better, even though the currency had only a pseudo-government behind it. The printing plates for the bills came from Switzerland, and the Kurds called the money "Swiss dinars." Satellite call centers could be found in the major cities, with clearer, cheaper, easier connections to the United States and Europe than at any of the dilapidated phone company buildings in Baghdad. Just as I arrived, the regional government announced that clocks would be set one hour ahead for spring; the Kurds didn't even want to share a time zone with Arab Iraq.

On my first trip out of Erbil I found a schoolhouse and recorded the kids singing the KDP national anthem. The teacher bragged that the children in the village hardly knew a word of Arabic. The village itself, just a few miles south of the city, was called Dal de Gan, which the teacher said meant "refuge of chieftains." In 1987, Iraqi troops and jahsh razed it to the ground as part of the Anfal campaign. Oil-for-Food money started to help rebuild the town in 1998, and forty-eight families had moved back into new mud-brick houses. Most of the men were out with their sheep, but a few of the women were willing to speak.

"We're not afraid of anybody here," said Sadiya Bassi, a young mother. Her family ran the gamut of the Anfal experience. One brother had been a pesh merga and fled into the hills when the pogrom began. Her mother described watching the village dynamited and bulldozed in 1987, then sneaking back to comb the rubble for a few belongings. Sadiya's father had invaded Kuwait as a soldier in the Iraqi army. He deserted when his commanding officer, an Arab, mercifully told all the men to go home to their families instead of being slaughtered by the coming American invasion. HABITAT, the U.N.'s settlement agency, helped the family return from the slums in Erbil, and two years along, life wasn't bad. Everyone mentioned the Oil-for-Food program as the reason, but it all seemed too good to be completely believed. "Since the U.N. is here, I'm not afraid, but when they go, Saddam is coming back, and they will destroy us again," said Bassi.

Destruction seemed like a fact of life for Kurds like Bassi—they could rebuild their villages, start printing schoolbooks in Kurdish, hold their own elections, and police their own streets, but they couldn't shake the idea that fate had plans to smash it all.

After the arrest—a bad first impression—the KDP graciously arranged to bring me up to the mountain resort of Salahudin, where I met Sami

Abd-al-Rahman. The KDP had absorbed his own party after the 1992 elections, and he now sat at the head of the KDP politburo. He was a bit stern—though I can't blame him. For the stories I was writing, my questions boiled down to a tricked-out version of "What's a Kurd?" I asked him if the Kurds had ever seen it so good. He resisted the hyperbole.

"Our people have seen better times, but since the genocide campaign, this is the best," he allowed. He gave good marks to the Oil-for-Food program but walked a careful line between singing the praises of "Free Iraq" and making sure I wouldn't try to put words in his mouth about Kurdish independence.

"We have never asked for separation [from Iraq] and no one would be dealing with us if we had," he said. "And that's why we are a factor of stability in the area. And we have been managing to ourselves for eight years."

Sami deflected questions about the Washington Agreement that had ended the Kurdish civil war, and claimed that the KDP was sharing with the PUK whatever they got from the Khabur bridge customs revenues, and that it was nowhere near a million dollars each day. He said the agreement at least had produced two and a half years without shooting. Much of Sami's nuance was wasted on me at the time, and only listening to my recordings of the interview years later do I hear the stress he put on certain historical events—repeating, for example, that the Kurds had not taken over the north but simply filled the vacuum created when Saddam withdrew. When I asked why he trusted the Americans to keep protecting the north, he enthused about a new world order, in which minority rights and self-determination were respected. That was a talking point with many of the leadership figures I met. He also gave me my first recitation of the standard disclaimer of a desire for a Greater Kurdistan

"It is a sweet dream," he said, "and no one can prevent us from dreaming this sweet dream. But we are pragmatic. We know that for the time it is difficult that this dream be fulfilled."

As Abd-al-Rahman's protocol officer took me out to the foyer, he saw Abu Soran waiting beside his orange and white Baghdad taxicab down in the parking lot. "They think we are so stupid that we don't know their spies?" he nearly spat.

The KDP had taken a small page out of Baghdad's book and kept my access limited in Erbil. They didn't sit in on all my interviews—as the Iraqis did in the south—but they did control my access. I had been given the name of Hussein Sinjari, the flamboyant PUK representative who had worked as the PUK liaison to General Jay Garner and later as Jim Muir's mountain escort. Disgusted by the civil war, Sinjari left the PUK in 1996 and founded a democracy institute in Erbil. He had never joined the KDP though, and they told me it would be impossible to see him. With my inexperience, I didn't know how easily I could have sidestepped them.

Instead I interviewed everyone in sight, and their stories overflowed. After one lunch I called the restaurant owner over for a chat and found that he was a former pesh merga from Kifri, on the southern tip of the safe zone. Because he had served as a bodyguard to a high-ranking official with the KDP, he couldn't go home to see his family, who were deep inside the PUK area. He said life was fine and salaries were much better here in the north than in the rest of Iraq. But he gave perfunctory replies about a lasting peace that conveyed his disgust for the war between the Kurdish parties. His family came across the cease-fire lines to visit about twice a year.

The other line that had people worried was the green line I had driven in across—the border with the government of Iraq, or GOI as those in the U.N. community called it. The three Kurdish provinces in the north made a contorted shape, reaching widely around Mosul to go from Erbil to Dohuk in the north. Traveling on the main highway between Erbil and Dohuk, through GOI-controlled Mosul, would have taken only a couple of hours, but that was a no-go area for many Kurds, and forbidden to any journalists or NGO workers in the north without Baghdad's permission. Anyone who might have problems with the regime had to drive a long, bone-jarring route to the north and then over toward Dohuk and Zakho. Even locals sometimes get lost, and making a wrong turn could have fatal consequences, as Sarteed Kakai, a medical school professor, explained to me.

Kakai was vice chancellor of Hawler University. His family had roots in Kirkuk, but he worried that talking about them could mean trouble for his relatives still living there. Like most people of prominence in the north, he couldn't safely travel back to Kirkuk or anywhere in Iraqi government territory. But the crossings weren't always well marked or patrolled.

One morning in July 1999, Kakai had set out with his young son and daughter from Erbil to visit Dohuk University. His driver took a wrong turn where the route skirts around Mosul, and before Kakai knew it, their car had rolled up to an Iraqi government checkpoint. The white license plate on their car gave them away as VIPs in the Kurdish region—Kakai had stepped into the bear trap with both feet. He and his children soon found themselves in a Ba'ath Party office in Mosul.

At first, Kakai received a small mercy. The clerk at the party office was a Kurdish Yazidi; in fact he recognized Kakai as the doctor who had treated his cousin in Erbil. He quickly tried to help the doctor, throwing out the paperwork on Kakai's children and sending them to shelter with his family in Mosul. But when the Yazidi returned for the doctor, he stiffened—Mukhabarat agents had arrived at the party office. He had done all he could, and Dr. Kakai feared the worst.

The Mukhabarat agents took Kakai, now praying quietly to himself, to their security office. It was getting to be late afternoon. They hardly needed to threaten the doctor—he knew what happened in offices like this one. Kakai carried some mild medicine with him for hypertension; he swallowed all of his pills. The director of the Mukhabarat brought him a confession to sign, admitting that he worked with the American corrupters in northern Iraq.

"I told myself good-bye," Kakaki remembered. They took him to a basement room full of other luckless men. Ropes hung off pipes in the ceiling, and blood made the floor sticky under his shoes. Greeting Kakai and the agents, a huge muscular guard asked, "So this is the newcomer?"

Kakai heard women screaming somewhere in the building, then silence, as he waited some hours in dread. But before his torture session could begin, an agent opened the door and asked which one was Kakai. Praying it meant something good, Kakai raised his hand. His children had contacted their mother back in Erbil, she had been able to alert the KDP, and Masoud Barzani himself had intervened. At midnight the Iraqi agents hustled him out of jail to a prisoner swap in the dark, and by morning he was reunited with his family.

"Tell me now if *you* love freedom," Kakai said.

As long as he stayed on the Kurdish side of the line, Kakai thought times had never been so good. He bragged about the greatest level of academic freedom he had ever known. Under Saddam, of course, Kurdish studies were unheard of, and all serious education was conducted in Arabic. Now the Kurds were studying their own history in their own language. Both the KDP and PUK broadcast from satellite television stations in the Kurdish language, airing pirated Hollywood movies with crude Kurdish dubbing. Kakai saw something as simple as a children's cartoon with Kurdish voice-overs as a major step forward for his people.

As WE LEFT Erbil after a few days, I had Abu Soran stop the car at an intersection. The KDP had raised a statue there for Gad Gross, the young German freelance photographer killed covering the uprising in Kirkuk in 1991. Seeing the Kurds' appreciation for the journalists who get their story out encouraged me for a moment, but it also made me a little paranoid about returning to Baghdad from the north. Besides the apparent execution of Gross during the war, Saddam had hanged British journalist Farzad Bazoft in spring 1990—in peacetime.

The three-hour drive east to Sulimaniya followed the road toward Koi Sanjaq, passing the cease-fire line at Degala. This time our papers were in order and the KDP pesh merga quickly let us pass over to their PUK counterparts on the other side of a rocky field, where a Kurdish artist had painted the rocks with peace signs. As we drove around the mountains toward Lake Dukan, I marveled at the colored lines in the hillsides—the cliffs along the lake looked like they had been painted by Jackson Pollock, with dark stains of water leaking from the rocks' endless lines of layered pigment. At first I mistook this for natural beauty, but I started to catch on when I saw rows of little pine trees planted along the hillsides in neat lines to reforest the countryside after the desperation of the early 1990s. The landscape's striking features came from horrible deforestation that had stripped away all the topsoil, leaving the bare bones of the earth showing. I started to feel differently about the beauty of the cliffs.

The welcoming committee in Sulimaniya was a good deal warmer— the PUK seemed much more attuned to the international media as a lifeline. I arrived in the late afternoon and met with a group of PUK politburo members, who said they would be happy to set up a meeting with Mam Jalal Talabani. They invited me to a late lunch, and instead of the usual tea with cardamom served after every meal, they offered Johnnie Walker Black Label. They assigned a young college student to guide me around the city and promised to show me anything I wanted. When *they* saw my Kurdish driver, they kissed him on both cheeks and exchanged a few jokes. After Abu Soran pulled away to return to the hotel, I asked Adil Murad, one of the politburo, to explain.

"Yes, he's a spy, but he's our friend," he said with a shrug. I must have looked a bit surprised, and Murad laughed. "He's a good guy. Hey—he's got a job to do," he said.

Sulimaniya suits the PUK: the city is freer with itself, people more often dress in Western clothes, and it has been the center of dissent in Iraqi Kurdistan for generations. On a clear day the snowy mountains to the north frame the city's few attempts at a skyline (two dumpy concrete hotels at the time). The climate is a few degrees colder than Erbil, and well into the spring a whiff of chilly air floats down from the mountains. Hajar Arif, the college student assigned to guide me, started off the tour by sitting me down with a group of his friends at Sulimaniya University. Most of them had been barely teenagers the last time Saddam controlled this city.

"I was a child, but I could understand what was happening around me," Hajar said, admitting that his taste of the regime and his memories of the entire nation fleeing across the mountains in 1991 kept him from taking the new Kurdistan for granted. "I appreciate this freedom and it's like food to me—saying, writing whatever you think."

Hajar had been living with his family in Zakho until the Kurdish civil war sent them fleeing to the PUK side in Sulimaniya. He would have been of military age during the civil war, but neither Hajar nor any of his college friends had fought; it wasn't a cause they took any pride in, unlike the struggle with Saddam's regime. Yet none of them laid on false bravado about that either, even lounging in the safety of the university campus. If Saddam came back, they said, everyone would head for the hills. Baghdad was just too strong. But they also peddled the notion that the world had somehow evolved beyond hanging the Kurds out to dry. "Saddam is stronger than us. But this is the age of globalization, and everyone hopes to live in peace and let other nationalities live in peace," Hajar reflected.

The next morning we drove toward Chamchamal, the last town under PUK control on the road west to Kirkuk. Along the south side of the highway a few thousand tents were set up—New Kirkuk refugee camp. I had expected to collect accounts of refugees who had been evicted from Kirkuk during the Arabization programs in the 1980s or had been living here since the 1991 uprising. After interviewing a few families living in the heavy canvas tents, I noticed a group with chairs, pots, and blankets in front of their tent, stacked neatly to keep them from the mud. A wiry man with jet-black hair stood at the door of the tent, looking a bit bewildered.

He introduced himself as Azat Omar. I asked what year he had fled Kirkuk. He looked around at his belongings and then at me, as if I were mad. The Ba'athist government in Kirkuk had kicked his family out the previous night.

Azat's family had been in Kirkuk for generations, but during his lifetime it became impossible for Kurds to live in the city. He had worked as a driver and had owned his own car. As his family grew to a normal Kurdish size— eight children—Azat tried to buy land and build a bigger house, but the municipality denied him permission, unless he agreed to officially switch his nationality to Arab on his identity documents. Azat refused. In the year before he left, he had tried to sell his house and was told that, as a Kurd, he couldn't be the legal owner—in fact there was an Arab family coming to live in the house and he would have to leave. When the final eviction order came, the authorities wouldn't allow Azat to take his car out of Kirkuk with him. He paid to rent a small flatbed truck to carry his family and all they owned to Chamchamal. There the PUK displacement committee had allotted a twelve-foot tent in New Kirkuk for his family of ten.

The term "ethnic cleansing" had entered my vocabulary only a few years earlier, a 1990s catchphrase for an ancient crime.[14] The PUK told me that about forty families moved to their side of the Kurdish region every week. They didn't have an exact breakdown of who came for pure economic reasons and who came looking for a place where they could be first-class citizens, educate their kids in Kurdish, and generally escape the dreadful Ba'athist administration. For those without families in the north to take them in, it couldn't have been an easy choice. The Oil-for-Food program had pumped up the Kurdish economy, but that was only relative to the terrible years after the uprising. Laborers in Sulimaniya hardly welcomed Kirkuk's refugees into the competition for scarce jobs. The politicians didn't really want them to assimilate either—for that would mean that the regime had won and Kirkuk would become Arab. People from Kirkuk were the Palestinians of Kurdistan—most of them would never accept another home, and their leaders didn't really want to take the pressure off by building them one.

Azat Omar got tired of my questions quickly. Besides the trauma of his predicament, he was fresh from Saddam's Iraq and still jumpy about journalists. The stories at other tents fell along similar lines—men hiding from the authorities as their family members were harassed or arrested until eventually they couldn't bear it. The food ration helped, but as in southern Iraq, it was pretty meager for these Kurds with no other source of income. There had been deaths in the camp, some from disease, a few when kerosene heaters set tents alight. A Japanese NGO, Peace Winds, came three times a week, listening to the refugee's grievances and helping them lobby the PUK in Sulimaniya.

Hajar took me back to Sulimaniya in time to meet with Kosrat Rasul, the PUK general who was now serving as prime minister for this side of Kurdistan (his nemesis, Nechirvan Barzani, was KDP prime minister). Meeting Kosrat for the first time was slightly unnerving. It might be his one lazy eye, or his reputation for ferocity in a country where everyone considers himself a fighter, but even when Kosrat smiles, he looks like he might tear you in half with his bare hands. He tore into the Washington Agreement instead.

"None of it has been implemented!" he said. Kosrat spoke as though the two sides were still at war. He charged that the KDP was happy with Kurdistan's divided status quo, making money off Saddam's black market oil trade with Turkey. "I'm concerned about a day when there are no sanctions on Iraq," Kosrat said, getting to the paradox of the Kurds' condition. As with so many times in their history, Kurdish prosperity was a side effect of greater powers' policies and conflicts. As soon as the international community stopped punishing Iraq with sanctions, said Kosrat, the world would stop providing Kurdistan with extra help and probably let Saddam have his way with the north. Many Kurds expressed the same irony: as much as they hated Saddam, they wished him a long healthy life so the world's opprobrium would keep helping them rebuild. Kosrat said Kurdistan needed to keep showing America and Europe that there was democracy growing here, so they would continue to be shamed into protecting the north.

"There are no permanent allies, only permanent interests," Kosrat said, ending with a paraphrase of Britain's Lord Palmerston. He sent me around the town that afternoon with his personal translator, Kawan, to show me the wonderful things the PUK had achieved, first among them the oil refinery they had built out of sugar refinery parts. Taking crude from the few wells north of the no-fly line, they now produced a small quantity of diesel and gasoline for domestic consumption. The PUK claimed they had had no help in setting it up.[15] There is no stronger symbol of independence in the Middle East than oil wealth, and the PUK proudly showed off this token amount of petro-power.

Kawan, my guide, had something of a split personality. As Kosrat's translator, he fully expected to work under some rough conditions—when we passed into the refinery grounds, he checked his Makarov pistol at the gate—but the job he loved was being chairman of the English Department at Sulimaniya University. Our discussion on the drive around town ranged from Saddam to Shakespeare, and he asked for help with the precise definitions of a few English words. After the oil refinery we took in Sulimaniya's amusement park—a long boardwalk along a canal with a zoo and a small Ferris wheel. People were taking leisurely walks along the water, including some young couples. My "plight of the Kurds" story had just wandered into the fun-fair and fed the ducks.

Talabani agreed to an interview the next day at Qalaat Chowlan, his old hideout above the city. One of his aides took me into a study crowded with books and papers where he sat behind a cluttered desk. Larger than life, Talbani draws you in with his warm smile and jovial demeanor. He is never without books and can digress easily into any number of topics, often contradicting his own arguments along the way. A few years worth of Oil-for-Food money to throw around had agreed with Talabani, and he shied away from picking fights over arrangements with the KDP. True to his reputation as an internationalist, Talabani seemed more interested in talking about Washington than Kurdistan.

"There is a law in the U.S. to overthrow the government of Iraq," he started in, "but Congress is more serious than the Clinton administration." I agreed with him. The Iraq Liberation Act was on the books, but it looked as though Clinton had inherited the Iraq problem and was hoping to pass it along cleanly to his own heir. The White House had spent about 2 percent of the ninety-eight million dollars approved and had provided nothing more lethal than a fax machine. Talabani thought it was a joke. "They are ready to give you computers. They will pay the salary in London of the Iraqi National Congress. It is not serious. In Iraq people are laughing when they hear this. They must cooperate with real opposition forces inside the country to remove the dictator," he said.

Given the lack of attention so far, I asked him if he wasn't worried the United States would lose interest in protecting the Kurds and withdraw their jets. "We have not received one dollar or one bullet from the U.S. If the U.S. disappears, we will still be here," Talabani said, and then he laughed and pointed out the window. "Maybe not here but in that mountain."

Talabani added that he didn't think Saddam's army was such a great threat these days—their morale was dismal, and the officers so poorly paid that the PUK could buy assault rifles directly from the Iraqi units across the front. He brought the conversation back to Washington again, claiming that the United States was still fixated on its one-bullet policy, and not the federal Iraq solution that the Kurds had been pushing. He worried that the United States really wanted another Arab strongman. But then, like the lawyer he once was, Talabani argued the other side.

"You know the United States wants a new Iraq. This century is different—this is the time of democracy, human rights. Even the U.S. Department of State has a department for promoting democracy in the world. The U.S. cannot blind its eyes. It cannot repeat like the time of cold war, with the U.S. supporting dictatorships. Even in Saudi Arabia they have an assembly now."

I asked if he wasn't better off just keeping the status quo, milking the world's anger at Baghdad, but Talabani, at sixty-seven, was the same age as Saddam, and hoping to outlive the Iraqi dictator. "Nothing lasts forever— even your president lasts for only four years," he said. I asked whom he was betting on in the 2000 elections. Talabani didn't rise to the bait.

Talabani said the Kurds, and the entire region, were ready to help take down Saddam, but only if Washington presented a real plan and gave solid guarantees they wouldn't pull out at the last minute. He said even the Iranians had sent him such signals. For the Kurds, they didn't expect to get independence out of it, but they were not moving backward. "No, my friend, I don't think Kurds will accept anything less than they have now. The big majority would refuse any kind of compromise," he said. He spoke as though he had run afoul of his own constituents before and knew he couldn't afford to do it very often.

We chatted for about an hour and then it was time for lunch. All the PUK lieutenants from my welcoming committee were there, and we tucked into a Kurdish banquet of turkey, lamb, stuffed leaves, white beans, okra, apricots, spinach, rice, and flat bread. The men all around me wore suits, but they still ate like mountain rebels who thought the next meal could be a while away. I was stuffed to the gills, but they chided me for my lack of appetite. That's usually a function of Middle East hospitality, a way to make sure that the guest eats his fill. But I hadn't been shy; I just couldn't compete with the pesh merga, and Talabani led them fearlessly from the head of the table. After lunch he had his official photographer take our picture together as he saw me to the door. I took a few shots with my own camera, but I intended to hide the film. When the photographer dropped off the photos later at the hotel, I thanked him and then surreptitiously tore them up and flushed them down the toilet—better not to drive back to Baghdad with an eight-by-ten photo of me with Saddam's least favorite Kurd.

With time to visit one more city on my tour of the north, we drove to Halabja. Kawan gave me a tip: Talabani was supposed to be visiting there that day to initiate a memorial to the victims of the chemical attack. This wasn't just a groundbreaking ceremony for the monument; it would be the first time Talabani had visited the city since the PUK had retaken control from the Islamic Movement of Kurdistan (IMK). Kawan helped arrange a ride to the city with some Kurdish journalists.

The road east from Sulimaniya skirts foothills just north of a long verdant plain above Darbandikhan Lake, the snowy peaks in the distance across the border in Iran. Halfway to Halabja, we passed the town of Sa'id Sadiq, where the road forks north toward the Iranian border town of Penjwin, and everyone in the car compared stories of walking or driving this road during the mass exodus of 1991. We veered south on the road toward Halabja, and the mood turned serious.

Every fifty meters or so, on both sides of the road, a pesh merga stood at attention. Many of the men had new American-style military uniforms, but they packed a hodgepodge of weapons—short Kalashnikov knockoffs with plastic stocks, aging Russian sniper rifles, the occasional rocket-propelled grenade, like a fat harpoon slung over the shoulder. They were Talabani's honor guard, but their purpose was more than ceremonial. The PUK had only a shaky hold on this region. The road swung around and entered Halabja from the south, looking up into the bowl of mountains that holds the city. I couldn't help but think of how the poison gas, heavier than air, must have sunk down and poured through the streets. We pulled up to the town hall just in time for an opening speech by the mayor.

Jamil Abd-al-Rahman, Halabja's Islamist mayor, welcomed all the visitors to his city. He was the first man I noticed in Kurdistan with a bushy beard—most men sported as big a mustache as they could grow, but in Halabja quite a few had beards and wore some sort of head covering. No women attended the meeting, but a group of them watched the spectacle from the flat roof of a nearby house.

"We wish we could make our heart the carpets under your feet to welcome you," said the mayor, who had a reputation as something of a poet. Abd-al-Rahman had been Halabja's mayor for years, and a moderate voice among the fighting Kurdish factions and even his own IMK supporters. He spoke of bringing the Kurds together to rebuild Halabja, starting with this monument, to make Kurdistan's worst atrocity into a symbol of unity.

Abd-al-Rahman announced that engineers would begin cleaning up the city today, taking out debris still standing from the attack twelve years ago. Dozens of trucks and bulldozers had come from Sulimaniya, and the work crews with shovels began to clear out the area where the monument would go—the exact design was still under discussion. Also in dispute was the health risk of moving all the rubble. According to Dr. Fuad Baban, the head of Sulimaniya medical school and of a new postgraduate research institute in Halabja, the town had unreasonably high rates of congenital abnormalities and a high rate of miscarriage. He ticked off a list of other ailments common in the city—chronic respiratory illness, heart problems, and aggressive cancers.

Baban worried the excavation would stir up more poisonous residues still in the soil. He looked out as the workers, many with simple shovels, started breaking ground. The institute Baban worked with had tried for international support to study the long-term effects of chemical weapons, but not much came. He couldn't understand why the world didn't show more interest, even a cold scientific interest, in Halabja.

Halabja would grab some attention soon enough, though not for the reasons Baban desired. Starting around 1998 a group of the most radical Islamists from around Kurdistan had trekked across Iran to Afghanistan to make contact with Osama bin Laden and enroll in his al-Qa'ida training camp near Khost.[16] Two years later, these men were returning and starting their own jihadi camp in the mountains above Halabja. The PUK may have had an inkling already that the group had formed, since Talabani never showed up in Halabja that day. Either he had called off the trip at the last minute or it had been a ruse from the start to test the security around Halabja.

By the following year several of the Islamist groups coalesced into one force, called Ansar al-Islam. They called their caverns above Halabja "little Tora Bora" for its comfortable similarity to their stronghold in eastern Afghanistan. Al-Qa'ida's leaders apparently took a strong interest in the Kurdish region as a safe place to lay low in 2001.

CHAPTER SIX

A Most Convenient Foe

FOR A DECADE AFTER THE COLD WAR, presidents and prime ministers routinely announced the dawning of a new era, but that new age truly arrived on September 11, 2001. Only hours after the attacks on New York and Washington, America's friends and foes around the world hastened to figure out where they fit in the terrifying new paradigm. Despite their revulsion at the massacre, possessing a terrorist threat suddenly counted like money in the bank in terms of U.S. aid. Afghans tempered their horror with hope that the world's attention would zero in on the Taliban government. In Israel, Ariel Sharon canceled peace talks and began referring to Palestinian leader Yassir Arafat as "our bin Laden." He sent tanks into the West Bank, counting on America to empathize with Israel's situation. Arafat charged him with exploiting the attacks and desperately tried to control the damage caused by some Palestinians caught on camera cheering on al-Qa'ida.[1] Countries from Central America to Central Asia scrambled their policies to fit with the fear and rage emanating from the wounded superpower. Iraqi foreign minister Tariq Aziz appeared on CNN from Baghdad, disclaiming any connection with bin Laden. Everyone with a scrap of information about al-Qa'ida—real, fabricated, or fantastical—airbrushed it for presentation.

Except the Kurds. A block from the Capitol building in Washington,

D.C., Qubad Talabani sat at his desk in the PUK office and didn't pick up
the phone. "All the people were saying, '*Oh, focus on me.*' Various countries popped up and said, 'Hey, we've got terrorists!' We just didn't want
to appear to be jumping on the bandwagon," said Talabani. He had another reason not to hurry. The PUK had already provided the White
House a dossier on Kurdistan's own al-Qa'ida-inspired group, Ansar al-
Islam, exactly one week before September 11.[2] This small gang of fanat-
ics would do as much to bring about a Kurdish state as years of struggling
in the mountains.

Al-Qa'ida connections would eventually draw the Americans' attention, but Ansar al-Islam was home-grown in Kurdistan. The Islamists
in northern Iraq trace their roots back to Halabja in 1986. A popular
preacher, Sheikh Othman Abdulaziz, and his brother Ali, led protests
against the regime in one of Halabja's town squares, and the Ba'athists re-
acted by reducing the plaza to rubble. The Shi'ite Islamic republic next
door in Iran took an interest. Kurdish Islamists are all Sunni, but their enmity with Saddam Hussein apparently trumped the sectarian difference,
and elements of the Iranian government helped recruit and train volunteers from Halabja. In the cross fire of the Iran-Iraq war, the Kurds happily accepted help. On their return to Halabja, the Abdulaziz family
founded the Islamic Movement of Kurdistan (IMK). The IMK drew
equal measures of inspiration from Khomeini's revolutionary tactics in
Iran and the religious teachings of Sayyid Qutb, the Egyptian Sunni fundamentalist thinker—an odd mix, but somehow fitting the Kurds' history
and geography.[3] The IMK fought against the Ba'athists in the 1991 uprising, though they never joined the Kurdistan Front. Othman Abdulaziz
ran for the leadership of the Kurdish region, one of the four faces ap-
pearing on the ballot. But his IMK got only 5 percent in the 1992 elections, short of the minimum of 7 percent needed for seats in parliament.
The ruling parties sidelined them completely.[4]

During those same formative years, global jihad concentrated on the
Soviet conquest of Afghanistan, and American money and weapons
flowed through Pakistan to the Afghan mujahideen. Thousands of Muslims from across the world traveled to base camps in Peshawar, Pakistan,
and then crossed the border to fight a holy war against the Soviets. Many
Kurds made the journey, and they found a friendly safe house along the way
run by an IMK member called Mullah Krekar (whose real name is Najmaldin Faraj Ahmad). Until 1991 Krekar taught at the Islamic University

in Islamabad, and he became close with Abdullah Azzam, a mentor to Osama bin Laden. Krekar may have fought alongside bin Laden in the 1980s.[5] The jihadis who returned home wore the experience in Afghanistan as a badge of honor, and for the Kurdish Islamists it was ideal. They returned to northern Iraq, where the terrain and conditions looked nearly identical to Afghanistan's Hindu Kush Mountains, and they had a big fat target in the Kurdish secular government and its Western visitors.

The desperate times of the early 1990s in Kurdistan, combined with the senseless conflict between the KDP and PUK, made fertile ground for the Islamists. Religious foundations from Saudi Arabia offered an unveiled, blatant exchange: food and medicine in return for Koranic students and fundamentalist behavior. As in many other poor Muslim countries around the world, the Saudis built hundreds of mosques, schools, and branch offices across northern Iraq. But the fundamentalists chafed against secular traditions in Kurdistan—and that friction often spiked to violence when a prominent "Afghan" Kurd returned. When Mullah Krekar came back from Pakistan in time for the 1991 uprising, he led a push to install a conservative version of shari'a, Islamic law, in Halabja. Attacks on immodest women and simple turf issues led the PUK to crack down on the IMK. Naturally the KDP exploited the situation and made some ties with the Islamists. Again in 1997, with the return of a fighter called "Mullah Aso," the IMK fought with the secular parties.[6]

Halabja and the surrounding region had always nurtured conservative religious traditions, but even there the extremists stood out, especially those preaching *takfir*—the idea that anyone practicing an alternative to their radical Islam was an infidel, and fair game for slaughter. Internal divisions broke the IMK into factions during the late 1990s. Officially, Ali Abdulaziz led the group, but members complained he had started to take personal control of the movement's funds—acting a bit too much like the secular party bosses. At a congress in August 2000, a significant portion of the IMK leadership split away from Abdulaziz. The splinter group, led by a charismatic young preacher named Ali Bapir, called itself the Islamic Group, or Komala Islami. He presented himself as more responsible than Abdulaziz and less radical than the "Afghanis" like Mulla Krekar.[7] Bapir's youthful looks and serene gaze belie a hard-as-nails reputation; he is rumored to have personally executed his own brother as a Ba'athist spy.[8] He and his followers set up shop outside Halabja in the town of Khurmal. But even deeper divisions remained.

While giving the impression of being unified, two factions within the IMK secretly arranged separate trips to Afghanistan in early 2001. Mullah Krekar used his connections with the mujahideen to help send his delegation to al-Qa'ida training camps. Coming straight from years of battle in Kurdistan, they skipped the basic training and started right in on advanced tactics for bombs and suicide vests. Another internal faction, Kurdish Hamas, had joined with the Erbil-based faction Tawheed. They arranged their own trip to meet with bin Laden through Abu Qatada al-Filistini, a London-based cleric. Over several months bin Laden and his associate Ayman al-Zawahiri pressured the Kurds to unify and form a training camp of their own in Kurdistan.[9] Events in Kurdistan took a hand in pushing the factions together.

The IMK showed no ability to control radicals inside the movement—the leadership eventually disavowed Tawheed after members started throwing acid on the faces of unveiled women in Erbil. KDP authorities swept up all the radicals they could find and forced them and their families out of the city. Tawheed moved to the Iranian border town of Haj Omran, where they clashed with the KDP again, losing several men. But a sleeper cell remained in Erbil. On February 18, 2001, its members took revenge, assassinating Franso Hariri, a prominent KDP leader and a Christian. The Islamists claimed afterward that Hariri had ties with the Israeli Mossad, their stand-by conspiracy justification for murder.

Hariri's death became another marker in the rivalry between Talabani and Barzani. The PUK allowed Tawheed to relocate around the city of Khurmal and possibly allowed Hariri's assassins to make their escape. Talabani may have been trying to placate the Islamists in his backyard or trying to curry favor with Iran. But allowing the Islamists to concentrate around Khurmal soon blew back on the PUK. Osama bin Laden sent a personal envoy to tell them he wanted an al-Qa'ida base in the mountains of Kurdistan, and the radical factions began to galvanize. The plan hit a small bump when three Kurdish mujahideen slipped up, crossing back from Afghanistan through Iran. The Iranians arrested them and discovered CD-ROMs full of al-Qa'ida training videos, but the IMK still had enough connections in the Iranian government to get the men released. On September 1, 2001, the Islamist factions created Jund al-Islam, or "Soldiers of Islam." Two days later the PUK briefed the White House that they had a new Islamist threat on their hands with connections to an

obscure Saudi named Osama bin Laden. For their trouble they received
a collective blank stare from the Bush administration.*

Interest in al-Qa'ida links to Iraq revived quickly after September 11, but
Saddam hawks in Washington wanted more than evidence of a few guerrillas plotting in Kurdistan, outside Baghdad's control. Their opening premise
was that the 9/11 attacks were simply too complex for a nonstate actor; only
a government like Saddam's could have organized it. The White House
desperately sought something large to punish, and Saddam Hussein's capital city looked much more satisfying than the caves of Tora Bora or Halabja. By the first week of October the hawks seized on a rumored meeting
between one of the hijackers and an Iraqi Mukhabarat agent in Prague, but
that turned out to be a red herring. Most of Washington's intelligence ana-
lysts decided that Saddam Hussein, at best a Muslim of convenience, was
exactly the kind of Middle East despot bin Laden had railed against. The
Kurds never claimed Baghdad had helped with 9/11. They had learned not
to overplay their cards, but they maintained that Saddam Hussein had at
least opened channels with the militants in the north.

"It was murky. It wasn't hands-on," Qubad Talabani admitted. Saddam
had good intelligence about the formation of Islamist groups in Kurdistan, including a significant number of Arab military officers from Mosul
who had joined the Islamists after deserting during the uprising in 1991.
Some of them may have reopened ties with the regime. Saddam's first
contact with the group may have involved catching them trying to operate
in Iraq. "Saddam was arresting some of these guys in Baghdad," said
Qubad. "But they were saying, look, we can help you; we're not here to
harm you. We've got another problem—these Kurds in the north are way
too secular, way too pro-American. We need to deal with this. So Saddam
started releasing some of these guys."

In retrospect the Kurds saw a rush of al-Qa'ida operatives moving toward Iraqi Kurdistan in the first week of September 2001, just after the
assassination of Ahmed Shah Masoud, the leader of the Northern Alliance in Afghanistan. Killing Masoud was bin Laden's preemptive strike
against the most important rival to the Taliban government that was giving him shelter. It looked to the Kurds like many radicals might have left

---

* In 2004 NBC News reported that the U.S. government had in fact considered
  and then tabled a plan to take out the Ansar camp in northern Iraq, later cor-
  roborated in congressional testimony.

Afghanistan in advance of September 11, when they expected things to heat up there. Soon things heated up in Kurdistan as well.

MULLAH KREKAR TOOK the leadership of Jund al-Islam just weeks after 9/11, and the group changed its name to Ansar al-Islam (supporters of Islam). They inaugurated the change by stepping up attacks on PUK positions in the Halabja region, taking strategic peaks around the city. On September 23 they defeated a large number of PUK pesh merga in the town of Kheli Hama, and took the conflict a step further. Ansar's fighters executed forty-three prisoners, torturing many and beheading some. In what would become a familiar al-Qa'ida tactic, they put video of the entire gory massacre on the Internet.

The video footage shocked Jalal Talabani's men into action. PUK fighters launched a major assault during the first week of October and drove Ansar out of the valley around Halabja. They retook Shinerwe Mountain, a frigid peak along the Iranian border with a commanding view of the city. Ansar defended Shinerwe fiercely; some of its militants even chained themselves to their machine gun nests to ensure they would fight to the death. When the dust settled, the PUK discovered a major piece of evidence: a dead Syrian known as Abu Abd-al-Rahman, a known associate of Osama bin Laden. Abu Abd-al-Rahman had come as al-Qa'ida's envoy to Kurdistan, with hundreds of thousands of dollars to help bind the fractious Kurdish Islamists together, and stayed on as a leadership figure. Some days after the fight on Shinerwe Mountain, a PUK informer overheard Ansar al-Islam leaders lamenting Abu Abd-al-Rahman's death in the battle.[10] Between the videotaped massacre and the death of a major al-Qa'ida figure, the Americans finally woke to the Kurds' al-Qa'ida problem.

Small groups of Americans arrived in Kurdistan, asking to interview detainees from Ansar al-Islam. The Americans pointed to two enemies they had in common with the Kurds: Ansar al-Islam and the dictator in Baghdad, whom the White House keenly wanted to peg as an international terrorist. The KDP, still bearing the memory of Barzani's betrayal, especially didn't trust the visitors. Agents reported back to CIA headquarters that the United States, and particularly the CIA, had a major credibility problem.[11] The Kurds had outgrown their habit of believing that every foreigner who trekked into Kurdistan was a secret envoy from the great powers.

"Before we didn't know how the decision making worked," said Masoud

Barzani. "We didn't know where the centers of power were. For instance, we thought that when a CIA officer says something, it represents the president or the administration or the Pentagon." Barzani wasn't going to be taken on faith again, and the Bush administration realized it needed the Kurds solidly on board to support and protect any team it might send into the north. To settle their doubts, in March 2002 Jalal Talabani and Masoud Barzani secretly traveled to the United States. Avoiding nosy Washington, the administration hustled them out to the CIA's training base near Williamsburg, Virginia, known as "the Farm." George Tenet hosted them along with some familiar faces: Zalmay Khalilzad, now on the National Security Council staff, and Ryan Crocker, deputy assistant secretary of state for Near Eastern Affairs.* The act of bringing them to "the Farm" almost made the rest of the message unnecessary, but Tenet drove it home anyhow: this time the United States wanted Saddam gone.

"It was then we realized they were serious," Barzani said. "I was convinced from April 2002 that the Americans were coming."

Tenet may have bluffed through it a bit, overstating his resolve with the Kurdish leaders in order to protect the men he sent into Iraq,[12] and of course the Bush administration busily denied any intention to go to war, even as military resources started to shift from Afghanistan toward Iraq. When Talabani and Barzani returned to Kurdistan, the CIA set up a permanent base near the town of Sa'id Sadiq, between Sulimaniya and Halabja. The location made sense for the agency's stated purpose—gathering intelligence on Ansar al-Islam—but its real mission involved prospecting for human intelligence inside Iraq. The trip to Washington finally convinced both Kurdish leaders that the Iraqi dictator would be taken down. They only worried how many Kurds Saddam might be able to take with him.

The United States upped the ante during the first week of April, with a public visit to the Kurdish region. Ryan Crocker swung through Salahudin and Sulimaniya. While his visit officially reaffirmed the U.S. commitment to the Washington Agreement, it meant more as a follow-up from the CIA meeting and as a shot across Saddam's bow. On the eve of

---

* Both major players on Bush's all-star war on terror team: Khalilzad was ambassador first to the Iraqi opposition, then to Kabul, then to Baghdad. Ryan Crocker was chargé d'affaires in Kabul, then ambassador to Pakistan, then took over for Khalilzad in Baghdad in 2007.

Crocker's meeting with Barzani and Talabani, however, Ansar al-Islam aimed its own cannonball.

Barham Salih had returned from Washington the previous year to serve as prime minister of the PUK's section of Kurdistan. He earned a good reputation in Sulimaniya as the next generation of Kurdish leadership, educated men in suits who would settle disputes around a boardroom table, not Kalashnikov-toting guerrillas. Dr. Barham embodied America's hopes for democracy in the Muslim world, and he could speak Washington's language perfectly. There was a flip side: no one better fit Ansar al-Islam's description of an apostate worthy of assassination. A three-man suicide team set out from Khurmal to ambush him on April 2, 2002.

The men staked out Salih's office in a red Volkswagen disguised as a taxi. On his home turf, and generally well liked in the city, Dr. Barham had fallen into a predictable routine of moving from his house to his office, but that Tuesday morning was an exception. A family friend, Thuraya Khan, had called from London the night before to tell him her brother had died. Dr. Barham promised to leave early in the morning for the funeral in Koi Sanjaq.

"I usually go to the office around eight o'clock, and that morning the Ansar team was waiting for me. [Instead] I left at six to go to Koi Sanjaq; I didn't go to the office. So they missed me in the morning," he said.[13]

Completely unaware, Salih drove an hour and a half to the west and paid his respects. He returned by way of Talabani's guesthouse at Dukan dam, where the Crocker delegation had arrived and were settling in for meetings with the PUK. The assassins picked him up again as he returned to his home, a block behind Sulimaniya's Ashti Hotel. At four o'clock they saw his driver ready the Land Cruiser again, and the jihadis stepped down from their car and drew their weapons.

"As I was stepping out, I was called back for a phone call," Salih recalled. It was Thuraya Kahn again. "This lady saved me twice. At four P.M. she called me, and she was crying for the death of her brother. It kept me from going out. Then I heard the bullets," he said.

With grenades and assault rifles, Ansar agents killed five of Salih's lightly armed bodyguards before two of the gunmen fell in a hail of bullets. A third assailant lost his suicidal fervor and fled with two bullets in his leg. The PUK authorities tracked him to a safehouse in Sulimaniya about fourteen hours after the attack. Qais Ibrahim Khadir, the twenty-six-year-old surviving attacker, had been a member of the original Tawheed faction from Erbil—which Talabani had allowed to cross over into his territory. The PUK at first put out word that he had been killed, perhaps trying to maximize his intelligence value. But what the wispy-bearded young man would say he said willingly. Khadir showed no remorse and only regretted failing in the attempt to kill Salih. He said he would try it again if they ever released him. When the PUK interrogators came to see him even months later, he tried to convert them into good fundamentalist Muslims.[14]

The narrow escape of Washington's favorite Kurd from an Islamist suicide team added leverage to those in the Bush administration talking about Ansar al-Islam, especially since the attack took place while Ryan Crocker made his official visit. The Americans had a great deal of work to do on the case for invasion, but at the time they felt quite pleased with their "War on Terror." As spring turned to summer, the Afghanistan war looked a total success. The Taliban had crumbled under air assaults with only a few Americans on the ground egging on the indigenous Northern Alliance. A meeting of Afghan exiles in Bonn, Germany, had selected a new Afghan government, and international donors pledged billions to rebuild the country. In June Afghanistan's bickering warlords had all come under the same tent to endorse America's handpicked president, Hamid Karzai (the huge air-conditioned tent near Kabul University had been built by the Americans). Even the optimistic neocons had thought Afghanistan might give them some trouble; in the early days after 9/11, Paul Wolfowitz opined that instead of Afghanistan, Iraq was the low-hanging fruit.[15] After Afghanistan had been such a pushover, taking Baghdad looked like a cinch. For act 2, the Kurds could play the part of the Northern Alliance, the indigenous force on the ground. The State Department commissioned the Middle East Institute, a Washington think tank, to convene an Iraqi version of the Bonn meeting. Only the Iraqi opposition had a different script.

The Kurds, bloodhounds when it came to a whiff of betrayal, started to harass Washington about promises made at the secret 2002 meeting with Barzani and Talabani in Virginia. They expected Saddam to lash out if cornered. He might save his dying curse for Israel, but the Kurds sat within reach even for the short-range missiles that the U.N. embargo allowed Baghdad to keep. All of the world's intelligence services believed at the time that Saddam still had chemical weapons; the Kurds wanted to know what sort of protection came with allowing Americans in. At the CIA meeting, the Americans had promised to protect the Kurds, but when asked about it over the summer, Vice President Dick Cheney had resorted to the old Clintonian language. He promised that any aggression by Saddam against the Kurdish safe zone would be met with retaliation "at a time and place of our choosing."[16] That same line had brought air strikes in southern Iraq while Saddam's tanks rolled through Erbil in 1996. Despite a constant chatter from the administration about Baghdad's chemical and nerve agents, the Kurds couldn't get any gas masks from the United States, which noted that delivering them would have violated the U.N. embargo on Iraq, an excuse that made the Kurds apoplectic.

"When they came and offered, there were around two or three thousand masks," said Masoud Barzani. The number implied that they were for the friends and family of the Kurdish leaders. "We said that if they didn't have enough for all the people, we don't accept."

The Americans first had four groups in mind for Iraq's "Bonn meeting," with a goal of uniting the fractious Iraqi opposition, to be held in Washington, D.C.: Ahmed Chalabi's INC, Ayad Allawi's INA, Barzani's KDP, and Talabani's PUK. The Clinton administration had started reaching out to Shi'ite groups as well, but the location of their leadership in Tehran bogged down the process, and by 2002, U.S. officials barely knew the names of the key Shi'ite figures.[17] Yet Washington couldn't afford to ignore them. Democracy in Iraq would of course mean Shi'ite majority rule, and the Shi'ite Supreme Council for Islamic Revolution in Iraq (SCIRI) boasted a ten-thousand-man militia, trained by Iran. SCIRI's leader, Ayatollah Muhammad Bakr al-Hakim, remained aloof, but he sent his brother Abdul Aziz al-Hakim, then a virtual unknown, to the talks in Washington. At the urging of Chalabi's INC, another group was added, the Constitutional Monarchist Movement, led by Sharif Ali bin al-Hussein, a London exile and would-be king of Iraq. But when the meeting convened in Washington during the sweltering first week of August, they were one man short.

Masoud Barzani snubbed the White House, even though he had been promised a face-to-face meeting with President Bush if he came along with Talabani. The latter went to Washington happily—he loved international travel, cameras, microphones, and meetings. The fact that the promises made in these meetings never panned out didn't seem to bother Mam Jalal, who had his own habit of letting his words run away with him and then backing off. While he was in D.C., for example, he told CNN that the Kurdish region would make an excellent base for U.S. attacks on Saddam. He "clarified" the remark the next day to say that the Kurdish region would *not* be an excellent base for U.S. attacks.

On August 8 and 9, members of the "group of six" held meetings at the White House and State Department, with the KDP represented by Hoshyar Zebari. At the State Department they met with Marc Grossman, now undersecretary of state for political affairs, and Douglas Feith, Wolfowitz's deputy from the Pentagon, and Secretary of State Colin Powell "stopped in" to visit. Barzani's absence made high-level decisions impossible, and the White House rescinded the offer of face time with Bush. Instead the group met at the National Security Council and spoke with Vice President Dick Cheney by video link from Wyoming. Khalilzad, Rumsfeld, and Joint Chiefs Chairman General Richard Meyers sat in on the meeting, asking specific questions about war planning. Talabani was his usual garrulous self, and he assured the vice president that the Iraq war would last only three weeks. The war would not be the issue, he told Cheney. It would be—and then Talabani leaned over to Barham Salih.[18]

"What is *farhud* ?" he asked Salih, who whispered him the translation.

"Looting," said Talabani. "The problem will be looting."

Zalmay Khalilzad smiled and later told Talabani he should be Iraq's next president.[19]

It was the strongest sign to date that the Bush administration planned to take action in Iraq, but Barzani was having none of this Washington love fest. Besides the undelivered aid and security guarantees for the Kurds, he had found other reasons not to go. The black market oil business between the regime and Turkey still filled the KDP coffers, and every week the war didn't happen made them that much richer. But Barzani could see this wouldn't last much longer. In fact he may have intended to go to Washington until a logistical problem gave him pause. At the last moment Turkey had, unusually, denied Barzani permission to travel across its borders (both he and Talabani held Turkish diplomatic passports, among several other travel documents). Barzani still could have headed out through Syria, but since Washington did nothing to protest, the Turkish snub showed him something important.[20] In a conflict between pleasing Turkey and keeping a promise with a Kurd, America was going to choose Ankara every time.

As it happened, Barzani wasn't the only one put on display as Turkey showed off its influence with Washington. On October 18, 2002, a group of medical doctors from Sulimaniya and Erbil left Iraqi Kurdistan at the invitation of East Tennessee State University. Traveling from an invisible state across a militarized border toward an international flight would have been a tall order, but the Kurds felt relaxed, as the U.S. State Department had arranged the seminar in Tennessee as part of a program to improve Kurdistan's health care system. The Appalachian communities had some similarities with the Kurdish ones, and perhaps for that reason Tennessee hosted America's largest Kurdish exile population. Like most Iraqi Kurds, the doctors carried black market forged passports—as Kurdish government employees, they could hardly apply at the passport offices in Baghdad or Mosul. Still, inside their fake passports were real Turkish transit visas that got them to Ankara, and there the U.S. embassy knowingly stamped in bona fide American visas. Thus the doctors were stunned when the Turkish police arrested them at Istanbul Atatürk Airport. Though such travel had been common, the Turkish government acted shocked to discover Kurdish doctors traveling with fake passports. They threw them in jail and pondered whether to deport them back to Iraqi Kurdistan—which the Turks officially said didn't exist—or to Baghdad, where Saddam might have a few questions for them.

In the end, after threatening them with being returned to Baghdad, the Turks took away the Kurds' passports and kept them in jail for two nights in Istanbul. The U.S. embassy finally interceded to gain their release, but the Turks wouldn't let the doctors carry on to attend the seminar in America, and by that time they felt lucky just to make it back home in decent health. Turkey had made its point. The Bush administration needed Turkish airspace and perhaps access to Iraq's northern border. As long as that was true, the Kurds were going to lose every round, and Turkey wanted to flaunt it.

In fact, though, one of the Kurdish doctors had made it to Washington, D.C., where Dr. Najmaldin Karim, the president of the Washington Kurdish Institute, arranged for him to meet with me. Before the interview I called the Turkish embassy, which said it had no knowledge of the case. Eventually embassy officials gave a simple confirmation: they had arrested thirteen Kurds in Istanbul traveling on false documents. A State Department spokesman was a bit less coy—he asked me to stop by Foggy Bottom the next day and he would give me the details on the Kurdish doctors.

Dr. Lezgine Ahmed, an internist from Salahudin, had avoided the trap in Turkey by leaving earlier for another conference in Vienna, where he picked up his visa for the trip to Tennessee. Now Lezgine was stranded in Washington, D.C., and the experience had reinforced his Kurdish sense of fatalism. He told a joke about a previous trip to Appalachia, when the airport shuttle driver had taken the mountain curves so fast that all the Kurdish visitors feared for their lives. Eventually one of them got up his courage to ask the driver to slow down.

"Please, sir, you don't understand," the visitor pleaded with the driver. "We can't die here—Saddam Hussein has important plans to kill us back in Kurdistan."[21]

Like many Kurds Lezgine was more of a cultural than religious Muslim—he fasted for Ramadan because he always had. He was also intensely nationalistic, considering Turkish history with the Kurds to be just as bad as what Saddam had done.

"To me genocide is not only killing people physically; you can also assimilate them. You can hardly find any Kurds in Iraq who can't speak Kurdish, but there are so many Kurds in Turkey who can't speak their mother tongue. The Turks want to eliminate the Kurds," he said.

Lezgine wasn't overly fond of the Talabanis or the Barzanis, who seemed to be settling into the role of dynastic rulers in Iraqi Kurdistan, but he shrugged off their many shifting alliances, as well as the behavior of the Americans, with a Kurdish proverb. "Everybody eats meat," he said. "Why do only the wolves get blamed?"

Lezgine had been e-mailing the other doctors, who all said they felt humiliated by their treatment in Istanbul, where the police have a terrible reputation for their treatment of Turkish Kurds. But Lezgine was just as stuck—he was afraid to travel through Turkey on his own fake passport and wasn't sure how to go home, where his wife was expecting to give birth within weeks. Somewhere back in history his family had become the victims of a map, and now he had no official nationality, no country to give him a passport.

Hoping for a reasonable explanation, I followed up the invitation to stop by the State Department, but my source had gone dry. I waited in the same lobby where Hoshyar Zebari had been stood up a decade earlier; when the receptionist called up to the office, no one answered the extension. I called several times on my cell phone and left voice mails, but apparently permission to tell me the State Department's side of the story had been rescinded. Najmaldin Karim, with uncharacteristic vehemence, explained the entire incident of the stranded doctors as another message from the Turks.

"I'm sure they get it! Turkey intended to show the U.S. that it's up to us!" he said, struggling to keep his typically measured tone. "The State

Department acted like this didn't concern them! They're more concerned with pleasing Turkey than helping these people who *they* invited."[22]

IN THE MEANTIME the State Department's plan for the next, larger Iraqi opposition conference was in the hopper. The Middle East Institute had dutifully started organizing an Iraqi version of the Bonn conference, planned for the fall, but the contract suddenly got the ax when the head of the institute committed one of the Bush administration's deadly sins: he publicly criticized the president's "axis of evil" speech. A former ambassador to half a dozen Middle Eastern countries, Ned Walker had thirty-five years of experience in diplomacy, but the Clinton years must have made him a bit too free with his opinions, and the Bush White House took the portfolio away. Walker's real offense may have been sidelining Ahmed Chalabi, who was still divisive enough to bust up Washington, D.C., cocktail parties. The CIA and State Department considered Chalabi a charlatan who had probably squandered all the money they had sent him since the 1990s. In the Pentagon, however, Chalabi had allies. Paul Wolfowitz and Douglas Feith, as well as many members of the Defense Policy Board advising Secretary of Defense Rumsfeld, saw Chalabi as the only one with the chutzpah to pull off the Iraq transformation they'd envisioned. To them, he was perfect—a secular Shi'ite Arab who could remake Iraq in his own Westernized image. Besides, Chalabi constantly told them exactly what they wanted to hear. It was the beginning of what Barham Salih described as "tribal warfare" between the Pentagon and the State Department over what to do in Iraq and how to do it.

The warring departments clashed a few times over the summer of 2002. The State Department let it be known that Chalabi's INC hadn't properly accounted for its recent disbursements of funding and put new accounting restrictions on INC programs, complaining that Chalabi was wasting their money. The Pentagon and its advisors had nothing but praise for Chalabi, noting that all the "best" leads on Saddam's weapons of mass destruction were coming through his INC. Toward the end of the summer Chalabi went to work again. At the August 8 and 9 meetings in Washington, the group of six had pledged to hold another opposition conference in November 2002, this time somewhere in Europe, without the taint of U.S. sponsorship. The meeting would have fifty or one hundred participants, and they agreed on the breakdown following a rough estimate of Iraq's population and the strength of opposition groups. Thirty-three percent would be Shi'ite Arabs like members of SCIRI and Da'wa Islamiya, another Iran-based religious party. Another third would be liberals and independents, including those from the INA and many Sunni Arab parties. The two Kurdish parties would split 25 percent of the slots, and the remainder would go to Turcomans and Assyrian Christian minorities.[23] Chalabi had nodded his assent to the numbers, but he noticed as well as anyone that all the other parties had battle-hardened troops inside Iraq that used to prop up his INC, now less of an umbrella party than a rain gauge. A proven chameleon, Chalabi suddenly became the champion of Iraqi civil society. He started bothering the two Kurdish groups, the INA and SCIRI, to expand the numbers of delegates up toward two hundred, which would have diluted the power of the traditional parties. Within a few weeks of the meeting, scheduled for November 22 in Brussels, Chalabi drew up a list of 376 names and demanded they be included in the name of democracy. He convinced several prominent Iraqi intellectuals to join his call, most notably Kanan Makiya, an Iraqi teaching at Brandeis University.

Under the pen name Samir al-Khalil, Makiya had written two books about Saddam's Iraq that first publicized the atrocities—including the Anfal campaign. Makiya wasn't easy to pigeonhole. He had a philosopher's habit of trying to challenge any assumptions that looked a bit too comfortable. His second book, *Cruelty and Silence*, took aim at Saddam but equally at the Arab heads of state whose silence countenanced Saddam's brutality. Makiya had bristled as most other Arab intellectuals fell in line with anti-American rhetoric against the Iraq war. He told an appreciative audience at the American Enterprise Institute in October 2002, "Unfortunately much of the debate over Iraq that has taken place in Europe, in the Arab world, and even in this country has been a selfish one, centered on the threats to the West and its friends on the one hand, and on the moral issues arising from American hegemony on the other. It has been all about 'us' in the West, and not about those who have had to live inside the grip of one of the most brutal dictatorships of modern times."

Makiya criticicized what he saw as the cynical manipulation by Arab regimes of the Palestinian issue that left no room for the plight of Iraqis under Saddam, and in more than one public forum he called antiwar speakers out on the carpet. Chalabi's plan to expand the opposition conference offered Makiya a chance to level his guns at the Iraqi opposition parties, which, to him, seemed theocratic or tribal and certainly corrupt. When the "group of four" pushed back against the attempt to open up the conference, Makiya made their e-mail correspondence public. Few people read the substance of the exchange; instead, anyone paying attention simply concluded that the Iraqi opposition couldn't organize a conference, much less a coup or a constitution.

"This isn't an election! He didn't need to bring all of his voters," exclaimed an extremely frustrated member of the Shi'ite opposition, who felt Chalabi had put his own personal inclusion above the success of the entire opposition, and over a meeting that most of them saw as merely symbolic.[24]

AS THE DRUMBEAT for an invasion of Iraq intensified, the opposition kept postponing their meeting, and it looked like the Bush administration might get its war finished first. Jalal Talabani, ever the big-mouth, predicted war after Ramadan, which in 2002 ended on December 6. At the KDP office in Washington, Farhad Barzani's brief was to get as many journalists into Kurdistan as he could, to witness either a preemptive strike by Saddam or another American double cross. The KDP had just pulled off a coup of sorts, getting a CNN team to set up a permanent office in Erbil. The TV crew took over the entire Hawraman Hotel, right across the traffic circle from the old Sheraton (still pockmarked with bullet holes from 1994). It delighted the Kurds to have a guarantee of the media coverage they thought had saved them in 1991. But after the crew was set up, CNN aired a feature detailing its team's arduous journey into Kurdistan through Syria. The Syrian government's collusion was still supposed to be a secret, even if it was an open one. Damascus slapped the KDP's wrist and shut the Syrian route—a disaster for the Kurdish publicity effort.

Visa problems and endless delays finally did in the Brussels opposition conference. Instead, the meeting would be held in early December in London, and following Ahmed Chalabi's push to expand the numbers, it had grown to the size of a Rolling Stones concert. London had long been the capital for Iraqi exiles. That December it felt as if they had all woken from a long suburban sleep on the fingertips of London's commuter railway. Ex-Ba'athists came into the city center from Wimbledon, Marsh Arabs from Queenspark, and secular Iraqi intellectuals from Surbiton. Hoshyar Zebari wore a three-piece suit and juggled his cell phone, cigarettes, and coffee cup at the InterContinental Hotel. Zebari's full, round cheeks and short dark mustache somehow make his face ideal for the transition from schoolboy laughter to threatening disdain. Zebari had spent a decade rushing out to meet every journalist who might possibly get a few inches of news copy for the Iraqi opposition. He had the Kurdish appeal to the world community down pat—he and Barham Salih had written the act. But Zebari is much quicker to let his guard down, or at least give reporters the impression that they're getting past the public relations.

In spring 2000, at our first meeting, he had ably delivered the set speech about how the international community, in its beneficence, would never let the Kurds be slaughtered again. When the microphone was off, Zebari had exhaled, and said, "Oh my God, but look what they're doing in Chechnya." The Russian military had been flattening Grozny with all the precision of a wounded grizzly bear. The precious international community had done nothing. In those days the Kurds fully expected Saddam might do the same to them.

Two years later Zebari had a bit more confidence—perhaps because the secret briefings in Washington had convinced the KDP that the war was a go. He laughed at attempts to poke holes in his optimism. The conference just needed to show a tiny measure of unity, he said. Chalabi needed to get used to the fact that he simply didn't have boots on the ground; that's why he was pushing so hard to form a transitional government in advance—he wanted to cash in his chips before everyone got to Iraq and discovered the INC had no support inside the country.

On December 13, a chilly Friday, the Iraqis took over the Hilton Metropole Hotel on Edgeware Road in North London. Half the businesses on the block bore signs written in Arabic anyhow, and the sheikhs in full regalia looked no more out of place than the lobbyists, the government operatives, and the horde of journalists. Everyone expected to spend a long weekend watching the parties battle it out, but the fight started early, before the conference officially began, with a preemptive strike by Ahmed Chalabi.

That Friday afternoon, Chalabi, along with Sharif Ali bin al-Hussein and Kanan Makiya, held a press conference in the grand ballroom and handed out an agenda for the conference. The document was bold and idealistic, outlining a vision for a new pluralistic Iraq. The only problem was, it wasn't really the agenda. The stack of paper was a report on the "Transition to Democracy in Iraq," largely authored by Makiya as part of a State Department initiative called the Future of Iraq Project. Makiya joined the project reluctantly, complaining that the diplomats would always sacrifice principle for consensus. Once inside, he just about took over the subcommittee on Transition to Democracy, and he seemed intent on ruffling as many feathers as possible among the traditional parties. By late 2002, the Future of Iraq Project completed a thirteen-volume report detailing every single thing that should be done after Saddam fell. Some of the project's members had presented their findings at the U.S. Institute of Peace in Washington that November. They appeared to have covered every contingency, some of them eminently practical (one presenter talked about the two gauges of railway line in Iraq and how they should be standardized), and others positively Disneyland—the suggestion, for example, that the new free Iraqi government might want to adopt Linux as a computer operating system. But few ever read the Future of Iraq Project report, just as the journalists assembled in London never read Kanan Makiya's agenda/manifesto.

For a moment, though, Chalabi looked like he would pull off his first coup. His panel never said it represented the entire Iraqi opposition, but most of the assembled press corps had no idea that wasn't the case and didn't know the characters well enough to note the absence of the Kurds and the Shi'ites. Reporters started asking questions as if the panel spoke for a unified opposition leadership, and Chalabi wasn't about to disabuse them of the notion. But during the questions, Kanan Makiya tipped his hand. When the reporters' concerns didn't seem to focus on the boldness of his document, Makiya proclaimed, "This is a fighting document! We intend to fight for it!"

Makiya's earnest timbre sounded out of key among the chorus of slick politicians. Suddenly ears pricked up. His pledge to fight gave the first clue to the assembled press that this agenda was not yet a fait accompli. As I walked out of the back of the ballroom, I saw Hoshyar Zebari coming in the doorway with some urgency, and I suggested that Chalabi might have hijacked the conference. "Nonsense," Zebari said. "They have no authority." Zebari kept smiling but he stepped up his pace to get into the room before the press corps left to file the day's story. A hint of doubt crept into his demeanor—to know Chalabi is to wonder if you've somehow become a cog in his latest machine. Zebari told everyone he could grab that the conference hadn't even started and that decisions would be made over the next several days. In the end, Chalabi's move was too clever by half. The next day the newspapers led not with the declaration by his pro-democracy intellectuals but with confusion and discord surrounding the conference before it even began.[25]

The next morning the party leaders sat smiling again onstage in the main ballroom of the Metropole. In front of the 330 delegates and countless hangers-on, they gave the sort of unquotably bland speeches designed to make an impression of official unity. Hoshyar Zebari introduced each of the main speakers, among them Talabani, al-Hakim, Chalabi, Sharif Ali, and Ayad Allawi. One woman sat among the big players, Safia al-Suhail, the heir to an important Sunni tribe who also happens to be married to Bakhtiar Amin, a Kurdish human rights activist. Masoud Barzani was hard to recognize in a suit and tie, instead of his usual Kurdish tunic and sash. The atmosphere of warmth and respect onstage just proved how unrealistic the entire process was, as each member's lackeys badmouthed one another in the lobby and the bar. No one in the audience cheered or booed, but they did occasionally perk up. Shi'ite leaders like al-Hakim and Bahr al-Oulum, in turbans and priestly robes, began their speeches with a long religious greeting in Arabic. The Shi'ites in the audience returned the greeting, and the Sunni Arabs in the crowd contracted bodily.

Zalmay Khalilzad addressed the assembly the next day, promising that Iraq would soon have a democratic government that protected minorities. He got the most audience response when he promised no "Saddamism without Saddam," going on the record to allay a common fear at the conference—that the United States would prefer another Iraqi strongman in place. That evening in a closed session he went a step further and said what the Shi'ites and Kurds had been waiting to hear, that "1991 was a mistake." The language, still somewhat coded, was designed to send a message back into Iraq that if the people rose up this time, they wouldn't be left hanging. After the speech, Khalilzad walked out with his phalanx of security guards and aides and retired to the hotel's fourteenth floor, which the U.S. delegation had taken over.

In response to a few questions in the elevator, Khalilzad downplayed the opposition's infighting. "It's a natural process—that people talk about how [the new Iraq] should be formed. We don't want any interference in Iraq. And we want a free Iraq where everyone's rights are respected," he said. Asked if that noninterference extended to the Turks, who already had demanded to send their own troops along if they allowed Americans to pass through their country, Khalilzad said the United States flat out wouldn't allow Turkey to interfere in Iraq.

Back in the hotel café Kanan Makiya still fumed to the concentric circles of reporters who had gathered around him about forming a technocratic leadership that would put the traditional parties out to pasture. "The parties are not competent enough to do otherwise," he said. "Let them be the symbols—but they're incompetent. They do not have the people to do what needs to be done."

Then Makiya's anger ticked up a notch, and he lashed out at his real enemy of the moment, the U.S. State Department.

"The U.S. State Department wants to give control of this to Iran!" he said. The statement seemed so outlandish that few stayed to hear his longer explanation about how the State Department had given too much weight to the Shi'ite religious parties living in exile in Tehran. In fact several delegates had complained that each minor decision sent the Shi'ite parties out of the room to consult with Tehran before they could make up their mind. In any case, the journalists began to move away from where Makiya had settled on one of the café's couches.

Late that night, Jalal Talabani, despite his sixty-nine years, was one of the last delegates still in the conference rooms. Asked what he thought about Makiya's criticisms of the traditional parties, Talabani waved his hand. "The role of anyone in the opposition is according to his sacrifice," Talabani said, searching for the right words after a grueling day of discussions in three or more languages. "It's not for an intellectual living far away from Iraq to send orders to us."

By Monday all the adrenaline was gone and anyone not in the thick of the arguing had forgotten exactly what the dispute was. The conference had only booked the hotel through Monday. Hoping to restore a little punch to the event, Khalilzad and Bill Luti, Douglas Feith's deputy at the Pentagon, convened a meeting in the small hours of Tuesday morning with the four traditional parties plus Chalabi and Sharif Ali, and rumors trickled out that the two representatives from the White House had upbraided the leaders for missing a simple deadline to produce a completely bland statement of unity.

Both Luti and Khalilzad were in the neocon camp, but Luti's Office of Special Plans over at the Defense Department had been cultivating much closer ties to Chalabi's INC. His late arrival to the conference, as well as the presence of the neocons' "prince of darkness" Richard Perle, gave rise to rumors that Luti had come to make a last-ditch push for Chalabi. Khalilzad denied that any interagency rivalry played out at the meeting, for which he had pretty low expectations from the start. At the time, he said, the U.S. government opposed Chalabi's push to set up some sort of government in exile and that both he and Luti wanted to avoid the appearance of an American anointment of the next leader of Iraq. The Kurds, he said later, formed a special part of the core group, because they needed to be on board to host the follow-up meetings—scheduled for Salahudin in mid-January.[26]

"These meetings were called 'meetings of exiles,'" Khalilzad recalled. "But we had to remind the media that some were exiles, but not all—there were powerful groups such as [the Kurds] that were in Iraq."

Still, Chalabi expected to get more of a boost in London, and his supporters at the Pentagon probably expected he would make a better showing. A subtle shift permeated the attitude of the INC delegates at the conference. At the beginning they had welcomed the appointment of Khalilzad as ambassador to the free Iraqis. By Sunday evening they were dropping hints about him in their typical style, implying that he had a lot to learn, that he might not be in his post for long. Chalabi's people also made free with the information that the CIA was now permanently on the ground in Erbil and Sulimaniya, referring to it indelicately as a "non-Pentagon agency of the U.S. government that sometimes carries out lethal operations."

By Tuesday morning, with the hotel management ushering the delegates out the door, it was clear that all the late nights had been unnecessary. The sixty-one delegates for the next opposition conference had been chosen, though by the end of the week the number had risen to sixty-five, with plenty of still-bruised feelings about the percentages from each group and not much change from the original formula. Laith Kubba, a former member of Da'wa who had transformed himself into a policy wonk at the National Endowment for Democracy in Washington, seemed to think the arguments would be moot pretty soon.

"The purpose was to give common principles," he said. "As far as percentages, I think everyone knows it's irrelevant, because the next meeting is likely to be in Baghdad."

Instead, the next meeting was in Kurdistan.

CHAPTER SEVEN

The Northern Front

FOR ALL THEIR EXPERIENCE WITH SADDAM Hussein's chemical weapons and the enclave of Afghan-trained suicide bombers in their mountains, the Kurds worried most about the one U.S. ally on their northern border. President Bush still claimed he didn't have an Iraq war plan "on my desk," but his generals had a plan, with a big left hook through Turkey.

Unlike in his father's Iraq war, the coalition Bush assembled this time could count its major players on one hand. Another handful of allies sat on the fence, caught between popular opposition to America's invasion plans and the enormous pressure to be either with the Bush administration or against it. Turkey struggled mightily with the choice. In March 2002, as the CIA convinced Kurdish leaders they would remove Saddam, Vice President Dick Cheney traveled to Ankara to secure Turkish support. Cheney consulted not only with the government in office but also with the Turkish military—not a ringing endorsement of civilian rule in a country that has hardly seen a generation without its military coup. But Turkey's democracy had matured, as the Bush administration learned that November. The Justice and Development (AK) Party, a group with Islamist roots, won Turkey's general elections, and Washington had to start the lobbying process from scratch. In early December Paul Wolfowitz visited Ankara to meet the new leadership and feel them out about the war. He came home telling the White House it would be a hard sell.[1]

Perhaps as a direct consequence, when President Bush met with Iraqis for the first time, on January 10, 2003, no Kurds were among them. Three exiles were ushered into the Oval Office: Rend Rahim, an Arab human rights activist; Hatem Mukhlis, a doctor from Tikrit; and Kanan Makiya.* Cheney, Condoleezza Rice, and Khalilzad sat in on the meeting, in which the exiles spent part of the time explaining to Bush that Iraq had two kinds of Arab Muslims, Shi'ite and Sunni. Bush was interested in the exiles' personal stories and also asked if Iraqis hated Israel.[2] The three Iraqis gave sometimes contradictory answers to Bush's questions about how Americans should proceed post-invasion, but no one appears to have mentioned that in addition to twenty million Arabs, the country was also home to millions of Kurds as well as some Turcomans and Assyrians. A week later Vice President Cheney quietly received the PUK's Barham Salih, visiting Washington from Sulimaniya, but it didn't have the same pizzazz as a meeting with the president. As far as the Kurds could see, they had been clearly snubbed to placate the Turks, as usual.

MY SECOND VISIT to the invisible nation of Kurdistan began in January 2003 with immigration officials in Tehran cheerfully fingerprinting me—their retaliation for the American policy that requires the same for Iranian visitors. With the Syrian and Turkish routes closed, I had lucked into an Iranian visa and arranged to get across the border with help from the PUK in Tehran. Iranian bureaucracy kept my head spinning for all of the ten days I spent there, like jet lag that never went away.

The government office that gave me permission to travel up to the border didn't seem to have any pull with the guards deciding who would be allowed to cross; upon arrival at the gate near the northwestern city of Mariwan, the guards looked at my papers and turned me back toward town. Bright sunshine made an unseasonably warm day for January, and I struck up a pantomime conversation with some young Kurdish Iranian men playing cards in the sun by the beautiful lake below the mountains along the

---

* Though they wouldn't make a point of self-identifying as such, Makiya is from a Shi'ite family, Mukhlis is Sunni, and Rahim is mixed.

Iraqi border. Quite naturally they invited me home for a meal, stopping to buy a chicken along the way. The visit lasted much longer than my dozen words of Kurdish, as we waited for the women in the kitchen to boil the chicken—I wondered how often they ate anything beyond rice and white beans. I felt even worse when they walked me back to my hotel, where Iranian security was waiting. A stern man in civilian clothes took the boys aside in the manager's office. Ten minutes later they came out looking scared and bade me an anxious farewell, caught between their cultural mandate of hospitality and a terrifying government security apparatus.

The next morning winter returned and both the mountains and lake disappeared in a blizzard. It took until noon to find a driver who would brave the snowy few miles up to the border, and this time I got through. The taxi couldn't pass though, and I walked the last hundred yards with all my gear on my back, tromping through the slush and over a plank that served as a footbridge across a running brook. Taxis waited on the Iraqi side, and I was driven down the mountain roads through the city of Penjwin toward Sulimaniya. The fresh snow gave way to bright green fields of winter wheat as we descended, and seeing how the beauty of his land impressed me, the taxi driver started to sing. He laughed as I got out my microphone to record.

The city of Sulimaniya bustled, with the addition of a faux-five-star hotel, the Sulimaniya Palace, standing a dozen stories at the edge of the old bazaar. I checked into the hotel just in time for a press conference given by the PUK's Fuad Masum, and there I noticed another major change: cell phones. Some enterprising Kurds had put up towers all over the north, and shop windows brimmed with the latest Chinese knockoff handsets. The PUK and KDP still wouldn't let each other's cell phone networks roam across the old cease-fire line, but they had figured out a couple of dummy area codes in the U.K. that would transfer a call into the exchange in northern Iraq.

First, Masum announced the postponement of the next round of opposition talks—blaming visa problems again. February 15 was the new target date for the talks, to be held in the KDP-administered city of Salahudin. Masum said he didn't think Saddam would attack the conference for fear of giving the Americans a clear excuse for war. At that point many of America's European and Arab allies thought the invasion could be averted, and that the Bush administration wouldn't go to war without a United Nations Security Council resolution. In response to a question, however, Masum betrayed greater concern about the possibility of chemical attack. The Kurds still had no gas masks, he said, and unlike Kuwait and Israel, the Kurdish government couldn't afford to buy them. Even if the Americans hadn't yet landed in Kurdistan, the Kurds were already traitors as far as Saddam was concerned, and they sat uncomfortably nearby. Someone then asked him if there weren't already American troops operating in the north.

"We have no troops," Masum said, choosing his words carefully. "We have civilians who come and go. There are no permanently based Americans here."

The "temporary" Americans had recently been spotted inspecting airstrips, one in a suburb west of Sulimaniya called Bakrajo next to what had been a secret PUK prison in the 1990s.[3] Kurdish workmen started fixing up the runway that ran along the valley by the main highway toward Kirkuk. Barely visible from the road, it now measured about two miles, long enough to land the AC-130, a massive armed transport plane, as well as to accommodate an emergency landing by a U.S. fighter jet.* The KDP had a new airfield as well, and Kurdish leaders couldn't understand the media's impatience in confirming such an obvious, open secret. One zealous television producer had even called the KDP's Fowzi Hariri around four in the morning to confirm that American troops had finally landed at the KDP's new airstrip (they hadn't).

The next day Hariri dressed down the press humorously with his slightly nasal British accent, saying something to the effect of "It's four o'clock in the morning. At four o'clock in the morning, I don't know if the Americans have landed, and I just want to say to you people: Get a life."

But the war drum beat on unmistakably in Washington, gaining a momentum that seemed impossible to reverse. President Bush closed his State of the Union address in January 2003 with a warning about Iraq:

> Evidence from intelligence sources, secret communications, and statements by people now in custody reveal that Saddam Hussein

---

* The Kurds closed off all public access to the area, and naturally that made it an obsession for journalists. At one point I snuck from the back side of the village of Bakrajo with binoculars and ran into a few high-level PUK officials doing the same thing. They chuckled and claimed to be out for a walk, and wouldn't talk about the airstrip being built by a government with no airplanes in an area where the United Nations still prohibited flights.

aids and protects terrorists, including members of al-Qa'ida. Secretly, and without fingerprints, he could provide one of his hidden weapons to terrorists, or help them develop their own . . . Imagine those nineteen hijackers with other weapons and other plans—this time armed by Saddam Hussein. It would take one vial, one canister, one crate slipped into this country to bring a day of horror like none we have ever known.

Bush promised that a detailed case against Saddam would be presented at the United Nations on February 5, just a week later, by Colin Powell—somehow an admission that a world that didn't believe the president would be swayed by the gravitas of his secretary of state. Powell would rely on Kurdistan to make a large part of his case. One of the "people now in custody" that Bush had referred to in his speech was Kadhim Hussein Muhammad, then sitting in a Sulimaniya jail. An Arab from Basra, Kadhim confessed to the Kurds that he had been sent north by the Mukhabarat to make contact with Abu Wa'el,[4] a key figure in Ansar al-Islam. The PUK claimed that Abu Wa'el simultaneously served Osama bin Laden and Saddam Hussein, information they shared with the CIA, and probably again with Dick Cheney on Barham Salih's January 17 visit. Taking the link a step further, in his earliest interviews Kadhim claimed to have worked security for Ayman al-Zawahiri, bin Laden's deputy, when he visited Baghdad in 1992.* Such a high-level visit was a smoking gun, even if it had happened a decade earlier, and Kadhim seemed tailor-made to support the case for war.

By January 2003, however, Kadhim had stopped telling the Zawahiri story. Sulimaniya's chief warden, Colonel Wasta Hassan, gladly allowed journalists to visit his star inmates. The prisoner had a cordial relationship with his jailers and didn't mind the interviews either; perhaps they were a

---

* The *New Yorker*'s Jeffrey Goldberg did one of the earliest interviews with Kadhim in the March 25, 2002, issue. He transliterated the first name as "Qassem." Filmmaker Gwynne Roberts also did early interviews, translated by the ubiquitous Ayub Nuri. In a bizarre coincidence, Nuri recognized Kadhim as his neighbor in a Sulimaniya apartment building in 2001 and recalled puzzling over why Kadhim said he was moving out to go live in Khurmal. A Shi'ite Arab moving to a Kurdish region dominated by Sunni extremists was enough for local authorities to raise an eyebrow.

break in the monotony of prison life. He was a heavyset man and graying, unkempt and unshaven after a year in prison, though he claimed no mistreatment. The way he joked with the jailers almost suggested he was getting some sort of perk every time he outlined the al-Qa'ida–Saddam link for a foreigner—perhaps a carton of the cigarettes he chain-smoked.

Kadhim didn't confess to having contacted Abu Wa'el; in fact he didn't seem to know the man. He only admitted trying to reach him, perhaps trying to establish the link. When asked what sort of aid Baghdad was supplying Ansar, he said weapons and cash were smuggled up to the north—not through the Kurdish region, but rather across the border into Iran near Baghdad and then back into Iraq from the Kurdish region of northwest Iran. It didn't make much sense—Iran and Iraq, archenemies, cooperating with a third party that despised both Saddam's secular depravity and Tehran's Shi'ite theocracy. Still, the Middle East often saw strange marriages of convenience, and it made some twisted sense to the Kurds that the Iraqis, Iranians, and Islamists should all gang up on them. Colonel Hassan didn't seem to dislike Kadhim, who, after all, was only a Ba'athist. Hassan saved his ire for the religious radicals, cursing with every breath the "Afghan Arabs" who had come to Kurdistan, and eventually ridiculing practicing Muslims in general, not an uncommon attitude among the PUK's soldiery.[5] Even with the Kurds' history of pain at the hands of the Iraqi regime, Colonel Hassan seemed to dread the Islamists even more: they promised a new long war, just as the old one gave signs of ending. He opened his Koran to the Anfal chapter and read out the sura about smashing fingers, and a few other choice verses.

"You see what lunatics I'm dealing with?" he said.

A combination of U.S. government officials and unconfirmed press reports hyped Ansar even more, suggesting the group had been experimenting with the deadly toxin ricin, which is made from castor beans. The previous summer an al-Qa'ida videotape showed footage of a dog convulsing to death in a crude weapons laboratory. Ricin was one of the poisons U.N. weapons inspectors suspected that the Iraqi regime possessed, and anonymous Bush administration officials hinted that Ansar al-Islam was running the poison lab shown in the video. In early January 2003 the buzz got even louder, when British police arrested several Algerian men in London who police said had conspired to use ricin in a terror plot. Again the officials hinted at a connection to northern Iraq, though all it takes to make ricin is castor beans and know-how.[6]

All the parsing of intelligence that has occurred since suggests that much of the al-Qa'ida-Ansar-Saddam link came from CIA raw data refried by the Pentagon's Office of Special Plans, which leaked to the media and then could be cited publicly by the vice president's office.* But it nonetheless scared a lot of people at the time—especially Kurds on the front line. The PUK was also tracking a militant it believed had studied poisons and chemicals in Afghanistan. He traveled to Kurdistan under the alias "Qudama the Engineer," but his other name would soon be well known: Abu Musab al-Zarqawi, a Jordanian.

One of my first trips out of Sulimaniya allowed for a peek at the Islamist groups, from not quite a safe distance. As I came upon Girda Drozna, the "liar's hill," the name made perfect sense. From the Halabja road it looks like a little bump, and only from a few hundred yards reveals itself to be a towering plateau with a commanding view of the entire valley west of Halabja. The mound rises up so suddenly that older Kurdish stories call it a fake hill, put there by a fairy-tale king who wanted to please his wife by adding more features to the landscape. Another explanation comes from local farmers: the hill hides an erratic freshwater spring shepherds have always known they couldn't depend on. By now it had a military derivation as well—from the distance one can't see how many men are on the top. But the mortar man from Ansar al-Islam had decided there must be enough to warrant a few rounds every day.

At his request, Barham Salih's workaholic press attaché Dildar Katani had loaned me her car and driver and worked as my translator and guide for several days without accepting payment. Dildar felt at home among the soldiers, and they seemed to know her. At Halabja's security office down in the valley, pesh merga commander Ramadan Dekoni began talking about Ansar's origins, but I had only one question: Why hadn't the PUK already driven the group out? The PUK estimated only about seven hundred fighters bunkered down in the hills, and the Kurdish militias numbered in the tens of thousands. Dekoni's eyes went completely lifeless, perhaps wondering how many of his men would die in such an assault.

---

* Thomas F. Gimble, the Pentagon's acting inspector general, told the Senate Armed Services Committee as much on February 9, 2007. This was Doug Feith's shop, which mined the raw data, desperate to find the links he and the vice president were sure the CIA had missed.

He then sketched out a map of why running up the hill to brush away Ansar al-Islam wasn't such a brilliant idea.

Ansar controlled the towns of Sargat, Biyara, and Taweela, which make a small triangle in the high mountains overlooking Halabja and Girda Drozna. Their backs nestled comfortably to the east against the Iranian border, and Dekoni claimed that the Islamists crossed it at their leisure. Ansar must have been getting food and supplies from Iran, Dekoni said, and probably arms as well. The quantity of mortars being lobbed at his positions every night indicated frequent resupply, and Dekoni seemed to be jealous of the quality as well. "We are using old weapons we've taken from the Iraqis," he said. "The mortars they have are from Iran, and they are brand new."

The PUK would no longer be underestimating Ansar. In December 2002, some militants had swarmed up Girda Drozna one morning before dawn, using accurate mortar fire to cover their arrival. Dozens of pesh merga died, some of them executed after surrendering. Ansar held the hill only briefly, but it proved the group's skill, or demonstrated the PUK's complacency. But Dekoni blamed the defeat on treachery. The two remaining splinters of Kurdish Islamism, the IMK and Ali Bapir's Komala Islami, had set up buffer zones on Ansar's flanks. IMK leader Ali Abdulaziz still lived in Halabja, but his son Tahseen had taken a large number of fighters north of the city on the mountain path to Taweela. They were officially at peace with the PUK, but they also had relations with Ansar, and the PUK didn't want to fight its way through them. Ali Bapir's men still controlled the town of Khurmal, at the foothills of Ansar's territory. Bapir claimed to be neutral as well, but the PUK said his Komala checkpoints had allowed Ansar fighters free movement. Distrust between the parties ran so high that PUK pesh merga, as well as any foreign visitors to Halabja, stopped using the main road, which passed too close to Komala territory. Instead we drove a muddy farmer's track through the fields that came out just below the PUK's military command post outside Halabja.

With Iran at their back, and Islamists to the north and south, the only way for the PUK to attack Ansar al-Islam's positions was straight up the throat of the valley from Girda Drozna, through minefields and naked to the mortar shells from above. "We're waiting," Dekoni said, "because we want the Americans to blow them up."

The PUK assumed the Americans would eventually take out Ansar al-Islam with air strikes, and perhaps want to comb their camps for evidence of a chemical or poison program. The CIA teams on the ground might have asked the PUK to wait, but equally Talibani's men didn't want to expend any extra force before the coming confrontation with Saddam Hussein. What's more, they wanted all their strength to compete with the KDP in the power scramble that might ensue when Saddam fell.

Dekoni took us up the winding road to the top of Girda Drozna, where some of his soldiers were keeping warm in makeshift tents and earth berms. The camp was pocked with little craters from well-aimed mortars, which Dekoni assured me came in like clockwork—at lunchtime and at dusk. The soldiers' big gray steel water tank had been perforated by shrapnel the night before and made a steady dripping noise. In the distance Dekoni pointed out Ansar's forts in the hills several miles away. The soldiers said that they didn't have it as bad as the pesh merga on Shinerwe Mountain, where the Ansar forts in Taweela were within shouting distance and the mortar rounds came in all night. But then they mentioned something curious.

Two days earlier, Ansar's afternoon mortars had come in as usual, except that the last one didn't detonate. It landed in the road outside the village of Kheli Hama, just below us. It hit softly and let out a dark cloud, and then everybody smelled something like rotting garlic.

"What does that mean?" I asked Dildar, who had been translating from Kurdish. It seemed to be just dawning on her, and she said, "Chemical?" and then her voice trailed off. Dildar, it transpired, had been with the pesh merga during the 1980s, and she knew the smell of mustard gas firsthand. Victims often say the poison first smells like garlic or rotting apples. She had seen many people die from it but never had more than that first whiff herself. I asked if we could go down to Kheli Hama.

The bumpy car ride down the hill lasted only a few minutes, but my mind raced the whole way. First I felt suspicious. Would the PUK set up a reporter to publicize that their enemy not only had ties to al-Qa'ida but also that Saddam was giving them weapons of mass destruction—just what Bush had laid out in his speech? PUK security officials had been briefing reporters on a suspected Ansar project to poison people by contaminating food and cigarettes, but they hadn't mentioned chemicals. We pulled into the village of Kheli Hama, now nothing more than barracks.

A soldier named Muhammad recounted how the mortar round had hit on Thursday evening and at first he thought it was white phosphorus, which lets out smoke. The smoke lingered in a dark cloud for about four hours though, and all the men in the barracks felt their eyes water. The wind had carried the fog away from Kheli Hama, but several of the men still felt nauseous. A lieutenant named Osman told the same story of burning eyes and runny noses; he said three of the men had gone to the hospital in Halabja with stomach cramps that night. Then they offered to show us the crater.

With characteristic nonchalance, eight pesh merga walked to the road and pointed out a small crater. One of the men brought a spade and turned over the soil where the shell had landed. He pushed aside a mix of dirt and a grimy golden dust, and then the spade hit metal. As air touched the shell fragments, they gave off a white smoke and made a small hissing noise. I caught a whiff of the sweet smell, but then moved upwind—if you can smell gas, it means you're inhaling it—and asked the men to please cover it back up again. The sun was sinking, and right on cue, the soldiers pointed to a white puff of smoke up the hill. A few seconds later we heard the sound follow. Ansar was lobbing its evening mortars, and it was time to go.

In Sulimaniya that evening Fuad Baban, the doctor from the Halabja postgraduate center, complained that he still couldn't drum up interest in studying the victims of Halabja. It seemed insane, he said, that no one was learning from Halabja's terrible experience, especially if U.S. troops really wanted to prepare for a possible chemical attack. He had already heard rumors about the mortar in Kheli Hama from the men coming to Halabja's hospital.

"It seems to me that it is some form of chemical agent, most probably a type of mustard," said Baban. But then he wondered about the fact that none of the men had developed blisters. If it really was a chemical, the wind must have blown it away from the soldiers before they got a real dose. Saddam had used mustard gas against Iran and the Kurds, and he mused about whether Ansar could have gotten its hands on some old munitions.[7] Despite the Kurds' history, Baban said, they still had little training for what to do under chemical attack, no protective equipment available, and no labs to test the soil.

I, on the other hand, had been carrying a full biohazard suit and mask, and sleeping with it next to my pillow. Most major news organizations had sent their teams to a course at Porton Down, the U.K.'s ninety-year-old chemical warfare institute near Stonehenge. We'd spent a few days learning how to put on a gas mask in a hurry and practiced pretending to jab ourselves in the leg with atropine, the supposed antidote to nerve agent. Most of us had a similar attitude to the chemical equipment as we did to the flak jackets and helmets that had become mandatory gear: they were heavy, they made interviewees nervous, and anywhere I needed them was a place I shouldn't be.

The next day I returned to Kheli Hama, put on the gas mask and over it a hooded polyurethane suit, boots, and gloves, and saw the pesh merga laughing their heads off. I borrowed their shovel and then had to ask them repeatedly to stay back or at least upwind as I unearthed the shell again. It started hissing and smoking once more, and I took out a chemical test strip and pored some of the soil over it. In contact with a chemical agent, the paper would turn dark. The test strip showed nothing.

My BBC colleague Dumeetha Luthra had come along with me and had managed to contact someone from Porton Down by satellite phone, who said that the description sounded like dusty mustard gas, where the gas has been bonded to a particle to make it more difficult to disperse. He said the Iraqi government had been known to possess it during the Iran-Iraq war, but the test strips I'd been using, he said, would only react with liquid and not the particles, if that's what it was. The right way to find out would be to send glass vials of the soil back to Porton Down for analysis. But all the soil around Halabja might well test positive, according to Baban. In the end I filed an inconclusive story about the incident, which was coupled to an interview with Ansar al-Islam leader Mullah Krekar.

Another BBC bureau tracked down Krekar in Oslo, Norway, where he had held political refugee status since 1991. Krekar brought his entire family over to Oslo and somehow maintained his asylum status there despite his regular trips to Kurdistan, including the times he went home for combat against the PUK. Only days before Colin Powell's speech, Krekar tried to preempt all the accusations against his group, denying that Ansar al-Islam had any unconventional weapons.

"I wrote a letter to Hans Blix and the U.N.," Mullah Krekar said. "We can bring them to our area—stone by stone, village by village, they can watch everything."

Krekar also denied any connection with Saddam Hussein. He dismissed the link through Abu Wa'el, whom, he said, was not a Mukhabarat agent but a loyal Kurdish Islamist—besides, he said, Abu Wa'el was a white-haired old man.[8] By 2003 Krekar also began to deny he had ever

met Osama bin Laden, despite earlier interviews claiming that he had.*
Mullah Krekar said Abu Musab al-Zarqawi had never been with him and
couldn't have possibly been in all the places the Americans claimed he was
(especially with a missing leg from the Afghan war). He wasn't all
denial—Krekar approved wholeheartedly of the video showing executed
PUK pesh merga and endorsed suicide bombing as a glorious tactic.

On February 5, Colin Powell took the podium at the United Nations
Security Council and made nothing any clearer.

"I cannot tell you everything that we know. But what I can share with
you, when combined with what all of us have learned over the years, is
deeply troubling," Powell said. He worked his way slowly through a detailed presentation but never seemed to shake a hint of reluctance—as if
he didn't want to be there. Perhaps his lack of messianic fervor made him
more convincing, because the following day many critics swung to his
side. The *Washington Post*'s editorial bore the title "Irrefutable."

The Kurds, who stayed up late into the night (local time) to watch,
found the presentation underwhelming. On the question of illegal
weapons, the Kurds didn't need any convincing, given the many survivors
of Halabja living among them. But Powell's description of the terrorist
connections started out on the wrong foot. Claiming that Abu Musab al-
Zarqawi had set up a chemical weapons lab in northern Iraq, Powell
turned to a satellite photo.[9] The heading across the top read "Terrorist
Poison and Explosives Factory, Khurmal." Powell went on gravely:

> The network is teaching its operatives how to produce ricin and
> other poisons. Let me remind you how ricin works. Less than a
> pinch—imagine a pinch of salt—less than a pinch of ricin, eating
> just this amount in your food, would cause shock followed by cir-
> culatory failure. Death comes within seventy-two hours and there
> is no antidote, there is no cure.

A scary statement, but one most Kurds probably missed—distracted by
the fact that Powell had named the wrong town! Ansar ran its headquarters and the suspected lab out of the tiny town of Sargat. Khurmal, a

---

* After 9/11 Krekar told *Asharq al-Awsat* newspaper that he had met bin Laden
once in 1988 in Peshawar. In subsequent interviews he began to deny it.

bustling market town at the base of the mountains, was the center of Ali Bapir's Komala Islami party. Kurdish officials tried to explain the error, saying that Powell must have just been reading the larger town's name off the map, and still had the right coordinates. On the ground, people had to hope the Pentagon would read the map more carefully when they programmed the cruise missiles.

Powell focused on Zarqawi as the human link between bin Laden and Saddam, and described his lightning movement around the region—in Afghanistan during September 2001, to Baghdad in spring 2002 for medical treatment, training the Baghdad al-Qa'ida cell to use poison and chemicals, arranging the October 2002 murder of U.S. diplomat Lawrence Foley in Amman, Jordan. Powell called the fighters in northern Iraq "Zarqawi lieutenants" and described the Jordanian militant as the leader of a network that reached to Spain, Britain, and Germany.

In retrospect Colin Powell would call his speech at the United Nations a blot on his record.* None of the claims he made about WMD facilities panned out. Powell later said that some in the intelligence community knew that his information didn't pass muster and had come from defectors, discounted by the CIA but reintroduced by Ahmed Chalabi's INC.

As for Zarqawi and Kurdistan, the presentation was wrong in both substance and implication. Zarqawi had been in Afghanistan around September 11, but was running his own training camp near Herat next to the Iranian border.[10] He considered bin Laden something of a rival and had never met the Saudi. Zarqawi eventually swore fealty to bin Laden by letter long after the U.S. invasion of Iraq. The claim that Zarqawi had spent time in Baghdad with Saddam's blessing also fell away later.[11]

"Secretary Powell did his best not to make a fool of himself," said Paul Pillar, a senior CIA official at the time of the speech. Pillar said he shook his head in frustration at several points in the speech, including the implication that Saddam was sheltering Ansar al-Islam. "It never was made clear that Ansar al-Islam's stronghold, and Zarqawi, was outside Saddam's control. It's rather an important point," said Pillar.

Pillar also disagreed with the Kurds' assertion that the Iraqi Mukhabarat had a role in commanding Ansar al-Islam. Abu Wa'el might

---

* On September 9, 2005, Powell told ABC News, "I'm the one who presented [it] on behalf of the United States to the world and it will always be a part of my record. It was painful. It's painful now."

Jim Jones, Jalal Talabani, General Jay Garner, and Masoud Barzani enjoying glasses of milk and discussing the withdrawal of U.S. troops from the north of Iraq in 1991.

Turkish border guard preventing Iraqi Kurds from crossing into Turkey in 1991.

Jalal and Hero Talabani in 1979.

Sheikh Mahmoud Barzinji (*center*).

Voting slip for the
Kurdish parliamentary
election of 1992.
From left to right:
Othman Abdulaziz,
Masoud Barzani,
Mahmoud Othman,
Jalal Talabani.

Jalal Talabani and Masoud Barzani shaking hands
during the 1991 uprising.

Ali Hassan al-Majid,
"Chemical Ali."

Tragedy in Halabja: this image of a man trying to shield his child
from the gas became iconic.

(Author)

Breaking ground for the Halabja Memorial in April 2000.

The Halabja Memorial after it was ransacked in 2006,
with debris still sitting in the yard.

(Author)

(Omar Abdulqadir)

A young Kurdish girl in Sulimaniya after
Saddam Hussein's capture.

April 9, 2003, Erbil celebrates the toppling of Saddam Hussein's statue
in Baghdad.

(Omar Abdulqadir)

Foothills of the Qandil Mountains.

Erosion marks the hills of Iraqi Kurdistan, which lost its forest cover through decades of war.

The hills above Koi Sanjaq.

Portraits of Mulla Mustafa Barzani can be found across the KDP section of Iraqi Kurdistan, like this one at Hawler University in Erbil.

Veiled Iraqi woman in front of a poster of Grand Ayatollah Ali al-Sistani.

Refugees' tent in a camp near Sulimaniya after having been expelled from Kirkuk in March 2000.

Hoshyar Darbandi and his family at their home in Salahudin in 2006.

Zalmay Khalilzad greets Hoshyar Zebari, with Masoud Barzani in the foreground, outside Jalal Talabani's guesthouse at Lake Dukan, October 2006.

From left to right: Kosrat Rasul, Masoud Barzani, Zalmay Khalilzad, Jalal Talabani, Hoshyar Zebari, and Fuad Masum at Talabani's guesthouse at Lake Dukan, October 2006.

PUK officials disembark from a U.S. Air Force
C-130 at Sulimaniya International Airport,
October 2006.

Pesh merga leader Mam Rostam in Kirkuk before the January 2005
elections.

Masoud Barzani.

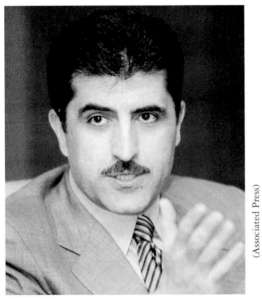

Nechirvan Barzani, first prime minister of
the Kurdistan Regional Government.

Hoshyar Zebari, KDP foreign
envoy and Iraqi foreign minister.

Qubad Talabani, George W. Bush, and Jalal Talabani at
the White House in 2005.

Bafel Talabani (*center*) and his pesh merga during the battle with
Ansar in March 2003.

Paul Bremer and associates in their CPA trademark suits and boots.

From left to right: Nuri al-Maliki, Jalal Talabani, and Adel Abdul-Mahdi.

General David Petraeus and Ambassador Ryan Crocker at a press conference in Washington, D.C., in 2007.

Ahmed Chalabi being fitted for a *khaffiyeh* in Nasiriya in 2003.

Islamist leader Ali Bapir.

Ayad Allawi and Barham Salih.

PKK press conference in front of a banner featuring Abdullah Öcalan's portrait.

PKK fighter in the mountains.

Abdullah Gül, current
president of Turkey.

Turgut Özal, president of
Turkey 1989–1993.

Abdullah Öcalan, leader of the PKK.

have been gathering information for the Mukhabarat, Pillar said, but he wasn't controlling Ansar. Pillar didn't accuse the Kurds of sexing up the intelligence on Ansar—the Bush administration hardly needed a push, and was eager to believe it.

The most immediate fallout of the speech hit the unlucky town of Khurmal. Assuming the Americans had them marked for bombardment, many families in the town of fifteen hundred began looking for relatives in Halabja to put them up. Ali Bapir's group maintained that no armed Ansar troops came through his town, but admitted that they sometimes passed through without their weapons. The next reaction came directly from the leaders of Ansar—they wanted to show the world they were clean. On February 8, using Bapir as a go-between and Khurmal as a way station, Ansar hosted about twenty Western journalists.[12] Escorted by Ali Bapir's gunmen, the militants drove half an hour from Khurmal, up a mountain road to Sargat. There Ansar's fighters, including Ayub Khadir ("al Afghani"), who had fought the Soviets in Afghanistan, gave the reporters a rushed tour of the building pictured in Colin Powell's satellite image. The militants kept many rooms off-limits, and the ones they showed held nothing more harmful than small arms and some empty plastic fuel containers.

"This is an isolated place and we haven't even got lavatories," one of the fighters said in a room he claimed had been a radio station. "The people who were here were officers of media. They left here because they feared an American bomb. According to news there will be an [air] strike. We hope that will not happen, because it will be catastrophic."

Skull and crossbones insignias marked many of the fences around the village, but they were the same triangular land-mine warnings as all over Kurdistan. The press walk-through proved nothing about what had or hadn't been in that building when Powell made his speech, though it may have shown that Ansar had a bit more media savvy than previously thought. But not much more—toward the end of the visit Ayub Khadir demanded that several of the journalists make statements into his own videocamera about the camp being clean. And whatever meager help the tour did for the group's reputation was undone only hours later, by an act of cold-blooded treachery.

The PUK still sought to avoid a costly direct confrontation with Ansar al-Islam on the eve of a war with Saddam, and Talabani thought he had the problem solved. High-ranking members of Ansar al-Islam had contacted the PUK and said they wanted to surrender; they were tired of the

Taliban-like conditions that the group had imposed in Sargat, Biyara, and Taweela. They insisted on meeting with a major PUK figure who they could be sure was speaking for Talabani, and requested his older son, Bafel. Instead, a founding member of the PUK, Shawkat Haji Mushir, agreed to sit down with the Islamists. They had two preliminary meetings, and the offer got sweet—the Islamists said they had more than one hundred members who wanted to surrender. But for the next meeting, on February 8, the would-be defectors said they needed a security guarantee and asked for three PUK hostages to hold during the meeting. Shawkat agreed.

No one in the tiny village of Gamesh Tepa knew they would be hosting the negotiations that Saturday evening, until the famous PUK commander showed up. "General Shawkat arrived without warning," said local resident Salih Hassan, who stepped out into his front yard to greet the delegation. "He asked me if he could please borrow a room in my house to hold an important meeting."[13]

Hassan agreed without question and let Shawkat in, moving his family into a separate room. Several strangers arrived at about eight thirty P.M. The newcomers carried Kalashnikov rifles, even though Shawkat wore only a sidearm.

Shawkat met alone with Ali Tezhia, one of the Ansar fighters. The meeting lasted about forty-five minutes. Then, as Shawkat began writing a letter containing the details of the agreement, Tezhia picked up a rifle and blew a hole in his head. On that signal the Ansar fighters outside opened fire on the unsuspecting PUK guards. Tezhia rushed outside and lobbed a grenade in behind him, and then joined the others in emptying his rifle clip through the windows of the house. In the back room, Salih Hassan and his family scrambled in vain to find shelter from the bullets and shrapnel flying everywhere. Hassan felt a round hit his calf and went down. A bullet hit his daughter-in-law in the neck and another hit his son. When the firing stopped, both were dead, and their eight-year-old daughter, Daroon Fazil, was bleeding from a bullet wound to the forehead. She died at the hospital the following day. The Ansar hit-team went overland to the nearby village of Girdi Go—inside Ali Bapir's Komala territory—where a car waited for them and they made a clean escape. The PUK hostages were never heard from again.

Following Muslim custom the funeral took place the next morning, and a drummer led thousands of mourners behind a truck bearing

Shawkat's body. The procession snaked out of Sulimaniya to the hilltop cemetery above the city. Hundreds of Shawkat's comrades wept openly as they lowered his casket into the ground, and a few threw themselves on the burial mound. The next morning the PUK commanders let their rage overcome their restraint and raced up to Shinerwe Mountain, personally touching off some of the artillery rounds they had been husbanding for the war. But knowing the mountains as they did, the PUK understood that rooting Ansar out of the caves would be a long and bloody fight. They waited for the help America had promised.

As THE PUK worried about the seven hundred or so Islamic radicals to the east, the KDP focused more on seventy thousand Turkish troops to the north—that was one of the numbers the Turks were reportedly asking to escort any Americans through the border into Kurdistan. The U.S. military made no secret about the importance of the northern front, and as the time grew short, high-ranking officials shuttled between Ankara and Washington trying to seal an agreement. The Turks said they needed troops in Iraq to forestall a humanitarian disaster and wanted to create a cordon fifteen miles deep. The explanation infuriated the KDP—in their minds Turkish troops would have only one goal: to destroy the fledgling Kurdish state.

"We refuse it," Sami Abd-al-Rahman told a small group of journalists at his home in Erbil. "If Turkish troops enter, it is a provocation. No patriot would welcome occupying forces. There is no rationale—nothing good would come out of it. Where is the humanitarian reason for it? Send us the International Red Cross; don't send us military forces."

Ankara cited the exodus in 1991 as an example, but Turkish troops then had mostly been involved in preventing freezing refugees from coming down from the mountains. In the dozen years since, Turkish-American relations had pivoted on American access to patrol the no-fly zone. Every six months, Washington had to come to Ankara with hat in hand and ask to renew the use of Incirlik air base. Hardly a household word in the United States, Incirlik, along with Iraq, dominated the relationship in the minds of the Turks. The isolation of Iraq denied Turkey access to a country that had previously been its second-largest trading partner. Opposition parties in every election made an issue of the U.S. operation and hinted about canceling it; every winning party then changed its mind in the face of the daunting prospect of denying Uncle Sam.

A tiny window of change had opened and closed in the early days of the no-fly zone, when President Turgut Özal began to test the limits of Turkish society. Özal started to publicly discuss that he had a Kurdish grandmother and mused privately that the new situation in Iraq might not be so bad for Turkey.

"Think of it this way," Özal said, according to a source he spoke with often during his presidency. "Let's say there's a Kurdish state in northern Iraq. It might have a little oil. It would be totally dependent on Turkey, because how else would they export or import their goods? The Iraqis would surely be pretty mad at them, so they'd be dependent on Turkey. For Kurds in Turkey, the government would be able to say, 'If you'd like to live in a Kurdish state, there's one—and please [go]. And if you'd like to live here, there are rules.' "

However, Özal died in 1993 of a heart attack, and any hope of a new attitude in Turkey died with him. Turkey returned to viewing Kurdish Iraq and their federalist idea as an existential threat. On the same day Colin Powell addressed the U.N., making war seem unavoidable, Turkish prime minister Abdullah Gül laid out his government's red lines. "Turkey is going to position herself in that region in order to prevent any possible massacres, or the establishment of a new state," he said at a news conference.

Turkish officials wanted their troops to outnumber the American army that came through, and made clear they would take the opportunity to hit PKK bases in northern Iraq and defend themselves robustly. Sami Abd-al-Rahman shot back at the United States, saying American troops were welcome as liberators, but not a single Turk should cross the border. "If the U.S. goes ahead, it would be the third betrayal in a generation. We will not allow ourselves to be sacrificed. The people will resist [the Turks]," he said.[14]

As usual the situation in Kurdistan wasn't black and white, since about five thousand Turkish troops were already inside Iraqi Kurdistan. They had chased the PKK across the border in 1997 and never gone home. The morning after speaking with Abd-al-Rahman, on February 13, 2003, I crammed into a Land Cruiser with a few colleagues and took a bone-jarring ride from Erbil up toward the town of Bamarni, along the border east of Zakho, to investigate the rumor that Turkey had massed troops on the border and maybe even sent some more across.

We drove the long way toward Dohuk, skirting Iraqi government territory. The February sky kept threatening snow but instead drizzled down a constant chilly rain. After several hours we reached the hillside base of Bamarni, where fourteen Turkish tanks were parked, their crews adjusting the oilcloths they had thrown over the artillery against the rain. A few helicopters with their blades tied down sat parked at the end of a long airstrip. We drove past the base slowly, not wanting to announce ourselves yet.

Over the hill in the tiny hamlet of Zewa, a few Kurdish villagers invited us in out of the damp, and soon a town meeting materialized. A young man named Azad Haj Shokri said he and the other villagers feared to get too close to the Turkish base. "They'll shoot us for PKK," he said. Shokri's wife served us a tray full of small teacups, in Kurdish fashion, with a finger's width of sugar sitting at the bottom of the glasses. It wasn't going to take much pushing to get these men to oppose a Turkish incursion.

"We are all pesh merga," Shokri said. He and his friends went on to list the horrible behavior of the Turkish government toward Kurds. "There a Kurd can't speak his own language or even give his son a Kurdish name. If we're told to fight the Turks, we will," Shokri said. At some point his older brother Barhan cut in through the young man's bravado.

"The Turks will do whatever they want," he said. "They're strong and we are powerless. Only the British and the Americans can protect us."

Eventually we drove back toward Dohuk and stopped in at the main gate of the Bamarni base. Naturally no one would talk—the Turkish government still wouldn't officially admit any of its troops were in Kurdistan. That seemed to be a fiction the KDP wanted to help the Turks support, because as we entered the city of Dohuk, the pesh merga stopped us at a checkpoint and claimed we weren't authorized to be in this zone for our own safety. In the end the only punishment was a chill that took hours to shake.*

On February 6 the Turkish parliament had voted to give the United States a green light to upgrade bases in the country, an obvious precursor

---

* Both Kurdish parties tried their hand at controlling the foreign press, but their tiny English-speaking staff was soon overwhelmed by the growing number of reporters, especially after several busloads of journalists arrived from Turkey. There was a tussle at the border when the KDP wouldn't let the Turkish minders accompany the journalists, claiming they were spies from Ankara. The Turks had agreed to let the journalists in to cover the Iraqi opposition conference if they promised to leave immediately afterward, and ultimately they all stayed.

to landing troops and moving them into Iraq. In a particular insult to the Kurds, America promised to help revise Turkey's defenses against chemical attack. The final vote on letting the U.S. Fourth Infantry Division through to Iraq was scheduled for February 18—before the Iraqi opposition would be able to meet in Salahudin. Some Kurdish officials maintained that wasn't a coincidence—the Americans wanted to prevent the "free Iraqis" from forming a government in exile. But Turkey took its time, haggling as if George W. Bush were a tourist buying rugs in Istanbul's grand bazaar. Dick Cheney contacted the Turkish foreign minister to push for a speedy resolution, but Turkey kept playing hard-to-get. Zalmay Khalilzad eventually arrived in Ankara at the head of a team designed to seal the bargain. Along with him were several other diplomats as well as a U.S. Treasury official to sign the checks—the Turks' asking price had soared into the tens of billions of dollars.

Concerned and in the dark, the Kurds sent a joint delegation to meet Khalilzad in Ankara. Jalal Talabani represented his PUK along with Adnan Mufti; the perennial "bad cop" Nechirvan Barzani led the KDP side along with Hoshyar Zebari. The Turkish military officials could barely stand to meet with the Kurds, much less treat them as representatives of a governing entity. In one meeting a Turkish general told the Kurds they couldn't possibly make assessments the way a real government did, and that the war would cause another exodus of six hundred thousand people. Nechirvan Barzani seethed.[15]

"I told him no, we are a government too!" Barzani recalled. "I said, I am a prime minister! Six hundred thousand will not come—not six people will cross the border!"

He went on to lecture the Turks about all the progress Kurdistan had made in reconstruction as well as command and control since 1991, but his words fell on deaf ears, and Turkish officials began telling the press that they would not consent to American supremacy of command when their troops entered Iraq. Though Khalilzad kept trying to reassure them things were fine, the Kurds came home believing that America had sold them cheap to the Turks. Likewise the Turks accused the Americans of pushing a secret agenda to create an independent Kurdish state. The Turkish negotiator, Ambassador Deniz Bölükbaşı, had a visceral reaction to the *K*-word. At one point America's "pro-Kurdish bias" became too much for him.

"If Barzani was sitting in your place, he might have contemplated saying what you just said, but he would not be able to say it. In view of your re-marks there is no point of continuing the negotiations," Bölükbaşı said as he gathered his things and left Ambassador Marisa Lino, the U.S. delegate, sit-ting in an empty room in the Turkish foreign ministry.[16] Negotiations con-tinued, but not pleasantly.

Not surprisingly, Khalilzad complained that all the sides in the region were "worst-casing" their neighbors' intentions.[17] When Hoshyar Zebari returned to Kurdistan, he laid out the Kurdish position as a warning to the Americans as much as the Turks.[18]

"No one should see us as bluffing on this issue. Any intervention under whatever pretext will lead to clashes," Zebari said. "No one wants another fight, of course, but if there's a forced incursion, done under the pretext of 'I'm going to give you forced aid,' then believe me, there will be un-controlled clashes. And it will be bad for the image of the United States, Britain, and other countries who want to help Iraq, to see two of their al-lies, Turkey and Kurdistan, at each other's throats."

Zebari tried to broaden the warning, claiming that Turkish intervention would only lead to other regional powers like Iran sending troops, but the Kurds' focus remained on the northern front. The Turks also obfuscated, stressing their concern for the Turcoman minority living in northern Iraq. The Turcomans claimed to be descendants of the Seljuks, left behind as the Turkic world shrank and fragmented. Saddam Hussein had ethnically cleansed Turcomans with his Arabization program, and Turkey hadn't made much fuss. Now the Turks started to claim the Kurds planned to do their own cleansing against Turcomans once they got to Kirkuk. The KDP response was to announce the arrest of the security chief of the Iraqi Turcoman Front (ITF), who was charged with hoarding dynamite. The ITF continued to operate its radio and television station in Erbil, but it claimed the arrest was a bad sign for the Turcomans' future. A KDP offi-cial responded, "When it rains in Ankara, the ITF opens their umbrellas."*

As negotiations continued in Turkey, the KDP decided to flaunt a lit-tle democracy. On the eve of the opposition conference, now set for

---

* Ankara provided money to fund the ITF in 1995, as part of the government's strategy to influence events in northern Iraq, according to the International Crisis Group, among others. The ITF held an International Turcoman con-ference in Erbil in November 2002 and brought some other groups under its banner.

February 25, Kurds in Erbil planned to "spontaneously" demonstrate their freedom of expression by protesting in favor of American intervention and against Turkish interference.

They had gotten the idea from popular protests worldwide on February 15, rallies *against* the American invasion, when hundreds of thousands of protesters voiced their frustration at the Bush administration's juggernaut. But the peace marches in Manhattan or London or Buenos Aires didn't fit the mood in Kurdistan. Kurds displaced from Kirkuk by the regime looked in worse straits than ever. The winter rains had turned their dirt roads into cake batter and weighed down their feet as they carried water from the well back to their tents. One of the Kirkukees said he wanted to stick a needle into Saddam Hussein and drink his blood dry. Around the same time a Kurdish woman showed up at the hospital in Sulimaniya with burns covering her body—the Iraqi police had caught her trying to smuggle fuel to the north and had set her alight.[19] The Kurds had trouble understanding why no one in the world's capitals had ever taken to the streets to protest the gassing of Halabja, or ethnic cleansing in Kurdistan, but now hundreds of thousands took to the streets to stop America from removing Saddam.

"These [antiwar protesters] are well intentioned; they care for peace and they care for the Iraqi people. But I have to say, as an Iraqi living here, that their understanding of the situation is not adequate," Barham Salih said in the upstairs living room of his house in Sulimaniya one evening, a few days before the opposition conference. "Peace requires a commitment of the world outside to help the people of Iraq overcome tyranny. If they want to be morally consistent, they should focus on the plight of twenty-two million Iraqis who are suffering terribly at the hands of this tyranny."

Dr. Barham already had his "Iraqi" hat on—few Kurds knew the American line as well as he did, and only he and Hoshyar Zebari ever went so far as to call themselves Iraqis in public. For most Kurds, Iraq was that frightening country to the south, but Salih genuinely believed he could make it in Baghdad and everything would be better for Kurds and Arabs. Next he offered an excellent rendition of the idea that Paul Wolfowitz had been promoting for years: America needed to foster democracy in the Middle East because it would bring more stability than dictatorships.

"American policy in the last fifty years has been a failure, depending on unaccountable, corrupt elites throughout the Arab world. Not only did it not contain their problems; they managed to export their problems to the

United States and convince their populations that it's all the fault of the U.S." As usual, Salih multitasked, giving a spotless radio interview over tea while watching satellite TV at the same time. Then his Iraqi hat fell off for a moment.

"She's playing right into the Turks' hands!" he said sharply as a close shot of Kurdish villagers hiding in caves played out on the screen. A large number of Kurds had been finding relatives to stay with outside the major cities, fearing that Saddam might bomb the north as his dying act. An American television journalist had discovered a single family of Kurds sheltering in a cave, and suddenly all of Kurdistan looked like it was filled with desperate troglodytes in need of Turkish humanitarian intervention. Salih quickly regained his composure: The Turks wouldn't defy the Americans, and the Kurds were in the loop.

"I'm not going to tell you what the plan is," he said. "But we are partners to the U.S. We are part of the coalition. We want to be partners in the campaign to liberate Iraq. We are freedom fighters. The way we look at it, others are coming to help us. Not that we are guns for hire—we are the ones who have been here, consistently. We welcome help, and we are going to do it together."

Kanan Makiya had just written a scathing op-ed upon hearing that the United States planned a military government post-Saddam, and not an immediate hand-over to the Iraqis. Salih exuded serenity.

"Removing Saddam will be easy, but governing Iraq will be difficult. Everything I know about the U.S. says it's not a colonial power. They don't want to run countries. I was asking a very senior official, would they want to be blamed for outages in electricity in Iraq? Do they want to be seen as liberators or as colonialists?"

Still, Salih admitted there were too many unknowns. Anyone who claimed to know what would happen was a liar. Of all the factors, he said, Kurdistan was the most predictable. In the rest of Iraq we would have to wait until Iraqis could speak freely for themselves. Unlike the Kurds, the rest of the opposition still had to prove it had support inside Iraq.

"Many will want to ride an American tank into Baghdad to be shown as the liberator. I think the key is to focus on a system of government, a proper system, with checks and balances—and not to let egos of Iraqi opposition run the show," he said.

He didn't need to mention names. After a chilly reception from Barzani, Ahmed Chalabi's INC delegation, including his nephew Sam and his daughter Tamara, had taken up residence in the Sulimaniya Palace hotel. Kanan Makiya traveled with them, as did Mudhar Shawkat, a Sunni exile who led the Iraqi National Movement, which had on and off supported the INC. Chalabi would occasionally sweep through the lobby in the middle of a huge posse, with his imposing bodyguard Hussein ready to stiff-arm anyone who tried to get close enough to ask a question. All the others could be seen sipping cappuccinos in the hotel lobby and were quite approachable. Shawkat opined that Iraq was a turnkey job, just waiting to become a modern, secular Arab state. And he said only one man could lead it.

"Ahmed Chalabi *will* be the next president of Iraq," he said.

Chalabi and his entourage soon moved out of the hotel to a guesthouse on Lake Dukan that Talabani had prepared for him, but not before several brief audiences with reporters. Chalabi knew he was the man the media loved to hate, constantly painted as a Pentagon puppet, but he used it to his advantage, letting people believe that Washington had anointed him. Yet time was short. Many of his rivals claimed Chalabi was at the peak of his power now—with the White House behind him and his true popular support inside Iraq untested. Chalabi had been giving the classic politician's line that he wasn't interested in any particular position in the post-Saddam government.

"There is no one who wants to make a power grab. There are elements within the Bush administration who want to control the process in Iraq entirely. I think it will lead to problems. It's not the best way to save American lives or Iraqi lives," Chalabi said, relaxing in his hotel suite.

Chalabi stressed that his INC was an ally, not an agent, of the Americans. He said there would be no government declared at the upcoming meeting, but that the opposition would elect a leadership—which he allowed could decide to declare a government at any time—and that everyone in the opposition was on the same page. I asked if there wasn't a problem being an exile so long out of the country, compared to the Kurds who had a standing army inside Iraq.

"This distinction is rather artificial," he bristled. "Many people who have been under Saddam will support those who have been outside, because they've been in contact. This problem of inside and outside is not a reflection of the reality." He said anyone but Ba'ath Party leadership would be welcome in the new government, and that those who had not split from the regime would be judged on a case-by-case basis. Asked if he thought Iraq's tribes might help keep order in the post-Saddam chaos, he practically spat: "What tribes!? Iraq is an urban society. Seventy percent of Iraqis live in cities. There are six million people living in Baghdad alone."

In any case, Chalabi said, there wouldn't be chaos post-Saddam; the Iraqi opposition would be able to control the country. At this point my interview ended. One of Chalabi's aides came in saying that a photographer had arrived, the same one who had shot the famous photo of Afghanistan's new president, Hamid Karzai, and she was ready to take Chalabi's portrait.[20]

At the end of February all the opposition figures took over the hotels around Erbil and Salahudin. The sixty-five members selected at the London opposition conference filled Erbil's comfortable Chwar Chra Hotel. The leader of SCIRI, Ayatollah Muhammad Bakr al-Hakim, had arrived from Iran with an honor guard of his Badr Brigade militia. Everyone from the communists to Detroit exiles had a delegation and the city buzzed with the latest gossip—General Tommy Franks would be installed as the leader of an American military occupation post-Saddam. U.S. envoy Zalmay Khalilzad entered town late one evening in a convoy of Toyota Land Cruisers.* Khalilzad's State Department security guards took over the KDP's politburo building in Salahudin, wearing wraparound shades, baseball caps, and webbed fishing vests with their carbines on a string across their chests. At one end of the building's driveway they rigged a nest with a long black .50-caliber sniper rifle pointing down the gullet of the road, powerful enough to shoot a driver through the engine block of his car. They ran several stringent security checks on everyone entering, provoking some muttering about a preview of American occupation. And in addition to hosting the conference, Salahudin sat right along the route to Baghdad for the Fourth Infantry.

If the soldiers came. The Turkish government was making the wait agony for Washington. The Bush administration had raised its offer up to two billion dollars in grants plus two billion dollars in military credits.[21] The leader of a Turkish delegation to Washington had even asked for

---

* The Land Cruiser is a favorite model in Kurdistan, with its bulbous fenders. In the mid-1990s the Kurds started to call them "Monicas" out of affection for the car's curvaceousness.

assurances—in writing—that Congress would honor the budget. Turkish ambassador Faruk Loğoğlu had to break it to him that a verbal commitment from House Speaker Dennis Hastert was the best he would get. Some Turkish officials later admitted they had been trying to delay until it was too late for the United States to go to war. They asked for a sum greater than the entire U.S. foreign budget—twenty-two billion dollars all at once or ninety-two billion dollars over five years. The American offer went up to six billion dollars, with a warning that the United States could do without Turkey if need be, but the military wanted time to turn the fleet through the Suez Canal and land it in Kuwait. The scheduled Turkish parliamentary vote for February 18 came and went with the boats still in the harbor. By the time the Iraq opposition gathered in Salahudin, the arrangement had been written up in three different diplomatic contracts involving two different U.S. ambassadors. Negotiations had been long and unpleasant, but the deal was done. The vote in parliament, a formality at this point, would take place on March 1.

The Salahudin conference lasted days, but there was one clear keynote speaker: Khalilzad spoke on February 26, introduced by Jalal Talabani as a friend to free Iraqis. The U.S. envoy used the barest minimum of conditional phrases—"should military action be necessary"—but everyone knew he had just come from sealing the bargain with the Turks. Heated discussions went on with the Kurds, who were still dead set against a Turkish intervention. The United States wanted them to sign off on letting Turkish troops in as part of the coalition. Khalilzad offered to make a statement against any unilateral intervention by "the neighboring countries" and promised that everyone who came in with the Americans would leave with them.

"We said no, you have to mention Turkey by name," Nechirvan Barzani recalls, "because they are the only ones who want to intervene." But the Kurds could see their concerns had been swept aside again, as sure as there were thirty U.S. warships waiting in Turkish waters to unload enough tanks and trucks to carry sixty thousand American soldiers across Turkey into Iraq.

In Salahudin, the audience of about one hundred opposition figures and advisors interrupted Khalilzad with applause several times—not least when he complimented his hosts. "The claim that Iraq cannot become a democracy is belied by the experience of northern Iraq," said Khalilzad, who also mentioned the right of Iraqis to choose federalism, a word he knew would upset the Turkish observers. He repeated his promise that there would be no "Saddamism without Saddam," but he implied that the Iraqi army would remain in place and encouraged its soldiers not to fight. He asked the Iraqi opposition leaders to form task forces to help the coalition forces when they arrived—should military action be necessary.

"The Iraqi people will never forget those who helped them in the difficult days, those who supported us," said Jalal Talabani, after Khalilzad spoke. Nonetheless, Khalilzad hadn't even been able to say the word "Kurdistan" after he had praised it as a democracy, for fear of offending the Turks.

Journalists, Kurds, and opposition figures alike started to speculate as to when U.S. forces would arrive, taking into consideration the phase of the moon and how it might affect U.S. night-vision goggles, the coming of warm weather, the time it would take for troops to drive across Turkey, the readiness and length of the Kurdish airstrips. Fuel and food hoarding drove up prices, and rumors flew about the Americans' deal to shut down all satellite phones and Internet connections—and even that missiles would home in on satellite phones and that electromagnetic pulses would fry them. As the opposition leaders met on February 26, Ansar al-Islam sent a suicide bomber hitchhiking toward Sulimaniya. The bomber detonated at a checkpoint outside Halabja, killing himself, two Kurdish soldiers, and the unsuspecting driver who had picked him up.

For the enemy to the south, the Salahudin conference was the greatest provocation yet—U.S. officials plotting with Saddam's archenemies on his own soil. Talabani closed the meeting with a call for the Iraqi people to rise up, but the real question was whether he and Barzani could keep their own people in line should Turkish forces enter Kurdistan—and if they even wanted to. If the Kurds started fighting against Turkish troops, would they also start to fight against the Americans? Turkey was America's NATO ally; wouldn't the United States have to side with the Turks against the Kurds?

On the afternoon of March 1, all eyes in Kurdistan watched live coverage of the Turkish parliament. Finally the ayes had it, 264 yes votes and 251 against. The American troops would be coming through on their way to Baghdad, and the Turks would be coming with them in equal numbers. But then there was confusion. Nineteen Turkish lawmakers had abstained, and passage of the measure required a majority of those present. The abstentions made it 264 in favor out of 534 total—less than a majority.

Washington requested a clarification and got it—according to the rules of Turkish democracy, the measure was defeated.

Kurdistan's most important battle for independence had been fought and won, in the Turkish parliament, without a drop of blood spilled. There would be no northern front.

IT WOULD TAKE years to realize, but failure to win Turkish assistance in March 2003 may go down in history as the luckiest thing that happened to America regarding Iraq, since it averted a guerrilla war between Kurds and Turks. At the time, however, the Americans in Salahudin hardly felt like celebrating. The Kurds, on the other hand, couldn't contain their glee. The greatest threat to the twelve-year-old enclave was neutralized.

"It was like a party," Nechirvan Barzani recalled, still unable to suppress a giggle years later. "For the Americans, you cannot imagine how disappointed they were. We smiled anyway! We said *alhamdulallah* [praise the lord]."

The American diplomats may not actually have been as upset as they were supposed to be. Neither side in the Ankara negotiations had come away endeared, revealing that decades of friendship had come down to a quid pro quo, measured out to the penny. "Khalilzad is a diplomat. He had instructions from Washington; he was unable to go beyond that," said Nechirvan. "I believe his heart was with us." Indeed, it was the considered opinion of many of the U.S. government's regional experts that America dodged a bullet when it didn't go through Turkey—most important, because it kept Turkish troops out of a quagmire in Kurdistan.

"We worked as hard as we could to get the Fourth I.D. through Turkey. That's what our military commanders wanted. We failed, and I don't like to fail," said Marc Grossman, then undersecretary of state for political affairs. "But I knew at the time, and I am convinced now, that moving ninety thousand Americans through Turkey would have been no small job. And our military had agreed to take fifteen thousand Turkish troops along with them. Getting them back out would have been a pretty big struggle."

The Kurds had plain guaranteed a fight, and in retrospect, Kurdistan could have ended up looking as bad as the Arab Sunni province of Anbar, with Kurds fighting the Turkish troops and the United States caught in the middle. "It's too horrible to contemplate," said Grossman.

"America would have had little leverage to pull the Turks out with, especially if they were under attack—the United States would have been obliged to defend them under NATO article five."

The inexperienced Turkish Justice and Development Party (AKP) delivered the blow to the Bush war plan without seeming to realize what had been done. In fact party officials may not even have been aware of the intricacies of their own parliamentary procedure. A straw poll earlier in the day told them they had the votes to win passage, but the party leadership didn't go to sit in parliament and enforce the result. Many parliamentarians may have thought the AK Party had the votes already and felt the pressure was off. Without a watchful eye, voting no was much more attractive, since Turkish popular opinion ran 9 to 1 against the war. Weeks later, at a second vote, to allow U.S. over-flight rights, the new prime minister of the AK Party, Recep Tayyip Erdoğan, went to the parliament and looked each member in the face as the ballots went into the box. That measure passed.

Washington, which had considered Turkish support a slam dunk, made some mutterings about wishing the Turkish military had taken a stronger role, but the Bush administration was forced for the most part to keep its mouth shut—it was about to go to war in part to bring democracy to the region, so criticizing the voting results of the region's only Muslim democracy wasn't going to fly.

"God and Turkish democracy saved us," said Qubad Talabani in Washington. The decision veered the Kurds away from a collision course with the U.S.-led coalition, but better still from the Kurds' perspective, it crippled Turkish-American relations for years to come.

"Fuck Turkey. Fuck their families. Fuck their dogs," was the attitude of General Tommy Franks, head of U.S. Central Command.[22] In Kurdistan sixty thousand pesh merga dearly wanted to be his new best friends.

CHAPTER EIGHT

No Friends but the Kurds

Guerrillas know something about contingency plans, the double-crossed Kurds more than most. The Kurds are fond of repeating that they have no friends but the mountains. Jalal Talabani always looked beyond those mountains to the day he might represent a Kurdish nation to the world, attending global summits and riding in a bulletproof limousine. Talabani's fast talking in four languages, his networking skills across cultures, and his charming sense of humor were meant for the world of political deals after the fighting ended. But the odds were long, and Talabani knew he might end his days practicing the trade of a warlord, not a president. Like a good guerrilla, he hedged his bets, and Talabani had one son for each outcome.

Qubad Talabani, his younger son, went to soak up the culture of Washington, D.C., and before he turned thirty, Qubad was briefing U.S. congressmen and taking calls from the White House asking for advice on Iraq. He married a young American woman he met through her work on Iraq for the U.S. State Department. If everything went well, Qubad Talabani would be just the kind of talent Kurdistan needed. If not, there was his brother, Bafel.

As a young boy, Bafel spent much time in the care of his father's pesh merga—so much that after his first day of kindergarten he came home angry, demanding to know why he had been sent to a place for children, instead of staying with the grizzled bodyguards his "own age." In adolescence, Bafel was sent by his father to live in London with his grandfather Ibrahim Ahmad. When Hero Talabani decided to join her husband in the mountains in 1979, she had the toddler Qubad with her, but she sent him back to London as well, reasoning that such a difference in experience could drive a rift between the boys. The brothers grew up as friends in the U.K., and while neither one felt any pressure to join the family trade, each discovered different interests. When his British schoolteachers asked him what he aspired to be when he grew up, Bafel answered incomprehensibly, "pesh merga." Bafel studied judo and became a bodybuilder. He completed a degree in graphic design, but then floated between different odd jobs, including some work in London restaurants and nightclubs.

After the uprising in 1991, Bafel made trips to Kurdistan every year, missing only the tumultuous summer of 1996. The following year he saw a small piece of the action, catching the very end of the Kurdish civil war. The KDP and Turkish army fought the PUK and PKK, and Bafel traveled with a cousin to see Kosrat Rasul at the front. The Turks used helicopter gunships and tanks, but the PUK held its own, clinging to the Kurds' friends, the mountains. Kosrat Rasul received the young visitors warmly in a blown-out shelter. As they drank tea, a small tapping noise kept interrupting, and Bafel noticed something small bouncing across the floor nearby.[1]

"Oh, those are snipers," Kosrat said nonchalantly of the spent bullets skipping by. "They've been at it all day. Don't worry—they're well out of range."

Bafel returned to London tantalized by the taste of war. When his grandfather died in 2000, he accompanied the casket back to Kurdistan and decided to stay for good. He briefly experimented with setting up a Kurdish weapons factory, but it produced guns as dangerous to the shooter as the target. When that venture fell through, Bafel became an unofficial liaison and interpreter and also took courses in intelligence gathering and close protection offered by the governments of several friendly countries. While Bafel studied interrogation and security, Qubad shadowed Dr. Barham Salih in Washington, D.C. The people of Sulimaniya, known for a vicious sense of humor, nicknamed the brothers "Uday and Qusay," after the sinister sons of Saddam Hussein.

During the long wait for the war to begin, Bafel and some of his men attempted to sequester the entire American press corps in January 2003.

Acting on a tip from the CIA that Saddam had marked us for assassination, Bafel called an urgent meeting in the dingy restaurant at the Ashti Hotel and announced that the PUK had to take protective measures. Bafel had been put in charge of the PUK's new counterterrorism force. He was a spitting image of his brother, Qubad, with the same sculpted black goatee, but the lines in Bafel's face cut longer down the sides of his mouth, and he spoke with great ceremony as he told us our lives were in danger.

All of the press bristled at the PUK's attempt to control us; a few of the journalists who had been in town the longest refused to go along to the PUK safe house, clearly annoying Bafel. A bit disoriented, the rest of us went. I got into the backseat of Bafel's SUV and nearly sat on an assault carbine. It's as easy to distinguish American weapons from Kalashnikovs as it is to tell Nikes from Birkenstocks, and I had never seen a Kurd carrying an M-4, the compact weapon carried by most U.S. officers. Bafel smiled sheepishly as he put the American gun behind the seat. He had been seen escorting a long convoy of white Toyotas between Halabja and Dukan dam, sometimes stopping to inspect the airstrip at Bakrajo. Everyone in the country knew it was CIA agents, but photographers who too obviously took a picture of the cars had their film or memory chip confiscated, sometimes by Bafel himself.

The cantonment of the press lasted less than twenty-four hours, then fell apart without ceremony—either the attempt to rein in the press had failed or the threat had disappeared. Several of us had called the CIA headquarters in Langley to make sure we weren't being wantonly jerked around, and the CIA confirmed the assassination threat. It didn't make much sense to anyone at the time, since Saddam Hussein was still trying to avoid any provocation of the West, and killing an American journalist would have done nicely in that regard. But Bafel shouldn't have been surprised if the CIA's tips were a little shaky—the agents had been meeting with some very strange people.

America's espionage agency had returned to northern Iraq after September 11, but it relied on approval from the Turks, who actually yanked the whole CIA operation out briefly in the summer of 2002.[2] Washington had sold the effort as a mission to gather information about Ansar al-Islam, which indeed its agents were. But the primary purpose had been to develop a campaign of sabotage and misinformation in Saddam Hussein's territory to the south. The CIA also desperately wanted human sources for intelligence on Saddam's WMDs—they hadn't found a reliable source since the disasters of 1996 had cleaned out their database and ruined their credibility in Iraq. While they set up liaisons with their Kurdish hosts, the CIA operatives naturally gathered information about them as well— Kurdish troop strength, command and control, the chance of conflict between the KDP and PUK. By the end of 2002 the team of about a dozen men had returned for good and set up headquarters at Qalaat Chowlan, Jalal Talabani's favorite old hideout. They brought thirty-two million dollars in Benjamin Franklins, enough for a considerable information shopping spree.[3] As soon as the new crisp bills started trickling out, would-be informants sprouted like desert flowers after a rainstorm.

Most of the information didn't withstand the tiniest scrutiny, but the Kurdish intelligence services helped to vet it. Early on, the leadership of both the KDP and PUK made separate decisions against trying to hype up the intelligence, not wanting to burn the latest bridge to America. The CIA team stayed in their headquarters and let the Kurds bring up potential informants. Some sources didn't get past the waiting room, with tales of James Bond caves and mechanical rotating garden walls that hid Iraq's nuclear weapons. Like most of the world's intelligence agencies, the CIA sincerely believed that Saddam Hussein still had forbidden weapons, judging by the agents' reaction when one reliable informant brought a cylindrical canister to the team. None of the CIA men spoke Kurdish but when they heard the word "uranium," they knocked over a table and shouted, "Get it out! Get it out!"

Their translator explained that the informant was warning about a scam involving phony uranium and had brought an example he had purchased. Another time, a layer of dust in the air had the agents searching for their anti-nerve-gas atropine injectors, only to have their hosts explain it was pollen.

The information wasn't all junk. In the summer of 2002, just before the CIA got pulled out, agents had been approached with access to an unbelievable source. A former friend of Saddam Hussein had fallen out with the dictator and fled to Sulimaniya, where he now lived in a razor-wire-encircled fort near Bakrajo. The man himself had no useful information, but he happened to be the head of the Kasnazani Qaderi Sufi order, commanding more than a million followers across Iraq. Sufism is the mystical side of Islam, and runs parallel to the Sunni-Shi'ite schism. The strictest Muslims consider it superstition (it's banned in Saudi Arabia), but Sufi groups remain popular throughout the Islamic world, allowing followers to reach religious ecstasy through singing, dancing, or in some extreme cases, performing rites of mutilation.

Sheikh Muhammad Abdul Karim al-Kasnazani, a Kurd, had enjoyed roaring good relations with Saddam Hussein in the 1970s and '80s, and had even used his influence to raise an army of jahsh against Talabani's PUK rebellion. In later years he became an important middleman in the Iraqi state oil business and became close with Izzat al-Douri, one of Saddam's vice presidents. The sheikh's power grew so great that in the mid-1990s one of his sons felt brazen enough to forge Saddam Hussein's signature on a contract. All three sons found themselves thrown in jail, sentenced to death. The sheikh managed to use his connections to get the boys out, and the family fled to the north. Ever malleable, Talabani offered the family his protection.

Now a disgruntled PUK member suggested the CIA start using Kasnazani's followers against Saddam, claiming they were placed in all the dictator's security services. At first the agents didn't know what to make of the Sufi order, which, after all, sometimes involved the practice of sticking knives through the faces of followers to prove how insensitive religious fervor can make them. What's more, the sheikh himself, paranoid that Saddam had assassins looking for him, refused to meet with the Americans at first. Instead his son Nahro, a smarmy mountain of a man weighing around four hundred pounds, coordinated the meetings. Nahro also happily accepted the cash.

The scheme hadn't looked promising, but the agents decided to give it a try and asked Nahro to produce a specific officer from the list of followers he claimed. The Kasnazanis smuggled the man into the north and brought him before Sheikh Muhammad. The CIA agents watched as the Iraqi officer dissolved, trembling in front of the Sufi leader. The officer produced a CD-ROM with the personnel files of thousands of Saddam's security agents. Before long the Sufis had a steady flow of informants shuttling up to Qalaat Chowlan, and the CIA was mapping out troop movements and security schematics. One follower even purloined a mobile phone belonging to Foreign Minister Tariq Aziz, which the CIA managed to bug. The intelligence checked out with aerial surveillance, and the myth of an impenetrable regime began to crumble. Information about troop rotations revealed an encouraging fact: The Iraqi military worried that any soldiers left near the Kurdish lines for too long would have a chance to contact the other side and arrange to surrender. In

Langley, Virginia, the Iraq desk couldn't believe its good fortune and code-named the Sufis "Rockstars." The CIA started paying Nahro a million dollars a month for the information that scores of faithful Sufis risked their lives to give the Americans. By the end of February the agency's human intelligence network inside Iraq had grown larger than ever, including eighty-seven men with Thuraya handheld satellite phones that could send GPS coordinates.[4]

Kurdish officials noticed both the string of informants slinking up to Qalaat Chowlan and, even more so, the flood of U.S. hundred-dollar bills into Sulimaniya. There was no way to replenish or reprint the local currency, the "Swiss" Iraqi dinar, and as the Kurdish bills became tattered, they surged in value against the dollar simply because of their scarcity—no one in Kurdistan seemed to have anything smaller than a C-note. The PUK leaders welcomed the cash (which the CIA also shelled out to them directly for protection), but they had a more pressing concern: Ansar al-Islam had also reportedly noticed the Americans.

Informants told the PUK that the Islamists had car-bomb squads on the roads, and the pesh merga at checkpoints around the city worked themselves up on to a hair trigger. The Islamists wanted to hit the CIA's convoy of white Land Cruisers, but northern Iraq was target-rich with infidels, between all the Western journalists and the Kurdish party leaders themselves. On the afternoon of March 4 an SUV full of bearded men pulled up to the pesh merga checkpoint on the main route leaving Sulimaniya to the west. Suddenly a shot rang out and then a cascade of bullets. Pandemonium followed, with jumpy pesh merga shooting everywhere, shouting that they had stopped an Ansar car bomb.

The men weren't with Ansar, but rather were members of Ali Bapir's neutral Komala Islami. All five lay dead inside the car, so riddled with bullets that blood leaked onto the highway. It wasn't even clear the men had gotten off any shots before the pesh merga opened up, but stray rounds wounded several bystanders, including a nine-year-old girl.[5] Bafel Talabani's counterterrorism team appeared immediately afterward, looking for the Ansar bombers but instead finding that the dead included Abdullah Qasri, a thirty-six-year-old Komala leader from the city of Ranya. Bafel began advising the pesh merga in a loud voice that there was nothing wrong with shooting since they had been fired upon. A few of the Western journalists on the scene couldn't help but wonder why Bafel was giving the instruction to the pesh merga in English—it seemed aimed more at the observers than the Kurds. The PUK issued an apology as soon as the dust cleared, assuring Ali Bapir that they still considered him an ally. But only a month had passed since Komala's questionable role in the death of General Shawkat Haji Mushir. Sulimaniya's rumor mill soon claimed that the PUK—specifically Bafel—had hit Komala at the checkpoint in revenge for Shawkat's killing. The PUK denied it, but in Khurmal, Ali Bapir and his men started to feel the heat between the PUK down the road and Ansar up the hill, preparing for a fight to the death. They didn't know the worst: the Americans still had Khurmal on their target list.

As the Kurdish New Year, Newroz, approached, Kurds left the major cities fearing the war might start, and once-jammed streets looked deserted. The universities and high schools closed for vacation over the holiday and didn't reopen, suspending classes until the war was over. On the world stage Europeans and some of America's Arab allies clung to the hope that President Bush wanted a second resolution from the United Nations before attacking Iraq, and they tried to push it off until the summer heat might dissuade the Americans for the season. But their delaying tactics backfired, and on March 17, Bush announced in a speech that he wouldn't wait any longer for the U.N. He ended with an ultimatum: "Saddam Hussein and his sons must leave Iraq within forty-eight hours."

Even to the ardently pro-war Kurds watching the speech, this sounded Wild West. One of them turned with his face screwed up and asked, "Who does he think he is?"

As Bush's deadline ticked closer, Khalilzad went to Ankara, accompanied by Talabani and Nechirvan Barzani, seeking to forestall any rash action by the Turks. The Turkish government seemed to be coming to terms with the two edges of standing up to the United States. Defying a global bully played wonderfully to the gallery of Turkish public opinion, but now that Bush had announced he was going to war anyway, Ankara seemed to have gotten the worst of both worlds: The government hadn't prevented anything, they now had no say in northern Iraq, and America had started to rethink even the one billion dollars in aid promised for Turkey's struggling economy. The Turks had thought they could politely agree to disagree with Washington, but to the Americans, all bets were now off—even Turkish demands that Washington never partition Iraq.

"U.S. policy had always been unity, sovereignty, and territorial integrity of Iraq," said one U.S. diplomat involved in the negotiations. "With Turkey we had a document that enshrined that, which obviously, when they voted no on March 1, was totally irrelevant as a document."

Washington still pushed for Turkey to grant over-flight rights, but now in a more menacing tone. Both Kurdish leaders promised that pesh merga forces wouldn't enter Kirkuk or Mosul during the war, but the Turks didn't believe them and wanted a written guarantee from the United States that Turkey could send in troops if the Kurds broke their promise. After twelve years of tiptoeing around the Turks, Washington was sick of them and gave nothing but strongly worded letters about letting U.S. planes through. Turkey's promise to intervene for humanitarian reasons looked even more transparent as some of the Turkish troops at the border caused delays for humanitarian aid shipments heading into the north.[6] The Kurds came back from Ankara reveling in the Turks' misery.

"Thanks to our friends in the U.S. and friends in Europe, Turkey was convinced not to come in," said Talabani, ever the politician. "And we want to assure our Turkish brothers we will do nothing against them, and the day there is need, we will ask them."

It was Talabani's favorite joke—his American friends and Turkish brothers. In private he would explain: your friends you get to choose; your brothers you have to live with. Talabani's closest American friends at the moment were the CIA agents living near his Qalaat Chowlan headquarters, and they thought they were about to win the war before it began.

On March 18, the morning after Bush delivered his ultimatum, one of the "Rockstars" reported the strongest-ever tip regarding Saddam's whereabouts. A Kasnazani follower called in from Saddam's wife's complex in Dora, south across the Tigris River from Baghdad, where he worked as head of security. He said Saddam had arrived on the premises, and the CIA picked up the GPS coordinates from his Thuraya phone. Back in Washington, satellite surveillance watched three dozen vehicles pull up to the compound, and it looked like there was a chance to decapitate the regime before the war even started. The "Rockstar" at Dora was understandably nervous and hard to keep on the phone. Thirty of the spies had been caught, and one of them was tortured into confessing on Iraqi television. Owning a Thuraya now carried a death sentence, but the spy ring still functioned through the cajoling of the Sufi leaders. Nahro screamed down the phone to the spy at Dora that he should keep calling in.[7]

The White House weighed the pros and cons as reports kept coming in that Saddam had arrived at Dora, that he had left, that his sons, Uday and Qusay, had come for the night, expecting their father. Finally President Bush decided the chance couldn't be wasted and ordered General Franks to ready the bombers—something big enough to penetrate the bunker that the CIA believed Saddam had constructed in Dora. This meant starting the war a few days early—after Bush's deadline, but before his planned start on Friday, March 21. As the bombs fell, Bush announced that the invasion was in the early stages. The Dora complex exploded under a barrage of forty Tomahawk missiles and two bunker-busting bombs from an American F-117 bomber. But in the end the most important person the CIA killed was its own source. A similar "decapitation" tip called in two weeks later near Baghdad's al-Saa restaurant also failed, killing only bystanders.

"It came to bugger-all. They destroyed a perfectly nice restaurant," was the assessment of one Kurdish official. America was discovering that all its precision technology amounted to nothing without good human intelligence to select the bull's-eye. The most elaborate infiltration of Saddam's networks in history amounted to tens of millions of CIA dollars in the hands of a cynical cult leader who gladly cashed in the lives of dozens of his followers. His sons prepared themselves to enter politics in the new Iraq.

The Dora assault didn't impress the Kurds, who were hoping to see the entire Iraqi army disappear in a cloud of pink dust the moment war began. Two days later they got some of what they were waiting for. The war began in Kurdistan on March 21, the first day of spring and of the Kurdish New Year. The Kurds christened it the "Newroz war" as America bombed targets along the green line to the south and specific locations within Kirkuk and Mosul. Late the same night the PUK's pesh merga cheered as Tomahawk missiles slammed into the hills from which Ansar al-Islam had fired mortars at them for months. The following day more bombs fell, but not just on Ansar.

In the predawn hours of March 22 an American precision strike incinerated Komala's base near Khurmal. Ali Bapir's men frantically pulled back to Khurmal's town center, and the PUK took over all Komala's forts and checkpoints on the Halabja road in a clearly preplanned action. Bapir could read the writing on the wall. Some of Ansar al-Islam's fighters were trying to flee down through his territory, and he suspected the Americans would soon be marching up it. He contacted the PUK and desperately sued for negotiations.

The newly opened road to Halabja bustled with traffic the morning of the air strike, as PUK pesh merga swept into their new positions, many civilians used the road for the first time in a year, and seemingly the entire stranded press corps raced in to cover the first development of the war. The PUK now held the ground up to the Khurmal turnoff from the Halabja road, and by late afternoon a mob of journalists congregated at the new line, cautioned back by a small group of PUK soldiers. Amid the chaos a white sedan pulled up and suddenly exploded in fire and shrapnel.

One of the Ansar car bombs had finally found a target. The blast rattled the windows of the Halabja police headquarters, a mile away, and sent the cops running outdoors to see a plume of black smoke push up against the mountains. Moments later, cars with blown-out windows raced toward hospitals in Halabja and Sa'id Sadiq carrying people wounded by flames, flying glass, and metal. Three PUK pesh merga died, as well as an Australian cameraman.* Twenty minutes after the explosion, the crowd at the intersection had cleared out in fear of more killers on the road. The skeleton of the bomber's car, now black, burned like a furnace beside a kiosk at the crossroads.

Within the week, the PUK had forged a deal with Ali Bapir's Komala party, all the while apologizing that the American bombing had been a terrible mistake.[8] Bapir didn't know whether to believe the PUK, but it hardly mattered—he had to get his people out.† On March 27, hundreds of Komala members convoyed from Khurmal to Qala Diza, where Talabani promised them a safe haven away from the action. The pesh merga shunted the wagon train around the city of Sulimaniya, lest a car should stray into town. Driving whatever they could find, including a few jeeps

---

* The cameraman, Paul Moran, was a freelancer working for the Australian Broadcasting Company, but he also had worked for the Rendon Group, a PR firm used extensively by the CIA, which had helped set up the INC. The coincidence of his death only days after arriving in Kurdistan gave rise to some absurd conspiracy theories that Ansar al-Islam somehow knew about his connections.

† A U.S. Special Forces officer with the Tenth Group, Third Battalion told me a few days after the bombing that the target had been selected by U.S. Central Command, acting on intelligence from the PUK and other sources. He said Komala had been sharing space with Ansar and planned to support them in the fight, so it wasn't an error from the U.S. perspective.

with plastic sheeting for windshields, the Komala men looked like they'd been through hell as they rolled through the PUK checkpoint below the city. Scraggly, filthy, and wide-eyed with fear, they peered out at the pesh merga, who in turn had their own concerns—each one of the vehicles screamed "car bomb" to their eyes, and more than once they couldn't help glancing around for something solid to dive behind. Later it appeared that some Ansar members managed to slip out within the ranks of Komala members. But the PUK didn't mind—the cavalry had finally arrived, though it was hardly a smooth ride in.

THE U.S. ARMY's Tenth Special Forces Group (Airborne) had been sitting in Constanta, Romania, since January, packing and repacking their bags each time it looked as if Turkey might let them fly through to land in Iraqi Kurdistan. The Kurds in Erbil and Sulimaniya had arranged to receive them and prepared Kurdish troops to work with the Green Berets, even tailoring Kurdish pesh merga costumes for them (but with elastic waistbands, since the Americans could never seem to get the hang of the cummerbund). By March the men were itching to go, and despite the Turkish no vote, they continued to plan a deployment into bases in southeastern Turkey, figuring that Ankara would relent. For several days running after Bush's ultimatum on March 17, the Americans boarded their planes and waited for the order to go, only to be stood down. Five days of getting psyched up and disappointed took its toll, and the Tenth Group's commanding officer, Colonel Charlie Cleveland, decided to switch to plan B. Instead of making the easy flight across the length of Turkey into the north, the first teams would fly for two days, secretly stopping twice in countries that didn't want their role publicly acknowledged. The last four and a half hours they would fly right across Iraq's western desert over batteries of enemy artillery. One of the noncommissioned officers quipped, "That's an ugly baby," and the route had its name: Operation Ugly Baby.[9]

The Special Forces, despite their confidence, had plenty to give them pause. As the U.S. Marines rolled up the highway in southern Iraq, they found the Iraqi army was not surrendering en masse, as many experts had predicted it would, and the irregular forces called Saddam Fedayeen were showing their zeal at setting urban ambushes.[10] U.S. Marines had seized oil fields in the far south of the country easily on March 21, and found the Iraqi army's marksmanship laughably poor. But the next day was a disaster for the Americans, when an antimissile maintenance company, the 507, somehow got ahead of the U.S. Marines and cruised through the unconquered city of Nasiriya. The mechanics were never meant to get so close to combat and had driven blind into a shooting gallery. Iraqi ambushes killed eleven Americans, and seven were captured, including two women, Specialist Shoshana Johnson and Private Jessica Lynch, who was knocked unconscious in a collision with a U.S. Army truck. It was a terrific propaganda victory for Saddam's forces, and Iraqi television aired interviews with the clearly shaken American prisoners.

On the same day as the disaster in Nasiriya, March 22, American bombs in the north rained down on Mosul and Kirkuk. With the scant cover provided by darkness and increasing bad weather, the Tenth Special Forces Group started barnstorming into Iraq, dodging Iraqi antiaircraft fire and throwing off chaff and countermeasures. The Iraqis, who had practiced shooting at the jets flying in Operation Provide Comfort for a dozen years, found the slow, fat troop transports a better target. They tagged three of the planes—one so badly it had to peel off to Turkey and beg for an emergency landing, while the other two made it to Kurdistan and touched down in a frightening state.

"Naturally, we fired an RPG at them," Bafel Talabani said with a grim laugh, recalling the Americans' arrival at Bakrajo airstrip. It was an accident—one of the pesh merga's rocket-propelled grenades (RPGs) went flying over the weary soldiers' heads, hardly a warm welcome. After the initial shock, everyone got down to business—they had only forty-five minutes to unload an entire C-130 cargo plane before the next flight would land. The flights stuck to a tight schedule to get all the Special Operations troops on the ground and into a PUK warehouse at the military base across the highway without being noticed by the sleeping inhabitants of Sulimaniya. The following day Turkey finally relented and allowed the rest of Tenth Group to fly directly, happily discontinuing the "Ugly Baby" route. Soon all fifty-two hundred military personnel were in place. They faced the thirteen divisions of Saddam's army still arrayed along the green line, about a hundred thousand men. On the U.S. side were about seventy thousand pesh merga—roughly the same number of men who would have come through Turkey in the Fourth Infantry Division. But working with pesh merga would be a bit different.

The Kurds harbored doubts even after the first Americans arrived. The CIA team had doled out money but hardly ever left their barracks in

Qalaat Chowlan, and never delivered the weapons and ammunition they had been promising.[11] The leader of the Tenth Group's Third Battalion, Lieutenant Colonel Ken Tovo, had come early to plan the attack on Ansar al-Islam, but the PUK soldiers didn't really believe he was serious until they saw the Tomahawk missiles hit the mountain. On the night of the first barrage, Tovo invited a few Kurdish commanders to go up on the roof of the command post at Halabja at the appointed hour. Bafel Talabani acted as interpreter.[12]

"Colonel Tovo told me the Tomahawks were coming, and to look over the horizon, the sound will come first," Bafel said. An awkward quarter of an hour passed with no sound or light on the mountainside. As it crept toward a half an hour, Bafel turned to Tovo and joked, "If these missiles don't come . . . you've got to get out of here."

Finally they heard an intense humming sound pass overheard and then saw a flash, and finally a loud boom and another and then another echoed down the valley. The pesh merga commanders watched, awestruck that the Americans could really call in such precise destruction from a thousand miles away in the Persian Gulf, all with a little laptop computer in the bunker in Halabja. The missiles crashed into the hills all night, but at dawn the Kurds were dismayed to look through binoculars at Ansar militants fleeing by truck, many of them crossing the border to Iran. As anxious as they were to attack, they had to wait until the rest of the Special Operations Forces battalion arrived over the following two days.

The pesh merga and the Special Ops made a good fit. Across Kurdistan many people who call themselves pesh merga are minutemen, to be called up every time Kurds flee into the mountains. For this mission the PUK had gathered its best professional soldiers, many from Halabja with personal scores to settle with Ansar al-Islam. The Americans impressed them with their high-tech gear—heading into battle with a heavy load of body armor, communications equipment, sleeping bags, and the most amazing thing of all, the meal ready-to-eat. The small, brown plastic MRE bag held enough calories for a whole day in combat, and the Americans could even heat up the little foil packet entrées by adding water to a chemical solution that came in the bag. It wasn't good Kurdish food, but still, it was terribly convenient for a guerrilla fighter.

Gadgets aside, the pesh merga liked the Special Forces work ethic. Most of the Kurds had at one time or another served mandatory stints in Saddam's army, where they were treated like dirt by Arab officers. The

Kurds feared the Americans might condescend or order them about, not realizing that pesh merga see themselves as patriotic volunteers. Instead the American officers ate on the ground right beside their soldiers, just like the Kurdish officers.

"Iraqi officers consider themselves God's deputies on earth," said one of the Kurdish translators. "Seeing that an American colonel is so simple and modest with his own soldiers—that increased their honor in the eyes of the pesh merga."

Mustafa Sa'id Kader, a PUK general, offered up a plan to Colonel Tovo, trying to mesh the fighting styles of the Kurds and the Americans. The major difference in philosophy centered on loss of life. The Americans planned to attack, secure a position, and then dig in to wait for air support to soften up the next target. Kader told Tovo that pesh merga don't fight that way—once they have momentum, they push the advantage without giving the enemy time to regroup, even if it costs some casualties. They agreed on a three-pronged attack, with two units coming in through Komala's old territory to the north of Ansar al-Islam, two traveling along the mountain ridge to Biyara from the south, and two going right up the gullet of the valley to the towns of Golp and Sargat. They gave the units color-coded names, yellow, blue, and green. When they finished planning, they realized that Tovo was working on the assumption that the battle would take several days. The pesh merga hoped to win it in thirty-six hours.

Eight thousand Kurdish soldiers began the assault on Friday, March 28, at seven in the morning, which was as close to "predawn" as the Kurds could assemble the division. Each prong had a dozen or so Americans along to communicate with Major George Thiebes, the company commander, who stayed back at Girda Drozna with Colonel Tovo calling in air support.[13] Throughout the preceding night, U.S. bombers and jets—including an AC-130 Spectre gunship, the Air Force's armored cargo plane, a flying pincushion of gun barrels—had pummeled the Ansar targets and minefields.

The Americans soldiers hung back as much as they could, letting the Kurds do the heavy fighting. They wore no helmets so they wouldn't stand out among the Kurdish fighters, who went into battle with little more than running shoes and a few magazines of ammunition stuffed in their cummerbunds. Now it was the Americans' turn to be impressed. The pesh merga moved through the terrain at what would have been a dead run for the heavily loaded Americans and controlled the first six kilometers in about an hour. A stable of Kurdish university students had volunteered to act as translators for the Special Forces, fortunately, because on the eve of the assault, the chief liaison told Colonel Tovo that he couldn't work for him that day at Girda Drozna.

"I know you need a good translator," Bafel Talabani told Tovo, "but there's absolutely no way I'm going to miss this."

Bafel swapped out with an interpreter from PUK security and joined the yellow prong, which would be led straight down the throat of the battle by Sheikh Jafar Mustafa, the gray-haired military commander of Halabja. Bafel's cousin Lahor joined the green prong, which would pass through Khurmal and move along the high ridge north above the towns of Golp and Sargat to Biyara. Lahor's group aimed to harass the Ansar mortarmen from high in the hills and allow Bafel's troops some cover as they charged into the towns. Both cousins had been too young to fight against Saddam during the 1980s, and their parents had kept them safe in England during the uprising and the civil war. They believed the American campaign against Saddam Hussein this time was going to be a pushover. The fight against Ansar al-Islam might be the last chance for the young men to prove themselves in a culture that still valued combat skill above all other qualities. This might be Bafel's best opportunity to step out of his father's shadow.

On the night before the battle Bafel didn't even try sleeping. He forced down several MREs to make sure he wouldn't run out of energy the next morning. Lahor couldn't sleep either—he was busy helping unload the last of the C-130s landing at Bakrajo until three A.M., and Bafel kept calling on the satellite phone to tease him that he would miss the fight. Lahor finally showed up at about five A.M., wearing a big Kurdish turban on his head like the one his father, Sheikh Jengi Talabani, used to wear. At dawn thousands of Kurds in baggy trousers and sash belts poured into the valley in cars, pickups, and even school buses. A few fingers of sunlight reached from the mountains behind Halabja, and the men in the yellow prong cast long shadows as they ran up the valley toward the town of Golp—in plain view of the deadly mortars Ansar had used so well from the peaks above.

The green prong moved ahead and to their left, hoping to close within shooting distance of Sargat before yellow prong made its headlong charge. The blue prong sped through the villages to the south, where the

Islamic Movement of Kurdistan, like Komala, had cut a deal with the PUK after seeing the American firepower. American air strikes should have helped to brush back the Islamists' mortars, but just to be sure, the green prong started mortaring and firing artillery at Ansar's positions. As the yellow prong, about a thousand men, pushed toward Golp, no shots fired from the hills. The Islamists had perhaps decided to pull back into their caves and bunkers—or maybe they had fled to Iran or been killed in the bombardment.

I snuck into Halabja that morning, though the roads into the city had all been shut to civilians for the assault. A Kurdish friend directed me to an unguarded route across the top of Darbandikhan Lake, on a rickety ferry that seemed likely to sink under the weight of my car. Spring weather had finally kicked in a few days before, and each day seemed to yield a new color of flowers alongside the roads. Early morning lifted a mist off the surrounding farmlands, and the countryside felt perfectly tranquil south of Halabja. Then I began to hear booms in the distance. On the spiral road up to Girda Drozna a strange mosquito noise caught my attention, and I turned around to see an oversize model airplane—a small "unmanned aerial vehicle"—buzz by on its way back from spying on the Ansar troops up the hill. At the bunker the Americans used laptop computers and small, collapsible satellite dishes, calling in air strikes on the mountains with the click of a mouse. In a brief conversation with one of the Special Operations soldiers I got the idea that things were going well and that the Kurdish fighters had made a real impression—especially the first wounded man of the morning.

One of the Kurds had come back from the battle, walking alone with labored gait. "He walked in, and everybody though he had an ankle problem. It turned out he'd been shot in the chest," the American said, adding, "these are hard people."*

"Look around—could you be in Ireland or something?" he said. It was about ten o'clock, and the low sunlight showed the green of the valley with a frosting of white nasturtiums and bloodred poppies. The American looked up at the snowy mountains and some of the little waterfalls running down. "I had no idea," he said. "It's well worth fighting over. If I lived here, I'd want to own it too."

---

* SOF soldiers almost never give their names for interviews.

ANSAR AL-ISLAM still wanted to own some of it as well, if only as burial plots. As the yellow prong reached Golp, the Islamists lit them up with sniper fire and heavy machine guns from the hills above. Grenades rocketed down and Sheikh Jafr called back to Bafel, who translated for the Americans that the front of yellow prong was completely pinned down a mile ahead. They radioed the company commander at Girda Drozna and before long saw tiny specks in the sky, the sound following as they approached. A pair of F/A-18s dropped two five-hundred-pound bombs, guided by lasers on the ground, to pulverize the Ansar machine gun nests.[14]

For the first time in the PUK's thirty-year history, airplanes dropped bombs on the other side. The pesh merga, accustomed to being underdogs, let out a cheer and charged up the open valley as if they were bulletproof. A few of the militants had survived the bombs and started shooting, but the momentum of the air strikes swung the battle. Sheikh Jafr's men sprinted the last mile into Golp and recaptured the town at nine A.M., fighting through the village house by house. The Special Forces colonel had planned the battle for Golp to last all day. The Kurds wanted to push on to the next target, Sargat, but the Americans insisted on securing the main road so supply vehicles and artillery could get to the front and take wounded to the rear.

"For us, in the mountains that's not the way to fight—move and then dig in again," said Bafel. "The way you fight is just speed and violence of action. Once we have them on the move, our job is keep them on the move. We're not used to air support."

The Kurds soon lost most of the advantage the air strikes had provided as they swarmed ahead of the Americans up the valley toward Sargat. Ansar fighters opened up with heavy machine guns from the hills, catching the pesh merga force in the cemetery just outside town. Grenades and Katyusha rockets also funneled down on the yellow prong from the surrounding hills. Bafel and an American captain found themselves huddled behind rock walls and tombstones. The captain called for artillery support and discovered that he had advanced well ahead of Sheikh Jafr and the Kurdish mortars. Close air support was impossible, with Kurdish soldiers scrambling ahead into the same hills around the Ansar positions. Then the enemy mortars began—the militants must have been saving them up. The eighty-two-millimeter shells Ansar lobbed down into the valley would kill everything in a huge radius of the impact, and they started to zero in.

Back at Girda Drozna the Kurdish and American commanders called the yellow prong and heard a storm of explosions crackle over the radio. They had discovered the problem with supporting the pesh merga with air strikes as well. At one point when the Special Forces commander started to call in a bomber, a Kurdish interpreter rushed up to him stuttering. The message was so urgent that the young man had forgotten his English. After a pause the translation came through—one of the prongs had moved into the kill zone for the next air strike. The American called off the drop in time, but the air advantage had been largely neutralized.

Bafel and the Special Forces captain had also outpaced green prong, which was supposed to get in position first to provide cover for them from the ridge, as Lahor discovered when his satellite phone rang. Bafel shouted at him down the line. "He said, 'We're in the shit!' and I said, 'So am I,'" said Lahor, each of them shouting in excitement over gunfire. Lahor told his cousin not to go into Sargat, advice Bafel hardly needed at the moment.

Lahor had had a busy morning. Heading into the town of Khurmal, one of the pesh merga lost his leg to a mine. Then a few snipers started taking shots at the advancing platoon from the old radio tower behind Khurmal. Lahor went with a few dozen Kurds to take the tower, already in ruins from a U.S. air strike. The snipers offered to surrender, but something about them didn't seem right. As they came a bit closer, Lahor's suspicions were confirmed. The pesh merga raised their rifles to shoot and the would-be prisoners of war detonated suicide vests, exploding before Lahor's eyes. They were the first suicide bombers of the day, but not the last.

Once they cleared the tower, one of Lahor's men scaled up the flagpole to pull down Ansar's white banner, which had "God is great" written across it. Of course all the pesh merga are Muslims as well, and when the man climbed down, a dizzy spell hit him, and he bent over with nausea, shouting, "God forgive me. God forgive me!"

When Lahor took Bafel's phone call, he was creeping up the ridgeline with two of the American soldiers he knew from the advance team at Bakrajo airstrip. One of them was along to "spot," or call in coordinates, for air support; the other worked the hill with a .50-caliber sniper rifle that could hit a target a mile away. After the call, the green prong realized they had to move faster to help yellow prong get out of the cemetery outside Sargat. The spotter traded his M4 rifle with one of the pesh merga for a massive PKM machine gun, with a long belt of finger-size shells.

"I've never seen anything like it," said Lahor. "He fired the thing with one hand and said, 'Follow me.'" Lahor did, moving from boulder to boulder, grenade to grenade. At one point he stood up to take a look at the enemy, with his big turban making him a head taller.

"I really wanted to impress the guys and say we shouldn't be scared. I felt the heat of the bullet pass my ear. And there was a tall pesh merga standing behind me," Lahor said. The round hit the tall Kurd in the chest, but the man didn't fall. As Lahor helped rip away the man's heavy clothes, the hot slug came away with his shirt—it must have been out of range and spent its force before impact. One of the Americans quickly wrapped the wound.

"Okay, guys, I'm not going to stand up anymore," said Lahor.

As part of the PUK's first family, both Bafel and Lahor had dedicated pesh merga following them, treating them with as much deference as a battlefield would allow. In the mêlée below, Bafel stood behind a low wall with an experienced soldier named Muhsin.

"Look, if you think it wise, perhaps we should move," Muhsin suggested. Bafel asked why, and he answered, "Because just a few feet from you there's an RPG that hasn't exploded." They scurried to another stone wall.

Finally the green prong got in position to see Bafel and the captain pinned in the valley below. As they started firing down the mountainside from a kilometer away, the Ansar gunners began to break. Alternating fire from down in the gully and away on the mountain, the pesh merga killed many of the Islamists and drove the others back up the hill. The last kilometer had taken almost four hours to win, but the PUK had Sargat.

None of the Americans in the yellow prong had been seriously wounded, but several Kurds were too badly shot up to walk. Bafel suddenly realized he was exhausted. Sheikh Jafr radioed from the rear for the men to halt, and a few minutes later a truck arrived with hot lamb kebabs and bread. The Americans looked on in disbelief as the Kurds stopped everything for lunch. Up on the ridge Lahor and his companions had simpler fare. "We'd stick our hands in the rice bucket and then stick our hands in the beans bucket. It was the most delicious thing," he said.

Along the ridges, Kurdish-American forces then began the painstaking work of clearing caves of the Ansar survivors. In Sargat, an American team searched for evidence of the chemical laboratory that had helped start the war. They found what they thought might be traces of chemicals and poison, but nothing conclusive. Bafel took several pesh merga to case the house that had belonged to Abu Musab al-Zarqawi, "Qudama the Engineer." He found a hole in the wall made by a U.S. bomb, but the room had been cleaned out before the missile hit. The most convincing evidence of an al-Qa'ida connection came in the form of the prisoners—foreign fighters from Palestine, Syria, Algeria, Saudi Arabia, as far as Pakistan, and as near as Baghdad—but few of them wanted to be taken alive.*

"One guy came out of a cave and surrendered," said Bafel. "We sent some pesh to arrest him. I turned my head away, and he exploded." The militant had been hiding a grenade and killed himself and one of the pesh merga. The Kurds changed tactics, firing rocket-propelled grenades down the mouths of the caves. They still lost half a dozen men to suicide tricks— sometimes the Islamists surrendered and then pulled out hidden weapons and began shooting again until the pesh merga blew them down. In the end the pesh merga insisted the prisoners strip naked before coming close and then sent them down the mountain that way, provoking some funny looks from the Americans.

Thirty-six PUK soldiers died in the battle with Ansar fighters, and none of the Americans was seriously injured. The victors couldn't be sure just how many of the seven hundred or so Ansar fighters had died, but they estimated about three hundred. They seized documents and computers from the bombed-out buildings, but the nickname "little Tora Bora" may have earned a second meaning. As had happened in the assault on al-Qa'ida in Tora Bora, Afghanistan, in December 2001, the time between the air strikes and the ground offensive allowed a large number of Islamists to escape over the border to Iran, where some faced arrest and others slipped through the cracks. Still, the towns belonged to the PUK, and the senior leadership hosted a banquet the day after the battle in Taweela, Ansar's deepest territory. Almost as soon as the shooting stopped, thousands of Kurdish civilians started their way along the road back to their homes, some of them leading their flocks up the same road the pesh merga had cleared only days before.

---

* This according to Sheikh Jafr at a press conference a few days later, as well as Ayub Nuri, who saw among the casualties an Algerian passport and a man whose name was "al-Baghdadi." I saw a dead Saudi near Sargat a few days after the assault. He had pretended to surrender and then shot one of the pesh merga who came to arrest him. The Kurds killed him.

As much as defeating Ansar, the Kurds delighted in proving their mettle to the Americans, and it seemed a natural next step to turn around together toward the Iraqi front. Many of the Americans seemed tempted to join the Kurds in taking back Kirkuk, but the orders coming down from Central Command were to keep the Kurds out of the rest of the fight, and the Pentagon sent some reinforcements. A thousand paratroopers from the 173rd Airborne Brigade had landed at the KDP's airstrip in Bashur on March 26th, amid great fanfare.

"Americans are asking you to make the world a better place by jumping into the unknown for the benefit of others," the brigade's commanding officer, Colonel William Mayville, said to the men as they left their base in Aviano, Italy.[15]

On the ground, the Kurds couldn't help but puzzle at why the Americans arrived by parachute to a long, friendly airstrip the KDP had spent a month refurbishing. Some of the parachutes missed the base by miles, and they spent the next day digging their heavy equipment out of the deep mud. Nor was the jump a surprise. Marine General Pete Osman had come into northern Iraq through Turkey and held a press conference advertising the paratroopers' arrival three days earlier. The show helped keep Saddam Hussein's army guarding the north, but the troops themselves had been placed under the control of Special Forces Colonel Charlie Cleveland, mostly to make sure the Kurds didn't overreach. As much as they wanted the Iraqi army tied down, the Pentagon wanted the Turks and Kurds to stay within their borders.

Less than two weeks into the war, many Americans' assumptions turned out wrong. Shi'ite Arabs in the south, who rose up violently in 1991, stayed indoors this time, and though the U.S. Marines had reached the edge of Nasiriya, the southern capital of Basra still hadn't welcomed American or British aid. American forces started to look dangerously overextended as they stretched toward Baghdad, surrounded by civilians still too scared to express support. The Iraqi opposition tried to rally the population, but not everywhere.

"Yesterday the Iraqi opposition called for uprising in Iraq, but Kirkuk is a special case," Talabani told a news conference the day after Ansar's defeat. "We don't want any kind of mistake that would cause problems for our American friends or our Turkish brothers."

U.S. envoy Zalmay Khalilzad smiled next to him and nodded in approval. Talabani and Khalilzad fielded questions from the foreign reporters, ignoring Barham Salih's attempts to take a few questions from Sulimaniya's own inquisitive press. Both men seemed a bit off their game. Talabani told a flat joke about a woman in Sulimaniya complaining that after all the money she had spent taping her windows shut, she now feared that Saddam wouldn't even gas Kurdistan. Khalilzad gave him a terribly staged laugh. The American envoy also stumbled through a list of the opposition forces who had agreed to coordinate with the U.S. coalition. Talabani nudged him and said, "You forgot Chalabi."

"Oh yes. I'm glad you mentioned that," Khalilzad said, and added with another awkward laugh, "I'm getting old."

The missing northern front had left Chalabi's small group of fighters stuck in Kurdistan, which seemed just fine with the U.S. State Department. But Chalabi hungered for Baghdad. I had taken a drive to the southernmost point of the Kurdish safe zone in late March and discovered several hundred INC soldiers busing in from Iran. A number of them, including some U.S. citizens equipped with Thuraya satellite phones, declared Chalabi their leader and the next president of Iraq. They took over some buildings in the town of Kalar, just two hours' drive from Baghdad. On the drive back to Sulimaniya I saw a tall white stallion in the back of a pickup truck headed for Kalar and couldn't help but suppose it to be the white horse Chalabi planned to ride into Baghdad. PUK officials had trouble with Chalabi's recruits and later arrested some of them, claiming they were all hired mercenaries from Iran.[16] In fact a small number of them had been trained in Hungary by U.S. Special Forces. When General Tommy Franks realized that his troops in southern Iraq had virtually no translators, the Pentagon flew Chalabi and more than five hundred of his soldiers to Nasiriya, apparently without the knowledge of the State Department, or the knowledge of the troops on the ground in Nasiriya, who treated them like refugees when they arrived.[17]

Things would go smoother in the north, Talabani promised. The opposition's leadership council, with its many committees, would help guide the liberating forces, but no one would be making any grabs for land or power.

"Every step will be done in full coordination, and there will be no movement of pesh merga towards Kirkuk or Mosul and other towns," Mam Jalal repeated, smiling.

He didn't mean a word he said.

CHAPTER NINE

Deeds to the
Promised Land

INSIDE THE CITY OF KIRKUK, U.S. MISSILES had been taking out specific targets for several days during the last week of March 2003, and rumors filtered out to the north that Saddam's fearsome Republican Guard there had rounded up a group of young men for execution. The Ba'ath Party headquarters in the center of the city looked as likely a target as any, but in his house just a few blocks away, Ramadan Rashid, a slight, gray-haired goldsmith, didn't fret about the bombs. Rashid was born in Kirkuk in 1953. He had left the city and lived in Erbil for some years, but moved back and opened up his gold shop again in 1996. As neighbors, the Ba'athists knew Rashid and had even tried to recruit him as a spy on his regular business trips to Erbil. He had begged off, claiming that he had too many responsibilities, supporting his family and his brother's on the shop's meager income. In fact, Rashid had even more responsibilities than he let on. He was calling in the air strikes.[1]

Rashid joined the Kurdish resistance as a teenager and wound up in an Iraqi prison before he turned twenty. His torture by the Ba'athist government only steeled his resolve, and when he got out of jail in 1974, he made his way to the hills and joined the pesh merga. That meant leaving his home—Kirkuk was the prize of all Kurdish independence struggles, but it was no place for guerrilla warfare. A citadel has guarded the eastern

entrance of the city for millennia, and overlooks an open-air bazaar
nearly as old, but otherwise the city is flat and bare. Even the Khasah
River seems denuded—five bridges and numerous dams and weirs cross it,
but only a trickle of water flows through. Rashid fought for the PUK
against Saddam in the mountains until 1991, when he joined the all-too-
brief Kurdish reconquest of Kirkuk.

Through the early 1990s Rashid lived in Erbil, helping out with the
CIA's bungled coup attempts. When Saddam's army busted into the north
to help the KDP in 1996, Rashid discovered to his surprise that he wasn't
on any of the Ba'athists' lists for assassination. He accepted a general
amnesty and headed back to Kirkuk. To avoid suspicion he moved into a
house as close to the Ba'ath Party headquarters as he could find, and auda-
ciously buried a few dozen Kalashnikovs in his garden.

Rashid had a few close calls over the years, including a forty-eight-
hour interrogation with Kirkuk's Mukhabarat. Rashid sensed in the beginning of that ordeal that the Iraqis didn't have solid evidence against
him, so he stayed calm and acted the part of a meek Kurdish grandfather.
The agents kept leaving him to sweat in a tiny cell.

"This is your file," one of the agents told him, holding up a thick
manila envelope, "and if I send it with you down to Baghdad, only the file
will come back."

Rashid knew they had hidden cameras on him and were watching for
signs he might crack after they stepped out, so even then he kept his cool.
His intuition paid off, and eventually the Iraqis changed tack, asking if
he would work for them. For a year after his release they kept on him before giving up, but saved his name for their files, checking in periodically
to see if he had changed his mind. After the arrest, Rashid's superiors in
the PUK offered to pull him out, but he wanted to stay on. He would periodically go north to report in person, always taking the road to Erbil
and then crossing over to Sulimaniya—which added an extra four hours
to the journey. If the Iraqis caught on, they would think he worked for
the KDP, and it would help throw them off the trail a bit.

Six months before the U.S. invasion, Talabani promoted Rashid to lead
all the PUK cells in Kirkuk. For the first time Rashid saw the scale of the
operation—not only the sources inside the Ba'athist government but also
his many friends, neighbors, and even his brother, who also worked for
the underground. They dispensed Thuraya satellite phones to spotters
around the city. It was death to be caught with one of the phones, which

couldn't be used behind closed doors—the phone needs an open sky to function. Rashid called at night or went to a friend's half-finished apartment building to make the calls during the day. Kurdish neighborhoods in Kirkuk had been put under a special curfew, and many feared that the Iraqi army would start rounding up young Kurdish men, but Rashid had no shortage of volunteers for the underground.

"The organization was so strong in Kirkuk. Kirkukee Kurds were risking their lives to do this job. And they were desperately glad to do it," said Rashid.

As the air strikes started taking their toll on the city, Rashid fed reports back to the PUK about where the bombs had hit and how many casualties they had inflicted. Rashid found himself getting more than information from his Ba'athist informants—now they requested protection from the Americans and Kurds, whom they assumed would soon flood the city.

JUST ACROSS THE battle lines in the PUK-held city of Chamchamal, Kirkukees were just as desperate to go home. Many had been waiting decades in refugee camps and were now watching the Iraqi army garrison at Qara Hanjir on the ridge. On the morning of March 27, the Iraqi army that had looked down on them all those years suddenly turned to smoke. Seconds later the sound from the American bombs echoed across the valley.

At the police station in Chamchamal, dozens of pesh merga, Kurdish civilians, and news-starved journalists had gathered to look up at the ridge. Some pesh merga raced out to the checkpoint on the road to Kirkuk, daring one another to go farther out of town. On the roof of the station a bear of a man in Kurdish fatigues stood surrounded by Kurdish police. General Rostam Hamid Rahim, a fifty-year-old pesh merga legend, peered up at the ridge through binoculars. Up the hill a small truck was moving back and forth—it looked like survivors were pulling out.

"Mam" Rostam, as everyone called him, wouldn't have lasted a minute undercover as a civilian. Everything about the man said fighter, from the scars all over his body to the violent gestures in his speech. Now he was smiling, laughing, and shouting with his friends at the ruined Iraqi bunkers up the hill. Rostam, like all his contemporaries, had seen time and torture in Kirkuk's prisons as a teen. As one of the first PUK militants, he had fought nonstop from the 1970s through the '90s. He counted his father and two brothers as martyrs for Kirkuk, and the

Ba'athists threw another brother in jail because of Rostam's activities. He sent his wife and children to exile in Germany for their protection. After the uprising in 1991, Ali Hassan al-Majid had singled out Shorja, Rostam's neighborhood in Kirkuk, as an example for the rest of the city's Kurdish inhabitants. With dynamite and bulldozers, Iraqi troops razed about four hundred houses, treating Shorja like so many Kurdish villages during the Anfal campaign.

Rostam had been a member of the Kurdish parliament but never quite learned political correctness—he hated Arabs and had no time for religion. While his comrades in the PUK repeated the mantra that any action on Kirkuk would be under American supervision, Rostam told anyone who asked that when Kirkuk fell, he intended to be there, taking back his old house, his old neighborhood, and probably the rest of the city, walking on the heads of Ba'athists all the way.

Rostam stepped down off the roof and announced that the Iraqi troops appeared to be pulling back in a ring around Kirkuk. A few hundred pesh merga would be sent to inspect the Iraqi trenches. Everyone looked at Rostam, waiting for the battle cry that would start a mad rush to Kirkuk. As if on cue, a convoy of Toyota 4Runners drove down the main road by the police station and quickly turned around; the Americans had taken a wrong turn in Chamchamal on their way to meet with the PUK leadership. Mam Rostam disappeared and didn't give any further statements that day. Thousands of Kirkukees in the camps around Chamchamal wrapped up their paltry possessions and arranged for a car, donkey, or long walk back to their city.

Still, the Americans forbade any attack on Kirkuk and everyone knew why. In the three months before the war, I don't think I once heard a Kirkukee say the word *nawt*—oil. Neither did the more discreet Kurdish politicians ever mention the oil pumping out of Kirkuk that could have turned their tiny landlocked enclave into another Middle East petrokingdom. They didn't have to say it, because the Turks said it for them. Ankara had been telling Washington its nightmare scenario for years: the Kurds take Kirkuk, use the oil revenues to buy an air force, and in short order start stealing swaths of southeastern Turkey.

The Turkish paranoia had some truthful foundation. The oil factor in the Kurdish claim to Kirkuk was conspicuous in its absence—the Kurds never talked about their right to Kirkuk's oil fields; they only spoke of history and geography. Similarly, the Kurdish claim to several towns arcing northwest around the city of Mosul didn't mention the economic interests. As it stood, Kurdistan had only a tiny bit of borderline shared with Syria, and the key pipelines from Iraqi refineries skirted south of Kurdish territory. For the Kurdish state to be viable, the Kurds needed to redraw some lines.

Those western cities of Sinjar and Tal Afar were the preoccupation of Masoud Barzani's KDP. Barzani had no less interest in Kirkuk, but as the American war carried on, his forces also stayed clear. The parties made a show of unity, forming a joint military command, with all action to be authorized by the Americans. Talabani's PUK would command all Kurdish forces in the theater of Kirkuk, and the KDP would supervise all pesh merga fighting in and around Mosul. Geographically the KDP was just as close to Kirkuk's oil fields as the PUK, but Talabani's men had a stronger base inside the city. Mosul's several hundred thousand Kurds leaned more toward the KDP, but the city, Iraq's third largest, wasn't a place the Kurds felt they could own—it was the Sunni Arab heartland.

Astride the Tigris River, Mosul is the pride of Iraq's military. Since the creation of the country, the Sunni officer corps of the national army has always hailed from Mosul, a tradition that even Saddam had to accept. Sunni Arabs dominate the western half of the city, which Iraqis refer to as the "right bank." The smaller "left bank" of the Tigris is heavily Kurdish, as are many surrounding towns like Makluob, Makhmur, and Debaga. Even if they didn't think they should absorb the city, as they did with Kirkuk, the Kurds felt they should be there to help liberate Mosul—especially those who had family connections there.

"Mosul is my town, so I'm going there. I have a house there, land in the downtown. Whoever tells you, 'Don't go,' I'm going," Hoshyar Zebari explained in his office at the KDP's Salahudin headquarters. The Zebari clan came from farther north, but the KDP chancellor had spent his youth in the city, and Zebari spoke nostalgically about Mosul's green riverbanks. Then he snapped out of it.

"This has to be done in an organized way," he said. "People already are edgy. Some of the inhabitants of Makluob—they are dying to go. They say this is the moment. We say no, don't go."

It was the first week of April, and "edgy" didn't come close. The U.S. Special Forces Second Battalion, along with thousands of KDP pesh merga under the command of General Babakir Zebari, had skirmished with the Iraqi army along the Great Zab River midway between Mosul and Erbil for a grueling seven days. Iraqi tanks and artillery clung to a high ridge just beyond a key bridge at the town of Kalak. Forces also laid siege to Debaga, on the highway between Mosul and Kirkuk. The pesh merga fired their antiquated artillery to little effect; even the American bombers seemed only to brush the Iraqis back temporarily.

Who had pinned down whom remained unclear. The Iraqis held the high ground for the week, but according to the Kurds, the Arab soldiers kept fighting only because Ba'athist officers were shooting deserters. The Americans—again numbering only about a hundred—began blowing up tanks with their fancy new shoulder-fired "javelin" missiles, but they needed a hundred times more troops before they could think about controlling Mosul. General Babakir would have delighted in providing those numbers, but the Turks had made it clear to Washington that Mosul, just like Kirkuk, was a red line, and Turkey would consider it a military provocation should the Kurds take either city. The White House had even signed off on a rule limiting the number of pesh merga in any given attack to 150, which the Special Forces on the ground mostly ignored.[2] Yet Hoshyar Zebari believed that the northern front, hollow as it was, had succeeded. Saddam devoted nearly half his regular army to protect against an American invasion through Turkey that never came, Zebari said.

"The Fifth Corps, the First Corps, and half of the Second are all tied down," said Zebari. "And the regular divisions have really fought very hard. The Republican Guard has melted away—he put them around Baghdad like sitting ducks, to be pounded day and night."

Zebari may have overstated the importance of the north—in fact Baghdad had moved the elite Republican Guard south after realizing that there was no major American assault coming through Turkey.[3] Still, the Iraqi regular army units in the north were giving a real fight over the key entry points to the city of Mosul. The lightly armed pesh merga and American Special Forces had engaged Iraqi tanks all week, and not without cost. On the morning of April 6, Masoud Barzani's brother Waji had taken a caravan of high-ranking pesh merga and a BBC team to see the frontline near Debaga, acting on false news that the city had fallen. They stopped a safe distance back, at a crossroads next to an Iraqi tank the Special Forces had rocketed earlier. The Kurdish troops poured out of their trucks to watch as an American F-14 thundered toward their enemies on the ridge. They could not have known that the pilot had instructions to hit a large mass of troops and trucks, standing next to a tank, at a crossroads. From thousands of feet above, he planted his bomb squarely in the middle of the Kurds.[4]

Red hot blades of shrapnel flew out for a quarter mile, killing a dozen of the pesh merga instantly and inexplicably sparing others who stood only meters away from the crater. Many of the vehicles burst into flames, and in the heat the Kurds' ammunition and rocket-propelled grenades started exploding, adding to the fiery mayhem. The Special Forces soldiers who had called in the strike rushed to the scene and started hauling the wounded to a low spot where they had some cover. In dispassionate but essential combat triage, the Americans left a few grievously wounded men to die, trying to save others. They might have left one Kurd with an ugly shrapnel wound to the head, but one of his comrades pointed to the crumpled man and shouted, "Barzani!" It was Waji. The soldiers quickly wrapped his wounds before the pesh merga rushed him back toward Erbil. Another American wrapped tourniquets around the severed legs of Kamran Abdulrazaq Muhamed, a young Kurd working as an interpreter with John Simpson's BBC television crew. Kamran succumbed to his wounds before he could be evacuated, making him the fourth member of the press to die in the Kurdish front of the invasion.* The U.S. military spirited Waji Barzani away to a hospital in Germany, but he never fully recovered from the brain injury. The KDP and Barzani kept remarkably quiet about the American error—Masoud toed the line of his agreement with the United States and kept his troops behind the tiny contingent of U.S. Special Forces. On April 7, the day after the "friendly fire," Debaga fell.

ON THE FATEFUL morning of April 9, Hoshyar Zebari traced out the other key cities around Mosul on a wall map in his office: Makluob to the north, then Gwer to the east, and Debaga on the road to Kirkuk. The Kurds had

---

* Casualties in the press corps were now greater than those of the U.S. military in the north. In addition to Paul Moran, the Australian cameraman, filmmaker Gaby Rado died when he fell from a hotel roof in Sulimaniya. The other was a BBC journalist I was lucky to call my friend for the last two months of his life. On April 2 Kaveh Golestan, a renowned photographer and cameraman, died when he and Jim Muir, along with Stuart Hughes and Rebeen Azad, were inadvertently directed into a minefield by a Kurdish soldier. Kaveh was a kind fellow with a great sense of humor, and he had been reporting from the front lines for decades, including during the Halabja massacre in 1988. Many young reporters in his native Iran saw Kaveh as a mentor and remember him today as they push the limits of journalism in the Islamic Republic.

Mosul surrounded and had seized the oil fields on the road from Debaga to Kirkuk. The KDP ordered civilians to wait before reclaiming their old homes and lands. To the south, only the hilltop town of Altun Kopri remained to be captured between Kirkuk and Erbil.

Zebari sat back down at his desk and turned to glance at the television news. Footage had been coming in for a few days of disorder in Basra and Um Qasr, of U.S. forces bogged down near Nasiriya and Kut. "Baghdad Bob," Iraqi information minister Muhammad Saeed al-Sahaf, had defiantly claimed to the media that no U.S. troops had entered the capital and then gloated at the scene of a destroyed American tank on the city's edge.[5] Suddenly Zebari reached over to turn up the volume—live footage was coming in from Baghdad. U.S. troops hitched up an armored tow truck to a statue of Saddam in Firdus Square, in the heart of Baghdad, and pulled it down. Zebari watched in silence and then nodded his approval.

"Wow," he said.

The Americans' strategy of demoralizing the Iraqi army had finally worked, after several rough starts. On April 5 and then again on April 8, the Third Infantry Division staged "thunder runs" into Baghdad, brazen assaults through the city's main traffic arteries designed to show that defense of the city had failed. The tactic looked daring to the point of madness, but on April 9 it paid off when U.S. Marines hauled down the statue and won the symbolic victory they had been hoping for. Baghdad fell the next day after a pitched battle around the Abu Hanifa mosque on the west bank of the Tigris.[6] Iraqis flooded the streets, but the outpouring of joy at the fall of Saddam soon took a backseat to a looting frenzy. The American military, expecting a much longer siege, had only a tiny fraction of its forces in the city, and they did nothing to stop Baghdadis from stripping down government buildings to the steel wire inside the concrete. The Americans did secure the oil ministry building, but other government institutions as well as the Baghdad Museum soon sat empty of their valuables, their furniture, and the copper wire from their electrical outlets. Even suspected WMD sites fell prey to the looters; short of shooting the civilians, the American soldiers felt they could do nothing but watch.

In the north, the Kurds took to the streets as well, and a flood of celebrants completely shut down traffic in Erbil. The sun was shining and the entire city poured out of doors, complete with marching bands, portraits of Mulla Mustafa Barzani, and Kurdish flags sporting their own yellow sun. A few soldiers from the 173rd Airborne had been passing through town and found themselves utterly immobilized by well-wishers.

"Here, a flower," said one old man, handing over a limp daisy. "You take to Mr. George Bush and Mr. Tony Blair. I love you, George Bush! I love you, Tony Blair!"

On the road to Kirkuk KDP pesh merga stood stoically at their new checkpoint—just below the Iraqi-held town of Altun Kopri. They had turned away hundreds of Kurds that morning, in keeping with their bargain with the Americans. Along the PUK border that deal began to fray.

Leadership from both parties had met almost continuously since the war began, to coordinate as well as keep an eye on each other. April 10 found them meeting at Koya, halfway between Sulimaniya and Erbil. The KDP sent General Roj Shaways; Kosrat Rasul represented the PUK. Colonel Charlie Cleveland, at that point commanding the entire U.S. contingent in the north, brought along both his battalion commanders, representing essentially the KDP and PUK sections of the Special Forces. Everyone knew the meeting would probably decide the fate of Kirkuk, and the Americans felt caught again. They didn't have the numbers to take Kirkuk or Mosul, never mind both. But the Turks had stated plainly that they would intervene if the Americans used Kurdish forces to take either city, especially oil-rich Kirkuk. Turkish military observers had insisted on coming from the north, secretly, with the Americans to police the agreement—the Special Forces called them "Canadians."

The complications might have already cost them a crucial opportunity. The day before, as the Saddam statue fell in Baghdad, the Americans had watched Kirkuk by satellite and seen a large convoy fleeing to the south. Without any confirmation on the ground they held their fire, but the Pentagon suspected it was Kirkuk's Ba'athist leadership evacuating. Inside the city Ramadan Rashid could have easily confirmed their suspicions.

"By the time we came out into the streets on April 9, there were not many left," said Rashid. He convened a meeting of the six top resistance leaders, and they decided it was time to come out in the open. The next morning, when the resistance put its plan into action, they found no enemies left in town to oppose them. Rashid sent his men out to protect important public buildings, but discovered he was also too late for that.

"We realized that the looters were much better organized. We didn't have enough power to secure these sites, and unfortunately the Americans didn't help us," he said. Many in Kirkuk had hidden televisions that could pick up the Kurdish channels from the north; they had seen footage of Americans allowing the chaos in Baghdad. Some even concluded that the United States wanted the looting to happen. "At the time the Americans had so much influence," Rashid recalled. "If there had been one American soldier in front of each building, no one would have looted."

The PUK forces had tried everything they could to get into Kirkuk, with Mam Rostam's pesh merga lining up at the border on racing blocks. Bafel Talabani, still high from his first combat experience alongside the Americans, even tried the ridiculous scheme of calling up the Americans on his satellite phone, pretending to be a U.S. unit on the edge of the city, and shouting in a poor American accent that it was time to go in. But when Rashid made contact with the PUK to tell them the looting had begun and a power vacuum was consuming Kirkuk, Talabani couldn't wait any longer. He called U.S. General Pete Osman and told him Kirkuk was now a humanitarian issue and he needed to send in the pesh merga.[7] About two thousand men, led by Mam Rostam and Omar Fattah, crossed the front lines, and the levy burst.[8] Thousands more Kurdish soldiers, refugees, and freelance looters inundated the city. The Kurdish troops at the PUK checkpoints had neither the means nor the will to hold them back. They would later claim that the pesh merga and Special Forces had intended only to tighten circles around Kirkuk but encountered such little resistance that they accidentally liberated the city.

The green line separating Kurdistan from Iraq vanished in the morning sunlight. Journalists' cars had been decked out with big "TV" symbols painted on the side in a language we hoped would be universally understood. Expecting a long war and shortages, we had packed our SUVs with canned goods, sleeping bags, flashlights, and extra car batteries with DC converters for our equipment, with jerricans full of gasoline tied precariously to the roof. Almost all the preparations turned out to be unnecessary.

Looking for the next Kurdish checkpoint, I suddenly found myself inside the town of Altun Kopri, which had fallen peacefully hours before. Any doubts fell away at the sight of a ruddy-faced U.S. soldier thronged by Kurdish children. The Special Forces had changed out of their pesh merga costumes and shaved off their mustaches—they no longer wanted to blend but instead to be recognized as part of the invading American army. I assumed the soldier was Special Forces, but he had no markings other than the American flag hanging off his mud-smeared jeep.

"It's good to be here," he said with a sigh. "I've been working with the Kurds. They love us; we love them. I think everybody's happy that it's over with," he said. I couldn't tell if he was giving me the party line or his own opinion, but then he went much further. "[Operation] Provide Comfort when we came in after the Gulf War really paved the way. The whole north of this country was Kurdish at one time, and Kirkuk too. And then Saddam did his ethnic cleansing. And this is a Kurdish town," he said, pointing to the kids from Altun Kopri who had swarmed around him.

The American said he had started to pick up some of the Kurdish language, but he wouldn't say when he had arrived. Perhaps he was part of the CIA contingent; he seemed to have gone a bit more native than even the Special Forces soldiers I had met. Some of the locals started singing and ululating for him.

"We're going to get this all the way to Baghdad," he said, and then drove away.

The Iraqi army had abandoned the military barracks at Altun Kopri and several truckloads of surrendering soldiers called out to the foreigners they saw. The Arabs—most of them from cities in the south—said they had been restricted to the base for fifty days and had heard occasional bits of news from hidden radios. They were a ragged bunch, with worn civilian clothes, packed into the beds of cattle trucks. They claimed not to be afraid of being taken into Kurdish custody.

"We've been waiting since the first day in the war," said an officer from Baquba, just an hour south of Kirkuk. "We're not afraid. We and the Kurdish people are the same: we are Muslims; we are brothers. Justice was done today."

A hint of doubt, or perhaps hope, trailed off in his voice as the transport powered up to leave. The Red Cross already had several hundred Iraqi soldiers under observation in tents north of Erbil. The Kurds weren't even calling them prisoners, insisting on the term "guests." But the civilians in Kirkuk were not as tranquil as the surrendering soldiers.

My first sight of the city Kurds describe as their Jerusalem was the smoke coming from a gas flare in the oil fields. The second was a Kurdish woman carrying a freshly looted porcelain sink out of a Pepsi bottling plant as men, women, and children ran into the gates of the building and stole everything they could carry—desks, tables, chairs, and case upon case of empty Pepsi bottles. Seeing a foreigner, some of the looters—all Kurds—paused to tell me what I would be hearing all day, often in broken English.

"I love you, George Bush! Bush! Tony Blair! Thank you very much! Kurdistan! Kurdistan!" shouted a Kurd who gave his name as "Ali." Ali said he had seen pesh merga inside the city in the early morning and knew the Ba'athists' reign had ended. "Today we are born again!" he said. "But we're afraid that U.S. make with us another 1991! The Iraqi helicopters and airplanes bomb us and U.S. do nothing."

The entire neighborhood had been built for Arab employees of the bottling plant in the 1980s, pushing the Kurdish residents into a ghetto alongside.[9] Ali said he hadn't seen any of the Arabs around that day; they must have fled. A man came out of the plant with a canvas portrait of Saddam Hussein, which he tore into strips. No one paused for too long—they would have missed the best looting.

Across town on the eastern bank of the river, the Arab neighborhood of Askari was as quiet as a funeral, but I could still hear the crashing sounds of looting and the occasional gunshot from a few blocks away, where Kurds busily ransacked the local high school. Some of the better houses in Askari had belonged to military officers, but they were long gone. The people remaining here were Shi'ites—what the locals called "10,000s." In the mid-eighties Saddam started paying poor Arabs from the southern slums to come north, promising them housing and even a 10,000-dinar stipend, which was more than 30,000 U.S. dollars at the time. Most knew that Kurds and Turcomans had been pushed out of the houses, but it was an offer they couldn't refuse.

Just such a family of Shi'ites in Askari invited me into their living room. They offered me tea, but I declined, knowing they probably had no running water or even tea bags to spare. Suddenly it was Saddam's Iraq again, with everyone in the room clearly petrified to speak with me. I asked what they were so afraid of.

"La, la," everyone answered—no, they had no fear. There was no difference between Kurds and Arabs, all brothers. Then cautiously one young man said, "We are not afraid. But it would be better if the Americans were here."

An older man erupted over the denials: "Yes, we are all afraid! Why not say it? They're looting the high school—the Kurds. We have children in that school. Do you accept this? We need a government here! There is no government."

Gunshots punctuated his comments from not far away. I asked what they thought would happen now. "It's best if *you* stay," an older woman dressed in a black abaya responded. "We'd like you to stay here."

In front of Kirkuk's city hall, a group of Kurds assaulted a twenty-foot statue of Saddam with a sledgehammer, tying ropes around the statue's neck so they could climb up and bust its head in. In a repeat performance of the previous day's celebration in Baghdad, the Kurds toppled the dictator—but they did it without American soldiers' help. They did spray-paint "USA" all over the pedestal and into the statue's eyes, and someone bashed a hole between Saddam's legs. Shots rang out in the distance, but no one paused, confident that they had been fired in celebration. Then the crowd turned to see a long convoy of white Land Cruisers swing around the traffic circle heading to the mayor's office—the PUK had come to town.

The leaders still sitting around the table at Koya had intended to design the best course for entering Kirkuk, with small numbers of Kurds from each side, Special Forces, and perhaps even paratroopers from the 173rd. But news that PUK pesh merga had entered the city unopposed made the planning moot. Kosrat Rasul and his men started to cheer and celebrate: Kirkuk had been liberated—this time, they hoped, for good. The Americans at the table watched in frustration as the PUK gloated, and the KDP's Roj Shaways flew into a rage, stood up, and stormed out. Colonel Bob Waltemeyer, the commander of the Special Forces battalion working with the KDP, followed suit, angry for his own reasons. If the PUK had taken Kirkuk, he feared the KDP soldiers helping him hold down the Mosul front might abandon their posts and make a rush for the oil-rich city as well.[10] No one knew how the Turks would react to the coalition breaking its biggest promise: that the Kurds wouldn't take Kirkuk.

Not one to let a few ruffled feathers interfere with his celebration, Kosrat Rasul grabbed a bunch of his old comrades and sped to Chamchamal, where they joined up with Barham Salih, also steaming toward the city of Kirkuk. As they entered the city, they made a phone call to Washington—they just wanted to wake an old friend. Dr. Najmaldin Karim, up early to perform surgery, answered his cell phone to discover that his hometown had finally been liberated.

When I saw Dr. Barham walking toward city hall, I didn't even think to ask him a question. Three years earlier I had met him, a dissident in his

Washington, D.C., office, and he now stood in Kirkuk. The war must be over. I and most of my friends had survived and the Kurds hadn't been victims of another chemical genocide. He smiled, and I gave him a big American hug.

Inside city hall, the PUK leadership toured a shattered facility—windows were broken, toilets fouled. At some point the electricity for Kirkuk had been cut. Citizens had no running water for several days before the city fell, and the sewers were backing up. Several PUK senior officials took over the mayor's outer office, a long room lined with couches. They said they were almost positive that the pesh merga invasion of Kirkuk had been done with American approval, but no Americans were to be seen.

Kurds began flowing into the city from the north, and all movable assets started flowing out. On the road to Erbil, a Kurd mounted on a thirty-foot-long yellow road-grading tractor bounced in the seat as he rumbled by KDP soldiers at a checkpoint, and he grinned in disbelief when they didn't stop him. By afternoon of the second day policemen from Sulimaniya came to town and started to confiscate stolen goods—at one rotary a traffic cop stood directing cars next to a dozen bags of grain he had taken from the looters.

One group was ready to play politics from the moment Saddam's statue fell. Just up the street from the fallen statue several storefronts had decorated their windows with the blue flags of the Iraqi Turcoman Front. A large group of Turcomans drove a pickup into the square that evening—next to the hotel where many journalists had taken rooms. In the bed of the truck was a boy whose skull had been crushed. The crowd told anyone who would listen that the pesh merga had killed the boy while attacking an ITF base. They broke into chants of "Atatürk!" and alleged that the Kurds were evicting Turcomans all over the city. Asked if they had brought their concerns to the Americans, they said they had no idea where to find them.

Soldiers from the 173rd also arrived in Kirkuk on April 10, but just like the U.S. troops in Baghdad, they only protected one facility: the Kirkuk oil fields. A few Americans had pulled razor wire across the entrance gates of the Northern Oil Company. A sergeant stood watch at the gate, his surname, "Hope," printed on the breast of his uniform. The paratroopers looked barely old enough to shave, compared with the weathered Special Forces the Kurds had seen around the north. Late in the day a gray-haired Kurd rushed up to the gate flailing his arms at Sergeant Hope, motioning at one of the buildings down the street. Smoke billowed out of the windows and flames began to flicker out the sides.

"Naw, we don't have a fire truck," he said, almost chuckling, and then, embarrassed, he tried to explain to the Kurd that he couldn't help. "If we had the resources to put out fires, we'd put out the fire."

Even if the Americans couldn't secure Kirkuk, they didn't want the PUK to do it. On the afternoon of April 11, Jalal Talabani arrived and tried to conduct a sort of town meeting at city hall. The building wasn't quite secure yet, and one young American soldier, looking scared and confused, stood outside the door of the conference room as the crowd pressed to get in. When Kosrat Rasul and his translator tried to get into the meeting, the soldier had no idea who he was but was finally convinced to squeeze the men past. By the end of the day, the Americans had convinced Talabani's pesh merga to leave the city as soon as GIs relieved them in place. Many did go, though a large number simply took off their uniform and stayed. The Americans found it much easier to accept Talabani's policemen than his soldiers. The residents of Kirkuk—Kurd, Arab, and Turcoman alike—started a backlash against the looting as well—as I discovered while trying to leave the city that day.

I was writing my day's dispatch on a laptop computer while being driven out of the city, sitting in the backseat of an SUV, a Thuraya satellite phone sticking out the window with its earpiece trailing back inside. The car stopped abruptly. Staring in my open window was a Kurdish Kirkukee with a sort of machete in his hand. An angry mob surrounded the car, armed with cleavers, sticks, and pipes. I glanced quickly around the vehicle, with its mess of blankets, provisions, and bags scattered in such disorder that they might have been freshly looted and thrown in the back. To my relief, Hamid Agha, the driver I had been working with for three months, convinced the mob that I was just a journalist, not a thief. They let us pass.

IT ONLY TOOK a look north to Mosul to conclude that Talabani's breaking of the deal regarding Kirkuk was for the best. The KDP pesh merga under General Babakir had been making forays into Mosul as early as April 9, but after Saddam's statues fell in Baghdad and then Kirkuk, nothing could hold them back. Colonel Waltemeyer raced headlong from the tempestuous meeting at Koya into an even bigger mess. The Iraqi Fifth Corps wanted to negotiate surrender, but the Kurds were already flowing past their lines into the city. Waltemeyer met with regional factions and invited them to enter the city with him, but no one came to his aid. With only a few dozen soldiers, Waltemeyer felt no other option but to go with the KDP into Mosul; but no hero's welcome awaited in the Arab city.[11]

While Kirkuk fell with only a handful of casualties, street fighting killed a dozen of Babakir's pesh merga before they even reached the center of Mosul.[12] No one there blessed, hugged, or thanked U.S. troops, and snipers started shooting at the American flags on their Humvees, probably from the irregular Saddam Fedayeen forces who had proven a hinderance to the Americans in the south. With Mosul as the heartland of Iraq's Sunni Arab military elite, its residents' animosity came partly from a loyalty to the Ba'ath Party and equally from a fear of the probable rise of the Shi'ites and Kurds after the regime's fall. Despite reinforcement by some marines flown into the north from the Mediterranean, Waltemeyer and his soldiers hung on in the city center for only a few days. Simply arriving at city hall wasn't enough in Mosul; the Iraqis wanted to know who would be in charge and what was coming next. Waltemeyer and the marines didn't really have an answer, but they thought it might be a good idea to present an Iraqi face to the crowd gathering around them. On April 14 they allowed a member of the Jibour tribe to address the crowd from the steps of city hall, hoping to calm things down. Unfortunately they picked the wrong Iraqi: Mishan al-Jibouri, a recently returned exile with a long and shady reputation. When they saw al-Jibouri looking like he was about to crown himself mayor with American backing, the mob rioted and burned several cars, and suddenly the Americans seemed to be caught in the city they meant to conquer.

The situation in Mosul teetered on the edge, as shots were exchanged between the Americans holed up in city hall and the increasingly emboldened crowd. The marines killed seven Iraqis whom they saw rushing the gate, and shortly afterward American fighter planes flew low over the city trying to spook the mob. It worked, but it was hardly a lasting solution. Waltemeyer held on one more night and then made a fighting retreat to the main airport, where his small contingent camped out for a week, awaiting reinforcements. Still concerned about how the Turks would react, he didn't want to ask for help from the Kurdish troops. The pesh merga left Mosul, but on their own terms—they looted the Iraqi Fifth Corps' base, taking munitions and every usable piece of artillery they could carry in their trucks. In a move that may have seemed like pure vandalism at the time, but later proved sensible, the Kurds detonated the Fifth Corps ammunition dump when they left, leaving less matériel to fall into the hands of insurgents. The base echoed with explosions and burned for days after the KDP troops pulled back outside the city limits. Finally, on April 22, the 101st Airborne and General David Petraeus arrived. Petraeus and his troops had been clearing up the rear of the American force in the south, around the Shi'ite cities of Karbala and Najaf, and they had little knowedge of the north, as the Kurds would later complain.

I DROVE BACK into Kirkuk on April 12, its third day of freedom from Ba'athist rule, past the still-smoking supermarket, the crowded hospital, and the Kurdish checkpoints now adorned with towers of loot, confiscated from Kurds who hadn't done their pillaging early enough. I wanted to visit the Kurdish neighborhood of Shorja, or whatever had been built on its remains after Ali Hassan al-Majid ordered it destroyed in 1991. On the way across the bridge in the southeastern quadrant of the city, we picked up a hitchhiker—Mustafa Fattah Mushir, a forty-eight-year-old man in a ragged gray coat, was walking along the side of the highway.

"I've been wandering the city like I was drunk since yesterday," he said. Mushir had walked to Kirkuk from his refugee camp near Chamchamal, looking for his old house in Shorja. I gave him a ride for the last mile. At the sight of an empty lot the size of a stadium, he asked Hamid Agha to stop the car. Mushir oriented himself by looking up at a nearby water tower and the apartment buildings across the road. Then he paced out a line into the empty dirt and turned around.

"This is my house," he said, drawing imaginary walls and a garden gate with his hand. "Three rooms from the side and one room there. This is where our house was."

Mushir told a now-familiar story of fleeing Kirkuk in 1991. He had never been a pesh merga, but half a dozen of his cousins had fought in rebellions going back to the 1970s. When the 1991 uprising failed, the Iraq army entered his neighborhood, killing Kurds at random.[13] Mushir and his family fled with only the clothes they wore and watched as the Arabs across the street looted their furniture. In the past twelve years he had worked when he could as a construction laborer in Sulimaniya, where he lived in a tent with his wife and three children. Mushir heard the rumors that the neighborhood had been flattened, but he hadn't seen it until now. The combination of joy at returning and grief at seeing the empty lot seemed to paralyze Mushir, and he stuttered answers to questions.

"My children told me they also wanted to see our house, but you see I am also sad here; they would also be sad. If I don't bring them, it's better," he said, but then contradicted himself. "I tell you, though, if you let me put a little tent on this empty land, I would be happy."

Mushir said Jalal Talabani had ordered returning Kirkukees not to use violence to take back their homes. Anyhow, Mushir just wanted the cycle to end. "If I kill him, maybe his children are going to kill my children, and it's going to be a big problem." He couldn't help glancing across the road to the apartment buildings, still standing next to the ghost of his house. A few kids were milling about the entryway to the apartment block. I could feel eyes watching us from behind the curtains and walked toward their door.

They were waiting for me inside, where the family of eight Arabs all began talking at once. On the wall hung a stylized picture of Imam Hussein, one of the founding martyrs of Shi'ite Islam. Next to it hung a black-and-white portrait of a young man, the kind seen all over Iraq of a family member killed in one war or another. Without asking who I was, the family unloaded a litany of complaints.

"Maku karabah! Mai maku! Maku aman"—there's no electricity; there's no water; there's no security. It would be the first phrase in nearly every conversation I had for the next three years. After decades under Saddam, the prospect of speaking to a foreigner was no less terrifying. In the past, the mandatory script was to complain about conditions because of American sanctions and to never criticize the government. Now confusion seized them—should they tell me the truth or try to figure out what I wanted to hear? Perhaps I could help them, but just as easily I might report them to the new boss, whoever that was going to be.

The family made no brave front—they were too scared to give me their names. When I asked what frightened them, they immediately answered, "Pesh merga," and a woman with a babe in her arms made a "Ta! Ta! Ta!" shooting noise, holding the baby like a machine gun. They had their own displacement story to tell. They were Baghdadis, from the poor Shi'ite slum of Thawra.

"There was a dictator in Baghdad, and he told us go to Kirkuk and then brought Tikritis to stay in our homes," said the woman, speaking over her husband, who was telling the same story simultaneously. "We came here in 1990, only because they gave us a new home and money. They said we could stay here twenty years. But these were new buildings, not Kurdish homes." She rushed into the next explanation: "In 1991 the Kurds came and took everything from us. They killed all the Arabs. When we returned to the house, there was nothing but the floor."

I asked if the Kurds killed anyone she knew, and her brother spoke up. "They killed only the Ba'athists," he said, but then he pointed to the photograph on the wall. "When we came back, he was gone. We don't know if he is dead." They had looked for their youngest brother, even going to the prisons when Saddam announced an amnesty, but there was no sign of him. I asked them if they saw what happened to the neighbors across the street.

"Yes," said the older man. "They killed a lot of people. Ali Hassan Majid exploded their houses with dynamite. We were friends with the Kurds there." He went on, "Ali Hassan Majid and the regime planted the hate between us. They made us afraid of the Kurds and the Kurdish people afraid of us. We are still afraid, and we don't know what will happen to us."

He said he trusted Barzani more than Talabani, because Masoud Barzani was the leader of a tribe and knew how to deal with other tribes. Cautiously, I asked if they would like to see the Kurds from Shorja again, but they had already noticed Mushir, pacing outside on his empty land. They came out and greeted their old neighbor, looking at each other like survivors of a head-on collision, neither one sure who was at fault.

Almost everyone that day claimed to have a title to their land, their house, their empty lot. As the sun sank low, I went looking for the land records at the central courthouse, a low, unguarded concrete building, back across the river in the center of town. Following a path of crumbled glass, I walked through the lobby and up to the second floor. Looters had removed all the furniture, apparently by throwing some of it out the upstairs windows. I could smell smoke somewhere in the building and braced myself to the idea of finding Kirkuk's official memory destroyed. Entering the main office, I could see a pile of trash burning in the corner. The record office door was closed.

Inside was a registry of citizens, with pictures and nationalities marked. Moishe Georgis Hann, a Christian Assyrian name for sure, marked as an Arab. Salahdin Mahmoud—probably Kurdish—marked as Arab. Among a few dozen files—mostly Kurdish and Turcoman names— only one was not marked as Arab.

At that moment, Moharam Mahmoud, a Kurdish clerk for the record office, came walking up the stairs. The records of landownership, he said, were safe. He and his coworkers had hidden them away before the looting, along with the office's air-conditioning units. All the evidence of who owned what, of who had been evicted, of what house had been granted to newcomers—nothing was lost.

"Why did they always keep records?" I asked, incredulous that Saddam's people would have kept such careful track of their own crimes. Mahmoud said that for a while the Ba'athists were too confident, never believing they needed to fear anyone's judgment of their actions. In the final days, he said, orders came down to destroy the records, but some of the lawyers in the office had banded together to protect them. By that time it was the Ba'athists who were afraid.

But why make a record in the first place, I wanted to know, if it would so clearly incriminate you later?

"They never thought they were leaving," he said and paused. "They thought they were gods."

CHAPTER TEN

The Believers

THE WAR TO TOPPLE SADDAM HUSSEIN, the greatest killer of Kurds in modern times, lasted twenty-two days. The fear of a last gasp of chemical revenge lifted—in fact the Kurds' side of the war cost them only dozens of casualties, was finished in two short weeks, and hardly touched Kurdish soil. They had partnered with the greatest army in the world, which had come to stay. The enemy within Iraq fled his palaces to hide in shacks and tunnels. The enemies without trembled at the proximity of the U.S. Army—Syria and Iran wondered which of them would be the next target on George Bush's crusade to remake the Gulf. To the north, Turkey had so alienated Washington that the two NATO allies seemed more like cold war enemies, with almost no communication between the American soldiers on the ground and the Turkish troops massed on the border. Ankara seethed with its two bad options: either pretend to support the U.S. program, which the Turks believed would end up creating a Kurdish state on their border, or challenge the superpower they had already perturbed by denying them access during the war. At that moment, Iraq's Kurds can be forgiven for believing that their history of struggle had ended in victory.

The fall of Saddam opened a thousand doors to the south. For some it promised a return home, to see relatives left behind the green line, to reclaim land and livelihoods. For others it unlocked the vault of the disappeared. As the Iraqi army drained away, many soldiers simply dumping their uniforms and going home, civilians all over Iraq converged on empty spots in the desert and began to dig—with bulldozers, with shovels, many with their bare hands—in the hope of finding a scrap of recognizable clothing or hair that might let their spirits rest, and confirm that their sons or brothers were not rotting in jail but had ended their suffering long ago. Rumors flew about the locations of the communal graves, many of them open secrets to villagers who had pretended not to hear the gunshots and earth-moving machines one night so many years ago.

For the Kurds, the secret graves were a wound on their national psyche that might finally close. Muhammad Ihsan, the Kurd from Zakho who had helped with the CIA's attempted military coup in 1996, had since been appointed by the KDP as minister for human rights. Ihsan started with the first few grave sites that became accessible in the north, but soon after the regime fell, he took a small team to Baghdad with one mission burning in his mind. Posing as a reporter, Ihsan started looking up some of Saddam's old secret policemen, names he knew from his time with the CIA, hoping that these orphans of the regime would be willing to tell him the location of Saddam's first mass grave. Twenty years before his downfall, Saddam had crossed a line and never looked back when he marched some eight thousand men from the Barzani clan through Baghdad to their doom. Ihsan suspected the bodies to be somewhere in the western desert. For him and thousands more, the new Iraq meant recovering their memory, their history, and perhaps finding some justice.

Others raced to Baghdad looking forward. Hussein Sinjari, the flamboyant former aide to Jalal Talabani, had his democracy institute primed to go, and he began publishing an English-language weekly newspaper. The first issue of *Iraq Today* was dated April 9, the day Saddam's statue fell, and Sinjari moved his Arabic paper *al-Ahali* (the people) to Baghdad as well. Still clean-shaven and wearing his French cuffs and wire-rimmed glasses, Sinjari had never quite fit as a mountain rebel or in drab, conservative Erbil. Baghdad meant finally laying claim to a cosmopolitan city as his own capital. It didn't matter that the city's bookstores, universities, and cafés had decayed in the past twenty years—Sinjari felt Baghdad would soon see the birth of a new intelligentsia, and he aimed to be a founding member. Months before the invasion he had dared to publish a poll in the north indicating that most Kurds preferred the United Nations or America to administer postwar Iraq, instead of their old familiar Kurdish leadership.

Now Sinjari's press could be the same critical voice for all Iraqis in their ancient capital.

Members of that leadership numbered among the most fervent believers in the new Iraq, none more than Kurdistan's two ambassadors, Hoshyar Zebari and Barham Salih. Zebari, his number in every news producer's cell phone, hit the airwaves like a rock star on a moral crusade. He presented himself as a member of the new Iraqi political class, replacing the absurd spokesmen for Saddam's regime. In Baghdad, Salih offered his experience as a Kurdish prime minister up to whatever new government would be formed.

"We have ten years of self-governing experience," Salih said, days after his arrival in Baghdad.[1] He served tea in a yellow stone mansion on the western bank of the Tigris, a house soon to be subsumed by the American Green Zone. Even as he sized up the mammoth task before the former opposition, he couldn't stop smiling.

"There is no such thing as a Kurdish position," Salih said a little cautiously, as if struggling to include himself when he spoke about Iraqis. "It is in our interest to be in Baghdad . . . In many ways the ball is in *our* court as Iraqis, to make the case that we Iraqis should shoulder primary responsibility. Ultimately this is our country."

In the early days after the invasion, Salih's comments rang true—for the first time Kurds felt no fear from Iraq. To the rest of Iraqis, the coming American occupation brought frightening uncertainty, while to the Kurds it wore a familiar face. A few months before the war, Secretary of Defense Donald Rumsfeld had struck upon the perfect man to lead the country post-invasion: General Jay Garner, whose effort during Operation Provide Comfort in 1991 had become the Pentagon's textbook for humanitarian intervention. Even better, the operation had been done quickly, cheaply, and with air power backed by small teams of Special Forces—pure Rumsfeld doctrine.

The secretary of defense couldn't have pleased the Kurds more if he had asked them to pick. Garner was an unknown in the outside world, Washington included, but the Kurds considered him a national hero. As a cherry on top, retired Special Forces Colonel Dick Naab also signed up with Garner's team. Since leading the small American ground force at the end of Operation Provide Comfort, Naab had stayed in touch with his Kurdish friends, who made him an honorary pesh merga. The Turks loathed Naab as much as the Kurds loved him.

Alongside Garner, Zalmay Khalilzad still served as the president's special envoy. With old friends in charge of setting up the new Iraq, the
Kurds started daydreaming about all the privileges of citizenship in a real
country. No longer would they need to travel on forged passports across
informal borders. Visiting businesspeople and diplomats might be able to
come to the north on the highway from Baghdad, instead of sneaking
across the river from Syria or haggling with Turkish border police. Most
of all, there was the matter of more than one hundred billion barrels of
oil. For the first time the Kurdish region might get its fair share of the
profits from export, not to mention all the wheeling and dealing to be
done around new contracts for foreign companies. Most of the Kurdish
leadership had studied in cosmopolitan Baghdad during their youth, and
they remembered a vibrant city with restaurants serving grilled fish under
the palm trees beside the Tigris River. The capital called to them as never
before.

The Kurds didn't head for Baghdad alone. All Iraq's would-be gover-
nors converged on the capital as the desert heat mounted in the spring of
2003. As Baghdadis looted their own city, the political parties did the
same thing, but on a larger and slightly more dignified scale. Ahmed Chalabi's INC seized the Baghdad Hunting Club, a huge fairground on the
west bank of the Tigris. Shi'ite factions set up in some of the great unfin-
ished mosques around the city. Even the pretender to Iraq's throne, Sharif
Ali, and his Constitutional Monarchy party assumed a large estate next to
the Babil hotel on the east bank of the river, which had belonged to his
grandfather. Talabani and his PUK grabbed a small mansion in the up-
scale neighborhood of Mansur, where many politicians secured homes.
The KDP took over a stubby concrete hotel in east Baghdad called the
Hayat Tower.

Joyful chaos rattled through Baghdad. In some ways the lawlessness
felt like a celebration—the violence hadn't yet begun in earnest, and Iraqis
found exhilaration even in making petty traffic violations, scratching the
itch of anarchy after decades of staring at their shoes. Most of the political leaders hadn't visited their home country in twenty years or more,
though the Kurds proudly noted they had ruled their part of Iraq for a
dozen years already. That didn't carry much weight with Baghdadis, and
the sight of the pesh merga inspired fear for many Arabs, who had been
hearing about the unruly, treasonous Kurds from Saddam's propaganda
for so many years. With the best organized force, the Kurds probably

commandeered more cars, houses, and hotels than any other faction setting up in the capital, but they may also have gotten a worse rap for it because they seemed to many Arabs like a foreign force. Furthermore, the sprinkling of American soldiers in town, walking freely in the streets and stopping in shops for ice cream, offered nothing to replace the old regime. The leader of the actual foreign force hadn't reached Baghdad yet. Garner couldn't get off the ground in Kuwait.

Garner's team of retired military personnel and diplomats started cramming for their Iraq assignment in January, expecting to find the same kind of humanitarian disaster as in 1991. The name of his organization, the Office of Reconstruction and Humanitarian Assistance (quickly shortened to "ORHA"), implied that Garner intended to use the same model and quickly hand over power. But before he even left the United States, Garner stumbled into a Washington minefield. The two most important agencies of foreign policy, the Pentagon and the State Department, weren't on speaking terms, and the White House neglected to make them cooperate. As Garner tried to pull together his team, the Pentagon blacklisted two of the most impressive Iraq experts from the State Department, apparently with Vice President Cheney's backing. When Garner briefed the White House on his plans for Iraq, including using the Iraqi army to rebuild the country, the assembled principals simply nodded and let him walk out the door without a single question or criticism. Garner took it to mean they were in agreement, and he went to Iraq believing he had the full backing of the Pentagon and the White House for his plans. Before leaving he snapped another trip wire when he gave a short briefing to the press at the Pentagon March 11. Garner described his plan for a quick transfer of power with a light footprint, and he went out of his way to debunk the idea that the United States supported putting Ahmed Chalabi's INC in power. Garner didn't want America to appear as if it would be anointing the next president of Iraq, and he privately considered Chalabi nothing better than a thug.[2] His faint praise for Chalabi at the press conference may have created the crack in the Pentagon's support of Garner, a crack that would soon become a chasm.

For almost two weeks after Saddam's statue fell, Garner and his team languished in Kuwait. Garner wanted to head to Baghdad immediately, but the ground force commander, Lieutenant General David McKiernan, still had combat operations going on and didn't want the postwar teams underfoot. Eventually Garner screamed loudly enough at Centcom commander

Tommy Franks, who allowed him to fly into Baghdad with a small advance team. On April 21 Garner set up ORHA in some government buildings on the west bank of the Tigris. Like all the other factions in postwar Iraq, the Americans appropriated a bunch of real estate, which would later metastasize into the sprawling "Green Zone." Garner stayed only one night in the heat and the dust. The next morning he jumped on another plane and flew to Kurdistan.

"It was like old home week," said Colonel Dick Naab, who traveled with Garner as they landed in Erbil and then flew to Sulimaniya. Men, women, and children filled the streets everywhere he went, throwing flowers. At the university hundreds of people crowded into a hall to cheer Garner, as much for his past deeds as his current mission. Garner can be a bit plain until he gets excited, and the crowds brought out some of his natural charisma.

"What you have done here in the last twelve years is a wonderful start in self-government, and can serve as a model for the rest of Iraq," Garner said. And then he went a bit further: "I think the time has come for the Kurds. The job they've done in the north is a tribute for free men and women."[3]

Garner had come up north on a specific mission. The Kurdish leaders, apparently putting their dispute over Kirkuk to the side, had started pushing for the creation of an interim government drawn from the core group selected with Zalmay Khalilzad at the London conference. Garner wanted them to allow for some U.S. consultation first, before they publically announced a government the United States might not agree with. From the adoring crowds in Sulimaniya, Garner went to the resort at Lake Dukan to meet Barzani and Talabani. Garner told each of them how happy he was to see them well and thriving in the Kurdish safe haven. Then they got down to business.[4]

"I hear you're trying to put up a provisional government," Garner said.

The Kurds backpedaled quickly. "What we're going to do is set up the group that Zal was working with and bring them to Baghdad, so you'll have a voice for the Iraqi people," Talabani told him.

Just as they had at the Salahudin conference, the Arab members of the opposition still felt cut out by America's plan to install an American general, instead of quickly looking for an indigenous leader as they had done in Afghanistan. But the Kurds at least weren't so worried with Garner in the role. They listed the seven factions they thought he should accept in

Baghdad: their two Kurdish parties, the two main Shi'ite parties, Ayad
Allawi's Iraqi National Accord, Ahmed Chalabi's INC, and a Sunni Arab
elder statesman named Adnan Pachachi, who had been Iraq's ambassador
to the U.N. before Saddam.

Garner objected that the list was mostly exiles, with the exception of
the two Kurdish leaders—couldn't they include some Arabs from inside
the country? The two Kurdish leaders turned his question aside, pointing
to the representatives of the majority Shi'ites, Ibrahim al-Ja'fari from the
Da'wa party and Ayatollah Muhammad Bakr al-Hakim, the head of
SCIRI, who was returning from Iran. Garner also raised concerns about
Hakim, who would be coming straight from a long exile in which he cooperated closely with Tehran. But Talabani knew that Garner was a prag-
matist. He put his hand on Garner's knee, just as he had done at their first
meeting twelve years before.

"Jay, it's better to have Hakim inside the tent than outside the tent,"
said Talabani.

Garner thought it was decent advice. He told Barzani and Talabani
that he would welcome the group as an advisory council and that he
planned to make them into a provisional government as quickly as possible. Garner let the two leaders know that he intended to use the former
Iraqi army troops for some public works projects. He also elicited a
pledge from both leaders that they weren't going to push for independence, and somehow took from that the idea that the Kurds would be
open to disbanding the pesh merga. Garner asked them to send their
deputies to Baghdad for a meeting at the week's end. None of the three
had any inkling that Garner's entire mission was a sinking ship.

Garner's image in Baghdad and Washington got off to a bad start and
went downhill from there. Since his comments implicitly criticizing
Ahmed Chalabi, the Pentagon had slapped a gag order on Garner, forbidding him to hold any press conferences. It wasn't a great vote of confidence for the man the White House had sent to rebuild Iraq. Garner had
a veteran image-maker with him, James Baker's former spokesperson,
Margaret Tutweiler, but the two of them couldn't seem to get the right
message out. After Garner had arrived almost unnoticed in Baghdad, the
pictures of Kurds rejoicing to greet him in the north would have made
great publicity, showing just what the Bush administration had predicted:
Americans greeted with sweets and flowers.

"This must be what it was like to enter Paris in 1944," recalled Gordon

Rudd, an army historian on Garner's team, who was awed by the pro-American reaction of the Kurds. "It didn't occur to me until later, but the press corps wasn't with us."

It wasn't just a case of hiding his light under a bushel—in his few encounters with the press, Garner didn't shine. Circumventing Washington's gag order, Tutweiler arranged to have members of the press "ambush" Garner, so it would look like he had no choice but to give a quick interview.[5] He made his points—that Iraq was not the humanitarian tragedy everyone had feared, that Saddam hadn't torched the oil fields or gassed anyone—but did so with a bit too much enthusiasm and not enough nuance.

"We ought to be beating our chests every day!" Garner said in one of his first reported comments since arriving in country. "We ought to look in a mirror and get proud and stick out our chests and suck in our bellies and say, 'Damn, we're Americans!'"

At the end of April, Garner held a "big tent" meeting in the Baghdad convention center with more than three hundred Iraqis interested in shaping their future government. Barzani and Talabani drove south to Baghdad the same day, but they didn't make the meeting, which amounted to an irrelevant free-flowing discussion. On May 5, Garner announced the plan he had arranged up in Kurdistan, to appoint within ten days the core of a provisional new government. The following day none of it mattered. On the evening of May 6, Hoshyar Zebari made a frantic call to his old friend Colonel Dick Naab.

"Dick, what the hell's going on?" Zebari said. President Bush had just announced that Garner would be replaced by former ambassador L. Paul "Jerry" Bremer, who would be named presidential envoy to Iraq. Naab hadn't heard about it until Zebari called him. Only days earlier, Garner had been warned that the president had picked a new envoy, but not much explanation accompanied the move. The Bush team tried to make it look like part of a long-term plan, but Bremer later revealed that he had gotten the call from the White House only two weeks before he deployed to Iraq. They felt Garner wasn't taking charge, and more important, he wasn't projecting success and control to the press.

Bremer didn't look good to the Kurds. Foremost, his résumé always started with his time as chief of staff to Dr. Henry Kissinger and later an executive at Kissinger's lobbying firm. In Kurdistan he might as well have said he was Satan's scribe and foot-page. Kissinger's involvement in the betrayal of Mulla Mustafa Barzani in 1975 made him one of the greatest villains in Kurdish history. Otherwise, Bremer was an unknown, not even clearly aligned in the blood-feud between the Pentagon and the State Department. Thought he had been briefly posted to Afghanistan in the mid-1960s, Bremer had spent the vast majority of his career in European countries—or in Washington, where he had a reputation as a shrewd bureaucratic infighter. In 1986 President Reagan made him ambassador at large for counterterrorism, and Bremer visited the Middle East, but not Iraq, never mind Kurdistan. He knew roughly as much about Iraqis as they knew about him.

Garner pledged to stay on through the transition, but he had lame duck written on his forehead, and so did Zalmay Khalilzad, who had been following Iraq and meeting with opposition figures since 1991. As the Middle East advisor for the National Security Council, Khalilzad was probably the only member of the George W. Bush cabinet with even a working knowledge of Iraq, but he suddenly discovered that the White House had picked another man with his same job description and title. Bremer had objected directly to President Bush that he needed unity of command. Khalilzad departed Baghdad quietly and without official explanation.[6] The Kurds had lost two familiar faces at the very top of the American occupational authority—men who didn't always give them what they wanted, but who at least knew their history. What's more, the American soldiers in the north who had worked so closely with the pesh merga had been replaced at the end of April by strangers from the 101st Airborne Division.

That change hadn't come gently either. The small teams of Special Forces, who had fought in baggy trousers alongside the pesh merga, disappeared as soon as reinforcements arrived. A few members of the original advance team stayed a short while longer—they seemed to have gone native after being stuck in the north so long.

"We were really sad when they left," recalled Lahor Talabani, who escorted many of the "special Americans" to the airport as they were called away to Baghdad. In particular the one he called the "cave blower," from their exploits in the attack against Ansar al-Islam, gave him a somber warning.

"They said, 'It's going to go downhill from here.' It was like they'd been through all this before. The next group will be worse, and the group after that will be even worse," said Lahor. He soon understood what the cave blower meant.

"We were the only ones linked to the Americans, and the first thing the

Americans did was disarm the Kurds! The pesh had just been through two fights, side by side with the Americans, and two days later they're getting their weapons taken off them. But the pesh didn't understand that these weren't Special Forces; they said, 'Americans are Americans,'" Lahor remembered.

In and around Mosul the Americans didn't seem to distinguish between the KDP's pesh merga and lingering enemy fighters. Upon their arrival at the end of April, hundreds of troops from the 101st Airborne got into a tense standoff around several KDP checkpoints. Instead of taking up the matter with the Kurdish command, the Americans called in attack helicopters and forced the pesh merga to yield their guns.

The soldiers from the U.S. Army 101st can't be blamed for a bit of disorientation. They had just completed a feat of military logistics, flying three hundred miles from south of Baghdad, refueling in the air along the way. Their commander, Lieutenant General David Petraeus, had prepared his men for pitched battles up to Baghdad, not stabilization and policing in a multiethnic powder keg. Petraeus, with thirty years in the army and a Ph.D. from Princeton University, was accustomed to a rapidly evolving mission, but when he arrived in Mosul, he didn't even have accurate maps to work with.[7] The general requested a meeting with the KDP leadership, who happily showed him their own very special maps—and gave him an earful. Nechirvan Barzani, still officially prime minister of the KDP section of Kurdistan, couldn't believe what he heard—that America was asking him to disband the pesh merga.

"I said, you know, Iraq is not Switzerland, and our neighbors are not Germany and France," Nechirvan Barzani recalled telling Petraeus. "My pesh merga fought side by side with you and shed blood side by side with you for this liberation. So your policy is this? Whoever is hostile to you, you respect them? And whoever is your friend you don't respect them?"

Petraeus had arrived in Salahudin to find ORHA liaison Dick Naab living in the KDP's guesthouse. It was far too close a relationship for the general, even if the Kurds had been allies in the war. "It is very easy to be sitting at the guesthouse or Lake Dukan and almost become beholden to them, or certainly become very partial. There's a natural inclination because of the nature of being allies during Operation Iraqi Freedom. They're more secular, more Western; a lot of them have been educated in the West. It is very easy to develop a feeling of kinship. But you have to try to do your best to be somewhat impartial," Petraeus said.

Accordingly, Petraeus demanded that the Kurds take down their checkpoints, remove their party flags, and stop displaying maps of Kurdistan
that laid claim to Kirkuk and the areas around Mosul. The border with
Turkey at Ibrahim Khalil would also have to fly an Iraqi flag, Petraeus
said. Nechirvan went ballistic.

"I told him, 'General, if you try to go to the Ibrahim Khalil border
crossing and try to bring down the Kurdistan flag or the flag of the KDP,
the next day we will have a bigger flag in its place. If you think that creating a problem for you is difficult, I'd like you to know that it's very easy
for us to create problems for you. Just like this [he snapped his fingers] I
can create a lot of problems for you. But you are our friends.'"

Nechirvan even threatened to bring protesters into the streets of Zakho and shut down the border—the only functioning crossing in hundreds of miles. Petraeus quickly retreated into diplomatic language—the
last thing he needed was unrest in the quietest part of Iraq. He learned to
call each of the Kurdish leaders by their title within the regional government; Nechirvan was "prime minister," even though Iraq had no government. He stopped referring to the pesh merga as a militia and opened
lines of communication with both major Kurdish parties. With the KDP
so near to Mosul, Petraeus made monthly trips to consult with Masoud
Barzani, often meeting him outside cities at the scene of some of Barzani's
more famous battles.

Petraeus stands out for his knowledge of Iraq among the division commanders during the invasion, some of whom never even learned to cor-
rectly pronounce the names of the cities (or the country) they were
occupying. After his first deployment in Iraq, Petraeus returned to Baghdad to train Iraq's security forces and then spent two years stateside over-
seeing the revision of the U.S. Army's counterinsurgency manual. In 2007
he would return to lead the Bush administration's last-ditch effort to take
control of Baghdad. "If you want one Iraq, you can't side completely with
one or the other. That's difficult to understand in a winner-takes-all culture," said Petraeus, reflecting on his experience in the north.

But Iraq's culture didn't change with the arrival or departure of the
101st Airborne. Petraeus was a disaster from the Kurds' perspective; in
many ways they saw that the war was still on and thought the Americans
should be reinforcing their success, not trying to rehabilitate Ba'athists,
an enemy they had never really defeated. To the Kurdish leaders, Petraeus's attempts to co-opt Mosul's majority Sunni Arabs stank of

appeasement. On May 5, Petraeus presided over a provincial council that voted in a former Ba'athist general, Ghanim al-Basso, to be the governor of Mosul and Nineveh province. With a leathery balding pate and a gray mustache, al-Basso addressed the council wearing a dark suit and checkered tie.

"I thank all the people who have come here from afar and made me responsible for all the province," al-Basso said in front of hundreds of delegates Petraeus had summoned from across Nineveh province. "I will be a loyal soldier."[8]

The Kurds screamed that al-Basso was a loyal soldier—*to Saddam* (and indeed a year later he was removed for corruption and aiding the insurgency). But Petraeus and the Kurds were already talking past one another. The general wouldn't accept the Kurds' numerous offers to help restore order in the north and began to doubt their intelligence tips (which Petraeus says were mostly dead ends). Although the Kurdish offers to pacify Mosul seemed nothing more than expansionism to Petraeus, they were also a bid to head off anarchy and nip the insurgency in the bud. Relations strained further when the Kurds arrested several infamous Ba'athist enforcers and handed them over to the 101st, only to see the men back on the street again. That summer the PUK tracked down Saddam's fugitive vice president, Taha Yassin Ramadan, the "ten of diamonds" in the coalition's deck of playing cards depicting the fifty-five most wanted Iraqis. The PUK offered his location to the Americans several times, but apparently the 101st had more important things to do. Finally, Kosrat Rasul, now based in his native Erbil, sent his pesh merga into Mosul, where they nabbed Ramadan in the middle of the night without firing a shot.

"I was not planning to hand him over to Petraeus," said Kosrat, who felt slighted by the American. Cooler heads prevailed. "Barham Salih is a friend of mine, and a friend of Petraeus, and he asked me to hand him over,"[9] said Kosrat.

Rocky dealings with one general in the north seemed like a glitch at the time, something that would soon be sorted out with the coming of a new Iraqi government. In any case the real authority was supposed to lie with ORHA, represented in the north by the Kurds' old friend Dick Naab. But ORHA was already limping—it had been sent to Iraq without any ready cash.

"We didn't have a pot to pee in," Naab said. He watched as Petraeus used the army's discretionary funding and other creative ways to get Mosul's civil servants paid. Naab waited for money, personnel, and plans sent from ORHA in Baghdad, but the organization was lost in the desert. Then three days after his arrival in Iraq on May 12, Ambassador Bremer scrapped what few plans Garner had.

AMBASSADOR PAUL BREMER landed in Iraq with a clear mission to bring the hammer down and get the country back onto the schedule dreamed up for it back in Washington. Bremer already considered "ORHA" a dirty word. His new outfit was called the Office of the Coalition Provisional Authority, or CPA, some Americans briefly called it "OCPA" until they realized how much it sounded like "occupation." In fact that word hit the mark. Bremer saw himself more as MacArthur—unlike either the unassuming Garner or the savvy Khalilzad. From the outset he sought to put the Iraqis in their place, postponing a meeting with Jay Garner's group of seven Iraqi leaders. "I wanted to signal to the Iraqi political figures that I was not in a hurry to see them. And finally I wanted to show everybody that I, not Jay, was now in charge," Bremer wrote in his memoir.[10]

Almost instantly he displayed his ignorance of Iraqi culture, and he compounded the problem by not understanding that in such a culture, no one was going to tell him to his face just how badly he was doing. He made a trademark of his appearance—a dark suit and tie worn over desert combat boots. Many of Bremer's staff, including a younger set who fancied themselves a conservative American peace corps, adopted his dress code, even though they would rarely leave the paved streets and marble halls of what became the Green Zone. The boots said it all: Bremer either didn't know or didn't care to learn the most basic rules of Middle East etiquette, and he often showed the bottoms of his garish combat boots to visitors in his office, an extremely offensive gesture across the region. Bafel Talabani recalled sitting in on a meeting in Baghdad between Bremer and a few of the Kurdish leaders. Years later Bafel couldn't recall what the meeting pertained to—he could only remember the bottom of Bremer's boot, hitched up across his knee and gesticulating to and fro as he spoke to his distinguished guests.

"I wanted to smash him," said Bafel. "This muddy shoe in my face—I thought, 'Leave it, Bafel, leave it' . . . but, his shoe in my face! And I've been twenty years in England. What does this man do in front of an ancient tribal leader?"

On the morning of his fourth day in Iraq, Ambassador Bremer began by signing the first of two earth-shattering CPA decrees, ordering a deep purge of Ba'ath Party officials from all of Iraq's institutions. That afternoon he met with representatives from Garner's group of seven, referring to them as "the exiles"—accurate except in the case of the Kurdish leaders. He summarily canceled Garner's promise to announce an Iraqi government any time soon, blaming the group for not bringing in a broad-enough spectrum of Iraqis. Soon afterward Bremer dropped his other bombshell: on May 23 he formally abolished Iraq's armed forces.* Iraq and its various American envoys would spend the next four years recovering from and reversing Bremer's decisions. But at the time he thought he was doing fine, thanks in part to what he did next. Bremer accepted an invitation to visit Masoud Barzani in the cool of the north.

"Congratulations on formally abolishing Saddam's army. It's a wonderful thing you've done," Bremer recalled Barzani telling him in one of the Kurdish leader's signature mountainside chats.† Bremer thought he had been credited with holding Iraq together by abolishing the hated army. More likely he had crippled the Iraqi state at a crucial moment. For

---

* The CPA order to abolish the army was drafted by Walter Slocombe, a former Pentagon official in the Clinton administration, a rare Democrat on Bremer's team. Bremer also consulted with Douglas Feith on the decision, which they saw as an easy way of eliminating a huge block of Ba'athist bureaucracy, since the army was almost completely AWOL at the time. Bremer said in press conferences in Baghdad that he had simply formalized the disappearance of the Iraqi army, but even as the order came down, members of Garner's team had been negotiating with former Iraqi officers about how to bring them back as a constructive force in the new Iraq. In September of 2007 Bremer made public a letter he had sent to President Bush advising him of the decision to dismantle the army, as well as Bush's approving response.

† This conversation is recounted by Bremer in his memoir. He goes on to say that he and Barzani discussed how abolishing the army had prevented the Kurds from seceding from Iraq and causing a regional war. Bremer recounts the conversation with such a brazenly exculpatory structure that it's worth doubting. Years later when I asked Masoud Barzani if he thought Bremer had made mistakes, he demurred. I asked him instead to name the things he thought Bremer had done well, and Barzani smiled, saying only, "Now that is a difficult question."

conspiracy mongers in and outside the country, Bremer's destruction of the institutions of Sunni Iraq, and then his willingness to travel up to Kurdistan to see Barzani instead of insisting that Barzani come down to Baghdad, showed that America was hell-bent on cutting up the country. For believers in a new Iraq, it didn't bode well, but most of the KDP leadership who were hosting Bremer were hardly champions of Iraqi unity.

"Bremer wanted to show that he's tough, he's in charge—I am the one who decides; you are nothing," recalled Nechirvan Barzani. While Nechirvan found Bremer arrogant, he couldn't argue with what the ambassador had done. "With one signature, he dissolved four Iraqi establishments, all four of which loved to antagonize us. The army, the Mukhabarat, the Istikbarat, and the Ba'ath Party—the most important Iraqi institutions and cause for suffering of the Kurds."[11]

The KDP leaders had received the new American viceroy with apprehension, fearing a puppet master trained by Henry Kissinger. The reality soon put them at ease. As the KDP welcomed Bremer in a long reception hall, he looked up at the portraits on the wall of General Mulla Mustafa Barzani. He nudged Masoud Barzani, who looks an awful lot like his father, and asked, "Who's that gentleman?"[12]

Nechirvan Barzani, standing next to Bremer, felt offended but nonetheless reassured. "Our impression was not positive. But once we realized that he doesn't know anything—nothing!—then we were more comfortable with him," Nechirvan recalled with a laugh.

"General Garner's policy was very wise regarding the Iraqi situation. He didn't want to destroy the whole system. He wanted to remove the bad elements, gradually to do everything else. His heart was with the Kurds, but his sword was facing us. When Bremer came, he was arrogant, but maybe he had not realized himself how much we benefited. We had to take politics over personalities," Nechirvan observed.

Bremer announced his plans to create a larger governing council and made a good faith effort to include more of Iraq's minorities—Turcomans, Christians, women. Hardly a set of American yes-men, the twenty-five on Bremer's list even included a member of Iraq's small but resilient Communist Party. The council itself set up a strange system of rotating its presidency among the nine power members—a slightly expanded version of Garner's list of seven. With a new president each month, the council was almost guaranteed to get nothing done, but just in case, Bremer gave himself veto power over the council's actions.* Then he proposed that the council members engage in a bit of theater with the Americans, which he apparently thought would help their image. Bremer would give them a list of the CPA's plans, and then the Iraqis could pretend to demand those exact objectives from him, and for public consumption he would bow to their orders. The Iraqis knew their council was a mess, but this patronizing attitude cemented their dislike of Bremer. His plan for Iraq's constitution was similarly paternalistic. Not trusting the Iraqis to hold a constituent assembly, as had been done in Afghanistan, Bremer proposed that a system of caucuses select the national committee that would draft the constitution. The members of the caucuses would be chosen by Bremer's CPA. Bremer's plans drove his strongest detractors together almost immediately.

To Bremer's annoyance, the Barzani clan would keep themselves mostly in the north, openly disdaining trips to their nominal new capital, Baghdad. Masoud in particular told Bremer that he hated Baghdad and delighted in pointing out how much more pleasant were his Kurdish mountains. But there was one power broker Barzani was willing to make a longer drive to see.

EARLY ON JUNE 5, Hoshyar Zebari sat waiting in the lobby of the Hayat Tower hotel in Baghdad, looking no more out of place than he had in London or Salahudin, chain-smoking and sipping Arabic coffee in his brown suit. Zebari had made the lobby his court and delighted in seeing all the journalists he had cultivated over the years as they called on him in Baghdad. He also gladly explained the situation to newcomers, at the price of an occasional prank—at least once he told correspondents from a major newspaper that he was the concierge. Today he was all business, as a swarm of white Land Cruisers filled the street outside at seven A.M. The convoy paused just long enough in Baghdad, on its route from Salahudin, to pick up Zebari, a few other KDP dignitaries, and three journalists.[13] About twenty cars long, the Kurdish caravan tore south out of the city, crossing the Tigris at stunt-driver speed, scaring the taxis and private

---

* In his defense, Bremer did prominently use this veto to prevent religious parties on the council from rolling back Iraq's family law, which, on the books at least, supported women's rights better than other countries in the region.

jalopies off the road with blaring horns. Their destination was a tiny alleyway in the city of Najaf, home to Grand Ayatollah Ali al-Sistani, perhaps the most powerful man in Iraq. Sistani sat at the head of the Najaf's
marja'iya (literally, "sources of emulation")—for Shi'ites, a sort of informal Vatican. In the post-invasion power vacuum, Iraq's 60 percent majority Shi'ites were turning to Sistani for guidance, and hanging on his every
word. As the cars slowed to navigate the crowded streets inside Najaf's ancient old city, passersby and shopkeepers asked each other, "Barzani? Is it
Barzani?"

Masoud Barzani had last traveled to Najaf as an emissary of his father
in 1967, bringing a letter of thanks to the previous leader of Shi'ite Iraq,
Ayatollah Muhsin al-Hakim. When the Iraqi state began to suppress
Mulla Mustafa Barzani's rebellion in the early 1960s, Hakim had lent his
support to Barzani by issuing a fatwa against the killing of Kurdish civilians. It was a courageous move that sapped the strength of the Iraqi
army, populated with many poor Shi'ite conscripts who suddenly began
wasting ammunition by firing over the Kurds' heads. This solidarity
formed a bond between Iraq's two victimized peoples, though they were
usually separated geographically by the Sunni-dominated region in the
center of Iraq and the Sunni-controlled government in Baghdad. On
June 5, 2003, Barzani would visit Sistani and also greet Hakim's son,
Ayatollah Muhammad Bakr al-Hakim, who had just returned to Najaf
from a long exile in Iran.

At first blush the Kurdish warrior and the two Shi'ite imams didn't
have much in common. Barzani was a man of action, a Muslim but not a
preacher. He mostly wanted to secure his beloved mountain home, and
perhaps south to Kirkuk, but nowhere near so far as the desert around
Najaf. Hakim, also a resistance leader of sorts, was the spiritual guide of
the Badr Brigades, which had been trained in exile by the Iranian military.
A lean man with a long face and a bushy beard that was equal parts gray
and brown, Hakim tried to retain some of the distance from politics that
Shi'ite leaders often profess. But in that regard he would never equal the
Grand Ayatollah. Sistani truly kept to the quietist school of Shi'ism, aloof
from politics, allowing him to weigh in simply on matters of what is permissible or forbidden behavior. Born in northeastern Iran, Sistani never
accepted offers of Iraqi citizenship after decades living in a tiny house
down a quiet alley in Najaf. His reaction to Saddam Hussein's rule had
been passive and nearly pacifist—after an assassination attempt in the

early 1990s, Sistani simply stopped leaving his house. Since the American invasion, he had made only one related fatwa—a prohibition on looting, which greatly reduced the disorder in Shi'ite areas.

Barzani first paid his respects to Sistani, sitting on a simple floor mat and drinking a single cup of tea with the seventy-four-year-old cleric. "He was a respectful man, very humble. We did not talk about politics," Barzani said later. "He said we can solve all the issues in a democratic way, and he said he will bless anything that the majority of the people in Iraq agree upon. These were our guidelines. We didn't go into specific issues."

The room was too small for many of Barzani's entourage to enter, and they milled about in the narrow passage outside with an equal number of Shi'ite functionaries. They chatted in Arabic and Kurdish, many of them hoping to be let in the door to peek at the historic spectacle. Sistani never appeared on television, and most had seen his face only on the placards that sprouted up all over Shi'ite Iraq after the invasion. The meeting lasted merely half an hour, and then Barzani's group sped across town to meet with Hakim. Afterward Barzani and Hakim, along with Hakim's younger brother Abdul Aziz, answered a few questions about their meeting. Hakim mostly deferred to Barzani, and for once the reticent Kurdish leader was the most talkative man in the room.

"We are in agreement that Iraq should be governed by Iraqis," Barzani said, looking bemused. "The important thing is how to achieve that, how to move forward together."

Barzani must have wondered at his own words on the long drive back to Kurdistan. His presence in Najaf had built a bridge between Iraq's two wounded peoples, yet all they had in common was a vanquished enemy. Barzani desired only to preserve the nationalist, secular freedom in the north that had flowed from cutting ties with the rest of Iraq twelve years prior. Hakim and Sistani saw Baghdad and Iraq's holy places as finally theirs, and felt their numbers would inevitably bring about their rule—not an Iranian-style rule of mullahs, their spokesmen assured, but certainly a system based more on the Koran than any other source. As for moving forward together, the Kurd and the clerics could only agree that the north and the south would have such drastically different systems as to be virtually separate states, presided over by a weak government in the center.

Barzani considered that an excellent foundation for cooperation, and making the personal trip south was just the kind of respectful diplomacy

that would keep the Kurds and Shi'ites unified where they could agree—
as in their opposition to Bremer's control over their government and their
new constitution. A few weeks later Sistani announced another fatwa, this
time prohibiting any constitution written by outsiders. Bremer would lose
almost every fight he tried to pick with Sistani, who refused to meet with
the U.S. viceroy. When the CPA tried to bargain with Sistani over the ruling, he famously replied to Bremer in a letter, "You are an American, I am
an Iranian. Let's leave the constitution to the Iraqis." Where the Kurds
could line up with the Shi'ites, it would be hard for anyone else to stand
against them.

The Shi'ites and Kurds had one more thing in common: between them
they sat atop almost all of Iraq's proven oil reserves. For the Shi'ite Arabs
in the south it was a simple fact; the wells dotted the southern deserts and
the country's only port lay in Basra, Iraq's second largest city and the
Shi'ite economic capital. The Kurds' claim was a bit more complicated.
The 20 percent or so of Iraq's oil coming out of the north was at the crux
of Kurdistan and Iraq's biggest pressure point—Kirkuk.

THE KIRKUK POWDER keg would turn out to have a very long fuse. In the
weeks after the regime fell, members of the U.S. Army's 173rd Airborne,
led by Colonel William Mayville, did their best to bone up on the history
of the city and its competing ethnic groups, who all seemed to be girding
themselves for a showdown. Mayville, a boyish-looking forty-two-year-old
with a master's degree in aerospace engineering, had a similar demeanor to
Petraeus's, embracing the role of soldier-diplomat and not shying away
from the complexity of Kirkuk, a city full of legitimate but contradictory
claims. Mayville had enough troops, alongside all the Kurdish police who
had come to town, to hold the city together. But there were nowhere near
enough soldiers to cover hundreds of villages in the countryside, where
claims were being settled, as I discovered during a quick tour around
Kirkuk province a month after it fell.

In a long arc, from Khanaqin by the Iranian border southeast of Kirkuk
all the way north of Mosul and west to the town of Sinjar, Kurdish forces
and eager Kurdish civilians pushed into their former lands. While there was
clearly intimidation, remarkably no revenge killings or massacres were reported, perhaps because the Arab settlers, motivated by fear or a guilty conscience, pulled up stakes and fled for the main cities of Kirkuk and Mosul.

The Kurds had achieved a fact on the ground and essentially picked up their green line and moved it a few dozen miles to the south, squatting on huge areas they considered Kurdish land. In many cases, Arab families with roots in the community predating 1975 and the first wave of Arabization stayed on, undisturbed by the pesh merga, who were acting with the blessing of both the KDP and PUK. Many of the Arabs who fled to the cities complained that the Kurds wouldn't allow them to return even to collect their belongings, and others said the pesh merga beat them or arrested them when they came back. The Kurds used force in a deliberate and controlled manner, confident that nothing could stop them, and even defied the occasional intervention by U.S. forces, who clearly didn't have the manpower to enforce the orders they gave.[14] Along the highway between Kirkuk and Altun Kopri, a Kurdish farmer in a hamlet called Nabiyawa prepared to make a trip to town, where he planned to rent a combine harvester.

"This is my house. I just haven't been able to see it for twelve years," said Sabah Haji Ali, a middle-age Kurd who had been living in Erbil. He allowed that the house was much bigger than he had left it—in fact it had two tall pillars in front of the door and several new rooms. As far as Sabah cared, the additions served as minimal interest on the debt owed to him by Saddam, who had given his house to Arabs. Sabah also had a clear conscience about harvesting the winter wheat crop that stood ready in the fields like a housewarming present. He had never seen the Arabs who had lived in his house and planted the wheat; they had apparently fled on the day Saddam fell.

Next to the Kurds, the most aggrieved party in Kirkuk was the Turcomans. By most accounts Turcomans had dominated the city, if not the countryside around it, until the 1950s. Saddam Hussein's ethnic cleansing had hit them as well, especially because many were Shi'ite and had been sympathetic to Iran during the Iran-Iraq war. In some of the outlying communities, they too intended to take back their homes. On the road to Hawijah I met a large group of Turcomans in a meeting hall painted with the blue flags of the Iraqi Turcoman Front. They were egging each other on to evict the Arabs down the road in the village of Bishar, who had been awarded all the Turcoman farms and houses in the late 1980s. The Turcomans claimed to have deeds for the property going back to the British occupation of Iraq. The Arabs, they said, had appealed years ago to the vice president of Saddam's revolutionary council, Izzat al-Douri, to give them official documents to the land.

One of the Turcomans told the story with a triumphant smile: "Douri told them, 'I am your papers. When I'm gone, you have no papers.' And now Izzat al-Douri is gone!"

The Turcoman said that he intended to take back the land, but representatives from the Shi'ite Supreme Council for Islamic Revolution in Iraq (SCIRI) had appealed to him to wait. This was the far edge of the new Kurdish green line, with no U.S. troops anywhere to be seen. Bidding farewell to the Turcomans, I proceeded down the road to talk with the Arabs they meant to evict and discovered in Bishar something completely unexpected—Saddam nostalgia.

"Saddam only did bad things to people for a reason," Yasir Hassan said, sitting in a sort of meeting hall in Bishar. All the other Arab farmers nodded their assent. Yasir freely admitted that the building he was sitting in had belonged to Turcomans, but claimed they had been in league with Iran. Perhaps several weeks of hearing Iraqis joyful at Saddam's downfall had made me naïve, but I could hardly believe my ears. "We didn't like Saddam before," Hassan continued, and it suddenly seemed so obvious, "but we do now. At least then we had security."

Hassan's chief concern was not the Americans but that the Kurds or Turcomans would come and take back their houses. He admitted that the Arab farmers around Hawijah had already formed defense groups to protect themselves against marauding Kurds, whom they accused of coming south to steal cars. A few days before my visit they had fired on a convoy in the middle of the night only to discover that it was not Kurds but Americans. Hassan and his friends retreated under withering gunfire from the U.S. Army patrol. His small group wasn't alone.

On May 17 about five hundred Arab tribesmen from Hawijah marched into Kirkuk, meeting at the gates of the city, where they distributed assault rifles. They poured into the city, attacking Kurdish neighborhoods in retaliation for the raids they claimed pesh merga had been making on their farms. Kirkuk became a war zone again for about thirty-six hours, and the Arabs attacked American troops as much as they did Kurdish civilians. At least five people died and dozens more suffered bullet wounds before troops from the 173rd Airborne managed to shut down the violence. Then, despite all the dire predictions, the trouble seemed to stop. Colonel Mayville credited the creation of a multiethnic city council that gave none of the ethnic groups a majority; it was led by a Kurd with an Arab deputy and three assistants—a Turcoman, a Christian Assyrian, and another Kurd.

"The different ethnic factions are starting to be a strength now. You have powers checking powers. No one group has a majority sufficiently large, [so] they have to work with each other. That's become a strength," Mayville said on the first day the council met at the end of May.[15]

Kirkuk's political parties did seem interested in promoting a peaceful resolution, but another factor played heavily into the equation. The CPA's representatives in Kirkuk put out the word that America was opening up a property claims commission that would soon adjudicate all disputes arising from Saddam's Arabization campaign. Word spread quickly that evicted Kurds and Turcomans would be able to return to their houses soon, but the Arabs placed there by the regime would receive money to relocate. The "house-jackings," as the U.S. soldiers started calling them, came to a halt, and streams of people started lining up outside the civil affairs battalion in Kirkuk to register their complaints. But the major effect of the compensation program was unintended.

"People started mentioning the big *c*-word," said Colonel Harry Schute, a reservist who had come into Iraq with the Special Forces as part of their civil affairs team. "As soon as compensation got mentioned, people didn't have an incentive to move out."[16]

Schute rapidly became enamored with the Kurds, as many of the U.S. military working closely with them did. He was glad to start registering property claims, and no one realized until more than a year later the major flaw: the CPA never properly funded the property claims commission. It might have been a fine plan, but as with many other CPA ideas, it was set adrift. Everyone in Kirkuk dug in their heels waiting for a settlement that would never come. Colonel Mayville even negotiated a fifty-fifty split of the grain harvest that was coming in, between Kurds and Arabs. But the deal was a nightmare to enforce for soldiers trained as infantrymen, not agronomists or lawyers. What Mayville hoped was the beginning of a beautiful new friendship between the Kurds and Arabs was more like a final divorce settlement from the Kurds' perspective. Suddenly the onus was on America to sort it all out.

"We end up ticking everyone off because we hadn't made a decision," said Schute. "I think sometimes we, as Americans, are so concerned about offending someone that we end up offending everyone."

THE AMERICANS WERE not the only ones trying to influence the outcome in the city of Kirkuk. Iran had agents there, and the young thuggish Iraqi

Shi'ite cleric Moqtada al-Sadr had sent a deputy up to Kirkuk to organize Shi'ite Turcomans and Arabs against what he assumed would be the Kurdish attempt to take over the city. But the keenest interest of all came from Iraq's northern neighbor.

Turkey had several unofficial observers with the U.S. forces, but the Americans soon began to notice the link between the Turkish forces and the Iraqi Turcoman Front. The ITF quickly annoyed the Americans when it tried to monopolize all the seats allocated for Turcomans on the city council. The ITF's demands were always maximalist; according to Mayville, it claimed that 1.2 million Turcomans lived in Kirkuk when, by Mayville's best estimate, the entire city was home to only 750,000 people. The ITF often eclipsed other Turcoman groups, which didn't help the cause of regular, moderate Turcomans in Iraq when Turkish-American relations started a tailspin.

In early May, Mayville's soldiers caught a dozen Turkish Special Forces troops, disguised as aid workers, bringing weapons into Kirkuk. The subterfuge alone was enough for the Americans to conclude that the Turks were up to no good—and besides, the Americans were not in the mood to cut the Turks any slack. Some of the U.S. soldiers now in northern Iraq had packed and unpacked their bags endlessly while floating off the Turkish coast in March; many in the U.S. Army even believed that the Turkish refusal to allow a northern front had prolonged the war and cost American lives. Mayville held the Turks overnight and returned them to the border. The colonel said he thought the Turkish Special Forces had come to link up with the ITF, intending to destabilize the city and give Ankara an excuse to intervene. Such actions by an ally weren't encouraging. What happened next, however, would scar Turkish-American relations for years, and delight the Kurds.

The news arrived on July 4, as American diplomats in Ankara sipped beer and grilled burgers at the embassy's Independence Day barbecue. The Turkish foreign minister was ripping mad and needed to see the American ambassador, Robert Pearson, immediately. Out of deference to the Fourth of July, the Turks downgraded the demand to the embassy's number two, an old Iraq hand, Bob Deutsch, who rushed home from the party to change and then sped over to the foreign ministry, where they all but set his tie on fire. Why was the U.S. Army suddenly treating Turks like their worst enemy? the foreign minister wanted to know.[17]

That day in Sulimaniya soldiers from the 173rd had arrested another group of Turkish Special Forces, who were in possession of not just weapons but also explosives. The Americans had acted on intelligence that the ITF was plotting to assassinate the Kurdish head of Kirkuk's city council, but when they swept the party headquarters, they scooped up eleven more Turkish Special Forces. This time there was no polite feeding them a meal and showing them to the border. The idea that Turks would be trying to stir up trouble in Kirkuk again made the Americans on the ground livid—and it was an opportunity for a little payback. The Americans not only handcuffed the Turks; they put their heads in black sacks like al-Qa'ida suspects on their way to Guantánamo.

In Washington the Turkish ambassador, Faruk Loğoğlu, received the news with shock and anger. His job had been difficult since March; now he had no choice but to protest at the highest levels. Loğoğlu spoke with both Marc Grossman at the State Department and Paul Wolfowitz at the Pentagon about the matter, and before long Bob Deutsch was heading home from the foreign minister's office with the proverbial backside of his suit hanging in tatters. When the embassy called the military in Baghdad and Kirkuk, however, the U.S. Army didn't want to let the Turks go. Their concern about the assassination plot was real enough that even with direct pressure from high-level Bush administration officials, it took almost two days to get the Turkish soldiers released.

The Turks stuck to an official line that the Turkish Special Forces were part of the same peacekeeping unit that had been in northern Iraq for years and that their intentions were peaceful and completely known to the Americans and the PUK. Officially, this explanation was accepted by Washington, and the diplomats set about the work of apologizing to Turkey for the treatment of the soldiers. But U.S. officials watched with interest as the Turkish military conducted its own investigation, and a few months later effectively ended the careers of the senior officers involved with the Sulimaniya operation.*

"My view was that this was an admission of guilt," said Deutsch. "It was confirmation that something was going on that either wasn't authorized or they weren't going to admit was authorized."[18]

Even if it had been a rogue operation, the bagging of the Turks was a

---

* Brigadier General Abdullah Kiliçarslan and Major General Sadik Ercan were quietly put out to pasture.

diplomatic disaster, which Ankara would fume about for years. "A big mistake on the part of our American friends," said Loğoğlu, "Once you take this action, it cannot be erased, and it's a permanent scar on Turkish-American military relations."

The incident became a symbol for the Turkish public that the friendship with America was over—but interestingly, the Turks had probably been the ones who leaked the news of the hoods used on the commandos. The Turkish press trembled with righteous rage and alleged that the entire incident had been arranged and filmed by Bafel Talabani. But again, it was the Turks who eventually put the incident out on film—a Turkish feature film. *Valley of the Wolves*, a blockbuster in Turkey a few years later, wove a tale of an American conspiracy to foment a state in northern Iraq and use it as a beachhead to help the Kurds destroy Turkey.*

For the Kurds, another crash in Turkish-American relations was like winning the lottery for the second time in six months. In Washington's view, Turkish concerns now ranked right down there with keeping "evil" Iran and Syria happy. Bremer made reference to the Turks as a "colonial" power that wouldn't be welcome in Iraq, even as the Turks prepared to offer troops to help the coalition in places like Anbar province. Even lip service was too much of a bother for America: for a full year no one in the U.S. government so much as mentioned Ankara's archenemy, the PKK guerrillas living openly in the mountains of northern Iraq, even though Washington considered the PKK a terrorist organization. The Turks lost their eyes and ears on the ground in Iraq and found themselves in the humiliating position of begging briefings from the U.S. embassy in Ankara. Without lifting a finger, the Kurds had bought themselves at least a few years of protection on the northern front.

THE NEW IRAQ was not following the script set out for it by the Bush administration of sweets and flowers, reconstruction and democracy. As the

---

* The opening scene of the film featured one of the Turkish soldiers nabbed on July 4 supposedly committing suicide because of his humiliation at the hands of the Americans. The movie details the wanton slaughter of Iraqis by Americans, and for good measure, there's a subplot about a Jewish vivisectionist harvesting organs from wounded Muslims. The Turkish first lady praised the film for its accuracy, prompting protests from Washington and Jerusalem.

summer wore on, bombs methodically erased all semblance of civility. An explosion that destroyed the Jordanian embassy was marked down to resentment against Jordan's support for Saddam in 1991. A bomb at the Baghdad office of the United Nations that killed twenty-two people, including the estimable leader of the mission, Sergio Vieira de Mello, was explained as lingering resentment of the U.N.-enforced sanctions. When the next bomb hit the International Committee for the Red Cross, it was clear something more sinister was at work. Coalition spokespeople, Governing Council members, and even wounded bystanders all spoke of outside agitators trying to ruin their great country (just as many had claimed Kuwaitis had done the looting). But in all their sweeps and cordon searches, coalition forces only apprehended a handful of foreign fighters. When Saddam Hussein's two sons, Qusay and Uday, died in a spectacular shootout with troops from the 101st Airborne in the city of Mosul on July 23, the Americans hoped in vain that the bombs and the insurgency would slow down. No one, Iraqi or American, wanted to face the reality that the wave of carnage was homegrown and independent of the regime's "dead-enders." But this was dawning on the Kurds who had come to Baghdad.

Returning home one night Hussein Sinjari flagged a taxi—one of the thousands of jalopies that Baghdad residents had taken to the street in hope of making a living. Getting into a stranger's car at midnight felt fine in the first months of Baghdad's happy anarchy—though it would look suicidal only a year later. Sinjari had a Thuraya satellite phone—there were still no cell phones in central Iraq—and he got a call from an American journalist. As the driver navigated the blacked-out streets, Sinjari chatted away on the phone, keeping his head crooked so the antenna could catch a signal through the window. After a few minutes Sinjari ended the call, pushed down the phone's stubby antenna, and looked up at the driver. The man stared at Sinjari, at his fancy shirt, cuff links, and the high-tech gadget he had just put back in his sport coat.[19]

"You are Mossad," the driver said.

The urbane and worldly Baghdad of Sinjari's dreams vanished into a cold sweat creeping up his neck. He looked out the open window into the dark and realized he had no idea where the driver had taken him.

"You were talking on the phone like Jewish people talk," the driver continued.

"English? Of course not," said Sinjari, and then thinking fast, "it's because I'm a doctor. You know that all doctors speak English." This was good Iraqi logic, but the driver wasn't sold, and a pistol materialized in his hand as the motor idled in a nameless alley.

"Even your Arabic you speak with a Jewish accent," he said.

"Not at all," said Sinjari, struggling to keep his voice steady. "It's a Moslawi accent."

Using the distinct Arabic of Mosul, which is just outside his hometown, Sinjari starting babbling, peppering his speech with as many colloquialisms as he could. The driver lowered the barrel of the gun.

"I'm sorry, Doctor! You're right. You know, I have cousins up in Mosul, and they speak the same way," said the driver, now a friend and brother Arab. "And to think I was going to kill you right here! My brother is a mujahid in Fallujah, fighting the Americans," the driver offered by way of explanation.*

Sinjari begged to be let off at the next corner, insisting it was his address. When he asked about the fare, the driver told him the ride was free of charge, and instead of arguing, Sinjari walked away as quickly as he could.

"I decided to be more careful and stopped taking taxis," recalled Sinjari, who still couldn't bear to dress down. "People advised me that I look European; they said, 'What are these stupid clothes? You have to look ordinary.' But I don't like mustaches," said Sinjari. Though his newspaper, *Iraq Today*, thrived at first, Sinjari became harder to find at the Baghdad office. Before long he had moved back to Erbil.

BY CONTRAST, MUHAMMAD Ihsan, the KDP's human rights minister, went looking for trouble. Posing as a producer for Beirut's LBC news channel, Ihsan looked up a former leader of the Mukhabarat, hoping for clues about where the eight thousand Barzani tribesmen were buried. Though reprisal killings had begun against senior Ba'athists in Baghdad, Ihsan wasn't on a "Nazi-hunting" mission.

"I was expecting these people to think that the game is over and maybe we can give them a chance to try for forgiveness," said Ihsan. But instead

---

* Fallujah had already proven a flashpoint since U.S. troops fired into a crowd of protesters, killing seventeen people on April 28, before the occupation had lasted a full month. Troops from the 82nd Airborne said they were returning fire from the mob, but Human Rights Watch later disputed the claim.

he found the agent to be unrepentant and undefeated. The Mukhabarat director told him that the mass graves in Iraq held only Sunni Arabs killed by revolting Shi'ites.[20]

"Saddam made only two mistakes," the agent continued, "withdrawing from Kuwait and not finishing the job he did on the Kurds."

Ihsan couldn't believe his ears and felt his anger rise, but he didn't want to blow his cover. Besides, the man had four burly sons hanging around the house and bragged about a fifth son whom the Americans had hired to do security up in Mosul. Fuming, Ihsan ended the "interview" and left. Returning to the house with Kurdish commandos a day later, Ihsan found it empty.

Buying information proved the most effective tactic. While many important records had been seized—some by the Kurdish authorities, others by Shi'ite parties or NGOs—the U.S. Army had no mandate to guard documents. By the time the CPA set up an office on the crimes of the regime and began preparing a case against the fifty-five most wanted war criminals, tons upon tons of documents had been looted, pilfered, or intentionally destroyed. Ihsan spent thousands of dollars in Baghdad marketplaces buying up documents that might suggest where the eight thousand Barzani tribesmen had been buried. The free market kicked in, and eventually Ihsan found he could get exactly the documents he wanted—for a much higher price. Through luck and persistence over two years, he finally located a town in the western desert called Bussia, near the Saudi border.

Throughout the process, Ihsan kept the CPA involved, letting them know what he was finding as he traveled around the country, eventually documenting 284 mass grave sites across Iraq. He assumed the Americans would have a keen interest—besides the WMD argument, Saddam's atrocities had been a major motivation to get America behind the war, and forensic evidence of Saddam's hundreds of thousands of victims would surely play a major role in the case against him. To his dismay, Ihsan discovered that the Americans had no interest in documenting the atrocities.

"They thought the history of Iraq started on April 9, 2003," Ihsan said ruefully.

American soldiers did nothing to secure the grave sites, and some civilians went out to the spots with bulldozers in a hopeless attempt to turn up an ID card or recognizable clothing of a loved one. Instead their efforts left much of the evidence in a jumble that would be almost impossible to decipher. Ihsan understood that the soldiers were not trained as forensics experts, but he expected the CPA, once it got running, to take on the issue—for the sake of the war crimes tribunal and also out of respect for the millions of long-suffering survivors wondering where and how their loved ones had died. He contacted the CPA staffer in charge of human rights, who assured him that technical assistance would be forthcoming.

"I got nothing from them. That's when I started calling the CPA 'Can't Provide Anything,'" said Ihsan.

Of the nearly three hundred grave sites, the CPA eventually performed forensic investigations at only two. With over thirty million dollars allocated for transitional justice and human rights, the Americans spent almost nothing to help Iraqis find their dead. Kurdish representatives in Baghdad lobbied the CPA constantly about the issue without effect. By the time Ihsan finally located the grave site of the missing Barzanis, Sunni insurgents controlled many of the mass graves—some insurgents no doubt the same people who had done the killings. If Ihsan had ever believed in the American vision for a new Iraq, his daydream ended with his last forays into the western desert, where Sunni sheikhs refused to help him find the bodies of Kurds twenty years dead.

"There is no way to reconcile with them," said Ihsan, "because if they have a chance, they would do it again."

CHAPTER ELEVEN

The Feast of the Sacrifice

"Can't Provide Anything" summed up the CPA's entire fourteen-month existence from the Kurdish perspective, and Ambassador Bremer seemed unable or uninterested in accepting anything either. The Governing Council spent so much time trying to divide the tasks of governance with perfectly equal patronage to every constituency that results became an afterthought. The Kurds had plenty to offer in terms of expertise and relatively disciplined manpower. Prominent Kurds took over the water ministry and the ministry of municipalities, and some were even hired by the CPA as outside advisors to Iraq's new government. But politics outweighed effectiveness, and no job was too small to be considered a crucial bargaining chip, even down to collecting the garbage.

"At one point we had a garbage crisis in Baghdad," recalled one CPA staffer. "I looked around and thought, where the heck can I quickly get garbage trucks. Then I saw Mam Jalal."[1]

Talabani was happy to provide PUK municipal trucks and workers, and the garbage got picked up. But it didn't last in the zero-sum game of Iraqi politics, where even collecting garbage looked like a power grab. Other parties complained, and Talabani sent his garbagemen home. The same process had taken place between the KDP and PUK when they set up their government in 1992; they had quibbled over every single driver, tea boy, and bodyguard job. But no lessons were accepted from the Kurdish experiment—many Arab delegates still considered the Kurds unruly rebels from the north. Kurds who prominently helped the coalition were often treated as foreign interlopers in Baghdad, as with Hero Talabani's collaboration with the CPA's bumbling effort to create a new Iraqi news network. Many in the CPA also resented the Kurds' independent attitude.

"People working in ministries would talk to Shi'ites and Sunnis and hear bad things said about the Kurds," the CPA staffer remembered. "They'd see the pesh merga running around like they owned the place and see the offices in the north under Kurdistan Regional Government control. There was some jealousy around that and a lack of appreciation of the model they could be for the rest of the country."

As mostly American advisors took de facto control of Iraq's provincial governments, three of the eighteen provinces remained in completely local control: Dohuk, Erbil, and Sulimaniya. The CPA disbursed funds to the Kurdish region but let the Kurds run their own affairs, which bred resentment among the Arab parties, who egged on CPA suspicions of the north.

"It was hard to convince the CPA that the Kurds were the good guys," said one State Department Iraq specialist. "They were meeting with all the Arab parties, most of whom don't like Kurds. They would be the ones telling the Americans, 'We're going to build our country, everything is going to be great, except we've got these wild Kurds up to the north.'"

Because the north remained calm, few in the CPA or the U.S. military made the trek to Kurdistan, and that made it even easier to take projects and resources away. One CPA project allocated six hundred million dollars for water and sanitation work in the north, but by the end of the CPA's term, USAID took away five hundred million dollars to devote to more troubled parts of the country.[2]

And the Kurds' position wasn't helped when their representatives in Baghdad took their new freedom of speech so seriously. An aging but still feisty Mahmoud Othman came out of retirement in London to take up a position on the Governing Council. He seemed an excellent choice, as a well-respected Kurdish leader clearly not in the pocket of the KDP or PUK. Othman soon became a self-appointed ombudsman for the council and began an affair of mutual love with the news media, much to the consternation of the many Republican Party loyalists coming out for short stints from Washington. Othman vigorously criticized the petty motives of many council members, but he saved his most withering words for the CPA and its contractors, who had begun to dwarf any other tribe in Iraq for waste, corruption, and ineptitude.

"Mr. Bush says this is the main front in the war on terror. He should put his best team here!" Othman said in an October 2003 interview in Baghdad.

Othman couldn't understand why the Americans weren't sending larger numbers of more experienced people to Baghdad. Those who arrived were either inexperienced Bush administration true believers or American private contractors on eight-figure reconstruction deals. Years later the CPA would admit to a nine-billion-dollar gap in its accounting, all of which might have been excused if the money had produced a functioning Iraq. At the time, while he was on the council, Othman was denouncing it to anyone in earshot.

"Iraqi firms or even some other firms could do it for half the amount. I don't know why they're just wasting money like that," said Othman. "And the Americans get salaries so high! Some of them get two thousand seven hundred dollars a day! The lowest get four hundred a day. What's going on? With four hundred dollars you could recruit ten Iraqi policemen!"

As the waste continued and the violence got worse, the ranks of believers shrank, but among those still hanging on to the American dream for Iraq were Kurdistan's most talented players: Hoshyar Zebari and Barham Salih. Zebari had been appointed interim foreign minister in September 2003, and he jetted around the world trying to put a professional face on the new Iraq. He had easy acts to follow—Baghdad's recent public faces had been either the ridiculous Muhammad Saeed al-Sahaf (a.k.a. "Baghdad Bob" or "Comical Ali") or the cold-blooded Tariq Aziz. As Iraq's new über-ambassador, Zebari pushed for debt relief at a donor conference in Madrid, asking European countries to put aside their distaste for the American war and support his new state. The Arab League debated about inviting Iraqi's foreign minister at all, arguing that the Governing Council wasn't a legitimate government for Iraq. When they finally invited Zebari to attend the September 10 summit, he let them have it—in flowing Arabic—for their years of unfaltering support for Saddam. Zebari's belief in the new Iraq made him almost cocky.

"Iraq is a founding member of the Arab League and should not be left out," Zebari told Secretary General Amir Moussa, no doubt aware that these words had special sting coming from a Kurd. "If you leave Iraq out, you will lose. Because among Iraqis, there isn't much love for the Arab League and its stance."

Even with Zebari's success as a globe-trotting diplomat, the Kurds' delicate position reared its head. If Zebari ever misspoke or even referred too strongly to federalism, his critics would seize on it as proof that Zebari's true loyalties lay in Kurdistan. In fact he was growing more independent by the day and building his own stature apart from the Barzani family. But in Kurdistan he also had to be careful not to seem too happy to work with Arabs; many nationalists thought Zebari wasn't being Kurdish enough and blamed him for not hanging a Kurdish flag next to his seat at the United Nations.

Barham Salih tried to bring to Baghdad some of the experience he had from governing in Sulimaniya. More than that, he could still play the part of a Washington insider. In Iraq's government only Salih remained on good terms with all the branches of the Bush administration, and at the same time he had realistic expectations of how little Washington understood about Iraq. Where many Iraqis saw conspiracies behind the erratic behavior of the Americans, Salih understood that the conflict between the State Department and the Pentagon was just as bitter, senseless, and tribal as Iraq's own divisions. He continued to play it straight with Bremer, but often his honesty made him something of a lone voice.

"You know how Middle Easterners are," said Salih. "You can't say no to the Americans in public. Many of my Iraqi colleagues in the leadership were going along with these American guys, just telling them what they'd like to hear. But because I lived in the West, I didn't have that complex. I could tell them, 'No, this is "not on," Mr. Bremer.'"

But as time passed, the rest of the Governing Council would learn to tell Bremer the same thing. After six months in power, departing Iraq became the CPA's central mission. Ayatollah Sistani's veto of the American plan to write a constitution before holding elections meant Iraqis needed some sort of transitional law for the interim government. Bremer hoped to finish to CPA's mandate by the middle of summer 2004. He convinced the Governing Council to set a deadline to write a transitional administrative law, or "TAL," and ratify it by the end of February 2004, under which Iraq would select an interim government that would rule once the CPA left Iraq on July 1. The interim system was to last until elections in 2005 would put a four-year government in place. All the parties dug in their heels.

The transitional law became the next arena for the factions. For the Shi'ites it would be a test to see if they would finally get the power accorded to their majority status; Sistani indirectly pushed for a religious tone in the new government. Individual Sunni Arab leaders hadn't really emerged but it was clear Sunnis were the most vulnerable in the negotiations and essentially wanted to return to some semblance of the strong central government they had once dominated. For the Kurds the question was basic: would they gain or suffer by fully rejoining Arab Iraq? The Kurdish negotiators knew that the rest of Iraq, Shi'ite and Sunni, was tilting toward religious government. Despite the landmark meeting between Barzani and the Grand Ayatollah Sistani, ancient divisions had resurfaced, stirred up deliberately by attacks on civilians. As car bombings increased, mostly at police and army recruitment centers, the rumors in the crowd around the wreckage followed a similar theme: these killers want to start a war between the Sunnis and the Shi'ites. And they seemed to be succeeding, as bodies of those killed simply for being a member of the wrong sect began turning up at Baghdad's morgue.

With the sectarian rift showing, several prominent Iraqis and Americans had begun to ask if Iraq would not survive better as three almost separate states. Some even suggested that Iraq should be cut neatly before it tore, with the natural divisions that existed before the British cobbled Iraq into a country in 1919 restored. When the "three-state solution" was pushed in Washington by several Iraq skeptics, it was decried as defeatist and unworkable, especially because the lines between the regions could not be drawn without a massive population transfer from mixed areas. The Kurds didn't say it publicly, for fear of being called separatists, but the three-state solution suited them perfectly. The crux of their message to the CPA was that they could survive without Baghdad unless their terms were met. They set out a list of demands that would drive Bremer mad, including retention of their armed forces, supremacy of Kurdish laws in the north, and shared control of local oil resources with the central government. The Kurds pushed for a referendum in Kirkuk, in which people from the city and the surrounding province could vote to join the Kurdish region, which all the other parties saw as a blatant bid for independence.

ON DECEMBER 14, 2003, American soldiers captured Saddam Hussein hiding in a dirty hole near Tikrit. At the news, Kurds throughout the

country poured into the streets to celebrate, and a picture of a haggard
Saddam obediently undergoing a medical checkup was pulled off the Internet and distributed across the north by gloating Kurds.* Four of the
Governing Council members had managed to see Saddam shortly after he
was captured, escorted by Paul Bremer to a small prison cell where they
woke Saddam from a nap.[3] The former opposition leaders were all Arabs,
though one of them did ask Saddam why he had gassed the Kurds in Halabja. The fallen dictator, unrepentant, claimed it was Iran that did the
gassing, and he responded with crude jokes to the other demanding questions of his visitors. Strangely, none of the prominent Kurdish leaders
ever met with Saddam in his jail cell, perhaps not wanting to revisit the
deals they had tried to make with Baghdad in the past. Talabani announced that he didn't support capital punishment and preferred to see
the ex-dictator suffer a long prison term and a full interrogation, but he
never deigned to go ask Saddam any questions himself. "Why would I go?
I don't want to see such a thing," Talabani said, and declined to answer
any more questions on the subject.[4]

The new year of 2004 should have ushered peace and stability to Iraq.
Most of the regime's top tier sat in a U.S. military brig, awaiting trial for
crimes against humanity, and coalition forces claimed to be mopping up
the last throes of the resistance. Instead, on New Year's Eve, three car
bombs rocked Baghdad, killing at least nine people, including an eight-
year-old girl standing too close to the U.S. Army Humvee that was the
bomber's target. Another of the bombs ripped through the Nabil restaurant, wounding three reporters who were enjoying what would turn out to
be the end of Baghdad's nightlife. Instead of reconstruction, the city saw
a rampant growth of ten-foot gray concrete blast walls, which turned the
capital into an apartheid maze, separating the powerful from unprotected
civilians and paralyzing traffic.

All Iraq shut down the first weekend in February, but for joyful reasons: Eid al-Adha, one of the most important holidays in Islam, which
celebrates Abraham's willingness to sacrifice his son to God. Shi'ites and
Sunnis sometimes disagree on the exact day the holiday starts, but it
doesn't usually matter much, because no one really goes to work on any

---

* The PUK's Kosrat Rasul insists that his men had a key role in helping U.S.
  troops get to Saddam; General Petraeus downplayed the Kurdish role in the
  capture.

of the few days before or after. Talabani returned to Sulimaniya, and Barzani remained up in Salahudin as usual, but both party headquarters in Erbil threw gala receptions. The KDP still dominated the city, but with the Kurdistan Regional Government set to resume its duties again, the PUK had also beefed up its presence. Eid al-Adha makes for a delightful holiday, which usually involves the slaughter of a sheep (which Abraham sacrificed in lieu of his son), lots of feasting, and spending a few days calling upon friends and neighbors. This time the one-upsmanship was more friendly, with each party trying to impress the other with their Eid reception.

Sami Abd-al-Rahman, now in his seventies and the deputy prime minister of the KDP region, spent the morning of February 1 at the KDP reception hall, sipping tea and greeting the two hundred or so well-wishers crowded into the hall. Some American officials came to pay respects, and just after ten thirty a.m. Colonel Harry Schute sat down next to Abd-al-Rahman. True to form, Sami was pleasant and cordial for a moment or two, and then he got down to business about a few bones he had to pick with the way the coalition had organized border patrols. They spoke for a quarter of an hour, and then Schute excused himself, anxious to spend exactly the same amount of time at the PUK reception across town. Abd-al-Rahman went back to the receiving line, to smile and greet the steady flow of visitors. Outside the building Colonel Schute ran into his colleague Army Major Randy Wade and took a moment to make fun of Wade's continuing attempts at speaking the Kurdish language. The two Americans chatted as dozens of Kurds pressed by them, barely stopping at a security detail that had relaxed in the spirit of the holiday. One of the men who passed was an unremarkable curly-headed fellow wearing jeans, a baggy black jacket, and yellow running shoes. A recording made by a Kurdish TV crew shows the man approach the line of KDP dignitaries as if to shake hands. At the last minute he reached inside his sleeve, as if feeling for a wristwatch, then everything went bright white.

The explosion seemed impossibly big for anything one man could carry in a suicide vest. It blew out the ceiling tiles and sent shards of glass flying out all the windows. The killer had planted himself expertly in the middle of a tightly packed holiday crowd, a murderer's dream. He had packed the vest with ball bearings, which flew out like a hundred shotgun shells. Across town, and almost simultaneously, another bomb—perhaps a bigger one—exploded inside the PUK reception, blasting through dozens of men, women, and children and blowing the southern wall of the ballroom clean off the building.

Harry Schute and his fellow officer called for American medical assistance and then rushed back in the building to administer first aid. Among the first pulled from the dust and carnage was Sami Abd-al-Rahman, carried by two pesh merga with a peppered red patch in his abdomen. Abd-al-Rahman asked repeatedly if his son was alive. Abd-al-Rahman's son, a London businessman, had arrived the night before to surprise his father for the holiday. He had been standing near his father in the receiving line and was killed instantly by the bomb. The medics lied to Abd-al-Rahman, who died on the way to the hospital.

The dead from the two blasts numbered more than one hundred, and twice that many suffered burns and shrapnel wounds. One survivor, his face and scalp glazed dark red and black from the explosion, said he had no doubt who was responsible.

"Ansar al-Islam, those Arab fascists," he said.

In fact, the killers were almost certainly Kurdish Islamist members of Ansar, since Arabs would have never made it so close to their targets unchallenged. Despite the fact that Ansar was homegrown, Kurds considered its members part of the plague of violent Islam and thereby connected to the Arab world. (Ansar later changed its name to Ansar al-Sunna, supporters of Sunnism, casting their lot with Iraq's increasingly bloody Sunni Arab insurgency against Shi'ites and secular Kurds.)

By the morning after the bomb, Kurdistan showed its reaction, almost literally shutting the door on the rest of Iraq. Kurdish security forces rounded up any Arabs discovered in the city of Erbil and took them in for questioning, even those who had come north from Baghdad to work with foreign companies. The former green line, now a dozen miles expanded in most directions, hardened into a real border again. Pesh merga at the checkpoints told Arabs they would be best advised to simply turn the car around and stick to their prewar side of the line. At a checkpoint on the road from Erbil toward the town of Makhmur, KDP soldiers roughed up an Arab newspaper reporter from Baghdad, though they stopped short when they noticed that a foreigner was watching. Perhaps Iraqis thought that the suicide bombs in the north would inspire the Kurds' sympathy and solidarity with the rest of Iraq, but the more common Kurdish reaction was revulsion toward everything to the south. Kurdish negotiators returned to the table in Baghdad wanting everything short of complete independence.

WHILE THE CPA and the White House offered condolences, they clearly didn't appreciate how hard it would now be to budge the Kurds from their demands in exchange for joining with a government based in Baghdad. In fact Talabani and Barzani had met with Bremer on January 27 and had been persuaded to sign off on a very weak form of federalism. Luckily for them, they never had to break off their deal with Bremer—instead the White House spiked it. The National Security Council, in charge of the Iraq portfolio since fall 2003, had made the ridiculous demand that all mention of the Kurdistan Regional Government be stricken from the TAL. Bremer was stuck delivering Washington's ruling, and the Kurds stomped their feet and stormed at having been betrayed. In fact they were delighted to avoid fighting their way out of the January agreement. On February 11, the Kurdistan Regional Parliament ratified its own set of conditions for the TAL, giving the Kurdish delegation in Baghdad the backing of the closest thing to a democratic body in Iraq.

The Kurds had one more advantage: ringers on their negotiating team. While both the Shi'ite and Sunni blocs had their patrons in the CPA, including some skilled Iraqi expats, the Kurds came around to the idea of hiring a small group of constitutional experts from universities in Europe and America. Among them was Peter Galbraith, the former Senate staffer who had worked so hard to bring attention to the Kurds' situation during the Saddam years. Asking for outside help was a sign of political maturity on the Kurds' part. It helped them stick to their guns and remain unintimidated by the Americans in the CPA and made for a much easier understanding of the legalese of Bremer's small team of lawyers who ended up drafting the TAL. As usual, the negotiations went down to the wire of the February 28 ratification deadline, and then another day past. Bremer seemed obsessed with the question of language and fought the Kurds hard over the putting Kurdish alongside Arabic as an official language in Iraq, something no one else made a fuss about. The Shi'ite block focused mostly on the role of Islam in the new constitution, and while Sistani of course wouldn't attend, he still had to be consulted, making for maddening delays. In the end the Kurds compromised on most of their key demands, allowing ambiguous language to be inserted and accepting

Bremer's promise that the real deal would be the Iraqi constitution, to be drafted later. Yet again, however, they felt like being so close to America had not brought them any benefit.

"Mr. Ambassador, you are asking us to join an Iraq in which we'll have less freedom than we had while Saddam was in power," Jalal Talabani said, according to Bremer's memoirs.

With that in mind, the Kurdish team pulled a masterstroke. At three A.M. on March 1, the Kurds inserted a short clause, article 61(c), that erased their worries about the entire process.[5] It stated simply that if any three provinces rejected the permanent constitution by a two-thirds margin, the document was dead. Only the next morning, after it was signed, did the rest of the Governing Council realize that the three provinces in mind made up the current Kurdish region, which had thereby granted itself a veto over Iraq's constitution. Sistani wrote to Bremer, telling him that this Kurdish veto was unacceptable. Finally, the "special relationship" with the Kurds actually came into play. Even with Washington pushing him to yield to Sistani, Bremer resisted, seeing that the Kurds were fighting for the same ideas as the Americans.

"If we forced the Kurds to cave while the US was still robustly present in Iraq, there was little hope for a secular, united Iraq once we left," Bremer wrote in his memoirs. After two days, Sistani gave in and accepted the signed document as it was. An elaborate ceremony on March 8 set the stage for the CPA to turn over power to an interim government by July 1. Then the real world of Iraq stepped in.

No one had bothered to explain the TAL to the public. Sunni Arabs, still without any clear leadership emerging from the ashes of the Ba'athist regime, felt they had been left out of the TAL drafting process. Sistani made clear to Shi'ites that the interim law didn't please him. On that point Moqtada al-Sadr outflanked the older cleric, declaring from the outset that the process was imposed by occupiers. The Kurds protested the idea that their pesh merga might be disbanded until they saw the reality—U.S. military forces on the ground in cities like Mosul, ignoring the madness from Bremer about disbanding the country's only friendly militia, essentially reflagged the Kurdish fighters and started calling them Iraqi forces. The Kurds took the cue and simply never enforced the parts of the law they disagreed with. The TAL seemed a triumph only to Bremer and the small coterie inside the Green Zone who had helped him write it.

Other realities soon came home to roost. Three weeks after the signing of the TAL, on March 31, an SUV carrying four American contractors mistakenly drove into downtown Fallujah, which had clearly become a no-go zone for all but the maddest journalists, much less small groups of Americans in baseball caps and wraparound sunglasses. The men were killed, mutilated, and finally hung in pieces from a bridge on the west side of the city; video of the incident showed Fallujans celebrating. The U.S. military resisted the idea of a retaliatory strike, but then Washington pushed for a show of force. The marines began an all-out attack, but then just short of them taking the city, politicians intervened again, saying that the assault wasn't playing well internationally. From a counterinsurgency perspective, it was like taking half a course of antibiotics and then stopping just when the infection was angry. A negotiated solution created the Fallujah Brigade, an indigenous force that pledged to control the city on Baghdad's behalf. By summer insurgents took complete command and control of the Fallujah Brigade and the city. Fallujah became a rallying cry for extremists worldwide, and for the first time the enemy had formally won territory from the U.S. Army.

Around the same time Fallujah ignited, the coalition forces tried to arrest a key aid to Moqtada al-Sadr on murder charges and lit up another open rebellion. Sadr's Mahdi Army took several southern cities, and again coalition forces fought bloody street battles. The counterinsurgency maxim that rebels win by not losing proved itself again: The coalition easily crushed Sadr's forces in every encounter, but when the dust settled with another cease-fire, Sadr's power and prestige had doubled.

As the two battles finally quieted, the coalition suffered a final, near-fatal self-inflicted wound. Back in January CPA officials had economically released news of the investigations into abuse at Saddam's notorious prison, which had become an American detention facility. At the end of April, however, the photographs taken by MPs at Abu Ghraib shocked Iraqis beyond their worst conspiracy theories. After seeing photographs of naked Iraqis stacked in a pyramid, threatened by dogs, and led on a leash, those who still believed in Washington's good intentions were finished. It didn't matter that Saddam had done much worse for decades—supporters of America didn't have a leg to stand on. With two months left to go, Bremer's CPA was a dead man walking.

The White House implored the U.N. to send back Lakhdar Brahimi, an Algerian diplomat who had shepherded the new Afghan government's constitutional process. Brahimi had been through Iraq in February, and he reluctantly returned to Baghdad to give some international legitimacy to the interim government that Bremer and the CPA were selecting. By that time Bremer's ship had so clearly lost its rudder that Condoleezza Rice sent her own man, former ambassador to India Robert Blackwill, to take matters in hand. None of this changed Bremer's unflappable autocratic style, as Brahimi's final press conference on June 4 in Baghdad made clear.

"I'm sure he doesn't mind my saying it," said Brahimi. "Mr. Bremer is the dictator of Iraq. He has the money. He has the signature. Nothing happens without his agreement in this country."

Indeed, it became clear that Bremer, with input from Blackwill, was handpicking the new government. For prime minister, they selected Ayad Allawi, the secular Shi'ite former Ba'athist who had worked with the British MI6 and the CIA in the 1990s. The Kurds expected the ceremonial position of president to go to Jalal Talabani, and Talabani, along with Barham Salih, had been to Washington to canvass old contacts to make sure this would happen. Upon their return to Baghdad, Bremer broke the news—he had decided that the president had to be a Sunni Arab.

"For too long, they have been underrepresented in the new Iraq, Mr. Talabani," Bremer told him. "We have to use this government as an opportunity to broaden Iraq's political base."[6]

With that lecture from a man whose knowledge of Iraq was a year old, Talabani returned to Sulimaniya without any position in the new government. Barham Salih had expected to become foreign minister but was instead named to a token position, deputy prime minister for national security. The KDP, which had sent more active lieutenants to Baghdad, fared much better. Hoshyar Zebari stayed on as foreign minister, and Roj Shaways took up one of the vice presidents' seats. Still, the KDP had been shut out of the power ministries like defense, finance, and oil, making it harder for the Kurdish believers to argue they would ever get a fair shake in the new Iraq.

In what he portrayed as a clever security move, Bremer decided to hand over power from the CPA two days early, to evade any major insurgent attacks. It wasn't paranoia—the Green Zone was clearly infiltrated by an increasingly sophisticated insurgency. Earlier in June, when the new government held its inauguration ceremony, insurgents had discovered the top-secret location and lobbed mortars nearby. So on June 28 Bremer quickly shook hands with Ayad Allawi and did what can only be described as "slinking off." He left a recorded farewell address for the Iraqi people. Bremer had an Iraqi honor guard of one, consisting of Barham Salih, ever the good host. The two men rode most of the way to the plane in silence, but at one point Bremer looked at Salih and shook his head.

"You Iraqis are a difficult bunch of people," Bremer said. Then Bremer climbed up the stairs into the waiting plane and waved good-bye.[7]

Bremer would be remembered in Iraq for two things. He introduced the new print currency without Saddam's picture on it, which Iraqis would thereafter refer to as "Bremers"—as in, "How many Bremers to the dollar today?" Also branded with his name were the hideous concrete blast walls that English-speaking Iraqis unaffectionately started calling "Bremer barriers." Bremer became a self-described punching bag for the American failure in Iraq, but it's hard not to take a swing, since he insisted on absolute control while in office for a year that battered the believers in the new Iraq and in America. Later in 2004 President Bush awarded Bremer the Presidential Medal of Freedom but didn't think for a second of offering him another job. Besides President Bush, only a few others will express their support for Bremer's actions, if not his style—they are, of course, Kurds.

"I don't like Bremer personally," said PUK deputy Nawshirwan Mustafa. "But for me it was very important to demolish the Iraqi army. The de-Ba'athification, the end of the Mukhabarat—these for me were favors from God. You cannot imagine."[8]

The KDP's Nechirvan Barzani stated it more brazenly, praising Bremer for the errors that have made Iraq's fragmentation, and therefore Kurdistan's independence, more likely. "No really, I like Bremer," Nechirvan is fond of telling guests, savoring the irony with a smirk. "If there is one Kurdish person who likes him, it's me. Because if not for Bremer, the situation in Iraq would never have been like this today . . . It would have been much better!"

CHAPTER TWELVE

Securing the Realm

ON THE EVE OF IRAQ'S FIRST DEMOCRATIC elections, January 30, 2005, Kurdish General "Mam" Rostam spent a long evening in his newly reclaimed Kirkuk home, answering phone calls from PUK pesh merga around the city as well as Kurds within the city's multiethnic police force. The elections, he felt sure, were finally going to restore the Kurds to their rightful place in control of the city. Rostam was still very grateful to the Americans; he said that if George Bush had been running, he would have won every single Kurdish vote. But the old warrior wasn't entirely pleased with what the Americans had done in Kirkuk. The police force was too multiethnic, Rostam thought, and the GIs were relying on too many Turcomans and Arabs. A Turcoman was in charge of the police in fact, and Rostam mistrusted that any of the potential saboteurs for the next morning's elections would be properly dealt with. He had given his men different orders. One of them called in to say he had apprehended an Arab with a rocket-propelled grenade in a car, driving after the Election Day curfew. Rostam was pleased until the pesh merga told him what he had done.

"You took him to the police? Why didn't you just kill him like I told you?!" Rostam said, then terminated the call and looked up at the guests around his dining room. "If it had been in my hands, you'd be looking at a dead body! They're brainwashed—raised on terror," Rostam said of the

Arabs, refilling whiskey glasses around the table. "They can't be reformed. So I've told my guys to kill whomever they arrest."

Late into the night before the vote, Rostam and his pesh merga patrolled the streets looking for anyone the slightest bit suspicious, which for Rostam meant any Arab out after curfew. Still wearing his pesh merga fatigues and a beige vest with many pockets, Rostam went personally to checkpoints around the city, glorying in the cheers he got from Kurdish troops and civilians when they recognized his weathered bulldog's face. One reclaimed Turcoman village had slaughtered a dozen sheep for him and his men, Rostam said, though it could have easily been more from fear than affection.

Almost two years since the liberation of the city, Kirkuk looked much the same—a dreary and bombed-out wreck that seemed to be full of refugees, either those returning or those soon to be turned out of their homes. The Americans had succeeded in stalling the reverse ethnic cleansing inside the city, but the process for adjudicating property claims had never gotten off the ground. The government in Baghdad didn't seem much concerned with enforcing the parts of the transitional administrative law dealing with return and compensation in Kirkuk. Thousands of Kurds had returned, but with their houses still occupied, they took to living in the soccer stadium, waiting every day for the news that the government had homes for them. The city felt frozen in time at April 2003, when the statue of Saddam came down. The term of the U.S.-appointed interim government had nearly gone. All in all, Mam Rostam was plenty glad he had ignored the law, and the U.S. Army, and simply reconquered his old neighborhood—no one else in Iraq seemed to be getting anything done.[1]

In Baghdad the interim government had taken power in June 2004, promising a firm hand—that of former Ba'athist Ayad Allawi. The secular Shi'ite had long painted himself as the man who could bring Iraq under control, and rumors spread that he was personally carrying out executions of terrorists at Abu Ghraib. Allawi let the rumors flourish, and the Western media soon noticed that the Iraqi prime minister's half smile and thick frame resembled that of television gangster Tony Soprano. Public opinion had been calling out for martial law and capital punishment, and Allawi quickly installed curfews and special powers over the police and military. Such sweeping power for a head of state might have raised concerns, except that the Iraqi police and army couldn't really carry out the

orders. During the first assault on Fallujah in spring 2004, the army had
fallen apart, and the police were no better. On the books Iraq had 115
batallions of combined security forces, but despite assertions by Secretary
of Defense Donald Rumsfeld, Pentagon officials admitted that few, if
any, could operate effectively without direct U.S. supervision.[2] Allawi was
now in effect the generalissimo of an empty barracks.

American leadership had also changed hands and style. Ambassador
John Negroponte delayed his arrival in Baghdad, avoiding the appearance
that he was taking over the reins from Bremer as viceroy. Like Bremer,
Negroponte had no Middle East experience, but his deputy, James Jeffrey,
was a plainspoken New Englander who had served as the deputy chief of
mission in two neighboring countries, Kuwait and Turkey. Both men also
had experience in Vietnam: Negroponte as a diplomat and Jeffrey as a soldier. The new ambassador would serve a short tenure, and make his most
important mark in reducing the U.S. government's patronizing role after
Bremer's overbearing CPA. Though the staff began to change over from
Republican-faithful CPA recruits, the majority still had next to no understanding about the quiet enclave in the north of the country.[3]

The U.S. military rotated in a team more cognizant of the reality—a
swelling insurgency—and more attuned to the fact that it could only be
defeated when Iraqi troops got on board. General David Petraeus was
assigned the task of retooling the army's training, but an entire year had
been wasted. Car bombs were now set off daily instead of weekly, and
the fight turned slowly from one against America and its Iraqi recruits
to an ethnic and sectarian war. In the absence of any order to replace the
twisted regimen of Saddam's dictatorship, Iraqis turned to co-religionists
and kin for safety. Americans coined a few dramatic terms that oversim-
plified the country nicely, most important, the concept of a "Sunni triangle" of stiff resistance, with arms extending roughly west from Baghdad
toward Fallujah and Ramadi and northwest through Baquba, Samara, and
Mosul. While the Kurds largely took shelter in their homogeneous north,
the new realities came home to them as Arab gunmen in Mosul began targeting Kurds along with U.S. troops. In mid-September 2004, three pesh
merga were ambushed and beheaded there, and soon Kurdish families
started moving away, or at least toward the eastern bank of the Tigris
River.

Americans fixated on Fallujah as a factory of suicide vests, car bombs,
and the roadside booby traps that had started to kill U.S. troops in large

numbers. The city was under the control of Iraqi and foreign mujahideen, and Taliban-like rules were being enforced. Since the Marines' half-finished assault on Fallujah in April 2004, the city's name had become a rallying cry in Friday sermons across the country, a one-word refutation of America's invulnerability and Baghdad's control. Though Mosul and Ramadi had become just as comfortable to insurgent forces, America had been girding itself for an all-out assault on Fallujah, advising civilians to leave the city in November 2004.

This time the Americans trusted only a token Iraqi force to join in the assault. Alongside U.S. Special Forces the Iraqi soldiers seized Fallujah's largest hospital on the west side of the Euphrates River, just across the bridge from which the U.S. contractors had been hanged six months earlier. The Iraqis guarded the hospital to prevent insurgents from grabbing it or claiming that the Americans had bombed it. As a deafening avalanche of munitions rained down on the few people left in the city, the Kurdish and Shi'ite soldiers in the hospital allowed the Sunni Arab doctors from Fallujah to come to work, preparing for wounded survivors from the city. But that didn't mean they got along.

"They're all terrorists here, even the doctors in the hospital," said one Shi'ite recruit. In turn, all the Sunni doctors claimed that the "Iraqi" soldiers had broken into storerooms, stealing medical supplies as well as cash and cell phones from the lockers of the hospital staff. Feelings of national unity did not abound among the Arabs, but one of the Kurdish commandos took the prize for intolerance.

"I hate all these Arabs," he said. "I've got a picture of Ariel Sharon hanging in my living room—he's the one who knows how to deal with Arabs. I wish I could send my children to live in Israel."

The hospital took mortar fire from insurgents inside the city, which hit so close that branches blew off the trees in the courtyard, inspiring a bit more fraternity among the Iraqis taking cover inside. The Americans responded with tanks, rockets from helicopter gunships, thousand-pound bombs guided in with lasers, howitzers, and the jackhammer of .50-caliber machine guns. Somehow the insurgents in Fallujah continued to shoot back with their rockets and small arms, drawing the Americans into the city street by street. Sniper fire on the west bank of the river also came from a cluster of houses southwest of the bridges, which the U.S. soldiers kept referring to as the "Kurdish village." Any Kurds who lived there were long gone to the north—which is where many of the insurgents had apparently gone as well. America's telegraphed punch in Fallujah showed the insurgency for the hydra it had become—U.S. forces retook the city, but the insurgents simply reared up elsewhere. Iraq was starting to look like a real war, and one America could lose.

Ten days into the Fallujah offensive, on November 17, 2004, the city of Mosul fell to insurgents. American officials admitted that the police chief and apparently his entire five-thousand-member force had disappeared or gone over to the side of anti-Americans. The Kurds could only shake their heads—this was the force set up by General David Petraeus, which they considered a rehabilitation program for Ba'athists. Masked gunmen surprised the head of Mosul's anti-crime task force and led him out of his house, which they set alight, and executed him along with his son and brother-in-law in front of the burning building.[4] Another group of insurgents burned down the governor's house but didn't find him at home.* Bodies appeared in the street, some of them beheaded, terrorizing the city's inhabitants. With the U.S. military's resources focused on Fallujah and units from all across the country pulled in, the Americans had nowhere else to turn yet again—they asked the Kurds for help, ethnic sensitivities be damned. The insurgency was driving the Americans and the Kurds closer together.

At first the Americans finessed this arrangement, announcing that "national guard" troops from outside Mosul had come in to help, and thus avoiding the sensitivities in Turkey and the rest of Iraq about Kurds taking over security in an Arab city. Of course "national guard" translated into Kurdish as *pesh merga*. Two thousand troops—half KDP and half PUK—streamed into the city, some wearing traditional Kurdish baggy trousers and cummerbunds, others wearing the uniform of the new Iraqi National Guard, created the previous June. This time they received the grateful cooperation of the U.S. Army First Battalion, Twenty-Fifth Infantry Division, which scrambled to call some of their units back from Fallujah to help. Nominally the Kurds came under the coalition leadership,

---

* The governor installed by Petraeus, Ghanim al-Basso, had resigned under a dark cloud in spring 2004 and had been replaced by Usama Kashmoula (whom the CPA referred to in official documents as "Oussama," in apparent distaste for the correct spelling of his name). Kashmoula, by all accounts a popular and effective public servant, died in a hail of insurgent gunfire in July 2004. His deputy, Khasro Goran, a Kurd, took over and remained prominent after Kashmoula's brother Duraid assumed the governor's office.

but they kept their old pesh merga chains of command intact. Their presence in Mosul was supposed to be a temporary fix, but the Americans had lost some illusions about needing help from their friends, and the Kurdish soldiers never left. Beyond the National Guard, the party offices began setting up checkpoints to protect the Kurdish neighborhoods, primarily on the eastern bank of the Tigris, in an attempt to stem the flow of Kurdish families fleeing the violence.*

IN MOSUL AND across the country Iraqis quietly pulled up stakes and moved away from mixed territory, like wild creatures sensing a tsunami. Shi'ites began to talk of forming their own autonomous region, as allowed in the TAL, and the Sunnis worried at the thought of being left with nothing but sand as Kurds and Shi'ites partitioned off the oil-producing lands. The Sunni figurehead president, Ghazi al-Yawar, denounced any talk of partition as treasonous, but an informal population transfer crept along into 2005, clearest along the Kurds' new green line.

For Mam Rostam the news of Kurds on the run was bittersweet—he hated the idea that Kurds would flee anywhere, but the fact that they were fleeing *to* Kirkuk pleased him to no end. He was having the last laugh. Twenty years earlier Rostam had joined Talabani's delegation to Baghdad when negotiations between the regime and the PUK had broken down over the status of Kirkuk. Then foreign minister Tariq Aziz had taunted the Kurds when the deal failed.

"Tariq Aziz told us you can only look at Kirkuk and weep, like we Arabs weep for Gibraltar and Spain," Rostam recalled. "Look how racist they are," he said. "The Arabs are all like that. Even their religion is the same—all about kill them, hang them, cut their ears. You can't find the word *love* in the Koran."

As my interpreter, a practicing Muslim, turned dark red but kept translating, Rostam complained that the Arabs in the city had not returned his friendly greetings when he passed through their neighborhoods—at least not the Arabs who weren't "original" Kirkukees. "That's the nature of an occupier. They're always scared and

---

* When I embedded in Mosul in October 2005, I found the U.S. Army there collaborating with the pesh merga nests about the city, without any concern that they were officially illegal.

expect you to come and kick them out. Those with blood on their hands, they'll never like us," he said.

According to Rostam, hundreds of Kurdish families had fled from villages south of Kirkuk—he had recently found homes for several families from Hawijah. He pointed me in the direction of Askari, a warren of houses just across the bridge from the city center. Sitting in the living room of Heybat Rostam (no relation), I had a rush of déjà vu, realizing when I had last been to Askari—visiting terrified Shi'ite families on the day that Kirkuk fell to the Kurds, April 10, 2003. This was the same street, maybe even one of the same living rooms, but the Shi'ites were gone—more ghosts of Kirkuk—replaced by the Kurdish woman for whom this house was most recently a shelter.

"Kill the Kurds first, then the Americans," Heybat recounted. "That's what they were writing on the walls in Hawijah."

Heybat and her twelve children had always lived in Hawijah, part of Saddam's tribal heartland. Her family owned a bakery and had a good life, relatively speaking. With the U.S. invasion they began having problems as their neighbors began to accuse Kurdish residents of secretly aiding the Americans. Months after the end of the regime, teachers in the schools still made the children pledge allegiance to the Ba'ath Party. Even so, Heybat didn't think of leaving until the night letters began arriving.

"Four or five times a month, they threw letters over our garden wall, telling us to leave or die," she said. "But we didn't want to go."

In January 2005, nine Kurds were found shot dead in Hawijah, and Heybat's nephew Isam was one of them. She had had enough and was now hoping to live peacefully in Kirkuk. The Kurdistan Regional Government had given her and her family a million Iraqi dinars in assistance, and they had used it to pay for six months' rent in this small house; one of her sons had found work as a baker. She said the house belonged to a Kurd, but he had bought it cheaply from a fleeing Arab. As we spoke, the room filled with her friends and relatives, all recent refugees from Hawijah. My experience from two years earlier repeated itself down to the small details—the family was so poor they didn't have tea and sugar to offer a cup of Iraq's national drink.

Officially, Hawijah was part of Ta'mim province, one of the provinces Saddam Hussein created in 1974 to gerrymander the ethnic balance around Kirkuk. Hawijah had been tacked onto Ta'mim to increase its Arab population, and as such, none of the Kurdish officials now in Kirkuk cared about hanging on to the town. The more important point was that families like Heybat's could vote in Kirkuk during the January 30 elections. In addition, encouraged by the Kurdish parties, Kurds "came home" to Kirkuk in time for the elections, staying in makeshift tents in the soccer stadium and other open spaces. No one denied that the Kurds had increased their voting population by tens of thousands, though the Iraqi Turcoman Front claimed that the number was in the high six figures. As for the Arabs from Hawijah, they were politically irrelevant—Sunni groups across Iraq had called a boycott of the elections, and the Kurds didn't mind one bit. The Kurds had won the right to allow the returnees to vote in the January elections by threatening nothing less than a full boycott.

Baghdad and Washington couldn't afford to have the elections fail, and Sunni Arabs clearly intended to stay home, either on principle or because of the threats that extremist groups had made against anyone who went to the polls. A Kurdish boycott would have meant a parliament entirely selected by Shi'ite Arabs, many of them with close ties to Iran. Suddenly the Kurdish politicians were being described as kingmakers, and they showed no sign of compromising this time. Unless Kirkukee Kurds were allowed to vote in Kirkuk, they told the Americans, Arabization would have succeeded in becoming a fact. And the Kurds saw no contradiction in denying the vote to the hundreds of thousands of Arabs Saddam had imported to the city.

"Kirkuk is the city of Kurds, Turcomans, Chaldo Assyrians, and real Arabs—those who were there before Arabization," Jalal Talabani explained. "We are for first normalizing—reuniting Kirkuk because Saddam divided it, ending this ethnic cleansing policy by returning those who left and sending back those [who came]. They must go back home first. We will never agree that they vote as Kirkukees; they must vote at their birthplace."

The loudest protests to this policy came not from Arabs, who still lacked organization in the city, but from the Iraqi Turcoman Front. In the ITF's Kirkuk office, its head of public relations, Fawzi Akram, claimed the Kurds would certainly steal a victory in the election. Akram had toned down some of the mad predictions and estimates the ITF originally pushed on the Americans—no longer claiming three million Turcomans lived in the city. But he stressed that with only a tiny number of election observers and journalists across the country to observe, no one could possibly certify the elections as free and fair. Holding to results from such an election, he said, was a recipe for violence.

"When the civil war comes to Iraq, it will bring a fire so hot it will burn the green wood with the tinder," Akram said. As he spoke, several assistants loaded up a truck with pamphlets and fanfare, including Turcoman Front flags, Turcoman Front lighters, stainless steel watches with the ITF symbol on the faceplate, and nifty pens that revealed a Turcoman Front symbol when turned upside down. When asked if Ankara gave the ITF any funding for all the swag, Akram said he accepted money from anyone who wanted to help the downtrodden Turcomans of Iraq. Would Turkey help the Turcomans in the coming war? "Of course the branch goes back to its root," he answered. "If there is trouble here, every group will have help."

The way to solve the issue, Akram said, was to return to the 1957 Iraq census. Today, as in 1957, the city of Kirkuk's population was more than half Turcoman, with the rest split between Arabs and Kurds. As almost everyone in Kirkuk did, Akram was using the scant historical information available and turning it to his side. The 1957 census had indeed shown a majority of Turcomans in Kirkuk, and the city was known as a Turcoman business hub.[5] But the Kurds used the same document to show that with all the outlying villages included, they had once held a strong majority in the province of Kirkuk. The city's demographics had been rigged so many times it became hard to tell the stacking from the unstacking. Rostam and the other Kurds in the city dismissed the ITF as a small bunch of troublemakers.

"They have told so many lies," said Jalal Jawher, the PUK rep in Kirkuk, "claiming that they have three million, but now it's clear they have less than one hundred thousand. And now they need to tell more lies in order to excuse their first one."

Ordinary Turcomans and Kurds in the marketplaces and kebab joints sang a more moderate line than any of the parties. "The most important thing to us is security and peace," said Omar Ghazi, a Turcoman storekeeper in the central market. He would vote for the Turcoman Front's list but didn't mind the idea of living under a Kurdish government either. "I've been to Sulimaniya, and they seem to be running things very well. If we are with them, that's okay. But we hope everyone will get along together here," he said.

The most powerful rivals in the north had found a way to get along, recognizing that the opportunity to hold some power in Iraq outweighed their personal competition. The election was designed so that Iraqis voted not for individuals but party lists, with seats in parliament awarded according to each party's support at the polls. Talabani and Barzani fielded a common list of candidates for the national elections, maximizing the Kurdish power inside Iraq, including even the Kurdish Islamist parties. It was called the Kurdish Coalition list, and for once, Kurdish internal politics appeared to end at the mountains' edge (inside Kirkuk it was called the Kurdistan Brotherhood list, which included some Turcomans and Arabs).

Assuming a good voter turnout and a Sunni boycott, the Kurdish list would win a big enough bloc to make an attractive ally for the larger Shi'ite list in the parliament, where a two-thirds majority was needed to select a prime minister. Officially the parliament selected a president first, who would in turn pick a prime minister and a cabinet. In fact all the political bargaining over the presidency, vice presidents, and ministers would be done in advance, as one package. The assumption was that the Shi'ites would agree to pick a Kurd for the ceremonial post of president if the Kurdish president pledged to select a Shi'ite prime minister. After that, the rest of the ministries would be painstakingly negotiated between the parliamentary factions.

Both Kurdish leaders could get their way. Even if the presidency was largely symbolic, Talabani yearned to hold the post. He would then be able to weigh in on matters in Baghdad and, just as important, jet about to capital cities around the globe, finally walking through the front door of the statehouses, not ushered through the back. The Kurdish autonomous region was enshrined in the new Iraqi government, and in neat symmetry, Barzani wanted only to become president of the Kurdistan Regional Government and never have to bother with the heat and dust of Arab Iraq again. The Kurds would play kingmakers in Baghdad and kings in Kurdistan. The hatchet that had cleaved Kurdistan so many times might finally be buried.

The quiet of Iraq's first Election Day felt like an early-morning dream across the country. Eight million or so Iraqis went out to vote, most on foot because of a strict curfew and ban on nonofficial vehicles. Without cars on the road, the streets lay open, free of traffic jams or car bombs. For the day, Iraqis recaptured a bit of the jubilation of the early weeks after the regime fell. In Kirkuk, Kurds crowded the streets of Shorja, many of them wearing their finest traditional outfits—the women in long flowing dresses with heavy coin jewelry and the men in baggy trousers and pressed tunics wrapped up in sashes. Many of those returning early from

the ballot boxes started to play music and dance—the Kurdish traditional step is something between an Israeli hora and a Texas line dance.
Most of the pictures of Barzani and Talabani still hanging inside the
polling stations had come down, but the Kurdish flag flew all over Kurdish neighborhoods. Kirkuk sounded more like a village, with no unex-
plained noises in the distance—Mam Rostam had sternly prohibited
celebratory gunfire.

In the face of stepped-up security and a driving ban, most of the insurgents wisely laid low, conceding the day. They did lob two mortars into
the city from a safe distance. The first one landed in the stadium full of
Kurdish returnees, killing a sixteen-year-old boy whose parents defiantly
buried him and then went out to vote anyhow. The second mortar landed
in an Arab neighborhood, wounding several people. The news failed to
dampen the spirit in the Kurdish parts of town, where the lines at polling
stations filled streets all day long.

The Turcoman neighborhoods also had full polling stations on Election Day, but none of the celebratory feeling of the Kurdish sections.
Outside the Iraqi Turcoman Front offices were empty streets and none of
the bluster promised days before. At several nearby polling stations, election officials said turnout had been high. But the Turcomans I spoke with
never lost the suspicion that it was all fixed. Toward the day's end, the
polling station at al-Tisayn neighborhood was close to empty, but the ad-
ministrators said they had had more than two thousand voters during the
day—a good showing. The staff made a good slice of Kirkuk: a Kurd, a
Turcoman, a Christian, and an Arab.

"You see the whole Iraqi family here," said Omar Muhamad, a Kurdish
engineer working at the center. Nearby a Turcoman newspaperman, also
on staff, agreed cheerfully. "Yesterday everyone was afraid, today we all
feel very strong," he said. But then the warmth disappeared: "Still, we have
heard that in Shorja, the Kurds are not allowing Turcomans to vote."

"Excuse me, but did you see this? Speak only of what you saw," said
Muhamad, the Kurdish engineer, who hadn't walked so far away. "No
please, I am speaking—he's not letting me speak," said the Turcoman,
who wouldn't give his name. "There was no problem, but some mistakes.
And some groups want to make trouble," the Turcoman continued.
"This is the first time we've tried this in Iraq. Maybe next time it will be
normal."

A brief foray into the Arab quarter revealed an even starker contrast.

With an orange election sticker covering the upper-right-hand corner of our windshield, my colleagues and I felt safe enough driving the city's empty streets, but pulling through the neighborhood of Nasr, we could feel the mood change completely. Here the silence felt oppressive, and the few people on the street looked at our car with fear. Sunni Arab groups across the country that had been ordered to boycott here were under threat to stay away from the polls, and any vehicle looked to them like a rolling fireball. The few pedestrians out on the street stared us down as we drove by, their faces heavy with the knowledge that today the insurgents would be killing their own—attacking Sunni Arabs who dared to break the ban. It didn't help that American helicopters kept ripping through the air at very low altitude, barely audible before coming so close they blew your hat off. In the Kurdish neighborhoods that was a reassuring sound, yet in Nasr it felt like the last thing you might ever hear.

With no one around to ask for directions, finding a polling station in an elementary school took some time. We sped toward the safety of razor wire around the schoolyard, but when we were about fifty yards away, the Arab police greeted us with a few shots in the air. We all began shouting "journalist!" in Arabic and pointing frantically to the sticker on our car. The cops responded by firing more shots, but these didn't look so much like warnings as poor marksmanship. The driver began to turn the car around—not easy in the narrow street—but in a moment the police had rushed the car. Wearing black ski masks that made me suddenly think I was in Fallujah again, they pulled us all out and frisked us as one of the men kept his Kalashnikov trained at waist level. When they finally realized their mistake, everyone calmed down, and my disbelief turned to anger for a moment. I asked them what the hell they had been thinking. The men apologized sheepishly, and then we all laughed a bit as the adrenaline left our systems. "You should put a bigger sticker on your car," one of the policeman said, though he must have known there was only one official size.

The bullet dodging seemed even more absurd when we realized that almost none of the local Sunni Arabs had come out to vote. A few men were there and didn't seem to know whom to vote for. One man said he had voted for the Islamists, though they were boycotting the elections. "We've had no problems, though," said one of the cops. "The only shooting was at you folks."

We had been hoping to quietly slip in and out of Nasr, but the gunfire had ruined that plan. The policemen advised us to wait for one of their patrol cars to escort us out of the area. The whole neighborhood knew we were there, and suddenly everyone down the block looked a little mean. I finally got tired of the stares from a group of young men on the opposite corner and walked over to chat with them, surprising them into their Middle Eastern hospitality reflex. After a few pleasantries I asked if it was safe around here, and they told me they couldn't promise beyond this block. We waited an hour for the police cruiser but then gave up and just made a bolt for the highway, driving back toward the fiesta in Shorja without incident.

AMONG THE KURDS returning to Kirkuk from the north and south, a small number had come from thousands of miles away. Though polling stations had been set up in Europe and America for millions of Iraqi expats, Hoshyar Darbandi made the trip from Stockholm, Sweden, in time to vote, in Kirkuk, in person. At forty-three, Darbandi looked younger than the cousins he was staying with in Kirkuk, even with his silvering hair. Other features marked him as a returnee, like his new ski jacket and flashy running shoes. Darbandi told me he had come back so he might vote not only in the national elections but also for Kirkuk's city council—Kirkuk was the only part of "Iraq" he really wanted to bother with.

"We've never written our own history," Darbandi said as he walked away from the polling station in Shorja. "It's always been forced upon us. We're dreaming that this time Britain and America will help us write our own history—not to build our country, but just help us live with the Turcomans and Arabs."

Darbandi had left his wife and two children in Stockholm this trip, with a mind toward bringing them back soon if things looked good. He wanted to come home to Kirkuk, but the mess around him started looking like a hard sell for his children, ages six and eight, who knew only European living. He was torn, and a bit hesitant in his manner, trying too hard to like being back. Having left Kirkuk in 1985 to avoid serving in the Iraqi army, he had fled across the mountains to Iran, where he stayed less than a year—including a six-month prison term for talking politics a little too loudly. After smuggling himself to Sweden, Darbandi joined the thousands of

Kurds in the European diaspora.* He had spent nineteen years in Sweden, marrying another "Swedish Kurd" and raising his kids bilingual, always with the hope of returning. During that time his older brother died in the 1991 Kirkuk uprising. Darbandi's blood was calling him back to Kirkuk.

"This is my father's city, my hometown. It's not about oil—not for us," Darbandi said, but he knew that the oil was what would bring the outside world to Kirkuk, and perhaps to Kurdistan. "One thing I learned in my years in Sweden—America and Europe want business. And if we lose Kirkuk to the Arabs, there will be no business here for the Americans. That's why the Kurds here are so much better off than the Kurds in Turkey: they have no oil," he said.

Not a member of either party, Darbandi felt the same ambivalence as many independent-minded Kurds. When Talabani and Barzani went to Baghdad, he wanted them fierce and maximalist; when they came home to Kurdistan, he wanted them to keep their peace and share their power. He hoped for an American-enforced truce that would help Kurds start to finally enjoy some of the wealth of Iraq. But if you asked Darbandi whether he preferred Iraq or a free Kurdistan, it was no contest. He wanted Kurdish independence, and Darbandi realized that it would require the return of many people like himself—foreign-educated and relatively wealthy—if Kurdistan were to have a chance. After the elections, Darbandi went home to Sweden and asked his wife to pack up their house.

EVEN AS THE Kurds got out the electorate for a new government in Baghdad, most Iraqis suspected that they would rather have been voting to separate and form their own country. If there had been any doubt, it disappeared on Election Day, when volunteers sitting at tables outside all the polling stations across the north presented voters with an informal ballot asking them if they wouldn't rather secede. Karwan Kader, one of the founders of the Kurdistan Referendum Movement, a group of Kurdish activists formed one year before the elections, presented it as a matter of setting right the errors of 1919.

---

* Reliable figures about Kurdish expats in Europe and America are hard to come by, but the Kurdish Institute in Paris puts it at 850,000. The large majority are from Turkey.

"When Kurdistan was attached to Iraq, no one ever asked us if we wanted to stay or not," he said. Kader and his colleagues, in a remarkably short time, had gotten some 1.7 million signatures on a petition to hold a referendum for Kurdish inclusion in Iraq. If Iraq was being created anew, Kader said, this time it should be done with the consent of the Kurds. "Saying what the Kurds really want is the best means to keep not only Iraq but the whole region safe and stable. It's not violence; it's the most peaceful and democratic thing," he said.

Kader's statements were more than a little coy—he knew what the result of the referendum would be, and that it would throw more dynamite onto the short-fused geopolitics of Iraq, since Kurdish politicians had to spend so much time in Baghdad persuading people that the Kurds could be trusted to work for a unified Iraq. At the same time, Kader's arguments were hard to refute; instead the Americans ignored them, refusing to see him when he brought a petition for a vote on Kurdish secession to the CPA in Baghdad. Bringing the same list of signatures to the United Nations got a more pleasant brush-off, since the U.N. had hardly any say in Iraq. The Kurdish parties, on the other hand, didn't mind seeing the volunteers with their makeshift ballot boxes outside the official voting centers. Both the KDP and PUK publicly disavowed any connection to the Referendum Movement, but the organizers would never have been able to set up without the blessing of the parties. Kader said his movement was neutral and saw this as a beginning of reform with the two entrenched parties.

"They shouldn't keep all their meetings in the dark," said Kader. "They can't exist without the people. We don't know if what we are doing serves them or not, but we'll continue our struggle."

Barzani and Talabani clearly had an idea that the Referendum Movement would serve a purpose, even if both leaders knew that the dream of an independent Kurdistan was a long way off. On Election Day, nearly two million Kurds stopped at the little tables outside their polling stations and picked up ballots with an Iraqi flag on the top half and a Kurdish flag on the bottom. Ninety-eight percent of them passed over the flag that had "God is great" written in Arabic script. Below it they circled the yellow sun of the Kurdish flag, the same flag that Mulla Mustafa Barzani flew briefly in the Mahabad Republic of 1946. The next time the Kurdish leaders went to Baghdad, they would have another fresh bargaining tool to pressure the Arabs with—the documented fact that only 2 percent of Kurds wanted to stay in Iraq.

THAT EVENING SPORADIC gunfire sounded across Kirkuk, but the party resumed at Mam Rostam's house, with old friends stopping in to congratulate him on the Kurds' presumed election victory in Kirkuk. "I've been facing death for thirty-five years for the sake of democracy, for the right to vote," said Rostam. "Anybody against democracy should be dropped in acid."

Two weeks after the elections, the results confirmed predictions, with massive turnout for the Shi'ite Arabs, especially the religious parties. The Kurds pulled in nearly 80 percent of their eligible voters. In Kirkuk the Turcomans had a very small turnout, suggesting that the number of Sunni Turcoman voters in the entire country was in the low hundreds of thousands, though some of them may have voted for the Kurdish list, which included a few Turcomans. Shi'ite Turcomans probably supported the Shi'ite Alliance, which had come away with 60 percent of the vote—a powerful majority but not the two thirds needed to select the president. For that they would need to woo the Kurdish leaders, who came to Baghdad commanding 26 percent of the vote, enough to make them the decisive minority. The deal was obvious: the Shi'ites would support Talabani in the ceremonial position of president in exchange for the Kurds' support in picking a Shi'ite Arab as the more powerful prime minister. But the procedure was front-loaded for endless bargaining, since the minority's only real power came at the moment of naming the prime minister. Every detail would have to be worked out before Talabani could take office and implement the deal. Candidates for each ministry were weighed for their qualifications, but much more for their ethnic and sectarian alignment. The horse trading began and seemed never to end.

Washington's clock was ticking much faster than Baghdad's, as February turned to March with no Iraqi government. One major dispute was the apparent Shi'ite choice for prime minister, Da'wa party leader Ibrahim al-Ja'fari. The Kurds would have preferred Adel Abdul-Mahdi, whom they thought of as more friendly to a secular Kurdistan—in fact more friendly all around. Ja'fari's long exile in Iran had taught him the trick of holding endless conversation without any discernible substance.

Ja'fari had led the opposition to the Kurds' key veto provision in the TAL, and they expected him to continue doing so in the upcoming negotiations over the constitution. As the haggling dragged through the month of March, the Iraqi power vacuum fed the insurgency, and Condoleezza Rice phoned both Kurdish leaders personally to push for action in filling the posts. But Iraqis could have easily asked her to do the same thing in Washington. Inexplicably, for at least the second time since America launched the most ambitious foreign policy venture since World War II, no one sat in the driver's seat in Washington.

In February, Ambassador Negroponte accepted the newly created job of director of national intelligence, the "intel czar" position designed to orchestrate all of America's competing spy agencies. Negroponte's zeal to leave Baghdad after about six months on the job wasn't unusual—the entire American operation seemed to be running like a temp agency. James Jeffrey took over as chargé d'affaires, but he soon found that Condoleezza Rice, having moved from the White House to the State Department in the second Bush administration, wanted a direct hand in Iraq policy. Rice was a Soviet expert, and her migration to a Middle East focus had been reluctant and slow—she brought weight but little understanding. Her crucial failure in the national security advisor's role had been an inability to synchronize the Pentagon and the State Department, and she still appeared unable to get them together for the Iraq effort.*

America needed a new ambassador on the ground quickly, and the logical choice was Zalmay Khalilzad. He belonged to the core group of neocon true believers, but all his time on the ground showed him to be pragmatic and free of the head-on arrogance that had bothered so many Middle Easterners. Khalilzad had just stage-managed a constitutional process in Afghanistan and left on excellent terms with the Afghan lead-

---

* This problem dogged Rice until Donald Rumsfeld finally left office in November 2006. One clear example was the initiative to set up provincial reconstruction teams in Iraq. The "PRTs" had successfully brought civilian experts into far-flung provinces in Afghanistan. During the year that Rice tried to push the same model in Iraq, she was unable to get the Pentagon on board (it sounded way too much like nation building) even though commanders on the ground were in favor of it. After a year, only a half dozen PRTs were in place because the State Department couldn't manage to get the U.S. military to agree on how to protect them.

ership. But there was a snag—Khalilzad made a diplomatic faux pas some-time in 2004, being a little too frank about American policy with the U.N.'s Lahkdar Brahimi. Somehow the need for leadership on Iraq didn't trump the White House's need to slap Khalilzad's wrist, and the administration held him out for a few months as punishment.[6] Washington finally named him ambassador in April 2005, but Khalilzad didn't arrive in Iraq until the third week of June, and even then he returned to Washington for a round of meetings before finally settling in Baghdad at the end of July—in all, a four-month gap in leadership at, arguably, the world's most important embassy.

With no other knowledgeable voice in Washington, Khalilzad essentially took over the entire Iraq policy and left for Baghdad. Other neocon planners had moved on: Wolfowitz to the World Bank and Feith to academia. Robert Blackwill left the National Security Council when Rice went over to the State Department. After Secretary Rice picked Ambassador Richard Jones as her Iraq advisor in the State Department, he stayed only two months in the post. I did a brief poll of Iraq watchers in the capital that summer, asking who was in charge of overall Iraq strategy, and the consensus was "Tell me if you figure it out." Eventually the thirtysomething Meghan O'Sullivan, by then a scarred veteran of the State Department Iraq desk, ORHA, and the CPA, would become the last person standing on the Bush Iraq team and take over the issue for the National Security Council. But for the time being, it was all "Zal," and the Kurds were delighted.

Before Khalilzad's confirmation hearing in Washington, Hoshyar Zebari and Barham Salih had lunch with him at the Ritz-Carlton on M Street, and the three friends discussed their concerns about Iraq and about Kurdistan.[7] The two Kurdish envoys also let Khalilzad in on a practical joke they had played on his predecessor.

"When Negroponte called them in to tell them I'd been appointed, they'd both told him it was completely unacceptable!" recalled Khalilzad. "Negroponte was startled, and they put him on for a while before they let him know it was fine, we were all old friends."

After Khalilzad was appointed, Salih met with him again, at a low-key Italian restaurant along with their wives. It was like 1991 all over again, but both men had grown powerful in the previous fifteen years. They focused their discussion on the Iraqi constitution, the Bush administration's key goal. Not only would it be a legitimate legal framework, but if Iraq had a constitutional democracy, no matter how weak, it would also really mean something of a "mission accomplished" for the White House. Salih had been made planning minister in the new government, but he also laid out the Kurds' concerns, knowing full well they now had a friend in charge. Khalilzad, Salih said, "knows the culture and understands the geopolitics better than anyone I know. If [he] had been there earlier, maybe some of the mistakes never would have happened."

THE NEW IRAQI transitional government was finally sworn in at the beginning of May, more than three months after Election Day. Talabani became president and, following the hard-fought bargain, named Ibrahim al-Ja'fari as prime minister. Hoshyar Zebari remained in the post of foreign minister, and Kurds held five of the thirty other ministries and one deputy prime minister position. In Kurdistan the event unraveled a Mexican stand-off of internal politics. The Kurds had waited for the final deal in Baghdad before they could go ahead and inaugurate the new Kurdistan Regional Government—which would be calibrated perfectly to keep the KDP and PUK in balance. Until Talabani was in for sure, Masoud Barzani had to wait to stand up as president of the KRG in Erbil. His nephew Nechirvan took office as Kurdish regional prime minister, with the PUK's Omar Fattah as his deputy and Adnan Mufti as speaker of the parliament. Just as in the greedy madness of the 1992 government, the rival parties needed balance down to the number of tea boys in the lobby. Parties representing Turcomans, Christians, Yazidis, and Islamists also held a few seats and smaller ministries.

Despite their internal competition, the Kurds preserved a unified position toward Baghdad, and the natural tension between the two capitals, Erbil and Baghdad, got a kick start when Condoleezza Rice came to Iraq on May 15. Contrary to any protocol, she stopped first in Kurdistan to talk with Masoud Barzani before flying south to meet with Prime Minister Ja'fari in Baghdad. The snub might have bothered Ja'fari, but it positively incited the Turks, who still opposed the idea of a federal system in Iraq and persisted in hoping the Kurdistan Regional Government was just a bad dream they would soon wake their way out of. And if Ja'fari resented the mirror government to the north, it was nothing compared to how much he disliked working with Talabani.

The Shi'ites and Kurds still shared compatible goals—each wanted to

dominate their own regions—but the goal of federalism always fit better
with the larger Shi'ite Party in southern Iraq, SCIRI, which could easily
see itself in charge of a huge autonomous "Shi'istan" spanning from
Basra to Karbala.[8] Ja'fari's Da'wa party was smaller, however, and beholden to the parliamentary support of another Shi'ite leader, Moqtada
al-Sadr, who opposed federalism as well as anything else the Americans ex-
pressly supported. Politics aside, Ja'fari's and Talabani's personalities were
like chalk and cheese. Ja'fari soon proved as inactive as he was untalkative;
Talabani, by contrast, a busybody at his quietest moments, couldn't stand
for a second of dead air coming from Baghdad. Within minutes of taking
office, he began making pronouncements about plans for employing fac-
tional militias to help the security situation, about the time frame for the
constitution, and about addressing the issue of Kirkuk. Talabani held security meetings that Ja'fari, indignant, refused to let his ministers attend.
By mid-summer the two were hardly speaking.

The dispute went public for the first time during the August funeral of
Saudi Arabia's King Fahd. Talabani flew to Riyadh as Iraq's head of state,
and the Sunni vice president Ghazi al-Yawar, believing he was filling in
for Ja'fari, went by separate plane. Unbeknownst to either, Ja'fari decided
he would attend after all and came on a third plane from Baghdad. However, Iraq had only an embarrassing two seats in the pavilion. Ghazi al-
Yawar graciously yielded his seat to the older Talabani. A similar dispute
saw two separate delegations go to the U.N. General Assembly, and the
two camps fought for physical turf inside the Green Zone. At one point
Talabani's pesh merga drew guns on partisans of Ja'fari's Da'wa party in
an argument over who would get to use one of Saddam's palatial buildings. Khalilzad intervened before shots were fired, and Talabani came
away with the building.[9]

Besides the petty arguments, the Kurds had a real objection to Ja'fari's
government, concerning the only piece of Iraq they wanted that remained
south of the green line—Kirkuk. Through the period of Iraq's interim
government and now into the first elected term, both the Kurds and
Baghdad selectively observed the transitional administrative law that Bremer's people had labored over. Within months of Ja'fari's inauguration,
Kirkukees were complaining that he had blocked funds for the "normalization" of Kirkuk. The Kurds had fought hard to get control of the oil
ministry but failed, and as a result the Northern Oil Company, based
outside Kirkuk, still had almost no Kurds among its twelve thousand

employees. The Kurds' overriding goal was to make sure that enough of them would be officially returned to Kirkuk, so that in an eventual referendum, the city would vote to join the Kurdish region. To the rest of Iraq this looked like a program of "Kurdification" was taking the place of the old "Arabization."

Ramadan Rashid, Kirkuk's underground resistance leader, was disgusted with the stalemate. The new government in Baghdad, he said, had pledged two hundred million dollars to help with Kirkuk, but Ja'fari wouldn't let any of the money come north. What's more, Ja'fari kept sending his own party members up to the city to take key jobs, a reminder of the way Saddam had sent Baghdad Arabs up to work in the oil company. Kirkuk's city council, dominated by Kurds after the election, refused to work with Ja'fari's appointees, and nothing got done. Rashid blamed both sides.

"If the Kurdistan Regional Government were serious, they could have easily implemented the normalization without a penny from the central government. But they say KRG funding needs to stay only in the Kurdish region," said Rashid, observing a construction boom in Kurdish cities like Erbil and Sulimaniya.

The Iraqi property claims office set up by the CPA had managed only about twenty-five hundred settlements since its creation, and had more than thirty thousand pending. Even for those adjudicated, no money arrived for Kurds to return or for Arabs to resettle elsewhere. Before one side had clear ownership over Kirkuk, it seemed, no one was going to put up the money to rebuild it, and into the vacuum poured Iraq's growing chaos. Insurgents found fertile ground among Kirkuk's nervous Arab population, and soon much of the city became a red zone, connected directly to the hotbeds of Tikrit, Samarra, and Baquba. The Kurdish parties did send as many Kurds as they could into Kirkuk's safer outlaying areas, where the pesh merga could still protect them. Along the wedge of land between the roads to Erbil and Kirkuk new houses sprung into new neighborhoods, with the clear blessing of the Kurdish authorities. Kurds even tried to lay their claim as far away as Tal Afar—a predominantly Turcoman city near the Syrian border—resulting in more charges of expansionism. As usual in Kirkuk, everyone had their own set of numbers and their own form of math.

"Kirkuk is a time bomb," said Zhala Nafwachi, a Turcoman councilwoman, after the elections. "The Kurds are always pretending they make the majority, but in reality Kirkuk is 70 percent Turcoman. They are sneaking into the city. We reject all elections and what they say. And there is no Turcoman house without its gun. If it continues like this, we will have no choice but to use them."

While some Turcomans had radicalized, many of them did so along religious lines, joining with the growing base of the Mahdi Army, led by Moqtada al-Sadr. Sadr had become as much the voice of the urban poor as a Shi'ite religious leader, and he knew he would find willing recruits in Kirkuk. Sunni Arabs also tried to hold on to their turf, and complained that Kurds were staging pogroms in the countryside. In the farthest southern reach of the old safe zone, the Arab governor of Diyala province tried to respond in kind and reassert control over the town of Kifri. Officially, Kifri had been carved off of Kirkuk province and added to Diyala during Saddam's Arabization. But as a Kurdish majority town, it had easily been taken in as part of the Kurdish safe zone in 1991. Kifri had been part of the safe haven under Kurdish administration for thirteen years, but the Diyala governor took advantage of the ignorance of American troops and almost convinced them to start shooting up the pesh merga guarding Kifri as if they were an insurgent group occupying the city.

When I spoke with residents of Kifri after the 2005 elections, they predominately wanted to stay within the safety of Kurdish region. The town had always felt a bit different from the rest of Kurdistan, being part of what the Kurds called "hot country," but for people in Kifri, the hot country was the rest of Iraq. Even Arabs preferred to stay in the northern Kurdish region rather than be reattached to Diyala, whose capital, Baquba, had become a byword for insurgency. "I've never been to Baghdad, but all I hear about there are bombs," one teenage Arab girl told me, summing up the opinion of most of the people I interviewed.

With car bombs exploding daily in the rest of Iraq, it should have been easy for the Kurds to convince minorities in the city of Kirkuk that their best interest lay in joining the stability and prosperity flowing from the north. The numbers also argued for joining the north. Turcomans and Christians, a tiny minority in Iraq, would make a proportionally larger minority in tiny Iraqi Kurdistan. The Kurdish authorities could have flooded Kirkuk with reconstruction funds and technical assistance to win over the population without resorting to strong-arm tactics. Instead the old rivalry between the KDP and PUK reared its head again, and the

Kurds seemed intent on stacking Kirkuk's government with party loyalists (an equal number from each party, of course) and shoving their demands down the city's throat. While there were Kurdish proponents for a charm offensive to win Kirkuk, voices like Mam Rostam's drowned them out. The United States also played a schizophrenic role.

While dire predictions of a civil war sparking in Kirkuk proved premature, Kirkuk was no longer safe for foreign-aid workers, journalists, or anyone outside their own ethnic quarter. The Iraqi National Guard in the north, nothing but reflagged pesh merga, happily cooperated with the Americans in the counterinsurgency but still took orders from the Kurdish parties. Many American units seemed to follow the same arc as the troops in the city of Mosul did—first trying to be balanced and then realizing that every faction in the country had an agenda and that the Kurds' was closest to the Americans'. When Arabs and Turcomans in Kirkuk began to report that scores of their young men had disappeared into Kurdish prisons in the north, it turned out that U.S. military intelligence was aware of the "abductions." The Americans apparently considered the Kurdish prisons a much more secure place to leave a detainee, where some of them might be held indefinitely.

"We know we can drop a guy in there and he'd be taken care of and he's safe," Major Darren Blagburn told the *Washington Post*. An intelligence officer from the 116th Brigade Combat Team in Kirkuk, Blagburn didn't admit to any U.S. role in the prisoner transfers, as the embassy and the U.S. military denounced it, but with Iraqi jails becoming a revolving door in the vacuum of the Iraqi judicial system, there was clear sympathy toward the idea of sending suspects north to Erbil or Sulimaniya, where they would actually be held, certainly interrogated, and perhaps even tried in a court. Barzani and Talabani were happy to provide the service, wanting to help American troops root out insurgents, and also to continue the close ties between the Kurdish and American security forces. Scores of Arabs and Turcomans who disappeared in coalition raids later wrote their families letters from Kurdish prisons through the Red Cross, and some complained of torture and poor conditions. The outsourcing of prisoners continued long after the story broke in June 2005; many prisoners sat in Kurdish jails for years, where they suffered regular mistreatment including beatings, stress positions, and solitary confinement.[10] In Kirkuk and Mosul, Kurdish soldiers in the police force and the army sewed a Kurdish flag onto their uniforms and flak jackets. If Arabs and Turcomans hadn't considered joining the insurgency before, the Kurdish and American co-operation probably helped many of them decide.

"Even the Kurdish police only join [the police force] because it's good pay," Ramadan Rashid admitted. "They have no experience, no training. And the Arabs who come in were mostly former Saddam Fedayeen. And because they live in those areas, they have no choice but to collaborate with the insurgents."

As THE SUMMER of 2005 burned away, the disputes only heated up around the keystone of the new Iraq, the constitution. Judging by the time it had taken to reach a consensus after the January elections, agreement on the constitution promised another interminable set of late-night negotiations. Bremer's CPA had left Iraq with the deadline of August 15 to draft a constitution—a good six months after the first elections. But with the Iraqi parliament still finding their chairs in early May, a constitutional drafting committee wasn't appointed until the middle of the month. Divided mostly between Shi'ites and Kurds, according to their share of the parliament, the committee in its original form contained not a single Sunni Arab among its fifty-five members. In early July, fifteen Sunni representatives were added after strong U.S. pressure.[11] When insurgents shot to death two of the Sunni framers, it became glaringly obvious that trying to write Iraq's first democratically drafted constitution in only a few weeks screamed of madness—obvious to everyone except Washington, which had just sent Zalmay Khalilzad with strict marching orders.

The deadline had built-in flexibility; by August 1 the committee could ask for an extension, and many outside observers suggested another six months. But after a punishing year, Washington couldn't bear the thought of letting the process slide and brought the hammer down. On the last day of July, President Jalal Talabani emerged from a meeting with Khalilzad and declared his full support for the August 15 deadline, and other leaders started to follow suit. Again, Mahmoud Othman, still a self-appointed Kurdish critic-at-large and a member of the new parliament, raised the voice of dissent.

"Iraq hasn't had a good constitution in eighty-plus years. Will it really make a difference if we wait a few more months to get it right?" he told the *Guardian* newspaper and the many other journalists who came to him asking for his opinions.[12] Other Kurdish leaders made less of a fuss, however, since they felt they were holding all the cards.

The Kurdish delegates came to Baghdad in the very comfortable possession of a veto for the process. Article 61(c) of Bremer's TAL still stood, meaning that any three provinces that mustered a two-thirds vote against the constitution could veto the document. If the constitution was to their liking, the three Kurdish provinces would ratify it. Otherwise they would knock it back and the whole process would begin again. It was much easier to be patient in the north, where car bombs weren't taking a daily toll.

The Kurdish negotiating team kept many of the same members who had worked on the TAL, including the outside advisors. The first time, Bremer had been able to split off the leaders and personally persuade them to yield some of their demands. This time the delegation was unified under Kurdistan Regional Government president Barzani, who was determined not to repeat the mistake. To that end, Barzani tied his own hands before coming to Baghdad. The Kurdish parliament passed a resolution for him to take to the committee, with a lengthy list of Kurdish minimum demands: retention of the pesh merga, control over local oil resources, a referendum over the status of Kirkuk, Kurdish representation in Iraq's foreign embassies, and the power of regional law to trump national law. With the resolution in hand, Barzani felt he could stonewall the negotiations, and with the most democratic of excuses.

"Kurdistan will never accept less. If [the constitution] fails, the next negotiations will be about independence," Barzani told one of his advisors.[13]

Adding to their confidence, the Kurds found a booster in SCIRI. Barzani's accord with the Shi'ite clerics in the south still held—they both wanted to be left alone by Baghdad. Abdul Aziz al-Hakim now proposed that the nine Shi'ite provinces in the south form a super-region—not just a three-province region like the KRG, but a federal state comprising all of southern Iraq. That would leave the Sunnis without any of Iraq's oil. Already feeling besieged, the Sunni representatives walked out of the constitutional talks more than once, but America kept pressing them back to the table, promising that controversial subjects in the constitution could be put off and then worked out as soon as possible, but after ratification. The Kurds, by contrast, were determined that their demands not be kicked down the road this time.

"In our experience, 'as soon as possible' means never," said Khaled Salih, one of the Kurdish delegation's advisors.[14]

But again, the Kurds found the Americans thrown into their arms. The Shi'ite and Sunni Arabs had found common ground on one issue: Islam. Though they prayed differently, both groups had radicalized along religious lines. Many of their suggestions regarded curtailing rights for women and letting Koranic law supersede the state. Washington was faced with the prospect of producing a new Iraq that looked an awful lot like Iran, and would probably become its satellite. The few secularists inside the Arab delegations had their voices shouted down. Of course the United States wasn't an official party to the negotiations, but it went without saying that the document had to be acceptable to America; otherwise the U.S. military might not be around to help the new government stay on its feet. America and the Kurds united in fear of the thought that Sunni and Shi'ite might find common cause in the creation of a theocracy. "Minority rights, women's rights, and a division of powers were always on the Kurds' agenda," said Salih. "We were the only force demanding it, so it was easy for the U.S. to back our demands."

With Ambassador Khalilzad shuttling between the groups, the usual all-night negotiations passed the August 15 deadline and went on on another night and then another week. After two weeks of trying to find a compromise, even Khalilzad gave up on trying to placate the Sunni delegates, who rejected the basic notion of federalism, which had become sacred to both the Kurds and the Shi'ites. On Islam the Americans and Kurds had eked out a compromise: the Koran would be considered "a main source" of inspiration for Iraqi law but not "the source." Equally vague was the provision that no law could contradict Islam, but it seemed enough to satisfy the Shi'ites. On August 28, forty of the constitution's framers, including only four of the Sunnis, drove across town from the parliament building inside the Green Zone to President Talabani's palace on the banks of the Tigris. They read out the document and Talabani signed it, but the ceremony was muted—the constitution still had to be ratified by a nationwide referendum, now a mere six weeks away on October 15, and they would still have to do some convincing in the streets.

The Kurds had the hardest time restraining their euphoria; they walked away from Baghdad as if they had written the constitution themselves. For the Kurdish negotiators this victory was as big as when Saddam fell—it was an Iraq they could live with, and the constitution did nothing to curtail their potential of living without Iraq. The pesh merga remained as National Guard, and no other Iraqi troops could enter Kurdistan without permission. The requirement of a referendum on whether Kirkuk should join the Kurdish region became law, to be carried out by the end of 2007, which left the Kurds plenty of time to assure they would win. Should things in Iraq start to go agley, a Kurdish attaché with each Iraqi embassy in all the world's capitals would have a chance to spin the story their way.

On oil they found what looked like a working compromise. Baghdad kept control over existing oil operations with a strict revenue-sharing agreement—the KRG was entitled to 17 percent of the country's oil prof- its, in accordance to their estimated population. Any new operations would be managed by the regions, and the Kurds were already prospect- ing around Taq Taq and Zakho, with foreign investment. Oil revenue would still flow to Baghdad, but the lucrative construction and manage- ment contracts would nourish the Kurdish region, not to mention the co- pious opportunities for graft. The only demand the Kurdish team had sacrificed in Baghdad was for a referendum for Kurdish secession in eight years' time.

Despite the great success, the Kurdish street greeted Barzani's victory with lukewarm applause; after all, the entire region had recently voted to secede. Still, most of those openly in favor of Kurdish independence took a more pragmatic view of the new document—it would do fine until the rest of Iraq fell off. Then the Kurds could say they had been playing by the rules. "They won't have forced the issue themselves," said Najmaldin Karim. "It's the events and the others that have forced independence—if that happens."

Masoud Barzani echoed his sentiments: "God preserve us from civil war, but if others start fighting among themselves, we will have no alter- native [but independence]."[15]

The civil war began with the New Year.

CHAPTER THIRTEEN

Something That Does Not Love a Wall

THE HALABJA MEMORIAL, WITH ITS TWO concrete hands clasped and reaching up to the mountains behind the town, was completed just a few months after the fifteenth anniversary of the infamous gas attack. Citizens of the city still suffered from the effects of the poison as it lingered in their lungs, in strange marks on their children, in the soil and water of their valley. With Saddam Hussein deposed, the inauguration of the memorial on September 15, 2003, had been triumphant, attended by the Kurdish leadership as well as then secretary of state Colin Powell and American viceroy Paul Bremer. Powell stood next to a bank of lit candles inside the museum beneath the memorial's dome and intoned: "By your actions here at this spot and by the construction of this museum, you have made sure that you will never forget; but above all, the world will never forget. And I will always remember Halabja."

The locals had watched the building go up slowly since breaking ground in April 2000, and the structure made something of a gate to their city, stopping visitors on the road from Sulimaniya before they reached the town. The circular walls inside bore the names of the victims, and for the inauguration the Kurdish parties had adorned the graveyard outside with pro-American banners, thanking the United States for toppling the dictator. Barham Salih, still the PUK's prime minister, mused before the hundreds of cheering Kurds outside that Iraq's war criminals, especially "Chemical Ali" Hassan al-Majid, should be tried here in Halabja, at the scene of their worst crime.*

Less than three years later, on the morning of the eighteenth anniversary of the attack, hundreds of Halabja residents came out again, the children and siblings and parents of the poison gas victims. But this time, on March 16, 2006, they carried banners denouncing corruption in their own Kurdish government. Students from Halabja attending universities in Dohuk and Erbil had organized the protest, frustrated that as other cities built and grew, their long-suffering town received only empty promises. Visitors that year had come from Hiroshima and Rome for the anniversary, making a tour of the scene and symbol of Saddam's genocide against the Kurds. In good faith and solidarity, they had no idea that such visits had begun to anger the residents of Halabja. Sitting as the memorial did at the entrance to the city, pilgrims like Colin Powell and survivors from the world's other atrocities could come to Kurdistan, visit the memorial, and promise aid and support to the Kurdish government, all without ever setting foot in the town proper. None of the international donors ever came to see that Halabja still had not one mile of well-paved road, that the town lacked basic water and sanitation—their tour guides, usually PUK, would whisk them away. The students planned to block the road and prevent any more visits that would exploit but never really help their town.

The adept Kurdish security service caught wind of the demonstration plan and called in a group of the students to meet with the PUK's Omar Fattah days before the anniversary. They handed him a list of demands, which he promised to address. But the students still wanted to make their point. On the morning of March 16, at about eight A.M. a hundred of them gathered in the center of Halabja and began to walk the mile to the memorial. The sun peered over the mountains in Iran, casting long shadows down the valley on a clear spring day in Kurdistan. To the left of the marchers the fields shone emerald green where the city gives way to the lake. When they reached the entry road to the memorial, a few young

---

* Ali Hassan al-Majid was sentenced to death on June 24, 2007, in Baghdad, but never brought to Halabja. Many Kurds complained that Saddam Hussein never directly faced justice for Halabja, since he was executed soon after his conviction for a much smaller massacre in the Shi'ite Arab town of Dujail.

men poured diesel fuel on some tires and set them alight to keep any visitors from reaching the museum that day.

"It was because of their broken promises," said one of the students. "They all come to Halabja and see the memorial and then they give money—but the government keeps the money and gets rich. Here in Halabja you can see how we are living."*

What began as a student protest captured the spirit of other Halabjans, impatient after seeing themselves endlessly portrayed in newspapers and magazines, with nothing new in their town but the polished monument. The crowd swelled with older men, women, and children. Now numbering a few thousand, the mob moved toward the museum and pelted stones at the sign outside that read "No Ba'athists Allowed Here." The sign fell, encouraging the rioters. Closer to the entryway the few dozen guards began firing warning shots, then bursts from their assault rifles. The sight of their own government's police firing shots at them must have been the last straw, and the mob surged toward the monument, scattering the guards. The protesters bashed their way through the plate glass doors and flooded the small circular hall inside, breaking everything in sight—the glass display cases, the plaques with survivors' names. A few young men found cans of diesel fuel for the museum's generator and poured it on the floor. Then they torched the building.

The outraged security guards made to retake the monument when they saw the smoke, and this time they fired straight into the crowd. The protesters broke and fled and by midday it was all over. Six protesters suffered wounds, and seventeen-year-old boy lay dying in the dirt outside the Halabja Memorial, a bullet hole gaping in his chest. His name was Kurdistan ("Kurdo") Ahmed Sayed.

Even months after the event, every young man in Halabja had either taken part or wanted to associate himself with the protest. While Halabja always has a strong Islamist current, suddenly the angry youths there could have been from Gaza or Karachi or Baghdad. They distrusted America and saw conspiracy everywhere, and they yearned to take quick action, like pistols with their hammers pulled back, just looking for a target.

---

* The students whom I interviewed on September 29, 2006, withheld their names to avoid retribution for continuing to speak out.

As they told their stories in an open-air garage in the center of town, an old man sat listening harmlessly—he could have been grandfather to any of the boys. When the conversation paused, the old fellow chimed in innocently that he still loved George Bush, that the Americans had done a great thing by removing Saddam Hussein, that destroying the monument was a crime. "I lost my wife and my children to the gas that day," said Kamal Hamisli. "I had no choice but to leave them and flee to Iran with my one surviving son. Later I came back and found them in our house, and buried each of them."

The younger men listened quietly as he spoke about the holocaust that had hit their town, of how the gas smelled like perfume at first, before it began killing. Most of the student protesters had been three or four years old in 1988 and had no memory of the massacre. A couple of them laughed in that unsettling way people in war zones do. They wanted grandpa to stop going on with his tired genocide stories that didn't match the zeitgeist of the angry Kurdish young men.

"Since 1991 the Kurdish government had said it's going to rebuild Halabja. Every sixteenth of March at the commemoration, they make promises, but nothing ever comes," said one student. "Any guest coming to Halabja just went to the monument, and saw the tiles and how fancy it was. They never saw the ruined streets of Halabja."

In fact a few "guests" had made it to town on the day of the protest—several international reporters, expecting to write the perennial Halabja story and to enjoy a corner of Iraq that was cool in spring, friendly, and free of death squads. The burning of the monument by Halabja's own people so shocked the Kurdish authorities that they held a hurried press conference, panicking over what the media coverage would do to their sales campaign of "Kurdistan: The Other Iraq," which advertised the business boom in the north. On the drive back from Halabja after the protest, PUK security repeatedly tried to confiscate film from photojournalists.[1] In Sulimaniya the authorities hastened to blame the incident on outside agitators, or perhaps Halabja's Islamists. The PUK leadership seemed genuinely shocked, but nonpartisan Kurds simply nodded their heads, well aware that while Halabja went without noticeable improvement, Jalal Talabani had built a new mansion on the hill above Sulimaniya, with a Porsche parked in the back. The leadership had no idea how to spin the horrible news.

Kurdish security was not so conflicted about what to do. In raids over the next several days they nabbed at least eighty young men and took them in for interrogation and beatings. A four-year-old boy and a fifty-three-year old man were wounded in gunfire during some of the raids conducted by the PUK. One local judge even suggested that such rabble-rousers would face the death penalty under an old Ba'athist law.[2] The aggressive local paper, *Hawlati*, took the hardest hits, refusing to cooperate with a government order to turn over any photos and notes taken at the protest. While the pro-PUK journalists' syndicate buckled quickly to the request, a *Hawlati* columnist was arrested and later released on bail. Much of Halabja's frustration was shared across Iraq, as promised American aid got shunted away from public works and put toward security and counterinsurgency, but the Kurds also had some specific bones to pick with their leadership, and *Hawlati* had been leading the charge.

The weekly newspaper had found trouble early on, most notably before the January 2005 elections. *Hawlati* reporters had discovered a small trove of Mukhabarat documents detailing which Kurdish officials had been working as spies on the Iraqi regime's payroll. Some of the informers had been acting under duress, but the revelations still enraged voters in Kurdistan. The scandal broke just as the Kurdish leaders had asked the public for blind support for the election of the still unpublished Kurdistan Coalition list; now many of the names on the list appeared to be Ba'ath Party collaborators. Voting in Kurdistan felt more and more like voting in one of Saddam's yes-or-no elections, in which he was the only candidate. At first the Kurdish leadership panicked and some of the former spies feared retribution, but the KDP snipped the thread before it unraveled further. Barzani's men simply stonewalled, claiming that all their "spies" had been double agents, fooling Saddam while remaining faithful to the Kurdish cause. The PUK suddenly looked like a leaky ship by comparison.

"It became a competition. The PUK began to punish them, and the KDP did nothing. The KDP said, 'Look, you were infiltrated and we weren't,'" said one Kurdish journalist. Both parties formed committees to investigate the charges, and neither investigation went anywhere. *Hawlati* continued to publish every scandal it could, as well as the occasional blanket call to protest the political order. Some of *Hawlati*'s staff split off to form another aggressive paper, *Awane*, and two years after the first revelations, the two publications revealed more names and alluded to a list of three hundred former Ba'athist collaborators, all of them KDP or PUK members.[3] In the end both parties swept the scandal under the rug rather than face the embarrassment, but the affair helped explain why the protesters in Halabja saw hypocrisy in a sign saying "No Ba'athists Allowed Here" outside their memorial—their own government appeared to be lousy with Ba'athist informants.

PUK officials did not halt the publication of the newspapers, though they regularly harassed the writers. But on the KDP side, *Hawlati*'s editors confessed they had a very difficult time keeping an office open under the KDP's constant pressure. The local press was feeling for its red line in the new Kurdistan, and in October 2005, a Kurdish lawyer with Austrian citizenship crossed it. Kamal Sa'id Qadir, a Vienna-based exile who wrote for many Kurdish Web journals, charged the KDP with nepotism—not hard to substantiate since the most powerful men in the KDP all have the same last name. That might have been enough, but Qadir went a bit further and specifically charged the Barzanis with skimming off Kurdistan's revenues for their own enrichment. The KDP's internal security arrested Qadir in Erbil on October 26, only a day after Masoud Barzani made his first official visit to the White House as the president of the Kurdistan Regional Government. A Kurdish judge sentenced Qadir to thirty years in prison after a one-hour trial.[4]

The arrest and trial set off a storm of criticism and pressure—from free press groups as well as the Austrian government—and the KDP found itself for the first time facing the flip side of the global media it had long cultivated. Amnesty International, Reporters Without Borders, and many prior champions of Kurdish rights quickly denounced the arrest and used the occasion to express concern about Kurdistan's two increasingly authoritarian halves. Three months later, the KDP released Qadir from jail. The Barzanis, as ever denying the corruption charges, acknowledged the arrest to be a blunder.

"I call this a mistake," said Nechirvan Barzani. "That guy was crazy, and we just gave him prestige. Now just let them say whatever they want to say. You can't shut everybody's mouth. For me it's better for them to say it than to hide it."*

---

* When Human Rights Watch reported in July 2007 on widespread torture and mistreatment in Kurdish prisons, the group made a note that the KRG had been very cooperative, much more so than the Iraqi government or the U.S. government regarding detainees in Iraq. Nechirvan himself endorsed the conclusions of the report and pledged to send copies to the Kurdish security forces—whether this was sincere or not, it played very well in the media.

The Kurdish press needed to educate itself about libel and incitement, Nechirvan said. But the KDP had just received a public education: if they wanted to talk of democracy and human rights, they needed to walk the walk. The arrest of Kamal Sa'id Qadir showed the tip of an iceberg that the Kurdish parties, long set in their ways, had started to scrape.

The Kurds' frustration with their politicians simmered, growing bolder with the referendum on the draft constitution in October 2005 and the elections for a permanent government in December. Still, the Kurdish leadership went strongly into both elections, counting on over populations to vote in lockstep with them to maximize their leverage over the Arabs. Kurds in the three northern provinces indeed voted overwhelmingly to endorse the constitution. Since their leaders had practically written the document, the fear that Kurdistan would combine its three provinces for a veto had disappeared. Now the threat of a veto came from elsewhere. Inadvertently, the clause allowing any three provinces to reject the constitution with a two-thirds majority now applied to Iraq's Sunni Arabs, who had been left almost completely out of the constitutional drafting process. The Sunnis dominated Anbar province, as well as Salahudin province, which included Saddam's homeland around Tikrit. The third province they threatened to carry was Nineveh, with its hard core of Sunni military men in its capital city of Mosul. In order to make sure the constitution passed there, the Americans were counting on the Kurds.

Kurds in Nineveh made up nowhere near half the population, but all the proponents of the constitution needed was to prevent a two-thirds majority. A last-minute deal by U.S. ambassador Zalmay Khalilzad gave the constitution a better fighting chance. Promising a lengthy session for amendments later on, the American ambassador persuaded one Sunni Arab faction, the Iraqi Islamic Party, to support a yes vote in the referendum. The constitution would still need all of Nineveh's Kurdish vote to pass. Kurdish towns around the city like Sinjar and Akre would vote yes, but the key Kurdish population in the city of Mosul was shrinking.

I embedded with the U.S. military for the October constitutional referendum and requested a unit in Mosul, expecting Nineveh to be the swing state. The embed process remained the only safe way to get a feel for the attitudes of Sunni Arabs.* In random interviews around the city, I found, predictably, that most planned to vote against the referendum. Although no one I spoke with had read the draft of the constitution, they had a one-word answer for what they thought of it: *taksim*, or partition. Their community leaders had told them the constitution was a recipe to divide the country between Kurds and Shi'ites. A few partisans of the Iraqi Islamic Party told me they planned to vote yes, but the surprise came from other minorities. The Christians I spoke with all opposed the constitution for the same reason. I would have expected them to embrace Kurdish influence, but they clearly feared it—the Kurds had failed again to set an appealing example for those outside their ranks.

Inside Mosul many Kurdish families were on the run, leaving the city daily in the face of death threats from Sunni Arab insurgents. Despite their domination of the Iraqi army deployed in Mosul, and their political dominance since the January 2005 elections, the Kurdish authorities faced much the same problem the Americans did in the city center—a murderous insurgency and a local population that was not on their side. Tens of thousands of Kurds had already fled the city for the safety of the surrounding Kurdish towns; others crowded in on relatives on the eastern bank of the Tigris. To some it looked as if the Kurds wanted to annex the eastern "left bank" of the city, but on the ground they felt lucky to hold it as a buffer zone.[5] As I visited nests of KDP pesh merga around the city, they appeared just as precariously hunkered down as the U.S. Army troops I traveled with. Crossing the river meant entering a red zone as hot as anywhere in Iraq.

Mosul also made an interesting place to gauge opinions about another historic event: the trial of Saddam Hussein, scheduled to begin on October 19, just four days after the referendum on the constitution. After Saddam spent nearly a year in American custody, Iraq's special tribunal had decided to bring him and seven of his cronies to trial for a relatively minor case, the 1982 murder of 143 Shi'ites in the town of Dujail. The inexperienced tribunal brought this case first because it was uncomplicated, and a good test

---

* Embedding with the U.S. military is a trade-off for a journalist. The military doesn't practice overt censorship of anything but operational and technical details, but it's near impossible not to become biased while under military protection, and a Humvee window is a narrow lens through which to see Iraq. Unfortunately, after 2004 this became the only prudent way for a foreign journalist to travel in Iraq, outside the Kurdish area.

of their ability to try Saddam without letting him turn the dock into a podium, as Serbia's Slobodan Milošević had done. But the choice was anticlimactic, especially for victims of Saddam's later atrocities, like the gassing of Halabja and the massacre of Shi'tes after the 1991 rebellion. Asked what they wanted to see at the trial, Iraqis in Mosul across the spectrum used a surprisingly similar phrase: they thought Saddam should get a fair, just hearing. But the tone differed. Kurds in Mosul said the word "justice" with such malice that it was easy to imagine what horrible punishment they thought could fit Saddam's crimes. Many Sunni Arabs in Mosul said the word as if Saddam, given a chance, could justify his actions. I did all my interviews with U.S. troops only a house away, so if there were any outright Saddam supporters, they probably kept quiet. But one Arab, busy at a bakery preparing sweets for Ramadan, said he considered Saddam to be a prisoner of war. "You can't hang a prisoner of war. That would start a civil war in Iraq for certain," he said. Voting on the constitution and bringing Saddam to justice were both intended to bring the country together; instead they combined to make Sunni Arabs feel under siege.

On October 15 the referendum went smoothly, again providing a quiet celebration as regular Iraqis, under heavy American security and a complete vehicle ban, turned out in large numbers to cast their vote for or against the constitution. Iraq's electoral commission projected it would take ten days to tally the results from across the country, and in the meantime, on October 19, Saddam took the stand in Baghdad.[6] Only one of Saddam's five judges allowed his face to be shown on cameras, Rizgar Mohammed Amin, a Kurd from Sulimaniya. Saddam Hussein marched into the court and refused to give the judge so much as his name, shouting that he remained president of Iraq. The judge smiled indulgently and asked Saddam to relax and sit down. After a three-hour session taking down the not-guilty pleas of all eight defendants, the judge calmly adjourned for six weeks, yielding to requests from Saddam's lawyers for more time to prepare. The trial would drag on for months, and Iraqis were mesmerized by the image and especially the voice of their former leader. But the courtroom drama felt like a relic of the past, only relating to the present day as a wedge, with a Kurdish judge calling on Shi'ite witnesses to condemn a Sunni Arab.

On October 24, the night before the referendum results were announced in Baghdad, insurgents staged their most spectacular attack to date: a three-car bomb assault on the perimeter of the Sheraton and Palestine hotels in the center of Baghdad, next to the square when American troops had pulled down Saddam's statue in April 2003. Two vehicles packed with explosives rammed themselves into the high concrete blast walls around the parking lot, pulverizing the barriers to clear a path for the third—a cement truck stuffed with munitions. The truck driver got his wheels caught in the rubble and detonated far short of the building, which housed many foreign journalists, but the blasts still killed seventeen people and sent footlong pieces of shrapnel flying half a mile around.[7]

No one suggested the bombing was specifically linked to the announcement the next day, but the result of the referendum did nothing to bring Iraq's factions closer to peace.

The Kurdish-Shi'ite coalition managed to push through the constitution, with the popular vote endorsing the constitution by almost 80 percent across Iraq. But Sunni Anbar and Salahudin provinces came in solidly opposed, and a majority in Nineveh also rejected the draft—but a majority of only 55 percent, falling just shy of the two thirds needed to invoke the three-province veto. Effectively, the Sunni vote had been discounted again. They had boycotted Iraq's first elections in January, and now they had, as a bloc, rejected a constitution that would become Iraq's law. Some had predicted this as the worst possible outcome—a constitution that passed with clear Sunni opposition, smacking down the Sunni Arabs' first attempt at participatory democracy.[8]

THE KURDS ALSO greeted the constitution with mixed feelings, albeit from a different perspective. Popular sentiment was for secession, though most still understood that their leadership had played the game well in Baghdad and that international constraints forbade a Kurdish state. The frustration with being stuck in Iraq may have helped to channel growing discontent with the KDP-PUK binary hegemony. In December 2005 the Iraqi interim government's term came to an end and elections were held for a permanent four-year government. By that time the Kurdish list showed a few stress fractures—and not all from the street.

While the KDP had always been a family affair, channeling the spirit of Mulla Mustafa Barzani, Talabani's PUK still billed itself as a more modern coalition of parties. In the dawn of the new Iraq, however, the PUK was, if anything, looking slightly more like its neighbor. Jalal Talabani still ruled the party and his sons seemed to be taking a more active role. But strong personalities remained inside the PUK politburo, and they had delivered Talabani a stinging rebuke a year earlier on October 17, 2004, in a private letter signed by eight of his comrades.

"We survived the gas attacks; why should we be afraid of Mam Jalal?" said Mam Rostam, riding high in Kirkuk. He proudly supported the "signers," as the group came to be known. "We saw a diversion from the PUK's main principles and lost our patience. We are not winning a revolution to remove a dictator and bring another one. Everybody, even in your own house, has to be democratic," said Rostam, still using the *d*-word a bit loosely.

The signers, including Talabani's top two deputies, Nawshirwan Mustafa and Kosrat Rasul, knew they were staging something of a mutiny, but while the letter demanded elections within the PUK, it was more of a call to share the spoils. Talabani quickly demonstrated why he had been able to stay ahead of the pack for so many years, deftly playing his old friends against one another, and their demands were soon watered down. Sulimaniya's rumor mill took up the story that Talabani had paid each of the signers a million U.S. dollars as well, which did plenty to clam them up. When the story of their protest leaked to the press in the following months, Talabani dismissed it with confidence.[9]

"There was no challenge of my leadership in the PUK. Some comrades, a minority of the PUK politburo, wrote a letter asking some kind of demands, but even when they asked for reform, they asked for reform under the leadership of Talabani. There is no danger of any coup d'état inside PUK at all," Talabani said.

Mam Jalal insisted that he had made no concessions but willingly sent out a sort of suggestion box across the PUK's middle ranks. The signers settled for a promise of some kind of primary election to be held in 2006—by that time Talabani would be seventy-three years old and most likely reelected to a four-year term as Iraq's president. It would probably be Talabani's last public post, and the primary would be more about succession than power sharing.

Barzani had no pesky lieutenants considering him a mere first among equals, but the KDP also felt tremors of discontent. Just weeks before the December 15 vote to choose a four-year government, Kurdistan's Islamist parties withdrew from the Kurdish alliance, complaining that they had been given no power inside it. This second election already threatened to diminish

Kurdish power in Baghdad; since Sunni Arabs had pledged to participate this time, there would be much more competition for seats in parliament. The desertion by the Kurdish Islamists was a threat, and not one to leave unanswered, especially since it came with divisive rhetoric about the Kurdish list being in the pocket of the Americans and the Israelis (the latter a gibe at Barzani, whose father had enjoyed good relations with the Mossad). In response, on December 6, a crowd of protesters gathered outside five Islamic Union offices in towns around the usually quiet province of Dohuk. In the city of Dohuk the crowd soon swelled to thousands. KDP-dominated police arrived at the scene to find the demonstrators had painted the walls outside of the Islamic Union's office with the Kurdish list's election number, and were pelting the four-story building with rocks, demanding that the Islamists take down the enormous Kurdistan flag hanging outside.

The crowd got angry as a few members of the Islamic Union taunted them from the roof of the building, swinging Islamist election posters. A large number of Kurdish security personnel stood by, unwilling or unable to prevent what happened next. The first gunshot reportedly hit a policeman, and the crowd attacked the office with more than rocks. The Islamic Union partisans took cover inside as bullets suddenly ricocheted off the concrete walls. Two Islamists died of gunshots to the head; another three were wounded. The crowd surged into the building, producing cans of gasoline, which they poured on the floor. When the day was over, the destroyed building still smoldered, as did four other Islamic Union centers across the province. The action had every appearance of an orchestrated retaliation by the only real organization in Dohuk—the KDP.[10] However, Masoud Barzani's son Masrour, the head of internal security for the KDP side of Kurdistan, said the protests had been spontaneous.

"They were provoking people from different parties, baselessly accusing them of corruption. The people wouldn't tolerate that and burned their office," Masrour explained, about a year after the attacks. Then he quickly remembered his talking points. "Oh, and of course it was an unfortunate incident. It wasn't planned," said Masrour. "We investigated the incident. It wasn't the KDP—just some loyalist students." The Islamists were using the incident as a preemptive excuse to explain their poor showing in the December elections, Masrour said. The Kurdish Islamist parties had indeed lost support by aligning themselves with Sunni Arabs, but the KDP had a little bit of explaining to do in that regard as well. Even if Barzani had no apparent problems with public protests or private putsches within his party, at the polls Kurds in northern Iraq demonstrated frustration with the KDP's monolithic style.

On another blissfully quiet Election Day, the Kurdistan list did well again nationally, losing a few seats as expected, but keeping their influential position alongside the Shi'ite majority. Talabani remained president, and the Kurds actually increased their number of ministries to eight, with Hoshyar Zebari staying on as foreign minister and Barham Salih becoming deputy prime minister. Inside the Kurdistan Regional Government, the parties retained their usual fifty-fifty split in government from deputy ministers to tea boys, but popular support didn't fall along such neat lines. The PUK still clearly dominated Sulimaniya, and the KDP controlled the much smaller province of Dohuk. But Erbil, a province under KDP domination since 1996, was becoming the functioning seat of Kurdistan's two-party government, and the PUK was growing in popularity there. Even with several smaller local parties throwing in behind the KDP, Talabani's party was drawing even with Barzani's. If there were a popular election across the north, the PUK would win—especially if Kirkuk, with a clear majority of PUK voters, were to someday become part of the Kurdish region.

The KDP's conservatism did have a flip slide: most international businesspeople and consultants preferred dealing with the Barzanis. With Talabani's PUK, everything always seemed negotiable, postponable, and downright unreliable. In the KDP's hemisphere, only one family mattered, and once they made you a deal, you could take it to the bank in Kurdistan— Barzani was the bank. Sitting as he did at the head of the Kurdistan Regional Government, Nechirvan Barzani admitted that his party needed to adapt.

"There will be lots of changes in the KDP, maybe within ten years. I don't think we are that far from having independent candidates," he said, meaning candidates not blessed by the Barzani family.

"Kurds have an insurgent mentality," Nechirvan continued, allowing that neither party had managed to energize a new generation of Kurds. But he added that despite the criticism, all across Iraq people were looking for protection, and in their fear, they had come home to the traditional parties. "It's not exaggerated. People support KDP and PUK. Some criticize, but in the end they will vote for the parties."

FOR ALL ITS troubles, Kurdistan looked like paradise to some of its neighbors. The Turks had long worried that an independent Kurdistan would encourage Kurds around the region to rise up, and their assumption proved correct. But the first signs came from a surprising direction: "little Kurdistan," in Syria.

A bit less than 10 percent of Syria's eighteen million people are Kurds, but the Syrian government blocks several hundred thousand of them from their most basic rights by denying them passports. Their identity cards label them as foreigners, but they have no home country to return to, and no document to travel with. The solidifying Kurdistan next door in Iraq began to beckon as far back as the mid-1990s, and Syrian Kurds across the border watched in envy. While the young ruler of Syria, Bashar al-Assad, had made some overtures toward Kurdish groups, the music stopped after the U.S. invasion of Iraq in 2003, especially since the Bush administration loudly implied that Syria might be next.

On March 12, 2004 the issue came to a head at a soccer stadium in the Syrian Kurdish town of Qamishli. Kurdish leaders allege that the Syrian government had been arming Arab settlers in the Kurdish corner of northeast Syria for days before the game. Fans of the visiting Arab soccer team poured into the stadium armed with knives and sticks. They began taunting the Kurdish side, praising Saddam Hussein and shouting racial slurs. The Kurdish fans responded by chanting Kurdish nationalist slogans and singing the praises of the great regime changer, George W. Bush. The game dissolved in violence, and Syrian security forces quickly came down on the crowd, firing live rounds into the mass of unarmed civilians. Eleven Kurds and four Arabs died.

"The soccer match was an excuse—the Syrian government used it to attack us," said Lawki Haji,* a member of the Syrian Kurdish Democratic Party. Haji, a writer and activist, said that the Syrian government—and all the neighboring governments—were terrified by what was transpiring in Iraq. "It happened because of the success in Iraqi Kurdistan," said Haji, "and because we Kurds in Syria showed them that we understood what was happening."

The soccer match only kicked off the killing. At a funeral the following day, security forces again attacked mourners using live ammunition. Riots over several days in half a dozen Kurdish towns cost millions of dollars in damage and left more than thirty people dead. When the March 16 Halabja

---

* A nom de guerre.

anniversary came around four days after the game, Kurdish groups in Syria tried again to stand up and be counted, demonstrating in larger cities, and again security forces met the peaceful marches with force. By March 21, 2004, the Newroz holiday, Kurdish groups reported about two thousand of their number were in detention. Interrogators in Syria lived up to their reputation, and at least two Kurds were beaten to death while in custody.[11] Haji and many others chose the holiday to protest again, in any public forum they could find.

"I gave a speech in Arabic and praised successes and achievements of Iraqi Kurds," said Haji. "I wanted to give some legitimacy to our martyrs. The Syrians were saying it was outside interference, and I wanted to say no, this was legitimate."

Haji had spoken out on an Arabic satellite channel, and government harassment began immediately. He paid smugglers to get him, his wife, and their six children across the border to Zakho, in Iraqi Kurdistan. If he was going to live without documents, he reckoned, it would be better to be illegal in a country that spoke his language and respected his culture. The government of Syria soon shut the border, though it probably worried less about dissidents escaping than about help coming in from the uppity Kurds next door in Iraq. The fledgling government of Iraq sent its foreign minister to Damascus as the crisis swelled, but again the message got mixed with the messenger—it was, of course, Hoshyar Zebari, who assured Assad that the Iraqi Kurds had nothing to do with the unrest. But the old Kurdish guerrilla's very presence in Damascus, now as an Iraqi minister, probably did its own bit to embolden Syrian Kurds.[12]

Lawki Haji found his way to Dohuk, and the KDP sent him to live in an empty refugee camp nearby called Bakisli—once the home to Arabs fleeing Saddam Hussein. About a thousand Syrian Kurds found their way there in the spring 2004, and they selected Haji as their spokesman. Haji and his family filled up their new one-room tent but tried to make it a home and office—with a desk, musical instruments, some papers, and a portrait of Mulla Mustafa Barzani he had hung from a post along with a large Kurdistan flag.

For two years, Haji and the hundred families living in Bakisli waited for America to follow through with its implied threats against Syria, but their hope began to fade. The KDP stationed a pesh merga office at the site, to observe the refugees as much as protect them. Haji was lucky to find employment at a radio station in Dohuk, but most others worked as day laborers. As much as Haji would have liked to see more assistance from the Kurdistan government, he was proud of Iraqi Kurdistan's achievements.

"It's a success for all the Kurdish nation. It's created a big fear in the hearts of the enemies of the Kurds. We hope it will improve and become an independent country soon," Haji said, adding that of course he would like the same invasion and liberation of Kurdish land to happen in Syria next.

Instead the situation in Syrian Kurdistan only seemed to grow worse. In May 2005, an important Kurdish religious scholar, Sheikh Mohammad Mashouq al-Khaznawi disappeared. Khaznawi had long been a moderate voice, and sometimes the Assad government even promoted his sermons to compete with Islamic extremism. But the sheikh also preached in favor of Kurdish rights, and following the American invasion of Iraq, he became an outspoken critic of Damascus. Khaznawi was found in a shallow grave three weeks after his disappearance, and his body showed signs of torture.[13]

Two years after fleeing Syria, Haji said he and the other refugees had little hope of returning home soon. The refugees sent their children to school in Dohuk if they could, which was about a dozen miles away and not an easy commute, but at least the education was in Kurdish. And for those of college age, something was available they had never dreamed of: a college degree, in Kurdish, for free. Both Jalal Talabani and Masoud Barzani had let it be known that any Kurd who showed up to study at Kurdistan's public universities would be welcome. And the students who came weren't shy about why they wanted to study.

"I need an education so I can go home and fight for change in my country," said Ahmad,* a college student from Mahabad, the capital of Iranian Kurdistan.

AHMAD SIPPED TEA in the smoky student café at Sulimaniya University. He sported a young man's thin mustache and wore traditional Kurdish baggy trousers, even though most of the students in Sulimaniya preferred Western clothes, including the women, who would have given an Iranian mullah fits with their makeup and loose flowing hair.

Ahmad had taken part in a peaceful demonstration at Mahabad University, also commemorating the Halabja massacre. The Islamic Republic's

---

* He gave a pseudonym for fear of problems upon his return to Iran.

paramilitary student thugs, the basijis, had broken up the demonstration, delivering Ahmad a nasty crack to the skull. His best friend had joined up with the clandestine Kurdistan Democratic Party of Iran, but Ahmad wanted to complete his education, so he slipped across the porous border to Iraqi Kurdistan.

"We have to keep struggling, and the first step is to define an ideology," Ahmad said earnestly.

About four hundred of these revolutionary exchange students attended Sulimaniya University in 2006, two thirds of them from nearby Iran (more Syrians would logically have gone to Dohuk or Erbil). The PUK-appointed dean at Sulimaniya estimated that in Iranian fashion, a good number of the students were probably government spies. It didn't seem to bother the visiting students that their degrees would not likely be recognized in their home countries, nor that Iraqi Kurdistan's colleges were among the weakest in the region. Many of the students had been expelled from their home universities for political activity, and figured Iraqi Kurdistan was their last chance. The Kurdish professors didn't mind their guests either.

"They will definitely go back and try to implement the same thing in their own country. That's how education should be—something that brings freedom and opportunity," said Kaywan Anwar, a history professor at Sulimaniya, who felt it appropriate to be training agitators to send home to neighboring countries. He also thought it was a good time to export the Kurds' attitude about America. "These students should see that the Americans are no longer the occupiers—that Europe and America want to make a change in Iraq," he said, before beginning a lecture on Kurdish history to about twenty young men and women.

Again, the success of Kurds in Iraq had emboldened the residents of Mahabad and the rest of Iran's 4.5 million Kurds. As with their cousins in Turkey and Syria, Iran's Kurds suffered from chronic economic depression and saw little investment from Tehran. While the Iranian government never denied the existence of their Kurds, neither did they tolerate dissent. The flashpoint in Mahabad came on July 9, 2005, when Iranian security forces surrounded three known Kurdish activists in a poor neighborhood of the city. One of the youths, "Shwana" Qadir, had a reputation as something of a Kurdish Robin Hood, and a smile that said rascal loud and clear. He had most recently used his popularity to push a Kurdish boycott of Iranian elections, and the authorities concluded that Shwana's nonviolent activism must stop.

The three young men tried to escape the cordon in a taxi, but government agents pursued them, shooting. Their taxi overturned and a round hit Shwana in the knee. At some point in the mêlée his two companions died of bullet wounds, but Shwana managed to limp into a crowd that had gathered. Undeterred by the large number of bystanders, the agents shot at Shwana again, and a bullet brought him down. But Shwana wasn't dead, not yet, when the agents proceeded to tie him to the back of their jeep and drag him bleeding through Mahabad. When his body was returned to the family, his head was swollen, his arms broken, and lit cigarettes had been applied to the bullet holes in his flesh.[14]

Photos of Shwana's barely recognizable corpse set off a wave of riots across ten Iranian Kurdish towns and the government called out helicopters to put them down. Kurdish sources—no one from outside was able to report events firsthand—claimed at least nineteen deaths over the following weeks. Those who spoke too loudly about the incident found themselves fleeing—to Iraqi Kurdistan. One prominent Kurdish doctor and writer on women's issues, Roya Toloui, took up the case of Shwana in her magazine, *Rasan*, demanding the killers be arrested.

"The regime does things in reverse; instead they arrested me," said Toloui.

On August 1 five policemen and three policewomen arrived at her home in Sanandaj and took her in. Toloui spent sixty-six days under constant interrogation, at least seventeen of them in solitary confinement under a light that was never turned off. When she refused to sign a confession that she was a leader of the protests, her interrogator beat her ferociously and raped her. Still Toloui refused to make any confessions, and kept insisting they bring her a lawyer. When the authorities threatened to bring her children to the prison and burn them alive, she relented and signed whatever form they gave her. Upon her release, Toloui collected her children and fled across the border to Turkey, and eventually to asylum in the United States. In Washington, D.C., in the spring of 2006, she made one simple point at a conference on Kurdistan on Capitol Hill.

"We want exactly what the Iraqi Kurds have achieved—at least, if not more," Toloui told the crowd assembled in the U.S. Senate Dirksen Building.

WHILE IRAN AND Syria woke up to the problem state next door in 2003, Turkey had already been obsessed with it for a decade. More than ever,

Turkey found itself pulled between the realities of the two continents it bridges. In December of that year, as Turkish-American relations sat in a trough, the European Union finally gave Turkey a date to start accession talks. The news gave hope to Turkish secularists and modernists, confirming what they had been working toward: the golden promise of membership in the European Union. For the Kurds in Turkey and in Iraq, this was a godsend. One clear condition for joining the E.U. was that Turkey improve the state's treatment of Turkey's estimated fourteen million Kurds. Any large military incursion into Iraq would scuttle Turkey's chances for sure.

Despite twenty years of war in the Turkish southeast, the Kurds living there did not immediately look across with yearning to Iraqi Kurdistan. Turkish Kurds speak a different dialect from their kin in Iraq, and even with no investment or economic aid coming from Ankara, the depressed Turkish Kurds remain decades ahead in terms of development. For a brief while after the encouraging news from Brussels, the Turkish government seemed to lighten up about the Kurdish issue, relaxing regulation of Kurdish language and culture. Cafés in the city of Diyarbakir suddenly featured Kurdish musicians singing rebel songs that would have previously brought police knocking the door down. Kurds across the southeast, and the mothers of Turkish soldiers sent to war there, breathed a sigh of relief, but two important actors didn't seem to like the tranquility—Turkey's Kurdish rebels and the Turkish army.

With the American-assisted capture of PKK leader Abdullah Öcalan in 1999, Turkey seemed to have broken the rebels.* The guerrillas unilaterally declared a cease-fire and retreated, many of them taking shelter in Iraq's Qandil Mountains—one of Jalal Talabani's old hideouts from Saddam and familiar terrain to the PKK since the 1980s. Pro-PKK politicians

---

* The PKK has reorganized and changed its name a half dozen times since 1984, including one with the unfortunate acronym "KKK" (Democratic Confederation of Kurdistan) in 2005, and then changing to KCK by 2007. The name changes are irrelevant to anyone but the poor PKK spokesmen who have to learn the new organizational chart and try to explain it to outsiders. The sympathetic political party in Turkey, currently the Democratic Society Party (DTP), changes its name about as frequently, six times since 1991, but with a better reason—the Turkish government keeps encumbering the organization with lawsuits, and it has to fold and re-form.

in Turkish Kurdistan remained popular, but for the PKK fighters the future looked bleak. They would never be an acknowledged political party, and Turkey's offers of amnesty never convincingly included them.

A few months after the 2003 U.S. invasion of Iraq, the PKK seemed even more bewildered, waiting to figure out what this strange new Middle Eastern order would bring. Near the Iraqi town of Makhmur, a small Kurdish enclave that had been outside the Kurdish safe zone on the road between Erbil and Mosul, a refugee camp as large as the town itself made home for about ten thousand Kurds from Turkey, part of the exodus that fled Turkey's twenty-year war with the PKK. Almost all the families in Makhmur left Turkey after an incident in 1994 when the Turkish air force bombed their villages. Both the Turkish state and the PKK fought dirty during the war, which claimed the lives of more than thirty thousand people, most of them Kurdish civilians caught in the cross fire in southeastern Turkey.

But there was no doubt about the allegiance of the Kurdish refugees in Makhmur—they had PKK flags and pictures of Abdullah Öcalan hung in nearly every house. One man showed me his paralyzed left arm, the result, he said, of being kept in a tank of freezing water while under interrogation in a Turkish prison. None of the refugees believed the Turkish offers of amnesty if they returned, although in all likelihood the PKK rebels don't really want the civilians at Makhmur to return to Turkey—they make a good symbol and a bargaining chip for the guerrillas.

In October 2003 I took a drive toward the Qandil Mountains, and found myself passing something of an international border. North of the PUK-controlled city of Ranya, I traveled through a PUK checkpoint, through some no-man's-land, and up to a hilltop radio checkpoint manned by PKK soldiers—passing from the de facto state of Iraqi Kurdistan to the rebel-held enclave of Öcalanistan. The PKK rebels had a small museum and cemetery there, honoring martyrs in their wars against Turkey and the Iraqi Kurds. There were also some fresh graves from clashes with Iranian Revolutionary Guards.

A PKK spokesman who went by the name "Habun" walked me in from the station a few hours into the mountains to a camp of PKK volunteers, many of them girls barely out of their teens. They dressed in drab fatigues and led an austere existence—cigarettes were the only vice I saw, with alcohol and sexual activity prohibited. Habun introduced me to a gamut of pan-Kurdish volunteers; recently, he said, many were coming across from Iran. They all spoke about freedom and cultural rights, much like the students at Sulimaniya University. The PKK still campaigned for Kurdish rights in all four of the Kurdistans, they said, but they seemed equally or more interested in winning improved living conditions for "the leader" Abdullah Öcalan in his island prison. Habun took me later that day to another camp deeper in the mountains, where the leader's brother Osman Öcalan gave a long lecture on the mission of the PKK, hoping that the United States would weigh upon Turkey to negotiate a meaningful amnesty.

"The U.S. should force Turkey to make a solution," he said. "The U.S. intervention is justified for Iraqis to live free. The desire for the Kurds to live free is just as legitimate." Öcalan said he expected the Americans to soon realize that the PKK was a much greater force for democracy than the government of Turkey. But he didn't sound very convinced himself, and his followers had been hard at work blasting deep bomb shelters into the cliffs around Qandil, deep enough to withstand attacks from American bunker-buster bombs, which they feared might soon fall on Qandil.

"The main point is to prevent the beginning of the war. War will not solve the problems, but Turkey has to give up its problematic policies," Öcalan said, standing beneath a billboard-size portrait of his brother Abdullah painted on the rocks halfway up the mountainside. The next day I walked back out, passing the joyful young recruits as they hand-carried lumber and supplies into the mountains.

On June 1, 2004, the PKK ended its five-year cease-fire. Secretly, some members of the Turkish army couldn't have been happier. The Turkish military always considered itself the true guardian of Atatürk's dream of a secular state, but international pressure had more recently pushed them to tone down their influence in government. The rise of a pro-Islamist party, the AK, also worried them. Another military crisis would bring them again to the center of power.

Despite the fiery rhetoric, the PKK took a while to rekindle the war from the Qandil base. The violence didn't start until 2005, when small bombs and booby traps were aimed at Turkish soldiers. In late 2005, elements within the Turkish military tried to fan the flames. On November 9, in the Kurdish town of Semdinli, near the PKK's hottest front where the borders of Turkey, Iran, and Iraq meet, a man threw two grenades into a bookstore and ran. One customer was killed. The shop's owner, Seferi Yilmaz, who had spent fifteen years in prison for pro-Kurdish activities, was unhurt in the explosion, and along with some townspeople was able to apprehend the attacker and two men waiting in a getaway car. A Turkish court later identified the attacker and the driver as government intelligence officers; the third man was an ex-PKK informer. The car was loaded with weapons. A senior Turkish general, Yaşar Büyükanıt, later commented that he knew the attacker and that he was "a good fellow." The following year Büyükanıt was promoted from commandant of the army to commander of all Turkish Armed Forces.[15]

The smoldering conflict helped create a perfect storm of Turkish, Kurdish, and American antagonism, which looked ready to burst in the summer of 2006. The PKK killed Turkish soldiers at a slow but determined pace, peaking with the deaths of eighteen soldiers in combat during the month of July. At the same time, Israel launched its cross-border raid into Lebanon against the militant Shi'ite group Hezbollah, a terrible blunder in everyone's estimation—except the Turks'. As Washington nodded its approval of the Israeli strike in self-defense, the Turkish public angrily took up the slogan "Why Lebanon and not Qandil?"

If America was unwilling to help the Turks against the PKK in 2003, by 2006 America was almost incapable. The U.S. military already labored under the strain of regular troop rotations to Iraq and Afghanistan and hardly wanted to open another front in the only peaceful corner of their occupation. Washington sent a former Air Force general, Joseph Ralston, as the "Special Presidential Envoy to Turkey for Countering the PKK." The Turks knew Ralston from his time as supreme allied commander of NATO, but Turkish-American relations still swirled in a pool of distrust. Upon Ralston's arrival, Ankara quickly figured out that his main goal was to prevent the Turks from making any major cross-border raids into Iraq. The local press started to label Ralston as the American envoy *to the PKK*. Turkey's upcoming general elections threw more fuel on the fire, as did the attitude of Iraqi Kurds.

From within the safety of Iraq, the Kurdish leadership gave Ankara a hearty Bronx cheer. Hiding behind the apron of the American military occupation, the Kurds felt no need to pander to Turkey and left the camp in Qandil alone, though its location remained an open secret. The Kurdish regional prime minister, Nechirvan Barzani, lectured the Turks from Erbil.

"They cannot solve the PKK problem through military means. In the mid-nineties we carried out joint military operations with Turkey," Nechirvan said. He paused and quickly added, "It will never happen again, but what was the result? Nothing. We have to help the PKK and Turkey understand that."

When I asked KDP security chief Masrour Barzani if he would arrest the PKK's leadership even if he stumbled upon them in his garden, he immediately answered no. Talabani, as president, spoke less stridently, but still proposed negotiation, chiding the PKK leaders that the age of guerrilla war had passed. "We have advised them to end the armed struggle," Talabani said. "This is not the era of Mao or Che Guevara. It's a new world—globalization is not permitting armed struggle to be successful."

Barzani and Talabani succeeded in pressuring the PKK into calling a cease-fire in October 2006, but this did nothing to stem the Turkish anger. Meanwhile, the guerrillas had reorganized yet again. Their effective leader, Murat Karayilan, explained that they now sought a confederation of autonomous Kurdistans in Turkey, Syria, and Iran—all based exactly upon the system enjoyed by the Kurds of Iraq.[16] "Turkey wants us to put our weapons down. They want disarmament for us; they are not satisfied with cease-fire. But if that's what they want, let's have dialogue about a democratic solution for our people and we are ready to put down our weapons," said Karayilan, on the day he declared yet another end to the fighting.

Karayilan explained that the movement now had political wings in each of the four countries. The Iranian members of the PKK had split off completely to form their own armed wing, the Free Life in Kurdistan Party (PJAK). Karayilan suggested that if the CIA wanted to use PJAK to destabilize Iran, it would be a splendid idea. The split seemed almost tailor-made, allowing the Turkish rebels to try for a settlement while letting their Iranian cohorts fight on. The possibility of American support for the anti-Iranian portion of the PKK seemed more plausible as time passed and the U.S. government dragged its feet about classifying PJAK as an official "foreign terrorist organization," though it had previously denounced the PKK by any of its fronts or pseudonyms.* The Turks

---

* At this writing, PJAK is not on the blacklist, though the State Department assures that the group is being studiously evaluated. On a visit to PKK officials in late October 2007, I was taken to a PJAK safe house near the Qandil Mountains for a meeting—the two groups seem to share everything and even answer the same mobile phone.

rejected the cease-fire out of hand within hours of the PKK announcement, saying they would not negotiate with terrorists. It seemed as accurate to say they wouldn't negotiate with Kurds.

The Turkish government repeatedly refused to discuss the PKK matter directly with Barzani as the president of the Kurdish region. Increasingly for Turkish politicians and the public alike, the issue of the PKK concealed an even greater threat: the rise of Kurdistan. While Iraqi Kurds remained invisible to most Americans and Europeans, the Turkish public watched their every move and decried how some Iraqi Kurds referred to their region as "southern Kurdistan," implying that northern Kurdistan— or southeastern Turkey—would also soon join the game. It escaped no one that when the Iraqi Kurds arrested a pro-PKK politician, he was released only days later. Turks continued to believe that America had a secret plan to found a Kurdish nation on their doorstep, and eventually inside their door.

One former Turkish Air Force officer explained it bluntly. "The main problem is how they use their oil," said Mesut Hakki Caşin, now a professor of international relations at Istanbul's Yeditepe University. "Within ten years the Kurds will have an army and air force, just like Israel, and they will be demanding Turkish territory."[17]

The long-term fear was not so unreasonable. Over the decades, Kurds in Turkey might decide they could never have their cultural rights there, and a Kurdish state in Iraq might well have designs on the rest of the Kurdish-speaking region. It was the American angle that really had Caşin spooked. He had spent twenty minutes explaining how much he liked the United States and valued his time there on a military exchange in Kansas. Real hurt mixed with the anger in Caşin's face when he said, his voice rising in pitch, "The U.S. says, 'Don't worry,' but now we have a confidence problem with the U.S. Do you want the Turks as allies or as enemies?"

By spring 2007, the Lebanon example had reared its head again. Even the Israeli government had concluded that its incursion had shown the trouble with fighting asymmetric wars, in which a huge, powerful army is embarrassed by a smaller elusive foe using guerrilla tactics. American officials cautioned the Turks that they might have the same problem in any operation across the border into Iraq. Washington also pushed the Iraqi Kurds to refrain from further Turk-baiting, but in April 2007 a months-old interview with Masoud Barzani sent the Turks around the bend. Commenting on the future referendum on Kirkuk, Barzani said: "Turkey is not allowed to intervene in the Kirkuk issue and if it does, we will interfere in Diyarbakir and other cities in Turkey."[18] He later toned down the rhetoric, but the damage had been done, and the Turkish military massed a hundred thousand troops along the border.

In the United States, Defense Secretary Robert Gates and Secretary of State Condoleezza Rice both resorted to warning the Turks publicly not to invade Iraqi Kurdistan, which implied that they thought the private diplomatic channels were not getting the message through. The tension ramped up and up until the July 22 elections, when the ruling AK Party won a much stronger mandate, with support not just from its religious base but also from secularists, liberals, and even Kurdish nationalists, tired of their entrenched politicians taking them for granted. The clear loser was the Turkish military. The day after the vote, the saber rattling looked to have been a preelection charade. An aide to the newly confident Prime Minister Recep Tayyip Erdoğan told the *Guardian* newspaper, "There's been 26 cross-border operations in 30 years. If Turkey had the feeling that a 27th would put an end to the PKK, it would not blink."[19]

Despite the setback, the Turkish military wasn't going to share its power easily and it got some unexpected help—from the PKK. In the months after the elections the rebels staged several raids from across the Iraqi border, killing dozens of Turkish soldiers. Turkish public opinion stirred itself into a frenzy, with every party competing to outdo the other with bellicose anti-Kurdish rhetoric. Scrambling for cover, Prime Minister Erdoğan pushed a measure through parliament on October 17, authorizing military intervention into Northern Iraq, and the language left unclear if the incursion would be limited to the PKK. While the Iraqi Kurds protested that they had nothing to do with the guerrillas, the PKK kept poking Turkey, clearly hoping to draw the army into the quagmire of Iraq. In one ambush on October 21, near the Turkish town of Daglica, the guerrillas killed twelve soldiers and took another eight prisoner.

The Turkish military never officially admitted that the soldiers had been captured, and when Kurdish politicians from Turkey flew to Erbil, where the KRG helped facilitate the prisoners' release, nationalist politicians didn't bother to celebrate. Instead they lashed out at the Kurds in Iraq, the Kurds in the Turkish parliament, and even Kurds in the Turkish army (some of the captured soldiers were of Kurdish origin, and that seemed enough to imply that they must have gone along willingly—all eight soldiers were charged with neglect of their duty). It was a tricky paradox for the Turks to handle: they wanted to hold the Kurdistan Regional Government responsible for the actions of the PKK, all the while trying to deny that such an entity existed. When Erdoğan tried to open up a back-channel negotiation with KRG prime minister Nechirvan Barzani, the Turkish military made it public and ruined the chance.[20]

PKK guerrillas maintained that they had only been acting in self-defense and were ready to observe their cease-fire from the previous October. According to a high-ranking member of the PKK, they had exercised this self-defense 485 times during the year, sometimes quite deep into Turkish territory.[21] As usual, interviews with PKK officials were a bit stilted. More to the point was a casual encounter with some rebels near the Turkish border.

"Why does everyone call us terrorists?" was the first thing a Kalashnikov-toting guerrilla asked. He then added, "We have a right to defend our nationality. The Turkish government for years has given the Kurds no rights, no schools, no language. We have a right to live in freedom like the Kurds of Iraq."[22]

But in Washington it was back to the old math—Turkish interests outweighed the Kurds without question—and suddenly the U.S. State Department also seemed unable to utter the word *Kurdistan*.* Inside Iraq the Kurds finally figured out that baiting the Turks was a bad idea and tried to cool down the conflict. In an hour-long interview, Masrour Barzani used the word *de-escalation* a dozen times.[23]

"Let's be optimistic, and hope that the ties and the friendly relations will win," Barzani said. But the KRG couldn't help but try to leverage the situation to get some recognition from Ankara.

---

* The State Department's top Iraq advisor, Ambassador David Satterfield, couldn't manage the word at a briefing with a few journalists at the Istanbul meeting on November 3, 2007. When asked directly why he was calling the KRG the "Kurdish Regional Government" without the "stan," he replied only that action was more important than words.

"What we can do depends on how willing Turkey is to get a peaceful solution. We are willing to play any constructive role if we are included in this process," Masrour said.

The Turks successfully transformed a long-scheduled meeting of Iraq's neighboring countries in Istanbul on November 3, 2007, into an emergency meeting on the PKK, and the pressure finally yielded some concrete results. Washington began to share real-time satellite intelligence with the Turks and pressured the Kurds in Iraq to shut off the PKK supply routes. With the onset of winter, the possibility of a major ground incursion receded, and the Turks limited themselves to air strikes and some small forays of ground troops across the border. Still, the Kurdish leadership couldn't help suspect that they, and not the PKK, would have been the primary target of a full-scale Turkish invasion, should it come.

QUITE APART FROM and undeterred by troubles with the PKK, a different kind of Turkish invasion had already taken place in Iraqi Kurdistan. Turkish businessmen, engineers, and contractors, indifferent to politics, had crashed across the border, investing about three billion dollars. The run on Turkish cement drove the price up as far away as Ankara, and Turkish logos hung over hundreds of new buildings. While American and European companies remained shy of anything associated with Iraq, the Turks, alongside companies from Jordan, Lebanon, and Dubai, snapped up multimillion-dollar construction deals. They started working on Erbil's airport, designed to be larger than most in the region, let alone the rest of Iraq. By 2006, the city of Erbil seemed to double in size, with competing shopping malls springing up along the highways, most of them full of Turkish consumer goods.

"There's really no alternative to Turkey," said Ilnur Cevik, a Turkish journalist who had covered Iraq for years and then cashed in on his close contacts with the Kurdish parties to facilitate a construction business. "Turkey sells 1.5 billion dollars in goods here every year—the volume is incredible," he said.

The Turkish government wasn't stopping Turks from working in northern Iraq, but Cevik lamented that Ankara wasn't really helping foster economic ties either. Some Turkish nationalists thought that boosting the Kurdish economy was like fattening up the Kurdish tiger that would soon consume part of Turkey. Cevik thought the economic ties

would eventually bring peace between the Kurds and Ankara, on terms
that would favor the Turks. Pointing out Iraqi Kurdistan's obvious landlocked condition, Cevik concluded that sooner or later, the Kurds would
need to make some concessions to Turkey, and then his investments, already topping a hundred million dollars, would be even more lucrative, as
Turkey became an economic pipeline to the new country. Trying not to
smile, he said, "Think if everything collapses in [Arab] Iraq—the Kurds
cannot sustain any autonomy without the Turkish blessing."

The Turkish business interests in Iraqi Kurdistan started to pull some
weight—by 2007 some six hundred Turkish companies were operating inside the KRG. Even as the Turkish army gnashed its teeth at the border, the
government did not close the lucrative crossing to Iraq, where Turkish merchants trucked in cement, fuel, and consumer goods. The Turks who came
south to staff the company offices in Erbil and Sulimaniya often got along
well with the locals—they were mostly Turkish Kurds from the southeast.

THE FINAL GROUP clambering over the lines to reach Kurdistan weren't
Kurds at all, but victims of the growing violence and economic desolation
in Arab Iraq. Hundreds of Arab day laborers booked rooms in cheap hotels or slept on the steps of the mosques across the north, turning out at
dawn in the hope of earning a day's wage working in the construction
boom. In Sulimaniya the PUK security forces estimated at least eight
thousand Arab laborers had come to the city of eight hundred thousand
by the middle of 2006. For the most part they were glad to have the jobs,
and the laborers getting ready to sleep on the steps of Sulimaniya's
biggest mosque told the same story as economic migrants the world over.
They came north for the chance to eke out a living in safety and hoped to
bring the rest of the family later. One day laborer, his tongue loosed by
some of the readily available alcohol, expressed what many Arabs probably felt about the new racial dynamic that put them at the bottom. "The
Kurds treat us like Jews—like Jews!" he said in disgust. By 2008 Arabs had
competition even for menial jobs, as laborers began to arrive from as far
as the Philippines and Ethiopia.

The relative peace and stability of Iraqi Kurdistan also attracted another
echelon of immigrants. Suddenly doctors, academics, and other professi-
nals from across the south began moving to Kurdistan. In Erbil thousands

of Arabs bought apartments in the high-rise buildings under construction near the airport—a development called "Dream City" sold flats at $150,000 apiece. The Kurdish authorities required Arabs coming north to register, more or less granting them a visa to own property and live in the Kurdish region. But the Arab professionals were more than happy to do the paperwork—in Baghdad kidnappers had declared open season on them.

"All the famous doctors have moved to Erbil," said Dr. Thamir al-Hasafa, sitting in the garden of a simple rented house. "The medical students here are very happy!" Hasafa, a general practitioner, and his wife, Karema, a gynecologist, rattled off a short list of Baghdad's best-known doctors and professors of medicine, who had all recently moved north, some of them taking sabbaticals or academic exchanges to Erbil's tiny medical school. Some said they wanted to wait for the violence in Baghdad to blow over, but Hasafa and his wife were making a more permanent move and had purchased a flat in Dream City. They still longed to return to their life and their family practice in Baghdad, but Hasafa had better reasons than most to stay in the north.

In December 2004, while driving home from his Baghdad clinic, three cars spun into the street and boxed him in, just a block from his house in the al-Wiya neighborhood. A dozen gunmen grabbed the doctor from his car, trussing him up with his own suit jacket. They kicked and punched him as they pushed his face down to the floor in the back of one of the cars—at some point in the scrum Hasafa broke his leg, but at the time it seemed the least of his worries. Medical doctors had become a favorite target of Iraq's kidnapping epidemic, and their families often ended up ransoming dead bodies. The Iraqi police had proven useless in preventing the for-profit criminal gangs.

Hasafa hardly had time to contemplate his horrible situation though, for miraculously the kidnappers stumbled into a police checkpoint. They started shooting at the cops, and in the chaos, Hasafa wriggled his way out of the car and onto the ground, shouting that he was a doctor and a kidnap victim. As the police overpowered the gangsters, it looked like a rare thing would result—a prosecution of kidnappers in Baghdad. Hasafa gladly pressed charges, and interrogations revealed that the watchman hired by his neighborhood had sold him out to the gang as a man rich enough to kidnap.

Then it all went wrong. Members of the kidnappers' families paid Dr. Hasafa a visit, asking him to drop the charges against the men, one of whom was a serving policeman. Hasafa refused, but soon learned that his assailants had been freed after promising to collaborate with American soldiers against the insurgents.[24] That pushed him over the edge. In January 2005 Hasafa fled with his family to Jordan and eventually to London, where one of their sons, also a physician, lived.

Watching from afar as Baghdad continued to deteriorate, the family had an idea. The two doctors had run a family practice in Mosul for many years until they returned to their native Baghdad in 1999, and it allowed for contact with many Kurds, even some influential people who would sometimes come to Mosul for treatment. Leaving his wife and children in London, Hasafa returned to Iraq, but this time directly to Erbil on one of the new international flights. He didn't mind that the Kurdish authorities asked him plenty of questions and made him register.

"This is normal," said Hasafa, keen that the Kurds should keep out a certain class of people from the south—like the ones who kidnapped him. "They asked us simple questions. They have the right—otherwise the terrorist will come up here."

In November 2005 his wife and daughters joined him from London, and within a year Hasafa and his wife had set up a clinic in Erbil. They were learning medical vocabulary in Kurdish, but still struggling with the growing number of Kurds in Erbil who spoke no Arabic. Both maintained there is no tension, no enmity between Arabs and Kurds. A few Kurdish friends nodded supportively as the doctors asserted that the Kurds loved Arabs; they only had trouble with Saddam Hussein.

"That's why we decided to come here. They are Iraqi; we are Iraqi. Even most of the Kurdish people, they are proud to be Iraqi," said Hasafa. And then he laughed as his Kurdish friends sat in incredulous silence, too polite to contradict him.

"If Kurdistan becomes a country, then we will become citizens," his wife added, more convincingly. By 2007, however, Hasafa was thinking he would rather move to London—between the Kurdish doctors and all the Arabs moving north, the competition was making business slow.

HOSHYAR DARBANDI RETURNED to Kurdistan from Stockholm to make a go of it in April 2006. This time he brought his wife and two children, obviously "Swedish-Kurds" with European clothes and mannerisms. His ten-year-old son, Paiv, sported a spiky Euro hairdo that looked out of place among other kids his age. Darbandi's wife, Torin, shared his eagerness to come back to their homeland, but the sacrifice weighed heavier on her. For all its progressive talk, Kurdistan was still a century behind Sweden's attitude toward women and was only beginning to tackle issues like honor killing and even female circumcision. Their eight-year-old daughter, Pelin, required an outright bribe to return to Kurdistan: her father bought her a puppy. "That dog is fifty percent of the reason I'm able to stay," her father joked. Darbandi himself still looked half convinced about returning, perhaps because he was only halfway home. He had moved his family to the comfortable hilltop town of Salahudin, not his native Kirkuk, and it was easy to see why.

As with the rest of Iraq, the political inertia allowed for the most violent forces in Kirkuk to rule the day. In the center, the city hall that the Kurds joyously liberated in April 2003 was its own little green zone by 2006, to protect against an epidemic of bombs, shootings, and criminal kidnappings plaguing Arab Iraq, and now Kirkuk as well. Mixed or contested areas had the most potential for violence, which saw Iraqis killing each other more than they attacked foreign troops. The only way to speak with members from all of Kirkuk's ethnic and religious factions at once was to attend the weekly city council meetings in the city hall. Ramadan Rashid, the former PUK underground leader, felt in more danger now than he ever did while eluding Saddam's security forces.

"I'm under constant threat of assassination," Rashid said, and recounted how his brother, who had also worked in the Kurdish underground before the war, was killed by Sunni Arab gunmen in January 2006 after dropping off his kids at school. On June 13 one in a long string of car bombs killed twenty-two people just outside city hall, shattering Rashid's office windows. He knew he didn't have adequate protection, but Rashid refused to leave the city he had fought so long to liberate from Saddam. But he didn't blame Kirkukees who moved out, or those like Hoshyar Darbandi, who decided against returning.

In October 2006, I drove from Sulimaniya to visit Hoshyar Darbandi, stopping first to see his cousins in Kirkuk.* Since the opening of Kirkuk

---

* Omar Abdul Qadir, another brilliant young Kurdish journalist, had introduced me to Darbandi in 2005. George Packer wrote about Omar in the Kirkuk chapter of *The Assassins' Gate*.

in 2003, it was a much shorter drive between Sulimaniya and Erbil, with lower mountains to cross. The highway passes through Kirkuk's new sprawling Kurdish section and doesn't really involve entering the red zone, which by now made up the southern three quarters of the city. Along with a relative of Darbandi's named Ali, I drove down the same old frontline route through Chamchamal and over the ridge at Karahangir that had been so forbidding for all the years before the war. The car driving in front of us showed just how much things had changed. The Chevy Caprice listed to one side as it motored along, crammed full of Arabs returning home from a day's labor in the prosperous north. The rear left tire looked so low it might blow out, but as we tried to pass, the Arabs sped up. When we finally overtook the car, I caught the driver's eye and pointed to his tire with concern, without considering what a hair-trigger everyone's nerves and pride were riding on. I got an angry look in return. The Arab had taken my pointed index finger as a common obscene gesture, signifying my intentions with his mother. He floored the Chevy and came after us.

Ali drove as fast as he could toward Kirkuk, and more specifically to the pesh merga checkpoint at the entrance to the town—the last formal sign of Kurdish control before the disputed city. They waved us through the checkpoint—a car with a Kurd and a foreigner was fine with the pesh. Then Ali pulled over to one side. When the Arabs came through, they all stepped out of their car, their driver marching deliberately toward my door, which I quickly locked, seeing the anger in the man's face. As he started wrenching away at the door handle, Ali opened his and spoke as fast as he could. The first word he said was "ajnabi." I was a foreigner, he said, and didn't understand what I had done. I was pointing to the tire. A mile south of here yelling out "foreigner" was patently suicidal. Even in this part of Kirkuk I had taken care not to wear sunglasses or my seat belt, the telltale signs of an American that people can notice even from the street. But within the last few hundred meters of Kurdistan, being an American still afforded some protection, and the pesh merga from the checkpoint rushed over to prove it.

The angry Arab outside my window paused at Ali's explanation—or perhaps because of the Kurdish soldiers nearby. I opened my car door. "Afwan—ana ajnabi," I said—pardon me, I'm a foreigner. He smiled for a moment and made a formal face, and in forced English he said, "I am sorry." We all had a good laugh, and I stepped over to look at his rear tire with him—taking care not to point my finger.

The approach to Kirkuk from Sulimaniya disoriented me in other ways as well—so many new neighborhoods had sprung up in the north of the city that I couldn't tell where I was. But when I reached the center, it was the same dreary destruction, with no improvement from my last visit or the one before. It looked as bad as it did in April 2003, and Darbandi's cousins agreed. His uncle Abdul Hamid Omar took me up to the roof of their tiny house as his wife cooked up a small feast for that evening's Ramadan fast-breaking. I surveyed the rooftops, and the neighborhood looked like a beehive. He pointed out the original walls of the houses, and then the new ones—during Arabization Kurds had been forbidden to buy new homes, so anyone who wanted to remain in Kirkuk had to subdivide.

"By 1996 we had divided up these two houses to hold nine families," said Abdul Hamid, pointing to the smaller thin walls in the courtyards.

All of that was supposed to have ended, to be reversed. But Abdul Hamid said things weren't changing at all. Despite dominating the city government and the armed forces in town, the Kurds of Kirkuk were mostly crammed into the same sections of the city. It wasn't the Ba'ath Party keeping them there—they were simply afraid to leave the safety of the Kurdish quarter. Before, getting a job had been hard; now it was potentially deadly if the job involved a commute out of the neighborhood.

Abdul Hamid had taught school for thirty-four years before retiring and had expected a grant of land from the government, a normal perk that came with schoolteachers' pensions. The Ba'athists had never given it to him, since he refused to change his nationality to Arab. Now the new Kurdish government wasn't giving him any help either. All the legal land was tied down in the dispute over how to "normalize" the city—Kurds wanted to move in, but Arabs in the city had dug in their heels, waiting for compensation. In the meantime illegal houses were springing up all over the northern fringe of the city. I asked Abdul Hamid how many Kurds now lived in Kirkuk.

"Anyone who tells you they know the answer is a liar," he said.

He asked me to stay for the fast-breaking, but I begged off, telling him I wanted to go see his nephew in Salahudin before it got too dark on the roads; he nodded in approval, as much for my caution, I think, as for Darbandi's decision not to bring his family back into Kirkuk.

Darbandi had moved into a new part of Salahudin I had never seen before, called New Massif.* Along the ridge past all the KDP official buildings, dozens of lavish three-story concrete houses perch on the hillside, looking south all the way to the lights of Erbil. Darbandi's house had a grand staircase out front and a modern kitchen with marble tile and new appliances. The roads around the houses would be paved soon, and the exclusive community already had underground sewage pipes and electric cables. Many of the KDP's top cadres had built in the same neighborhood. The ostentatious homes up here matched the shopping centers down in Erbil, made of mirrored glass and reinforced concrete. One supermarket boasted a massive video screen outside, usually showing a soccer match. The Kurds loved the malls and went to see and be seen as much as they went to buy the Chinese electronics and clothing stacked on the shelves.

"For us a supermarket is big news!" said Darbandi. The Kurdistan he had returned to was a strange combination of modern boomtown and the scarred and neglected land of the Anfal campaign. Kurdistan was building in leaps and bounds, but it had started decades behind Arab Iraq with its oil riches, not to mention the European paradise Darbandi had left behind in Sweden. Electricity generation had stalled, leaving Kurdistan with rolling blackouts, but up here in the posh neighborhood of New Massif, a separate power plant kept electricity running twenty-four hours, and Darbandi's kids could watch the same cartoons they knew from Sweden on satellite television. Fancy sports cars suddenly could be seen around the north, including a few Hummers, looking like rich-kid toy versions of the military vehicles still patrolling the country. Some locals sported the sort of conspicuous consumption notorious in the Gulf States—ten-thousand-dollar designer cell phones and jewel-encrusted watches. Darbandi looked a bit uneasy talking about the wealth around him. He had taken a job as an advertising executive with Korek, the cell phone company that dominated KDP-controlled Kurdistan. I tried not to grimace.

For any visitor to Kurdistan, Korek spelled an enormous headache, a screaming symptom of the third world monopoly mind-set. Before the

---

* *Massif* means "resort" in Kurdish, and that is what most Kurds call the hilltop of Salahudin.

U.S. invasion, the KDP and PUK each ran competing cell phone networks—Korek in the northwest and Asiacell in the southeast. Each denied the other roaming rights and forced foreigners and Kurds alike to buy two phones and switch back and forth when crossing between cities. At the time it didn't seem much of a hardship—in 2002 using any kind of cell phone in Kurdistan felt like a miracle, and visiting businesspeople and journalists would gladly pay a few hundred dollars for a local phone line, knowing that a large portion of the money kicked straight back to the KDP and PUK. After the invasion, Paul Bremer's CPA bid out licenses to set up Iraq's new cell phone networks. Three companies won contracts dividing the country into south, middle, and north—where Asiacell got the contract.*

But Korek's CEO, Sirwan Barzani, was a nephew of Masoud. As Asiacell expanded into Kirkuk, and even into Mosul, Korek let it be known that no rival cell phone towers would last overnight in KDP territory—a threat that Asiacell crews took seriously, given the family name.[25] Even officials coming up from Baghdad couldn't use their Iraqi cell phones in the provinces of Erbil or Dohuk. Preferring to be an incommunicative island and taking their citizens with them, the Barzani family clung to the monopoly, and many others. Kurdish businesses who refused to offer KDP party members a percentage of their profits were not only prevented from working; some were thrown in jail. Korek was probably not the dirtiest deal in Kurdistan, just the most obvious. For its part, the PUK also was milking the corruption in Baghdad and Erbil, but with more than one family name in the party, it looked less obvious. The telecom scam seemed to further divide Kurdistan into two halves, but both had a common interest in keeping the graft flowing steadily, and family connections trumped technical ability.

"The two parties are dangerously united in the protection of incompetence," said one longtime Kurdish insider, adding that no single Kurdish official was untouched by some degree of corruption.

---

* The bidding process was roundly criticized as closed and nontransparent. For example, Mudir Shawkat, a prominent member of Ahmed Chalabi's Iraqi National Congress, was a major shareholder in one of the three companies, Atheer. There's no reason to suppose that Asiacell didn't cheat to get the contract, but it's hard to imagine how they outcheated Korek—maybe it was fair after all? I did not discuss Korek or any other KDP businesses with Darbandi.

Sitting in his new house on the hill, Darbandi said he enjoyed his work and that it was allowing him to get reacquainted with his home country. His wife had taken a job in the same office, and their children were fitfully adjusting to the Kurdish schools. Despite the Kurdish leaders' continued divisions, Darbandi had come to admire them in their new roles— Talabani for his image as an international statesman, and Barzani for his strident Kurdish nationalism, especially in standing up to Turkey.

"Honestly, I never liked the Kurdish leaders before, but they've been courageous—especially in saying that Kirkuk is Kurdish," Darbandi said. Asked if he was afraid of Turkish or Arab interference in Kurdistan, he quickly said no—there was only one thing that scared him.

"Henry Kissinger! We are thinking about it every minute." Without needing to explain that he meant the American betrayal of the Kurds in 1975, he added, "It's promises from the U.S. that scare me."

Darbandi quickly added that he meant no offense to his American houseguest, and that he was forever grateful for what the United States had done by removing Saddam Hussein. "If I have another son, I swear to you I'll name him Bush," said Darbandi, without a trace of irony.

As his son slowly fell asleep at the table amid a late night of grown-up talk, Darbandi returned to his main fear, that the American commitment to the Kurdish experiment would waiver. Turkey would invade or Iran would infiltrate, or Arab Iraq would smash Kurdistan again—without American pressure and protection, Kurdistan wouldn't stand a chance.

"As long as I see Americans, I'm staying in Kurdistan," he said, looking down at his son. "I'm leaving with the last American."

Visible Nation

BEHIND THE BLAST WALLS AND WIRE of the armed camp that is Baghdad, Mam Jalal Talabani smiled with pure joy as he welcomed his cabinet to the palace in October 2006. If he felt any disbelief at his great reversal of fortune, he didn't betray it. A full sixty years after joining the hapless Kurdish resistance, he now presided over Iraq's government. The men he greeted in front of the massive columns of the entryway had stories nearly as long as his own, each one a survivor of the same wars. The palace itself once belonged to Saddam Hussein's wife; now after looting and refurbishment, it hosted a continuous emergency meeting to discuss Iraq's worsening violence. Upon winning his second term as president, this time a four-year position, Talabani had insisted on more than just symbolic duties; he now presided over national security meetings twice a week, which became the most important regular convocation of Iraq's new leaders.

Mam Jalal sat on an ornate chair in the central hall of the palace, at the top of a long red carpet that stretched forty feet across the floor, under an impossibly heavy chandelier, then out the door and down the steps. Depending on the age, stature, and standing of each arrival, Talabani hefted himself out of his seat and simply rose, walked halfway down the carpet, or even trundled all the way out the door to greet his guest. Now seventy-three years old, Talabani walked with a bit of labored breath, the consequence of a well-known love for feasting that numerous dieting attempts couldn't overcome. He greeted each visitor warmly, kissing cheeks and exchanging a quick joke before dropping himself back in the chair. The parking lot jammed up with SUVs, and each arrival added a dozen rough-looking men in suits milling about the antechamber.

In the pantheon of Iraq's former resistance, the least recognizable man at the meeting was a balding, bespectacled Shi'ite Arab with his mouth curved in a perpetual hint of self-doubt. That was Nuri al-Maliki, Iraq's prime minister, who arrived among the last. Maliki was a compromise candidate and everyone knew it. After months of deadlock over Ibrahim al-Ja'fari's campaign to stay in office, the factions settled for Malaki, another Da'wa party member. Like Ja'fari before him, Malaki owed his position to support from Moqtada al-Sadr, who still managed to cross back and forth from insurgent to parliamentarian. The Kurds and the dominant Shi'ite party, as well as the small secular parties, would have preferred SCIRI's Adel Abdul-Mahdi, but at least Maliki was easy to push around. After an hour discussing the endless violence afflicting Baghdad, the ministers and party leaders adjourned chatting jovially, just as they had at countless opposition meetings over the years. They had managed to get rid of Saddam Hussein after all, and no challenge could be more daunting than that. From the outside, however, making peace in Iraq looked as though it might be.

IN FEBRUARY 2006 a bomb, probably planted by the Sunni group al-Qa'ida in Mesopotamia, had taken down the stunning gold dome of the Shi'ite Askaria mosque in the city of Samarra (more bombs took down the minarets eighteen months later). For Shi'ites the attack compared to blowing up St. Peter's Basilica—even for Grand Ayatollah Sistani, restraint was no longer an option. The Bush administration would point to the Askaria bomb as the one trigger that somehow undid all the alleged progress being made in Iraq. In fact it was more a symptom of how bad things had become.

No longer could anyone claim that the war in Iraq had to do with defeating remnants of Ba'athism or terrorist dead-enders, or even that it was a nationalist struggle that would cease with the end of American occupation. While roadside bombs still took the lives of American soldiers,

Iraqis began to slaughter one another by the thousands. Sectarian cleansing washed through Iraq's mixed cities and Baghdad's sprawling neighborhoods. When Saddam Hussein was finally executed in December 2006, there was no sense of triumph or closure for Iraqis.[1] His trial for the relatively small mass execution of Shi'ites in Dujail had resulted in a death sentence, which was carried out before the other trials—including a charge of genocide for the Anfal campaign and the mass murder of the Shi'ites in 1991—could be completed. The Kurds had the satisfaction of seeing some survivors of Anfal confront Saddam in court, but Iraq was so dangerous that few witnesses chose to show their faces. They would never see him convicted of genocide or of gassing Halabja, because halfway through the Anfal trial, the Shi'ite-led government rushed Saddam to the gallows, in the middle of the night on a Sunni Muslim holiday. The crudity of the affair lent the Butcher of Baghdad a dignity in death that he had never achieved in life. In Saddam's final moments, masked policemen nearby chanted the name Moqtada, who was considered the leader of many of the Shi'ite death squads terrorizing Sunnis in Baghdad. A tawdry cell phone video soon appeared on the Internet.

The mockery of Saddam by the security forces hanging him woke American soldiers to the fact that their allies in the police and army might be moonlighting as death squads—except the Kurds, who began all the more to distinguish themselves. Most of them fought around the edges of their own territory, which remained remarkably safe, benefiting from the most decisive factor in counterinsurgency: a civilian population completely aligned with the government against suicidal car bombers and mass murderers.

TOWARD MIDNIGHT IRAQ's democratic leaders left Talabani's presidential palace—the meeting had started a few hours after Ramadan's sunset fast-breaking, and now the men were anxious to get home for Suhur—the supper many Muslims eat late to give them sustenance through the next day's fast. Inside the hall, among the empty teacups and fruit plates, two men stayed behind: Talabani and Prime Minister Maliki. In the public eye Talabani deferred carefully to Maliki and seemed to genuinely want him to succeed. In this private setting it was different: Talabani stood with a Dominican cigar smoldering in his hand; Maliki sat at his side jotting down notes as Talabani spoke.

Talabani had now spent three years in the post-Saddam government and had seen three different prime ministers in Baghdad, each one less convincing than the last. Talabani had pledged to make Maliki into a strong leader, but the man was almost impossible not to upstage. Talabani charged forward, visiting coalition allies as well as France, Iran, and even China, constantly cultivating his mandate as president. Maliki, on the other hand, couldn't resist looking down the chasm, wondering if the Shi'ite factions he straddled would widen their differences. When President Bush called from the White House, Maliki made no demands other than to ask if it was true that Washington had decided to replace him. Talabani made the best of an impossible paradox. He possessed the famous ability to multitask contradictory policies, to charm and outwit his enemies and his allies, and to always be forgiven. But the more visible Talabani made himself, the weaker Maliki appeared, treading water at the head of a sinking parliament.

The two men finished speaking and walked out together like a student and professor finishing up a lesson. Maliki bid the president good night. His security men swept him back to the Green Zone.

Unusually, Talabani was fasting this Ramadan. It was the subject of great mirth in his entourage of Kurds, who now had to sneak their secular snacks while Talabani became grumpier as the day wore on, but failed to lose weight. After Maliki left, the president sat down to a mouthwatering spread of fruit and sweets, which Talabani tucked into, making sure that all his guests did the same. The president's aides stepped up close to his ear; as often as not, Talabani might perceive that one of the leaders at the meeting might have left feeling slighted, and after any heated argument the president's aides took orders to send over baskets of fruit, Kurdish honey, and yogurt, as well as other trinkets, to patch things up. The president was famous for his gifts, and his personal assistant always kept count of what was in the larder to send out. Tonight's meeting had gone well and no amends needed to be made ("Even Ja'fari behaved himself," remarked one of the aides, long accustomed to the two men locking horns, even now that Ja'fari was just a party official). Talabani's habit this month had been to stay up late with his old guerrilla cronies playing high-stakes poker, but most of them had already gone north to get ready for the end of the Ramadan holiday, so he lingered a while longer with his staff.

The palace entourage included many familiar faces from the Kurdish diaspora, including a few prominent journalists who had come on board to manage his media relations. Seemingly all the best-known independent Kurdish academics had also decided it was finally time to pitch in and try to make Iraq, or at least Kurdistan, succeed. A number of Arabs also worked for the president, including Wafiq al-Samarra'i, the Iraqi army general who had plotted the coup with Talabani back in 1995. After a brief foray into politics, Samarra'i had joined Talabani's staff as his security advisor, and he now lived in a riverside villa close by Mam Jalal's residence.* The house and palace sat only a hundred yards apart along the Tigris riverbank, but the president still rode home in his black bulletproof BMW with several white Land Cruisers escorting.

As they saw the American-administered Green Zone grow enormous and cumbersome, the Kurds had concluded they would rather take care of their own security; they kept to their own enclaves in Baghdad and many of the functions of government stayed with them. Talabani's PUK had seized a strip of land along the Tigris in 2003, and with his inauguration it became the presidential compound. More often than he drove across the river to see the U.S. ambassador or the prime minister, they came to see Talabani. The KDP's Hoshyar Zebari felt the same way. Though his foreign ministry sat just outside the gates of the Green Zone, Zebari kept it apart from the American canton, now a pretzel of annoying security layers. Sometimes not even high-security credentials plus a flawless command of English, Arabic, and Kurdish sufficed to easily get through the checkpoints, which were often manned by coalition soldiers from the Ukraine or Peru. Some of the problems were more conceptual than

---

* In January 2004 I tracked Samarra'i down in his hometown of Samara, which had not yet become a red zone of the insurgency. He was working out of a ground-floor office in the middle of town, trying to get a political party going as if he were running for mayor of a small Midwestern town. Samarra'i had been in charge of Saddam's military intelligence during the years of the Anfal campaign, and it seems impossible that he wasn't complicit in the gas attacks ordered against the Kurds (not to mention against Iran). I asked Samarra'i what he thought about the possibility of a war crimes tribunal. He misunderstood me— deliberately, I think—and answered that he wasn't interested in helping with the formation of the tribunal. When I asked him more emphatically whether he was afraid of being dragged in front of a tribunal in handcuffs, he acted shocked and said he had never participated in any war crimes.

linguistic. One day, late to a meeting, Zebari had erupted after being refused entry by American soldiers at a checkpoint.

"I am the foreign minister of Iraq!" Zebari yelled at the clueless GI. "Where is your passport?! Do you have a visa to be in my country?"

Zebari made his own secure enclave in the neighborhood behind the foreign ministry, where he and his staff lived quite comfortably in some of the mansions there, built in nouveau riche glory by black marketers during the years of sanctions. Once out of the American zone, Zebari felt comfortable to move his wife, children, and even grandchildren down to Baghdad with him—protected fastidiously by platoons of loyal pesh merga. As lifelong rebels, the Kurds in Baghdad perhaps felt nothing strange about the fact that every time they wanted to go five hundred yards up the road, they needed to cordon off the street, search for roadside bombs, stop traffic, post a soldier on every corner, and perhaps ask for American air cover.

Across the aisle in the PUK, Barham Salih also stayed on in the capital, still working desperately to convince Baghdad and Washington that the Kurds believed in Iraq. His title in the latest government was deputy prime minister, but Salih remained the consummate inside man, with his office as well as his home in the center of the Green Zone, not far from the palace serving as the American embassy. Like Zebari, Salih was caught in the middle, with Kurds back home wondering why he had expended so much effort in Baghdad, and the Arabs and internationals in Baghdad never quite believing that he wanted anything more than the time and money necessary to declare Kurdish independence and pull out. Salih stuck to his party line and never let on if he was tired of repeating it.

"We all want independence, but we think, genuinely so, that if Iraq becomes a democratic federal state, it is so much better for [the Kurds]— with all the resources of this country, a bigger entity," he said.

Indeed the Kurds' slice of the Iraqi pie had measured to 17 percent of Iraq's oil revenues, a mountain of cash that would be the envy of many countries in the region. While the constitution had allowed the Kurds to authorize new oil exploration in their region, the proceeds from any new wells would still go to Baghdad for redistribution. And Salih quickly laid out the madness of declaring independence: Turkey, Syria, Iran, and Arab Iraq would all declare war, with the Turks invading almost immediately to preempt the spread of a "Greater Kurdistan." Kurdistan's oil would be landlocked by hostile forces, and the Kurds wouldn't even have a refinery capable of meeting their own gasoline needs, much less getting rich off the stuff. An independent Kurdistan would unite the region in opposition, and it would lose the one friend it had: the United States. In fact, more than any other group, Salih said, the Kurds needed to keep Iraq going along the American program of federal democratic rule.

"The mother of all ironies is that the perennial victims of the state of Iraq may end up being the saviors of Iraq," he said. But with mortars landing daily even inside the Green Zone, it sounded a tall order. Salih added a disclaimer, "The Kurds will not be the cause of the breakup of Iraq; it will be the Arabs. And if they decide to break it up, there is nothing we can do about it."

If America left prematurely—before Iraqi security forces were up to the task of maintaining order—Salih predicted first that Iraq would fall to civil war, and then spark a regional war across the Middle East between Shi'ites and Sunnis, between Arabs, Kurds, and Turks. From Baghdad, it seemed impossible to think that the Americans could ever consider pulling out, not with such a tense standoff in the region. But in Washington, as even Republicans starting finding language to distance themselves from President Bush, it seemed impossible to contemplate staying. The 2006 midterm elections turned on the issue of Iraq, and the Democratic Party won back both houses of Congress. President Bush immediately accepted Secretary of Defense Donald Rumsfeld's resignation. The 2008 election season begun immediately, also pivoting on plans to get America out of Iraq.

WATCHING FROM THE hills of Kurdistan as Iraq trembled in daily explosions felt oddly like watching from America. The violent images on television transfixed the Kurds, and though they felt a safe distance away, they couldn't help but wonder what consequences lay in store. If Iraq fell apart, would it take them with it? Would America stand by the safe zone it had created fifteen years earlier? Would their own leaders rise above their petty rivalry to secure a peaceful and even a democratic future for the ever more visible nation of Iraqi Kurds?

Seeing that they were the only functioning part of the country encouraged the KDP and PUK to cooperate, and the rivals refrained from fighting over a few key posts in the Kurdistan Regional Government. Nechirvan Barzani led the KRG, with his uncle Masoud acting as president, but after

the December 2005 elections, they had willingly filled some key ministries with independent and PUK Kurds. Ali Bapir's Komala Islami party
held seats in parliament and the environment ministry—a token post to
say they were part of Kurdistan's government.* Masoud Barzani's chief of
staff, Fuad Hussein, had worked with the CPA and then for Talabani,
who sent him over to Masoud. The all-important Kurdish oil ministry
went to a PUK man, Ashti Hawrami, apparently chosen for his expertise,
not his affiliation. Hawrami got right to work, using some of the same international consultants to work on Kurdistan's oil law as had negotiated
the Iraqi constitution. Also unified was the Kurdish representation in
Washington, where Qubad Talabani pushed the agenda of the Kurdistan
Regional Government, declaring with a smile that his boss's name was
Nechirvan Barzani, one of the men who had sent him running up a
mountainside ten years earlier.

Qubad had briefly shared the post with a KDP partner, but soon took
over the operation himself. He kept in constant contact with Nechirvan,
and the two men gave the impression that the next generation of Kurds
would work together. Qubad's job description only included the KRG's
concerns in the United States, but of course he helped coordinate whenever his father came to Washington or New York, and often collaborated
with Hoshyar Zebari's staff as well. Just as his father had slowly slipped
into a much larger role than he had signed on for, Qubad evolved from
the Kurdistan liaison to the de facto Iraqi ambassador. Iraq's official embassy to Washington, the same run-down building near Dupont Circle,
had been a revolving door, eventually taken over by a secular Sunni businessman with no pull in Baghdad's Shi'ite government. Qubad, on the
other hand, had a direct line to the president of Iraq and almost a decade

---

* Bapir had disappeared from the scene most literally—in the summer of 2003 he
  had gone to meet some American officials and found himself suddenly arrested
  and sent to Baghdad. There, to his surprise and horror, he shared a prison compound with the former cabinet of Saddam Hussein: Tariq Aziz, Ali Hassan al-
  Majid, Barzani al-Tikriti—everyone but Saddam. Bapir said that the men still
  lived in a dream world, calling each other "minister" and "vice president" as if
  they would someday return to power. According to Bapir, the men warmed to
  him and let him lead them in prayer; they promised that when they returned to
  office, they would make him important. The Americans let Bapir go, without
  charge, in April 2005, after twenty-two months in prison.

of experience in Washington. During his time alongside Barham Salih he earned a sterling reputation for information with minimal spin. Qubad had been meeting with U.S. presidential hopefuls since the 2004 elections, and Dick Cheney's office regularly called him on his cell phone for advice.

Qubad lobbied both sides of the congressional aisle, with the goal of making protection of Kurdistan a political litmus test in Washington, like Israel or Taiwan. The Kurds had even sought out Israeli advisors to show them how it was done, and eventually in June 2004, the Kurds turned to a top Republican lobbying firm, Barbour, Griffith & Rogers. After paying the small sum of $29,000 for one month's representation by the Washington insiders, the Kurds had secured $1.4 billion of leftover frozen funds from the United Nations Oil-for-Food program. Results were near instantaneous—in the final days of the CPA, three U.S. helicopters delivered the cash to the Kurds' central bank in Erbil, in bricks of new Benjamin Franklins, weighing fifteen tons.[2] The Kurds kept BG&R on the payroll, and soon saw another familiar face—Robert Blackwill. The former ambassador whom Condoleezza Rice had picked as her point man on Iraq had left the public sector, waited the mandatory "cooling off" year, and then gone to work as a lobbyist for the Kurds.

Success had its problems though. The Kurds' strength spooked the Arabs, and Nechirvan Barzani kept holding Baghdad's feet to the fire—for example, making sure that Iraq delivered Kurdistan's 17 percent of the oil profits in current oil prices, pushing one hundred dollars per barrel in 2007, and not at the twenty-six dollars per barrel when the deal was made. And while Iraq's oil minister, Hussein Shahristani, failed to push through a national hydrocarbons law, he did find time to decry the Kurdistan regional law as illegal. Nechirvan fired back that the KRG was following the one law that had been ratified in the new Iraq.

"Everyone in Iraq voted for the constitution and all these articles are a constitutional commitment. No government in Baghdad can deny this. We are patiently waiting to see how the constitution will be implemented," Nechirvan said.

The oil law negotiations had broken down in December 2006, with a draft that the Kurds had signed off on sitting on Shahristani's desk in Baghdad.[3] Disputes settled around the KRG's authority to sign its own deals, and whether the government in Baghdad would have a right to veto them. There was also a difference in philosophy—the Kurds were pro-American, pro-investment, and willing to make attractive deals in order to get foreign companies into Kurdistan as soon as possible. They had made oil a priority and put their best technocrats on it, as well as hiring some outside experts. Shahristani, on the other hand, had no experience in the oil sector and apparently got the post only because of his close ties with Ayatollah Sistani. His Baghdad office was subject to pressure from many directions—from those against autonomy in Kurdistan, and from others who opposed any and all foreign profit from Iraqi oil. In late January 2007 the Iraqi government announced that the law was finished, but when the Kurds read it they found all of their hard-fought concessions had been deleted. The dispute went public, and it took a month for the KRG and Baghdad to get back to the language they had been working with the previous year; then negotiations froze again. Winter turned to spring and to summer, and no deal. Shahristani's office claimed they were still consulting with important experts in Baghdad and even said vaguely that they wanted to make the new oil law conform with a later version of the constitution that might emerge someday. With oil at its highest price in human history, Kurdistan's oil minister Ashti Hawrami, was pulling his hair out.

"Ninety, one hundred dollars a barrel and our oil stays in the ground! And everybody else who competes with us: flourishing with money for investment in their own country as a result of the boom in oil. And we, month after month, have less production. It's a crime—the Iraqi people deserve better," Hawrami said.

Hawrami pushed ahead with the Kurdistan projects, but what frustrated him was the rest of Iraq. The KRG planned to be pumping new crude by 2008, and had contracts for more exploration, drilling, and even a new pipeline. Hawrami said the KRG's actions were all in line with the Iraqi constitution and therefore wouldn't be in conflict with any law Baghdad eventually passed. New oil discovered in Kurdistan would go out of Iraq through the central government and be divided—83 percent for Baghdad and 17 percent for the KRG. Likewise, Hawrami insisted, the rest of Iraq should also be pumping at capacity, and giving 17 percent of that to the KRG. Instead Iraq's production was stagnant and the fastest-growing sector seemed to be the massive smuggling of Iraqi oil to Iran.

European, Canadian, and Turkish companies had already begun exploration for new oil in the north, but the deals stayed under the radar until September 2007, when a Texas-based company with ties to the Bush family, Hunt Oil, signed a deal with the Kurds. Baghdad screamed again that the deal was not valid, but even the major oil companies started to wonder if access to the fraction of Iraq's oil in Kurdistan was better than waiting for peace in the land above the titanic oil fields to the south. Hunt denied it had made any consultation with the White House, but later admitted to a meeting at the State Department, where diplomats warned the American company that the deal might be null and void once Iraq passed a federal oil law. But Washington wasn't deaf to the siren of one hundred dollars per barrel for American companies, or Iraq's potential to bring down the price if its oil got on line. In October 2007 the State Department suggested the government in Baghdad simply use Iraq's old Saddam-era oil law and sign some contracts.[4] The two systems would have to be homogenized at some point to both fit under Iraq's constitution.

But the constitution itself was looking endangered. The Sunni Arabs, of course, had never really supported the document, and the Kurds were the only ones to ever mention it. Their insistence on following the constitution seemed almost a provocation in Arab Iraq—especially the provision mandating a referendum on the city of Kirkuk before the end of 2007. While everyone knew the vote was impractical—no census had been taken in Kirkuk since 1957—the Kurds felt they couldn't back down from the commitment, especially since skipping the Kirkuk referendum might be the first blatant violation of the Iraqi constitution. As the end of the year approached, the Kirkuk referendum was quietly kicked down the road, leaving the Kurds to wonder what strength remained in the Iraqi constitution's other provisions. Kurdish officials promised that a high commission in Baghdad would get the measure on track early in 2008, but the referendum started to look like it might be added to the Kurds' list of forgotten documents full of promises.

The fact that they knew the referendum was on the rocks didn't prevent the PUK and KDP from posturing about it. When Talabani said Kirkuk was the "Kurdish Jerusalem," Barzani declared it "the beating heart of Kurdistan," each one trying to seem more of a patriot. Barzani had won a clear point when he banned the Iraqi flag in the Kurdish region until a new flag was designed to replace the Ba'athist symbol. The Arabs and the Turks were outraged, the Kurdish street delighted, and Talabani could only nod in approval and quietly fly an Iraqi flag wherever he traveled as head of state.

The divisions between the parties were more than rhetorical. Despite their political rapprochement, the PUK and KDP still had separate militias. The Kurdistan Regional Government still waited to unify the ministries of defense, finance, justice, and the interior. With plenty of mature political talent, Kurdistan's bipolar system had no future. The KDP had stability at the price of stagnation; the PUK's coalition looked like it might end or at least splinter with the retirement or passing of Talabani. Even as he struggled to assert his role in Baghdad's government, Talabani had flown home to Sulimaniya in the fall of 2006 to settle disputes among his lieutenants, when the PUK's first internal primary resulted in violent clashes between commanders. His son Bafel appeared keen to follow his father into the PUK leadership, but by year's end Talabani's longtime deputy, Nawshirwan Mustafa, formed his own separate party for the Kurdish parliament. Optimists saw the beginning of a multi-party system in Kurdistan; others feared chaos as Jalal Talabani's health began to look fragile.

Also looking fragile was the American commitment to stay in Iraq. In December 2006 the long-awaited bipartisan Iraq Study Group released its report. Congress had appointed the group to canvass the world's Iraq experts, under the leadership of Republican godfather James Baker and Democrat Lee Hamilton. From the Kurdish perspective, the report could have been called "The Arabists Strike Back." Among the group's members (including Robert Gates, who then replaced Rumsfeld as secretary of defense) were all the rational, realist voices that had let the Kurds down in 1991 in the name of regional stability. Somehow, in their deep study of Iraq, they had neglected to visit the Kurdish north, and none of their "experts" were Kurds. Their recommendations, blended into a soft pap by committee consensus, said nothing about federalism and favored central government control as a step closer to national reconciliation. They also stressed negotiating with Iran and Syria, and the Kurds looked once again like a big, but still expendable, bargaining chip.

The Kurds breathed a sigh of relief when President Bush completely ignored the ISG report and instead announced plans for a troop surge to take control of Baghdad. Their leadership cooed even more when the Americans finally accepted Kurdish help and announced that two brigades of pesh merga would form part of the surge, helping the Americans try to clear and hold some Baghdad neighborhoods. It seemed that America finally wanted to reinforce the success of the Kurdish region and take advantage of what its stability could offer. Ambassador Khalilzad flew north to open a trade fair in Erbil. A large number of Iraq watchers in America had begun to think that if Iraq were to fall apart, Kurdistan might be the one salvageable part. But the Kurds couldn't help fearing that this surge was the last gasp of the Bush administration in Iraq. The realists on the Iraq Study Group waited to clean things up with whoever took the White House in 2008, Republican or Democrat.

Khalilzad moved on sooner than that, to take the post of ambassador to the United Nations in 2007. He spent some of his last days in Iraq on an overnight trip with Masoud Barzani to the sacred hills around Barzan village, after celebrating the end of Ramadan with both Kurdish leaders at Jalal Talabani's new house on Lake Dukan. Khalilzad looked right at home in Talabani's gilded reception hall, sitting between Talabani and Barzani. Both "Zal" and Mam Jalal wore tailored blue suits; Masoud sat more comfortably in his pesh merga fatigues and turban. They joked in English and Farsi (Khalilzad's mother tongue is Dari, which is closer to Iranian Farsi than Kurdish), pausing to greet the endless stream of Kurdish VIPs who came to call. Khalilzad's relaxation was patent after so long in Baghdad, and he smiled widely when some of Talabani's guards asked to have their photo taken with him—surely this was the only place in Iraq where anyone would dare hang such a photo. Even as their oldest friend in the Bush administration, Khalilzad voiced the Kurds' lingering fears.

"The Kurds have only one friend: their mountains," Khalilzad said, a bit theatrically. "Now at least they tell me they have greater confidence in the U.S. But there's a sense of insecurity that's there. The Kurds say, 'The Shi'ites have Iran, the Sunnis have the rest of the Arab world, who do we have?' That does come out in the conversations. Any statement made that is not abundantly clear in favor of them, they get insecure."

Khalilzad allowed that plenty of forces in the region wanted Kurdistan to fail—chauvinists, he called them, the same word Kurds always use to describe Arab racists. "The tradition in this part of the world is for whoever is dominant to oppress the other. If the [Kurds] can make it work, that will be a different model. That's why it's so difficult. It hasn't been done for a long time in this region."

The Kurds looked like they had a decent shot at making it work, but Arab Iraq continued to slip. General David Petraeus returned to Iraq in 2007 as commander of the U.S. military effort and was cast as the administration's savior, ahead of the troop surge, which eventually brought total troop levels back up near the number that invaded Iraq in 2003. The surge made some military gains in Baghdad, but like squeezing a balloon, it pushed insurgent activity out to the provinces, and sectarian divisions only hardened. American troops made a breakthrough by helping Sunni tribes against al-Qa'ida-inspired fighters, but feared the tribes might turn their guns on Shi'ites later on. The Shi'ite factions continued to infiltrate Iraq's security forces, but in areas under Shi'ite control, violence broke out internally between rival militias. No country in the region was immune to the spillover—in Jordan and Syria millions of Iraqis appeared seeking refuge. Saudi Arabia watched in fear as they saw Iran's influence grow in Baghdad, and the war of words between Washington and Tehran heated up. As the Bush administration accused the Iranians of exporting bomb technology to Iraq, the Shi'ite Iraqi government kept clear lines of communication open with the Shi'ite religious government in Iran.

In America, lawmakers had found the scapegoat they needed with Nuri al-Maliki—if the surge failed, they reasoned, it was because Maliki and the Iraqi politicians weren't stepping up to the plate. America, having given its best shot, could head home with a clean conscience. But beneath the rhetoric they knew it was not so simple. Even as Democrats assailed Bush's war as a fiasco launched by misleading the public, the situation had changed. At least one of the false reasons for invading Iraq—the connection to al-Qaida operatives—was now true, as the country had become the haven for extremists that it never was under Saddam.

A quick withdrawal would almost certainly see complete degeneration of the Iraqi government into sectarian war, with the region inevitably pulled in. The Iranians would arm the Shi'ites; the Gulf Arabs would arm the Sunnis. All of Kurdistan's enemies would have a free hand to wreak havoc in the north, and perhaps stir up tension between the Kurdish leaders. General Petraeus invoked the genocide in Sudan as a warning of what would happen if the United States left: "If you didn't like Darfur, you're going to hate Baghdad."[5] If such a war began, the pesh merga could surely hold their own against the other Iraqis, defend their territory and probably expand it. But that was only within Iraq, where none of the factions had significant amounts of artillery, and the war would be fought by men with small arms. The neighboring countries had fighter jets, bombers, helicopter gunships, and missiles. Without the presence of the United States, the Kurds feared that Iran and Turkey might make sure the dream of Kurdistan never thrived.

If America couldn't prevent a civil war, the question was whether to try to stay as a referee. The scenario for trying to break up the fight came back to the three-state solution, or "soft partition." Some Americans, including Democratic presidential candidate Joseph Biden, concluded that Iraq was never meant to be one country, and a loose confederation of Sunni, Shi'ite, and Kurdish areas already allowed for in the constitution was the only path to peace. With so many mixed and contested areas, separating Iraq into three would be a bloody business, but perhaps less bloody than keeping it together. The problem for Washington was that both options would look like a failure, and history would never reveal what course had saved lives. In fact the population transfers had already begun, as hundreds of thousands of Iraqis displaced themselves from contested areas.

For the Kurds, the soft partition looked like a perfect path to independence. They could continue to develop separately from the Arabs and would be protected if the Shi'ites and Sunnis splintered and made war. They might even be able to convince America to use Kurdistan as its staging ground in Iraq and to finally build the permanent military base the Kurds had been begging for. If the chaos in the south lasted long enough, Turkey or Syria might see their way clear to exporting some of the Kurdish oil. If reunification ever threatened, the Kurds would be so far ahead that they would be able to dictate their terms to Baghdad. The key was to keep American patronage, and to do that, they would need to stay a tiny bit invisible. The Kurds could have a country in everything but name, and that way none of the neighbors could accuse them of trying to redraw the map.

As WITH ALL his trips from Baghdad, Talabani had started this journey home to Sulimaniya for the end of Ramadan 2006 by ordering his pesh merga to shut down a mile of road through the busy Karada neighborhood between him and the Green Zone. Talabani's entourage then sped down the gauntlet to the Fourteenth of July Bridge, where three rings of American soldiers waved them through to the suspension bridge over the Tigris. Once inside the Green Zone, Talabani's crew waited at a helipad to make the jump out to Baghdad International Airport in U.S. helicopters. After half an hour on the tarmac, and watching all their luggage being strapped to pallets, the presidential posse boarded a U.S. Air Force C-130. Though they had done it many times, the American airmen never looked quite at ease loading up Talabani's dozen Kalashnikov-toting bodyguards. Inside, Talabani squished into the web seats lining the plane just like his men—his one luxury a pair of noise-canceling headphones.

The mountain air of Sulimaniya soothed the nerves of every Kurd on the plane. As the propellers grunted to a halt, bulletproof vests were stowed and rifles left to hang loosely at the shoulder. All of Talabani's old friends and rivals came to meet him at the airport, some of them now moving a bit slowly with the years. Every homecoming to Kurdistan was joyful, but the Kurds still weren't over the thrill of landing in an American warplane in a Kurdish international airport, and they all grinned irrepressibly. This much they could defend: for the first time in a century, perhaps, they had a homeland and it was safe.

A small dispute broke out as the convoy saddled up to drive back to Talabani's house—the president, it seemed, was refusing to enter his armored Lexus. He had just lit one of his long Davidoffs and wanted to ride in a car where he could roll down the windows for the smoke. One of his titanic South African security guards, hired by the U.S. State Department, went over to plead with him. A head taller than Mam Jalal, the guard begged him to ride in the bulletproof car.

Talabani put the cigar in his other hand and reached up to pinch the soldier's cheek.

"Relax, my boy," he said. "You're in my country now. You're in Kurdistan."

Key Events in Iraqi Kurdish History

1918 With the end of the Ottoman Empire and World War I, British forces hold the oil-rich Ottoman province of Mosul, heavily populated by Kurds.

1919 The new Iraqi state expands to include Mosul province, which comes under a British mandate.

May: "Sheikh Mahmoud" Barzinji rebels against the British and declares himself the king of Kurdistan, laying claim to all of Kurdish northern Iraq. The British put down his rebellion by June and exile the sheikh to India.

1920 The Treaty of Sèvres, signed by the defeated Ottoman government, includes a provision for a referendum on Kurdish independence, subject to approval by the League of Nations. Article 64 of the treaty gives Kurds living in Mosul province the option of joining a future Kurdish state.

1921 Emir Faisal, son of Hussein bin Ali, sharif of Mecca, is crowned king of Iraq.

1922 The British try to control continuing unrest in Kurdistan by bringing Sheikh Mahmoud back. Within months he declares himself king again, and fights the British a second time.

1923 Kemal Atatürk wins international recognition for the newly founded Turkish Republic with the Treaty of Lausanne. The Treaty of

Sèvres and its provision for Kurdish independence is abandoned by the international community.

1924 British forces retake Sulimaniya, ending Sheikh Mahmoud Barzinji's second rebellion.

1932 Sheikh Ahmed Barzani leads an uprising based in his home village, Barzan, in favor of Kurdish autonomy. Iraq becomes officially independent of British mandate on October 3.

1943 Mulla Mustafa Barzani leads a new uprising and captures parts of Erbil and Badinan.

1946 Iraqi Kurdish rebels cross into Iran, where they join Iranian Kurds led by Qazi Muhamad. The Kurdistan Democratic Party (KDP) holds its first congress in Mahabad with Soviet support and announces an independent Kurdish "Mahabad Republic" with "General" Mulla Mustafa Barzani in command of its armed forces.

1947 The Mahabad Republic collapses under attack from Iranian forces, and Barzani flees to the Soviet Union.

1951 The KDP holds its second congress, led by Ibrahim Ahmad and a left-leaning younger generation, though Mullah Mustafa Barzani remains president in absentia.

1958 On July 14, Brigadier Abd-al-Karim Qassim and Colonel Abd-al-Salam Muhammad Arif stage a military coup pushing out Iraq's monarchy. Qassim becomes prime minister. The Kurdish nationalist movement comes out in the open and Mullah Mustafa Barzani returns from exile.

1961 Barzani agitates for Kurdish rebellion again in the north. Baghdad splits off support from many Kurdish tribes.

1963 In Feburary Qassim is overthrown by a Ba'athist Nasserite coup. In November the Ba'athists are pushed out by Arif and a group of officers.

1968   The Ba'athists return to power in a coup that puts General Ahmad Hasan al-Bakr in the presidency. Saddam Hussein, officially vice president, gradually becomes the power behind the government.

1970   The Iraqi government and Kurdish parties agree to a peace accord, which grants the Kurds autonomy on March 11. The Iraqi constitution is amended to affirm that Kurds are Iraq's second nationality. Cultural and language rights are recognized, but the status of Kirkuk is unresolved.

1971   In September the peace deal sours and Mulla Mustafa Barzani appeals to the United States for aid funneled through U.S. allies Iran and Israel. Barzani survives several assassination attempts (including the "exploding imams").

1972   Iraq aligns with the Soviet Union and nationalizes its oil industry.

1974   Mulla Mustafa Barzani rejects the autonomy offer from Baghdad on March 11 and rebellion begins in earnest.

In Turkey Abdullah Öcalan ("Apo") founds the Kurdish Workers' Party (PKK) and begins an insurgency to create an independent Kurdish state in southeastern Turkey.

1975   The March 11 Algiers Accord between Iran and Iraq ends Iranian support for the Kurdish uprising, which instantly collapses. Barzani flees to Iran and then to America for medical treatment. Mam Jalal Talabani, a former leading member of the KDP, announces the establishment of the Patriotic Union of Kurdistan (PUK) from Damascus.

1978   Clashes between the KDP and PUK.

1979   *In Iran* The shah is overthrown in February and eventually replaced by a Shi'ite Islamic government led by Ayatollah Ruhollah Khomeini.

March: Mulla Mustafa Barzani dies of cancer outside Washington, D.C., and his son Masoud Barzani takes over the leadership of the KDP.

July: Saddam Hussein formalizes his near absolute power in Baghdad.

1980   The Iran-Iraq war begins in September. The KDP aids Iran along Iraqi northern border; the PUK negotiates with Baghdad. Shi'ite leader Ayatolla Mohammad Bakr al-Sadr (uncle to Moqtada al-Sadr) is executed by the regime.

1983   Iranian troops cross into northern Iraq and take the town of Haj Omran in cooperation with Masoud Barzani's KDP. In revenge, Saddam Hussein executes eight thousand men from the region of Barzan. The PUK begins a cease-fire with Baghdad and negotiates about autonomy.

1984   *In Turkey* Abdullah Öcalan's PKK starts major guerrilla operations in the southeast, which leave as many as 35,000 people dead and 1.5 million displaced over the next fifteen years, most of them Kurdish civilians.

1985   Turkey helps to quash negotiations between Baghdad and the PUK. The talks permanently break after jahsh militiamen kill Jalal Talabani's half brother and two nieces.

1986   The KDP and PUK unify against Baghdad with Iranian support, forming the Kurdistan Front.

1988   Saddam Hussein's cousin Ali Hassan al-Majid is put in charge of the north and begins the "Anfal" campaign against the Kurds. Systematic killings begin, with Kurdish civilians herded into camps as their villages are razed. Called "Ali Chemical," Majid uses cocktails of poison gas against combatants and civilians. At least fifty thousand, but perhaps as many as a hundred thousand, people are killed.

March 16: Iraq gasses the town of Halabja, killing as many as five thousand Kurdish civilians.

July: Iran accepts a U.N. cease-fire, ending the war, but the Anfal campaign continues with gassing and executions through August.

1990   August 2: Iraq invades Kuwait.

1991   January 15: The United States leads an international coalition against Iraq.

February 27: The Iraqi army is routed and has withdrawn from Kuwait.

March: The Americans accept Iraq's surrender on March 3. By March 5, Kurds and Shi'ites rise up against the regime, believing they have U.S. support. America does not help the rebellion, and Baghdad brutally suppresses it, killing tens of thousands. In April around 1.5 million Kurds begin to flee across the mountains to Turkey and Iran. Turkey closes the border.

April 6: A U.S.-led coalition creates a tiny safe haven inside northwestern Iraq, the world's first U.N.-approved humanitarian intervention against the will of a sovereign state.

August: U.S., British, and French jets begin patrolling a no-fly zone in northern Iraq.

October: The Kurdistan Front has moved into the provinces of Duhok, Erbil, and Sulimaniya. Saddam withdraws from the Kurdish provinces and begins a blockade against them. The Iraqi government continues a policy of Arabization in the area around Kirkuk, evicting thousands of Kurdish families, most of whom flee to the northern safe zone.

1992   Elections in the Kurdish area split the government equally between Barzani's KDP and Talabani's PUK.

1994   Tension between the KDP and PUK becomes a low-intensity civil war. In July the KDP and PUK sign a peace agreement, which disintegrates by December.

1995   Ahmed Chalabi's INC, operating in Kurdistan, launches a coup attempt with the PUK and elements of the Iraqi army. A small CIA team on the ground supports the plot without Washington's full awareness. The coup fails.

1996   June: Another plotted coup attempt, this one based in Jordan with full CIA backing and the collaboration of Ayad Allawi's INA and Barzani's KDP, is foiled by Saddam.

July: Talabani allows Iran to enter his territory to attack Iranian Kurds based there.

August: With the PUK threatening to defeat the KDP, Masoud Barzani allows the Iraqi army to enter Kurdistan and pushes the PUK out of Erbil.

1997 The U.N.'s Oil-for-Food program begins to deliver humanitarian goods in exchange for Iraqi oil (approved in 1995 but delayed in negotiations with Baghdad). Kurdistan is supposed to get 13 percent of the proceeds from the program.

1998 Talabani and Barzani sign the Washington Agreement in September, providing a cold peace with the KDP, based in Erbil, controlling the northwest of Kurdistan, and the PUK, based in Sulimaniya, controlling the southeast.

1999 *In Turkey* On February 16, PKK leader Abdullah Öcalan is imprisoned after his capture in Kenya (with American assistance). The PKK ends offensive operations.

February 19: Grand Ayatollah Muhammad Sadiq al-Sadr, spiritual leader of the Shi'ite community (and father of Moqtada al-Sadr), is assassinated in Najaf, presumably by government agents.

2001 September 3: The PUK delivers a report to the White House about Jund al-Islam (later Ansar al-Islam), an Islamist group operating in Kurdish territory with links to al-Qa'ida members in Afghanistan.

2002 March: Barzani and Talabani make a secret visit to "the Farm," the CIA's training facility in Virginia, where Director George Tenet tells them to prepare for an American intervention.

April: The PUK's Barham Salih narrowly escapes an assassination attempt by Ansar al-Islam.

December: Hundreds of members of the Iraqi opposition, including the main Kurdish parties, meet in London.

2003 February: Kurds protest the possibility that Turkish troops could enter Iraq with the U.S. invasion.

February 5: U.S. secretary of state Colin Powell addresses the U.N. Security Council, making the case for military intervention in Iraq. His key link between Iraq and Osama bin Laden is the Ansar al-Islam group in Kurdistan.

February 8: Ansar al-Islam assassinates PUK leader Shawkat Haji Mushir.

March 1: The Turkish parliament rejects a bill allowing American troops to transit through Turkey and form a northern front against Iraq.

March 18: America's first bombs land on the Dora complex south of Baghdad in a failed attempt to kill Saddam Hussein, acting on intelligence gathered by the CIA in Kurdistan.

March 22: Coalition forces launch missiles against Kurdish Islamist groups including Ansar al-Islam in the north. Dozens are killed in the headquarters of the Komala Islami, separate radical Islamist faction, when a missile hits the Khurmal area.

March 26: Paratroopers from the 173rd Airborne land at airstrip near Erbil.

March 28: PUK fighters and U.S. Special Forces take control of all Ansar al-Islam territory, though many of the Islamists escape across the border to Iran.

April 9: U.S. soldiers enter Baghdad and topple a statue of Saddam Hussein. Saddam's top officials all go into hiding.

April 10: Kurdish forces rush into Kirkuk despite American requests and Turkish threats against their entry. KDP and U.S. Special Operations Forces enter Mosul.

July 13: American proconsul Paul Bremer appoints a governing council in Baghdad, including Talabani and Barzani among its rotating presidents.

July 23: Saddam's sons, Uday and Qusay, are killed in a firefight with U.S. troops in Mosul.

August: Car bombs in Baghdad target the Jordanian embassy, the U.N. headquarters, and the International Committee of the Red Cross.

December: Saddam is discovered in a dingy underground hideout near Tikrit by U.S. troops.

2004 February: At least one hundred people die and more than two hundred are wounded in simultaneous suicide bombings of KDP and PUK offices in Erbil during a Muslim holiday party.

March: Bombs at Shi'ite festivals kill at least 140 people.

In Syria A March 12 riot at a soccer stadium sets off weeks of protests by Kurdish nationalists, as many as two thousand are arrested by the government and at least two die in custody.

April–May: U.S. Marines assault the city of Fallujah after four U.S. contractors are lynched there. Moqtada al-Sadr's Mahdi Army engages coalition forces in Najaf.

November: American forces attack Fallujah again, this time destroying large sections of the city and retaking it for the Iraqi government.

2005 January: A combined list of Kurdish parties comes second to the Shi'ite Arab Alliance in a national election. Sunni Arabs boycott.

In Turkey In April the PKK resumes attacks in the southeast after a six-year cease-fire. They use northern Iraq as a base to launch attacks into Turkey.

May: After months of haggling, an interim government is sworn in for a one-year term. Jalal Talabani is president; Ibrahim al-Ja'fari is prime minister. Approximately 672 civilians are killed in May (up from 364 in April), according to the Iraqi government. At least 50 people are killed by a suicide bomber in Erbil.

June: Masoud Barzani inaugurates the first session of Kurdistan's re-unified parliament as president of the autonomous region.

In Iran The July 9 murder and mutilation of a popular young Kurdish activist, "Shwana" Qadir, sets off weeks of protests in Mahabad region; at least nineteen Kurds are killed by Iranian security forces

August: A stampede on a Baghdad bridge, caused by rumors of a suicide bomb, kills up to thousand people during a Shi'ite holiday.

October: Iraqis vote by a large majority to ratify a new constitution creating a federal democracy with Islam as a main source of law. Sunni Arab opposition to the constitution falls just short of the three-province margin needed to block ratification. Saddam Hussein and seven codefendants go on trial for crimes against humanity.

December: A Norwegian firm begins drilling for oil in Iraqi Kurdistan with cooperation from the Kurdistan Regional Government.

December 6: Kurdish rioters in Dohuk attack the headquarters of the Kurdish Islamic Union after the party withdraws support for the joint KDP-PUK legislative slate.

December 15: Iraqis vote again, this time for a four-year government. Sunni Arabs participate this time, but the elected government is still dominated by a coalition of Shi'ites and Kurds.

2006 February 22: A bomb destroys the Shi'ite Askaria mosque in the city of Samarra, marking for many the clear beginning of a civil war between Iraq's Sunni and Shi'ite Arabs.

March 16: Kurdish protesters in the town of Halabja clash with Kurd-ish security forces and destroy the memorial to victims of the 1988 gas attack.

April 22: After months of bargaining, the permanent government is se-lected, with Jalal Talabani again as president and Nuri al-Maliki as prime minister.

May–June: The U.N. reports that as many as one hundred civilians per day are dying in Iraq's violence.

September: Masoud Barzani orders that the Iraqi national flag not be flown in Kurdistan Regional Government buildings. One suicide truck bomb and four car bombs kill twenty-three people in Kirkuk.

December 30: Saddam Hussein is hanged in Baghdad.

2007   January: President Bush announces a plan to "surge" U.S. troop levels in order to pacify Baghdad.

April: A bomb blast in Iraq's parliament inside Baghdad's American-protected Green Zone kills one Iraqi member of parliament.

August: Truck and car bombs kill at least 250 people in a Yazidi village just outside the Kurdish region, near the Syrian border.

October: PKK clashes with the Turkish army bring tens of thousands of Turkish troops to the border. Turkey threatens invasion unless KRG and U.S. forces rein in the PKK. Turkish prime minister Erdoğan meets President Bush at the White House on November 5, apparently diffusing the standoff, at least until spring.

December: Turks mount minor cross-border action and air strikes.

December 31: The constitutional deadline passes for a referendum to determine whether the oil-rich city of Kirkuk will become part of the Kurdistan Regional Government. Kurdish officials continue to push for the referendum in 2008.

Sources: BBC and author's notes

Notes

1: The Stolen Sheath

1. McDowall, *Modern History of the Kurds*, p. 22.
2. James Reston Jr.'s *Warriors of God* is an enjoyable account of the Third Crusade. I relied on his book as well as Behâ ed-Dîn's contemporary account, *The Life of Saladin*. Tariq Ali also wrote a fictional biography, *The Book of Saladin*.
3. Jwaideh, *Kurdish National Movement*, pp. 19, 33.
4. McDowall, p. 4.
5. The book was penned by Douglas Layton, who is accomplished in the realms of building emergency shelters in disaster areas, securing U.S. government reconstruction contracts, and extreme-sport missionary organizations, like Shelter Now International (now called Shelter for Life International), which seems to specialize in sending Christians into modern-day lions' dens like Afghanistan under the Taliban. Layton has lobbied Washington in favor of Kurdish interests and also pushed for a genocide case against Saddam Hussein in the 1990s.
6. Jwaideh, p. 12.
7. McDowall, pp. 105–8.
8. Jwaideh, p. 126.
9. McDowall, pp. 117, 125.
10. Observed by David Fromkin in *A Peace to End All Peace*, among others.
11. McDowall, p. 137.
12. Fromkin, p. 450.
13. Ibid., p. 451.
14. Jwaideh, p. 175.
15. Ibid., p. 180.
16. Ibid., p. 176.
17. Ibid., p. 183.
18. McDowall, p. 161.
19. Jwaideh, p. 198.

20. Ibid., p. 187.
21. Randal, *After Such Knowledge*, p. 183.
22. Barzani, *Mustafa Barzani*, p. 1.
23. Nijyar Shemdin, KRG representative in Washington, presented in an address to commemorate Barzani on March 1, 2000, in Tysons Corner, Virginia.
24. Jwaideh, p. 219.
25. Shemdin address on March 1, 2000, in Tysons Corner, Virginia.
26. Jwaideh, p. 230.
27. Ibid., pp. 232, 239.
28. Shemdin address on March 1, 2000, in Tysons Corner, Virginia.
29. McDowall, p. 243.
30. Ibid., p. 252.
31. Interview with Najmaldin Karim, June 1, 2006, in Washington, D.C.
32. Jwaideh, p. 123.
33. Barzani said that his enemies in Iraq and Iran always tried to blame their failures on some foreign training, when in fact he learned to fight so well by making war all his life. As recounted in Schmidt, *Journey Among Brave Men*, p. 111.
34. McDowall, p. 303.
35. Ibid.
36. Jwaideh, p. 283.
37. McDowall, p. 307.
38. Baghdad has been at many times in the past century the Iraqi city with the largest Kurdish population; especially the elites would send their children to be educated there. In the absence of any reliable census, people often spoke of a million Kurds in Baghdad, mirroring their roughly 20 percent size in Iraq's general population. But the elections in 2005, assuming that Kurds voted for the Kurdish candidates, revealed only about fifty thousand to a hundred thousand. Baghdad once had a huge population of Fayli (Shi'ite) Kurds, until Saddam Hussein began deporting and exterminating them. The surviving Fayli Kurds may have voted with the Shi'ite religious parties—this analysis thanks to Brendan O'Leary of the University of Pennsylvania.
39. Schmidt, pp. 123, 254.
40. Interview with Najmaldin Karim, June 1, 2006, in Washington, D.C.
41. McDowall, p. 320.
42. Ibid., p. 325.
43. Interview with Fuad Hussein, September 21, 2006, in Salahudin.
44. Interview with Mahmoud Othman, October 31, 2006, in London.
45. Randal, p. 156.

2: Betrayal and Holocaust

1. Charles Tripp, *A History of Iraq*, p. 201.
2. Kissinger, *Years of Renewal*, p. 583.

3. Ibid., p. 591.
4. Interview with Brent Scowcroft, July 25, 2006. It should be noted that realists like Scowcroft and Kissinger were feeling smug around the time of the interview, after having warned George W. Bush not to invade Iraq and being told to go away. I spoke with Scowcroft in Washington's pork-packing district; in his corner office you can just about see the old executive building of his former fellow realist, Dick Cheney. Scowcroft and other members of George H. W. Bush's war room had long been criticized for not "going all the way to Baghdad" in the 1991 Gulf War. By 2004, with 140,000 U.S. troops bogged down in Iraq, no one was handing them that line anymore.
5. Saleem, *My Father's Rifle*, p. 45. Saleem describes how just a few years earlier, in perfect Orwellian style, the broadcasts were exactly the opposite, with Moscow calling Barzani a liberator and the Voice of America calling the Kurds "rebels and bandits."
6. McDowall, *Modern History of the Kurds*, p. 331.
7. Ibid., p. 333.
8. Ibid., p. 336.
9. Kissinger, p. 592.
10. McDowall, p. 338.
11. Kissinger, p. 594.
12. Interview with Najmaldin Karim, June 1, 2006, in Washington, D.C.
13. Saleem, p. 49.
14. McDowall, p. 338.
15. Ibid., p. 331.
16. Nijyar Shemdin, KRG representative in Washington, presented in an address to commemorate Barzani on March 1, 2000, in Tysons Corner, Virginia.
17. Interview with Najmaldin Karim, June 1, 2006, in Washington, D.C.
18. Interviews with Fuad Hussein and Masoud Barzani, September 21, 2006, in Salahudin.
19. Interview with Salah al-Sheikly, December 2002, in London.
20. Interview with Sa'id Aburish, March 2000, in London. Aburish was an arms negotiator for Saddam and later wrote a biography, *Saddam Hussein: The Politics of Revenge*. Aburish says Saddam got his penchant for documentation by studying the East German secret police.
21. Human Rights Watch, *Genocide in Iraq*, a Middle East Watch Report, 1993.
22. Interview with Jalal Talabani, March 2000, in Qalaat Chowlan.
23. Interview with Nawshirwan Mustafa, September 29, 2006, in Sulimaniya.
24. Mahmoud Othman, "The Kurdish Internal Conflict, Peace Process and Its Prospects," *Kurdistan Observer*, March 14, 2001.
25. McDowall, p. 343.
26. Tripp, p. 233.
27. McDowall, p. 347.
28. Interview with Fayek Mahmud Golpi, October 3, 2006, in Sulimaniya.

29. Interview with Muhammad Ihsan, October 23, 2006, in Erbil; Human Rights Watch, *Genocide in Iraq*.

30. McDowall, p. 350; interview with Fayek Mahmud Golpi, October 3, 2006, in Sulimaniya.

31. Interview with Sandra Charles, National Security Council staff member during Ronald Reagan's second term, July 18, 2006, in Washington, D.C.

32. "Shaking Hands with Saddam." Declassified documents compiled by the National Security Archive at George Washington University in Washington, D.C.

33. McDowall, p. 353.

34. Interview with Mahmoud Tofiq, September 2006, in Sulimaniya.

35. Human Rights Watch, *Genocide in Iraq*.

36. This account of Taimour's story is drawn from interviews by Human Rights Watch, Kanan Makiya's cross-examination of the boy in his book *Cruelty and Silence*, and Taimour's appearance at the Foreign Press Club in Washington, D.C., in 2004, as an adult and English speaker.

37. Dozens of interviews in Halabja; Human Rights Watch reports.

38. Interview with Mike Amitay, July 14, 2006, at the Open Society Institute, Washington, D.C.

39. Interview with Sandra Charles, July 18, 2006, in Washington, D.C.

40. Interview with Peter Galbraith, September 2006, in Salahudin.

41. McDowall, p. 359.

42. Galbraith, *End of Iraq*, p. 19.

3: Shame and Comfort

1. Michael R. Gordon, "The Iraqi Invasion: Iraq's Advantage Limits U.S. Options," *New York Times*, August 3, 1990.

2. Information about Hoshyar Zebari's life comes from a dozen interviews between March 2000 and October 2006. This story is from interviews in Salahudin and Dukan, October 24–25, 2006.

3. McDowall, *Modern History of the Kurds*, p. 370.

4. George H. W. Bush and Brent Scowcroft, *A World Transformed* (New York: Knopf, 1998), p. 472.

5. Gates was interviewed by phone from Texas A&M University, August 18, 2006, just weeks before the younger president Bush would ask him to take over the helm of what was looking like a disastrous Iraq policy.

6. Interview with Zalmay Khalilzad, October 25, 2006, in Dukan.

7. Interview with Morton Abramowitz, July 24, 2006, in Washington, D.C.

8. Interview with several history professors at Sulimaniya University, February 10, 2003.

9. Faleh Abd al-Jabbar, "Why the Intifada Failed," *Middle East Report*, May–June 1992.

10. Schwarzkopf, *It Doesn't Take a Hero*, p. 470.

11. Abd al-Jabbar, "Why the Intifada Failed."

12. Schwarzkopf, p. 489.

13. Interview with Fuad Hussein, September 21, 2006, in Salahudin.

14. Interview with Frank Smyth, December 22, 2006, by phone from Washington, D.C.

15. Interview with Jim Muir, October 16, 2006, in Baghdad.

16. Randal, *After Such Knowledge*, p. 101.

17. Galbraith, *End of Iraq*, p. 54.

18. Interview with Marc Grossman, July 17, 2006, in Washington, D.C.

19. As quoted by George Church, "Saddam Crushes Iraq's Rebels Making His People's Tragedy Complete," *Time* magazine, April 15, 1991.

20. Independent journalist Frank Smyth and photographer Gad Gross went south with the pesh merga to Kirkuk and never made it out of the city. Gross was executed by Iraqi troops, and Smyth was captured and taken to Abu Ghraib prison near Baghdad. Smyth was later released, shaken but unharmed. The Kurds built a statue of Gad Gross, with a camera around his neck, at a roundabout in Erbil.

21. The aggressive French position was thanks to two old friends of the Kurds. The first lady, Danielle Mitterrand, had been active in Kurdish causes since the early 1980s. President Mitterrand had also appointed Dr. Bernard Kouchner, the founder of Doctors Without Borders, to the curious position of "Minister for Humanitarian Action." Kouchner had deep knowledge of the Kurds from his work with nongovernmental organizations. Between the two, they pushed Paris to take a hard line in the U.N. on behalf of the Kurds. Paul Berman wrote about Kouchner in his book *Power and the Idealists*, serialized in the *New Republic* in June 2007, after Kouchner was named French foreign minister.

22. Notably this included many of the men who would later direct U.S. military operations in the Gulf. General James Jones would become NATO's supreme Allied commander. General Anthony Zinni would become head of U.S. Central Command and a U.S. special envoy to the Middle East. General Jay Garner would become President George W. Bush's first pick to supervise the reconstruction of Iraq in 2003. Then Colonel John Abizaid was the most senior Arabic speaker in the U.S. military until he retired as a general in 2007, after a record four years at the head of Central Command.

23. Interview with Jalal Talabani, October 24, 2006, in Dukan.

24. Interview with Mahmoud Othman, October 31, 2006, in London.

25. Graham-Brown, *Sanctioning Saddam*, p. 28.

26. Rudd, *Humanitarian Intervention*, p. 117.

27. Interview with Jay Garner, September 6, 2006, in Crystal City, Virginia. Fred Cuny didn't really fit in with the peace-and-love crowd—he was from Texas, very American, and knew he was too good at his work to care about what people thought of him. He worked in more than seventy disaster areas, from Biafra to Chechnya, where he disappeared in 1995. A great source of information about him is the PBS *Frontline* program "The Lost American" (www.pbs.org/wgbh/pages/frontline/shows/cuny/.

28. Graham-Brown, p. 29.

29. Rudd, p. 211.

30. Interview with Nawshirwan Mustafa, September 29, 2006, in Sulimaniya.

31. Interview with Robert Gates, August 18, 2006, by telephone from Texas A&M University.

4: Burning Down the House

1. This information comes from dozens of conversations with Qubad Talabani over several years, including one all-day interview on July 31, 2006, in Washington, D.C.

2. Interview with Omar Sheikhmus, December 10, 2006, by phone from Washington, D.C.

3. Interview with Nawshirwan Mustafa, September 29, 2006, in Sulimaniya.

4. Interview with Qubad Talabani, July 31, 2006, in Washington, D.C.

5. Interview with a former Department of State official with knowledge of the daily operations of Operation Provide Comfort, December 12, 2006, by phone from Washington, D.C.

6. McDowall, *Mordern History of the Kurds*, p. 381.

7. Fred Cuny, "Northern Iraq: One Year Later, A Special Report to the Carnegie Endowment for International Peace," undated (approximately July 1992).

8. McDowall, p. 382.

9. Cockburn and Cockburn, *Saddam Hussein*, p. 165.

10. Interview with Fuad Hussein, September 21, 2006, in Salahudin.

11. Interview with Ghanim Jawad, November 1, 2006, in London.

12. Hussein Tahiri, in Lennox, ed., *Fire, Snow and Honey*, p. 383.

13. Interview with Nawshirwan Mustafa, September 29, 2006, in Sulimaniya.

14. These details come from an excellent, if inconclusive, "he said, she said" between the KDP's Haval Dasko Aziz and the PUK's Sarbast Fatah in Lennox, pp. 385–96.

15. Interview with Najmaldin Karim, November 30, 2006, in Washington, D.C.

16. These recollections are from Ayub Nuri, January 20, 2007, by phone from New York City.

17. *Human Rights Abuses in Iraqi Kurdistan Since 1991*, Amnesty International, February 1995. Neither party has ever held anyone to account for the alleged war crimes during this period, which seem to have disappeared today in some kind of unwritten amnesty for participants in the war. When Saddam Hussein and his gang went on trial in Baghdad for crimes against humanity, a Kurdish Web site circulated a picture of the courtroom with Talabani's and Barzani's heads pasted in over those of Saddam and Ali Hassan al-Majid.

18. Cockburn and Cockburn, p. 180.

19. Baer, *See No Evil*, p. 183.

20. Interview with Warren Marik, December 7, 2006, by phone from Washington, D.C.

21. Cockburn and Cockburn, p. 178.

22. Interview with Warren Marik, December 7, 2006, by phone from Washington, D.C., and with Jalal Talabani, October 24, 2006, in Dukan.

23. Interview with Tony Lake, July 18, 2006, in Washington, D.C. Though he has always kept good relations with Tehran, Chalabi might not have been alone in encouraging Iranian participation. One former INC source maintains that Bob Baer made overtures to the Iranians. Baer couldn't talk directly to the Iranian agents who were visiting Salahudin, the source says, but arranged to appear in the lobby of their hotel at an appointed time as a sign that the Americans wanted them in on the plot. This is not the normal INC spinning, but a source who no longer has a good relationship with Chalabi and has no clear motive to implicate Baer.

24. Baer, p. 173, and confirmed by Lake.

25. Interview with Warren Marik, December 7, 2006, by phone from Washington, D.C. Marik couldn't disguise his distaste for the KDP, which sat out the attack and even obstructed it. He described Zebari's checking with Washington about the reality of American support as "snitching." This was years later, but it implies that he and Baer knew they were off the reservation, and shows their frustration with the do-nothing CIA of the Clinton years.

26. Interview with Jalal Talabani, October 24, 2006, in Dukan.

27. Cockburn and Cockburn, p. 184.

28. Graham-Brown, *Sanctioning Saddam*, p. 227.

29. Randal, *After Such Knowledge*, p. 297.

30. Interview with Muhammad Ihsan, October 23, 2006, in Erbil, and then November 16, 2006, by phone from Baghdad.

31. Cockburn and Cockburn, p. 229.

32. Interview with Muhammad Ihsan, November 16, 2006, by phone from Baghdad. Shahwani returned to Baghdad after Saddam fell to head the new Iraqi Mukhabarat, but in 2007 his mostly Sunni organization, again aided by the CIA, was put on the run in Baghdad by rival Shi'ite organizations with Iranian backing.

33. Human Rights Watch; Cockburn and Cockburn, *Saddam Hussein*, p. 233. The Surchis had been jahsh until 1991, but then joined the uprising. When Operation Provide Comfort began, they were considered important enough to be represented in meetings with the coalition; General Jay Garner remembers working with Omar al-Surchi, a hulking sheikh with huge hands, whom he nicknamed "JR" after the character on *Dallas*. When I met Omar Surchi many years later, he was a broken man, the leader of a tribe still subservient to the KDP. He hinted at the story of the 1996 raid, but I suspect he was under some sort of gag order, living in a very comfortable home in Erbil at the pleasure of

the KDP. A few KDP officials arrived to see him about twenty minutes into our meeting, I think by coincidence.

34. Dasko and Fatah, in Lennox, p. 390. This is the same group that Mulla Mustafa Barzani sold out in 1967.
35. Interview with Jalal Talabani, October 24, 2006, in Dukan.
36. Dasko and Fatah in Lennox, p. 390.
37. McDowall, p. 338.
38. Graham-Brown, p. 232.
39. Interview with Ghanim Jawad, November 1, 2006, in London.
40. Interview with Kosrat Rasul, September 18, 2006, in Erbil.
41. Hero Talabani told me the story of her escape from Erbil on October 26, 2006, in Sulimaniya.
42. Graham-Brown, p. 233.
43. Cockburn and Cockburn, p. 245.
44. Interview with Marc Grossman, July 17, 2006, in Washington, D.C.
45. Among the seven thousand, the FBI and INS discovered six suspicious characters, whom they put into detention. Two years later the men still sat in jail, deemed security threats by secret evidence their defense lawyers couldn't see. They were all Ahmed Chalabi's men. Chalabi finally enlisted former CIA chief James Woolsey to help them out—Woolsey took the case pro bono. What he discovered enraged him: the secret evidence was hearsay and conjecture by FBI agents with no background on Iraq. After a scorched-earth campaign through his own Washington Rolodex, Woolsey got a plea deal for five of the men, whereby they could settle in Nebraska with their families while awaiting a charge of entering the United States without a visa—even though the U.S. government had flown them in. One of the men refused to accept the deal on principle—Ali Habib Karim. His offense apparently consisted of being a cousin to Arras Habib Karim, the INC's intelligence chief. Woolsey and Warren Marik both went to bat for Karim, who was finally released after four years in detention. Most of this story was well told by Andrew Cockburn in his article "The Radicalization of James Woolsey" in the *New York Times Magazine*, July 23, 2000. James Woolsey spoke to me about it in an interview on August 15, 2006, by phone from Washington, D.C. But it gets a little worse. A few other of the 1996 evacuees, after living happily for ten years in Harrisonburg, Virginia, got nabbed by the FBI for violating the 2001 USA Patriot Act for running an informal money wiring service, which they used to get money back to their families in Kurdistan.
46. Interview with Qubad Talabani, July 31, 2006, in Washington, D.C.
47. Interview with Clinton National Security Council official, July 20, 2006, in Washington, D.C.
48. Interview with Bruce Riedel, January 10, 2007, by phone from Washington, D.C.
49. Interview with Wayne White, January 7, 2007, by e-mail.

5: Carnival in Limbo

1. Kenneth Katzman, "Iraq: US Regime Change Efforts," Congressional Research Service report for Congress, October 22, 2004.

2. Associated Press, "Turks Say Offensive Killed 1300 Kurds," May 21, 1997.

3. Interview with Stafford Clarry, October 24, 2006, in Erbil.

4. Graham-Brown, *Sanctioning Saddam*, p. 83.

5. Interviews with Kosrat Rasul and with Bafel Talabani, October 21, 2006, in Sulimaniya. And Kosrat wasn't wrong. He didn't see Erbil again until 2003.

6. Mahmoud Othman, "The Washington Agreement," Kurdish Media (www .kurdmedia.com), May 1, 2001.

7. Interview with Najmaldin Karim, June 1, 2006, in Washington, D.C.

8. The International Reporting Project Fellowship at Johns Hopkins School of Advanced International Studies helped me with my first trip to Iraq, providing a travel stipend, but it burned up very quickly. Freelance assignments from the *Christian Science Monitor*, NPR, the *Boston Globe*, and the *Chronicle of Higher Education* helped pay off the trip.

9. There's an old joke told in my native Maine, about a tourist who asks a farmer for directions back to the highway. The tourist follows the directions perfectly and finds himself right back at the old Yankee farmer's porch. "I wanted to see if you knew how to folla' directions before I waste my time giving 'em to you," the farmer explains. I sometimes wonder if the Kurds wanted to see if I could make it in on my own steam before they helped me out.

10. Wolfowitz spoke with me and seven other International Reporting Project fellows at Johns Hopkins School of Advanced International Studies in January 2000. The Sunni from the INC who opposed his plan was Mudhar Shawkat, with whom I spoke on February 7, 2003, in Sulimaniya.

11. Wolfowitz was speaking with my class of IRP fellows in January 2000 at SAIS.

12. Albright was responding to a loaded question on *60 Minutes* on May 12, 1996. The interviewer, Lesley Stahl, brought out the figure of half a million Iraqi children dying in one year because of the sanctions, and Albright didn't dispute the figure, saying only, "The price is worth it." Albright later regretted the remark, and the number was probably inflated. It came from a letter to the British medical journal the *Lancet* by researchers with the U.N. Food and Agricultural Organization (FAO) that was subsequently challenged. A good summary of the controversy is "A Hard Look at Iraq Sanctions" by David Cortright in the *Nation*, December 3, 2001.

13. After the fall of the regime investigators concluded that Saddam Hussein made about $1.7 billion in cash kickbacks and had bribed some U.N. officials and foreign politicians with illegal oil vouchers. The Council on Foreign Relations printed a good primer on Oil-for-Food in the *New York Times*, October 15, 2004, compiled by Sharon Otterman.

14. It's strange how the obvious can be controversial. When I wrote stories about

this trip for various newspapers and radio programs, the term "ethnic cleansing" was still fresh and charged from the massacres of Bosnian Muslims in the former Yugoslavia. Some editors thought it was hyperbolic. Iraq in those days, incomprehensibly, was a nonstory. I was used to yelling at editors about the importance of my pieces about unpronounceable far-off places, and they were used to freelancers like me trying to pump up stories that no one back home cared about. Notably Loren Jenkins from NPR was happy to use the term "ethnic cleansing" for Kirkuk on the air. I had the same problem a few years later trying to call the American presence in Iraq an "occupation," until it became painfully (and legally) obvious.

15. Interview with Qubad Talabani, February 2000, in Washington, D.C. Washington claimed they had had help from Tehran and vice versa.
16. Interview with PUK security official, October 21, 2006, in Sulimaniya.

6: A Most Convenient Foe

1. James Bennet, "Seeing Arafat Hurt by Attack on U.S., Sharon Cancels Plan for Peace Talks," *New York Times*, September 15, 2001.
2. PUK document, September 3, 2001; interview with Qubad Talabani, July 31, 2006, in Washington, D.C.
3. Ayub Nuri, with whom I had the pleasure to collaborate in Iraq from 2003 to 2006, provided me with information and analysis about Kurdish Islamism. Nuri is a reporter and interpreter from Halabja, and he lived through all the events of this book. Specifically his late father formed part of the early IMK and received training in Iran.
4. Interview with Ali Bapir, October 6, 2006, in Sulimaniya.
5. Interview with PUK intelligence official, October 2006, in Sulimaniya.
6. Burke, *Al-Qaeda*, p. 225.
7. Interview with Ali Bapir, October 6, 2006, in Sulimaniya; and PUK documents.
8. Interview with Ayub Nuri, January 20, 2007, by phone from New York City.
9. Interview with PUK intelligence official, October 2006, in Sulimaniya; and Burke, p. 226.
10. PUK document, October 16, 2001.
11. Woodward, *Plan of Attack*, p. 72.
12. Ibid., p. 116.
13. Interview with Barham Salih, October 6, 2006, in Baghdad.
14. Interviews with intelligence officials, January 2003 and October 2006, in Sulimaniya. Also Scott Peterson, "How a Young Iraqi Grew into a Terrorist," *Christian Science Monitor*, November 27, 2002.
15. Woodward, *Plan of Attack*, p. 21.
16. Patrick Tyler, "Kurd Chief Shuns Talks on Ousting Saddam," *New York Times*, August 15, 2002.

17. Interview with Frank Riccardone, then Iraq transition coordinator, U.S. State Department, April 27, 2000, in Washington, D.C.; and with Hamid al-Bayati, SCIRI spokesman, December 9, 2002, in London.

18. This account is from Qubad Talabani, July 31, 2006, in Washington, D.C.

19. Interview with Zalmay Khalilzad, October 25, 2006, in Dukan.

20. Patrick Tyler, "Kurd Chief Shuns Talks on Ousting Saddam."

21. Interview with Dr. Lezgine Ahmed, November 14, 2002, in Washington, D.C.

22. Interview with Najmaldin Karim, November 14, 2002, in Washington, D.C.

23. Ibid.

24. Interview with opposition member, November 6, 2002, in Washington, D.C.

25. George Packer details the process in chapter 3 of his excellent book the *The Assassins' Gate*. I used his book as well as Charles Glass's *The Northern Front* to compare with my own notes and recollections from the London conference.

26. Interview with Zalmay Khalilzad, October 25, 2006, in Dukan.

7: The Northern Front

1. Gerry J. Gilmore, "Disappointed Wolfowitz Still Supports US-Turkish Defense Ties," Armed Services Press Service, May 7, 2003.

2. Packer, *The Assassins' Gate*, p. 96; Galbraith, *The End of Iraq*, p. 83; Woodward, *Plan of Attack*, p. 258.

3. Interview with Hania Mufti of Human Rights Watch, January 10, 2007, by phone from New York City.

4. Abu Wa'el's real name is some variation of Satbun Mahmud Abdul Latif al-Aiai or Saadan Mahmoud Abdul Latif al-Aani, according to Jason Burke and Jonathan Schanzer, respectively.

5. Hassan gave me a rundown of the returning jihadis that was consistent with documents later made available to me in 2006 and detailed in chapter 6.

6. The "Wood Green Ricin Plot" never really became operational, a fact only revealed several years after the tabloid frenzy at the time. Only one of the men was charged—for possession of instructions on how to make the poison. By the time of his trial he was already serving a life sentence for stabbing a policeman. See BBC, "The Ricin Case Timeline," April 13, 2005.

7. Later, when the Iraqi insurgency ramped up, there were at least two incidents of chemical weapons use I am aware of in roadside bombs. The insurgents probably didn't even know the rounds they had daisy-chained together had chemicals in them. When I tried to follow it up with the Pentagon, a spokesperson refused to confirm or deny any cases of unconventional improvised explosive devices (IEDs). I wondered why the Pentagon didn't want to publicize the cases, which, after all, confirmed the existence of chemical weapons. But a few stray rounds would never be a solid ex post facto justification for the invasion, and I think at that point the military was probably more concerned about the issues with morale if soldiers had to worry about getting gassed by the IEDs. It

also wouldn't flatter them that the insurgents had found these weapons by raiding all the munitions dumps left unguarded in the immediate postwar period.

8. Krekar made his most extensive explanations in a February 2003 documentary, *Mullah Krekar*, by Jonathan Miller of Insight News Television. Ali Bapir told me in a 2006 interview in Sulimaniya that Abu Wa'el was a refugee from the Mukhabarat and wanted by Saddam. Bapir said Abu Wa'el had joined Ansar al-Islam because he felt there was no place else he could go.

9. This was slide number 39 of his presentation.

10. Interview with Paul Pillar, August 23, 2006, by phone from Washington, D.C.

11. Abu Musab al-Zarqawi would become the bogeyman of post-invasion Iraq, with every car bomb and suicide attack added to his name. CIA reports and the 9/11 commission eventually decided he had no working relationship with Saddam Hussein, but Vice President Dick Cheney continued to cite the link during the 2004 elections and beyond, still using the wrong town, Khurmal. Secretary of Defense Donald Rumsfeld clung to the notion as well, mentioning it to reporters as late as May 2006 as the enduring justification for invading Iraq. That spring the *Washington Post* reported that the U.S. military had deliberately pumped up Zarqawi's image, hoping to activate Iraqi xenophobia against him and other foreign fighters. When Zarqawi died during a U.S. air strike in June 2006, his removal had no discernible impact on the operational capacity of the insurgency.

12. I missed the bus on that trip—my BBC colleague Jim Muir filmed the visit.

13. I cross-referenced my notes with "Threats and Responses: Northern Iraq; Kurdish Leader Is Assassinated in Militant Raid," the February 10, 2003, *New York Times* article by C. J. Chivers, with whom I shared interviews of survivors at Sulimaniya's main hospital on February 9.

14. Interview with Sami Abd-al-Rahman, February 13, 2003, in Erbil.

15. Interview with Nechirvan Barzani, September 24, 2006, in Erbil.

16. Sedat Ergin, "US Made Concession in Stormy Pre-war Talks," *Hurriyet*, September 23, 2003; and interview with member of the American negotiating team, April 2007, in Washington, D.C.

17. When he made that remark at a press conference, I asked him if the United States might not be guilty of "best-casing." He disagreed.

18. Zebari made these remarks at a press conference on February 15, 2003, in Salahudin.

19. My colleague Ivan Watson reported this story for NPR and got a deluge of angry mail accusing him of supporting the war by villainizing the Iraqi police.

20. Kate Brooks had taken the iconic photo of Karzai, the face of the new, free Afghanistan.

21. Interview with Faruk Loğoğlu, September 11, 2006, in Ankara; and Glenn Kessler and Phillip P. Pan, "Missteps with Turkey Prove Costly," *Washington Post*, March 28, 2003.

22. Gordon and Trainor, *Cobra II*, p. 112.

8: No Friends but the Kurds

1.   Interview with Bafel Talabani, October 21 and 22, 2006, in Sulimaniya.
2.   Woodward, *Plan of Attack*, p. 144.
3.   Ibid., p. 208.
4.   Interviews with PUK officials, October 2006, in Sulimaniya. Also Woodward, *Plan of Attack*, p. 302. The Kasnazanis have refused all my interview requests over the years.
5.   "Kurdish Government Says Its Soldiers Killed Five in a Mistaken Attack," by Borzou Daragahi, AP, March 4, 2003. Daragahi happened on the scene, as did several other journalists (I got there almost an hour later). That evening Daragahi summed up the incident as a case of "driving while bearded."
6.   Glenn Kessler and Phillip P. Pan, "Powell Warns of 'Difficulties' if Turkey Remains Noncompliant," *Washington Post*, April 2, 2003.
7.   Information of the "Rockstars" comes from Woodward's *Plan of Attack*, with many missing details filled in by interviews with PUK officials. The information about the results of those strikes comes from a 2004 *Frontline* documentary "The Invasion of Iraq," by British journalist Richard Sanders, and an interview with Marc Garlasco, July 6, 2007, by phone from New York City. Garlasco was at the Defense Intelligence Agency until April 11, 2003. He quit the DIA in part because he realized that the targets he helped hit with perfect accuracy were all based on faulty intelligence. The United States made fifty precision air strikes aimed at high-value individuals during the war and killed none of them.
8.   Interview with Ali Bapir, October 2006, in Sulimaniya.
9.   Interview with Harry Schute, September 15, 2006, in Erbil. I also relied on Linda Robinson's biography of the Special Forces, *Masters of Chaos*, chapter 13, "Viking Hammer (and the Ugly Baby)."
10. Gordon and Trainor, *Cobra II*, p. 240.
11. The PUK eventually got so frustrated with CIA promises that they went ahead and purchased a cargo convoy full of weapons from Iran, which they unloaded conspicuously in plain view of the CIA station in Qalaat Chowlan, according to George Tenet's book, *At the Center of the Storm*, p. 391.
12. The details of the assault on Ansar al-Islam are reconstructed from interviews with Bafel Talabani and Lahor Talabani, October 21 and 22, 2006, in Sulimaniya; Kurdish translators who requested anonymity; American and Kurdish soldiers interviewed at Girda Drozna the day of the battle, March 28, 2003; and a press conference with Special Forces officers and pesh merga leadership the day after. I also consulted Robinson's *Masters of Chaos*.
13. Robinson, p. 307.
14. Ibid., p. 312.
15. Steve Vogel, "Troops Parachute in to Open a New Front," *Washington Post*, March 27, 2003.

16. Glass, *Northern Front*, p. 223.
17. Gordon and Trainor, p. 317.

9: Deeds to the Promised Land

1. Interview with Ramadan Rashid, October 3, 2006, in Kirkuk.
2. Robinson, *Masters of Chaos*, p. 328.
3. Gordon and Trainor, *Cobra II*, p. 347.
4. Frank Antenori, a retired Special Forces sergeant, wrote an account of the battle with Hans Halberstadt, *Roughneck Nine-One*, p. 173. BBC cameraman Fred Scott kept his camera rolling, and John Simpson reported on the incident immediately, despite both of them suffering minor wounds in the blast.
5. Ibid., p. 390.
6. Ibid., p. 411.
7. Ibid., p. 448.
8. Interview with Saadi Ahmad Pira, September 18, 2006, in Erbil.
9. Talabany, *Arabization of the Kirkuk Region*, p. 45.
10. A source who attended the meeting, and Robinson, p. 332.
11. Information about Mosul is from interviews with Iraqi civilians and U.S. soldiers in the city on May 28, 2003, including Captain Trey Kate, a public affairs officer with the 101st Airborne; interview with Mishan al-Jabouri, May 28, 2003, in Mosul; interview with General David Petraeus, December 16, 2006, by phone from Fort Leavenworth, Kansas; as well as Gordon and Trainor, and Robinson's accounts of Waltemeyer's entrance to the city. Waltemeyer declined several e-mail requests to be interviewed.
12. Interview with KDP general Jemil Mahmoud Suleiyman Besefky, by Mike Tucker, in *Hell Is Over*, p. 23.
13. The Iraqi army wasn't alone. Mushir told me the Mujahideen-e-Khalq Organization (MKO), a group of secular Iranian militants, helped put down the uprising, cementing a reputation for brutality among Kurds. The organization began as part of the 1979 Iranian revolution but split away as clerics consolidated control. Thousands of members of the group, along with their weapons and artillery, took shelter in Iraq. The asylum came with a price—one they didn't mind at first. Saddam Hussein required the MKO members to fight against their countrymen during the Iran-Iraq war. But after the war, Saddam began using the group against his internal enemies. The fighters had little choice—except for Saddam, the world considered the MKO to be made up of terrorists. In their isolation they became more cultlike, keeping to themselves in the town of Khanakeen, one of the Arabized villages just south of the Kurdish safe zone. But the story has more twists. The MKO took advantage of America's twenty-year feud with Tehran, and its political wing in the United States managed to generate support in Washington. In 2002 this political wing

convinced 150 members of Congress to sign a petition supporting the MKO as freedom fighters, the congresspeople not realizing that the State Department considered the MKO terrorists for their bombings against civilians in Iran. According to Linda Robinson, U.S. Special Forces signed a treaty with the MKO in spring of 2003 to keep them out of the fight. They were later cantoned and protected by U.S. troops, and some of the more extreme Iranophobes in the U.S. government favor using them as agents against Tehran.

10: The Believers

1. Interview with Barham Salih, May 27, 2003, in Baghdad.
2. Interview with Jay Garner, September 6, 2006, in Crystal City, Virginia.
3. Brian Knowleton, "US Administrator in Iraq Pledges a 'Mosaic' Government," *International Herald Tribune*, April 22, 2003.
4. Interviews with Jay Garner by phone and in Crystal City, Virginia, September 6, 2006; Dick Naab, July 21 and December 1, 2006, in Crystal City, Virginia; Gordon Rudd, July 19, 2006, in Virginia; and many conversations with Paul Hughes between 2003 and 2006. I also referred to *Iraq and Back* by Kim Olson, who was Garner's executive officer at ORHA, as well as Bob Woodward's *State of Denial* and Peter Galbraith's *The End of Iraq*.
5. Woodward, *State of Denial*, p. 170.
6. Gordon and Trainor, *Cobra II*, p. 475; and Bremer, *My Year in Iraq*, p. 11. Khalilzad took up the job of U.S. ambassador to Afghanistan in November 2003 and would return to head the embassy in Baghdad two years later after a generally well-reviewed tenure in Kabul.
7. Interview with General David Petraeus, December 16, 2006, by telephone from Fort Leavenworth, Kansas.
8. U.S. Army Pfc. James Matise, "Mosul Delegates Hold Iraq's First Election," 101st Airborne Division Web site.
9. Interview with Kosrat Rasul, September 18, 2006, in Erbil. General Petraeus had no recollection of Ramadan's capture when I interviewed him in 2006.
10. L. Paul Bremer, *My Year in Iraq*, p. 43.
11. Interview with Nechirvan Barzani, September 21, 2006, in Erbil.
12. This was related to me by two people who were standing within earshot. The question astounded not only the Kurds in attendance but also Bremer's staff and the U.S. military personnel standing nearby.
13. Ghaith Abdul-Ahad, then working with Patrick Tyler of the *New York Times*, and myself were the three.
14. Human Rights Watch, *Claims in Conflict: Reversing Ethnic Cleansing in Northern Iraq*, August 2004, p. 28.
15. Interview with Colonel William Mayville, May 30, 2003, in Kirkuk.
16. Interview with Harry Schute, September 15, 2006, in Erbil.
17. Interviews with two Bush administration officials involved in the case; interview

with Faruk Loğoğlu, September 11, 2006, in Ankara; Michael Rubin, "A Comedy of Errors: American Turkish Relations and the Iraq War," *Turkish Policy Quarterly*, Spring 2005.

18. Interview with Robert Deutsch, July 26, 2006, in Washington, D.C.
19. Interview with Hussein Sinjari, October 2, 2006, in Sulimaniya.
20. Interview with Muhammad Ihsan, November 16, 2006, by phone from Baghdad; interview with Hania Mufti, January 10, 2007, by phone from New York City; as well as Gwynne Roberts's documentary about Ihsan's journey, "Saddam's Road to Hell," which aired on *Frontline*, January 24, 2006.

11: The Feast of the Sacrifice

1. Interview with CPA staffer, 2006.
2. Interview with Stafford Clarry, October 24, 2006, in Erbil. By that time Clarry was a consultant for the KRG.
3. Bremer, *My Year in Iraq*, p. 258.
4. Interview on October 24, 2006, in Dukan.
5. Details of the TAL negotiations come from numerous interviews with principals, cross-checked against Bremer, *My Year in Iraq*; Galbraith, *End of Iraq*; and Diamond, *Squandered Victory*.
6. Bremer, p. 356.
7. Interview with Barham Salih, October 6, 2006, in Baghdad.
8. Interview with Nawshirwan Mustafa, September 23, 2006, in Sulimaniya.

12: Securing the Realm

1. I spent the days around the election with Rostam as well as several other journalists for security and camaraderie: Ayub Nuri, Nir Rosen, and Lynsey Addario. Nir wrote about Rostam in his book, *In the Belly of the Green Bird: The Triumph of the Martyrs in Iraq* (New York: Free Press, 2006).
2. James Fallows, "Why Iraq Has No Army," *Atlantic Monthly*, December 2005.
3. Interview with former embassy official, July 2006.
4. Thanassis Cambanis, "In Mosul, Kurdish Militia Helps Keep Order," *Boston Globe*, November 18, 2004; Dexter Filkins and Robert F. Worth, "U.S. Troops Set for Final Attack on Fallujah Force," *New York Times*, November 13, 2004.
5. In addition to the census, this was the impression of former U.S. ambassador to Iraq William Eagleton, interviewed August 15, 2006, by phone from Marrakech.
6. Woodward, *State of Denial*, pp. 375, 391.
7. Interview with Zalmay Khalilzad, October 25, 2006, in Dukan, and a press briefing July 13, 2005, in Washington, D.C.
8. SCIRI leader Abdul Aziz al-Hakim suggested the three regions as early as December 2003, in a PBS *Frontline* interview.

9. "Talabani and Ja'fari Have Dispute over Palace in the Green Zone," *Al Sharq al-Awsat*, November 7, 2005; "Mr. Big," by Jon Lee Anderson, *New Yorker*, February 5, 2007. Talabani later made the building available to Ja'fari's successor, another Da'wa party prime minister, Nuri al-Maliki, making it clear that his tiff with Ja'fari was almost purely personal.

10. Interview with Hania Mufti, January 10, 2007, by phone from New York City; Steven Fainaru and Anthony Shadid, "Kurdish Officials Sanction Abductions in Kirkuk," *Washington Post*, June 15, 2005; Human Rights Watch, *Caught in the Whirlwind*, July 2007.

11. Diamond, *Squandered Victory*, p. 343.

12. Michael Howard, "Iraqi Constitution in Trouble as Sunnis Walk Out," *Guardian*, July 21, 2005.

13. Interview with Peter Galbraith, August 30, 2005, by telephone from Erbil.

14. Interview August 30, 2005, by telephone from Erbil.

15. AFP, November 18, 2005, quoting Turkey's NTV.

13: Something That Does Not Love a Wall

1. Robert F. Worth, "Kurds Turn Violent in Protest Against Their Leaders," *New York Times*, March 16, 2006; AFP reporting the same day.

2. Amanj Khalil, "Halabja Protesters May Face Death Penalty," IWPR, March 23, 2006.

3. Farman Abdul Rahman and Zanko Ahmed, "More Alleged Kurdish Spies Revealed," IWPR, ICR no. 221, May 11, 2007.

4. Michael Rubin, "Dissident Watch," *Middle East Quarterly*, Spring 2006; Amnesty International 2006 Annual Report; AFP reporting based in Vienna.

5. By 2007 both American and Kurdish authorities put the number of Kurds who had fled Mosul at around seventy thousand; Edward Wong, "In North Sunni Arabs Drive Out Kurds," *New York Times*, May 30, 2007.

6. I watched on a video link from the press gallery in the Green Zone.

7. I watched but mostly listened, flat on the floor of the nearby BBC office, after our windows shattered in the first explosion. The cement truck stuck in the rubble was caught on security camera from the top of the hotel.

8. Noah Feldman, "Agreeing to Disagree in Iraq," *New York Times* op-ed, August 30, 2005.

9. Unbroadcast portion of interview by Jim Muir in February 2005; also author interviews with high-ranking members of the PUK who requested anonymity.

10. Jonathan Finer, "For Kurds, a Surge of Violence in Campaign," *Washington Post*, December 14, 2005; Kathleen Ridolfo, "RFE/RL Newsline," Radio Free Europe/Radio Liberty, December 9, 2005.

11. "Added Grievances Underlying Kurdish Unrest," Human Rights Watch, March 19, 2004; Gary C. Gambill, "The Kurdish Reawakening in Syria," *Middle East Intelligence Bulletin*, April 2004; and wire reports.

12. "Hoshyar Zebari Denies Involvement in Syria Unrest," AFP, March 22, 2004.

13. Nicholas Blanford, "A Murder Stirs Kurds in Syria," *Christian Science Monitor*, June 15, 2005.

14. Interviews with several Kurdish students; interview with Roya Toloui, June 2, 2006, in Washington, D.C.; purported pictures of "Shwana" before and after his murder at pak-us.com/English/Aug172005-RUK-Shwane.pdf. Further details provided by Roya Boroumand, of the Abdurrahman Boroumand Foundation (abfiran.org), which interviewed Shwana's brother after his murder.

15. Matthew McAllester, "A Renewed Threat," *Newsday*, June 25, 2006.

16. Interviews with Murat Karayilan and Adam Uzun (European spokesman for the PKK), September 30, 2006, in an undisclosed location near the Qandil Mountains.

17. Interview with Mesut Hakki Caşin, February 10, 2005, in Istanbul.

18. Associated Press, April 7, 2007, though Barzani's remarks had been made in an interview with Al-Arrabiyah Television months earlier.

19. Ian Traynor, "Turkey Raises Hopes of Peace with Kurds," *Guardian*, July 24, 2007.

20. Henri Barkey, "A Missed Moment in Iraq," *Washington Post*, October 27, 2007.

21. Interview with Bozan Teken and Mizgin Amed, members of the management council of the PKK (now calling itself the KCK), on October 25, 2007, at a location near the Qandil Mountains.

22. Interview with "Yezdin Sher," a PKK guerrilla, on October 26, 2007, near the Iraqi town of Kashani, along the Turkish border.

23. Interview with Masrour Barzani, October 24, 2007, in Salahudin.

24. Patrick Cockburn wrote about Hasafa's case for the *Independent on Sunday*, "US Frees Iraqi Kidnappers So They Can Spy on Insurgents," March 20, 2005. I met Hasafa in September 2006, in Erbil, and again in October 2007.

25. Nicholas Birch, "Political Rivalries Divide Kurdistan Mobile Networks," *Daily Star* (Beirut), June 7, 2004; Glenn Zorpette, "Iraq Goes Wireless," *Spectrum On Line*, 2006.

Conclusion: Visible Nation

1. John Simpson, "Saddam Hanging Taunts Evoke Ugly Past," BBC News, December 31, 2006.

2. Miller, *Blood Money*, p. 192; Rajiv Chandrasekaran, "Kurds Cultivating Their Own Ties with US," *Washington Post*, April 23, 2007.

3. Interview with Ashti Hawrami, October 30, 2007, in Salahudin. Also many posts by UPI International Energy Resources desk editor Ben Lando at http://iraqoilreport.com.

4. Ben Lando, "U.S. OK's Saddam Law Oil Deals," UPI, October 31, 2007.

5. John F. Burns, "David Petraeus, a General Who Won't Sugarcoat," *International Herald Tribune*, August 13, 2007.

Selected Bibliography

Aburish, Said K. *Saddam Hussein: The Politics of Revenge*. New York: Blooms-
bury, 2000.

Anderson, Liam, and Gareth Stansfield. *The Future of Iraq: Dictatorship,
Democracy, or Division*. New York: Palgrave Macmillan, 2004.

Antenori, Frank, and Hans Halberstadt. *Roughneck Nine-One: The Extraordi-
nary Story of a Special Forces A-Team at War*. New York: St. Martin's
Press, 2006.

Baer, Robert. *See No Evil: The True Story of a Ground Soldier in the CIA's War on
Terrorism*. New York: Three Rivers Press, 2002.

Baker, James A. III. *The Politics of Diplomacy: Revolution, War and Peace,
1989–1992*. New York: Putnam, 1995.

Barzani, Masoud. *Mustafa Barzani and the Kurdish Liberation Movement*. New
York: Palgrave Macmillan, 2003.

Behâ ed-Dîn. *The Life of Saladin*. Elibron Classics (reprint 1897 Committee
of the Palestine Exploration Fund, London). Adamont Media, 2005.

Bremer, L. Paul. *My Year in Iraq: The Struggle to Build a Future of Hope*. New
York: Simon & Schuster, 2006.

Burke, Jason. *Al-Qaeda: The True Story of Radical Islam*. London: I. B.Tauris, 2003.

Bulloch, John, and Harvey Morris. *No Friends but the Mountains: The Tragic
History of the Kurds*. New York: Oxford University Press, 1992.

Chaliand, Gerard, ed. *A People Without a Country: The Kurds and Kurdistan*.
Translated by Michael Pallis. New York: Olive Branch Press, 1993.

Clancy, Tom, with General Carl Stiner and Tony Koltz. *Shadow Warriors: Inside the Special Forces*. New York: Berkley Books, 2003.

Clancy, Tom, with General Tony Zinni and Tony Koltz. *Battle Ready*. New
York: Berkley Books, 2004.

Cockburn, Andrew, and Patrick Cockburn. *Saddam Hussein: An American Obsession*. London: Verso, 2002.

Cuny, Frederick C., with Richard B. Hill. *Famine, Conflict and Response: A Basic Guide*. West Hartford, CT: Kumjarian Press, 1999.

Diamond, Larry. *Squandered Victory: The American Occupation and the Bungled Effort to Bring Democracy to Iraq*. New York: Owl, 2005.

Fromkin, David. *A Peace to End All Peace: Creating the Modern Middle East 1914–1922*. New York: Henry Holt and Company, 1989.

Galbraith, Peter W. *The End of Iraq: How American Incompetence Created a War Without End*. New York: Simon & Schuster, 2006.

Glass, Charles. *The Northern Front*. London: Saqi, 2006.

Gordon, Michael R., and Bernard E. Trainor. *Cobra II: The Inside Story of the Invasion and Occupation of Iraq*. New York: Pantheon, 2006.

Graham-Brown, Sarah. *Sanctioning Saddam: The Politics of Intervention in Iraq*. London: I. B. Tauris, 1999.

Gunter, Michael M. *The Kurdish Predicament in Iraq: A Political Analysis*. New York: St. Martin's Press, 1999.

Hamilton, A. M. *Road Through Kurdistan: Travels in Northern Iraq*. London: I. B. Tauris, 2004.

Hazelton, Fran, ed. *Iraq Since the Gulf War: Prospects for Democracy*. London: Zed Books, 1994.

Hiltermann, Joost R. *A Poisonous Affair: America, Iraq, and the Gassing of Halabja*. Cambridge: Cambridge University Press, 2007.

Isikoff, Michael, and David Corn. *Hubris: The Inside Story of Spin, Scandal and the Selling of the Iraq War*. New York: Crown, 2006.

Izady, Mehrdad. *The Kurds: A Concise Handbook*. Washington, DC: Taylor & Francis, 1992.

Jabar, Faleh A., and Hosham Dawod, eds. *The Kurds: Nationalism and Politics*. London: Saqi, 2006.

Jwaideh, Wadie. *The Kurdish National Movement: Its Origins and Development*. Syracuse, NY: Syracuse University Press, 2006.

Kissinger, Henry. *Years of Renewal*. New York: Touchstone, 1999.

Lennox, Gina, ed. *Fire, Snow and Honey: Voices from Kurdistan*. Melbourne: Halstead Press, 2001.

Makiya, Kanan. *Cruelty and Silence: War, Tyranny, Uprising and the Arab World*. New York: W. W. Norton, 1993.

McDowall, David. *A Modern History of the Kurds*, 3rd edition. London: I. B. Tauris, 2004.

McKiernan, Kevin. *The Kurds: A People in Search of Their Homeland*. New York: St. Martin's Press, 2006.

Miller, T. Christian. *Blood Money: Wasted Billions, Lost Lives, and Corporate Greed in Iraq*. New York: Back Bay Books/Little, Brown and Company, 2006.

Natali, Denise. *The Kurds and the State: Evolving National Identity in Iraq*. Syracuse, NY: Syracuse University Press, 2005.

O'Leary, Brendan, John McGarry, and Khaled Salih, eds. *The Future of Kurdistan in Iraq*. Philadelphia: University of Pennsylvania Press, 2005.

Olson, Kim. *Iraq and Back: Inside the War to Win the Peace*. Annapolis, MD: Naval Institute Press, 2006.

Olson, Robert. *The Goat and the Butcher: Nationalism and State Formation in Kurdistan-Iraq Since the Iraqi War*. Costa Mesa, CA: Mazda, 2005.

Packer, George. *The Assassins' Gate*. New York: Farrar, Straus and Giroux, 2005.

Pollack, Kenneth M. *The Threatening Storm: The Case for Invading Iraq*. New York: Random House, 2002.

Powell, Colin. *My American Journey*. New York: Random House, 1995.

Power, Samatha. *A Problem from Hell: America and the Age of Genocide*. New York: HarperCollins, 2003.

Randal, Jonathan C. *After Such Knowledge, What Forgiveness? My Encounters with Kurdistan*. New York: Farrar, Straus and Giroux, 1997.

Reston, James Jr. *Warriors of God: Richard the Lionheart and Saladin in the Third Crusade*. New York: Doubleday, 2001.

Ricks, Thomas E. *Fiasco: The American Military Adventure in Iraq*. London: Penguin, 2006.

Robinson, Linda. *Masters of Chaos: The Secret History of the Special Forces*. New York: Public Affairs, 2004.

Rosen, Nir. *In the Belly of the Green Bird: The Triumph of the Martyrs in Iraq*. New York: Free Press, 2006.

Rudd, Gordon W. *Humanitarian Intervention: Assisting the Iraqi Kurds in Operation Provide Comfort, 1991*. Washington, D.C.: Department of the Army, 2004.

Safire, William. *Safire's Washington*. New York: Times Books, 1980.

Saleem, Hiner. *My Father's Rifle: A Childhood in Kurdistan*. Translated by Catherine Temerson. New York: Farrar, Straus and Giroux, 2005.

Schmidt, Dana Adams. *Journey Among Brave Men*. Boston: Little, Brown and Company, 1964.

Schwarzkopf, H. Norman. *It Doesn't Take a Hero*. New York: Bantam, 1992.

Talabany, Nouri. *Arabization of the Kirkuk Region*. London: Khak Press and Media Center, 1999.

Tenet, George. *At the Center of the Storm: My Years at the CIA*. New York: HarperCollins, 2007.

Thornhill, Teresa. *Sweet Tea with Cardamom: A Journey Through Iraqi Kurdistan*. London: Pandora, 1997.

Tripp, Charles. *A History of Iraq*. Cambridge: Cambridge University Press, 2000.

Tucker, Mike. *Among Warriors in Iraq: True Grit, Special Ops, and Raiding in Mosul and Fallujah*. Guilford, CT: Lyons Press, 2005.

——. *Hell Is Over: Voices of the Kurds After Saddam*. Guilford, CT: Lyons Press, 2004.

Woodward, Bob. *Bush at War*. New York: Simon & Schuster, 2002.

——. *Plan of Attack*. New York: Simon & Schuster, 2004.

——. *State of Denial*. New York: Simon & Schuster, 2006.

Yildiz, Kerim. *The Kurds in Iraq*. London: Pluto Press, 2004.

Acknowledgments

First and foremost, thanks to all of the people who generously gave me their time and lent me their thoughts, often complete strangers in the middle of terrible chaos. They must believe that telling their stories might help their world; may their faith not always be in vain.

I would have been deaf and dumb without Ayub Nuri, Shaho Hawezi, Rebeen Azad, Birzo Abdel Qadir, Yerevan Adham, Ali Adeeb, Yilmaz Akinci, and Omar Abdulkader. Thanks to Rebeen for his company and for answering so many questions by e-mail. Omar gave endless amounts of knowledge, encouragement, and friendship. Ayub provided comments on drafts and years of insight as he progressed from fixer to family. Thanks to IWPR for putting me up in Sulimaniya and to Sohini Sarkar for smuggling out a disc of Omar's excellent photos.

At the BBC I'd like to thank the staff of the PRI/WGBH coproduction, who are the finest bunch with whom a hack could ever bash out a day's news. On the ground in Iraq many crews at the Baghdad bureau gracefully put up with an American in their midst who always claimed to be working for the BBC; it is a great honor to work with you all. Thanks to Jim Muir for lending his recollections, photographs, and good humor.

I owe a debt to the International Reporting Project at SAIS, where John Schidlovsky, Louise Lief, and Denise Melvin helped me get out the door on my first trip to Kurdistan. Before I even met him in Jordan, Stephen Glain gave me the journalistic shirt off his back and set me up with Abu Ahmed in Baghdad (he also came up with my working title "Prodigal Republic"). Scott Peterson also gave a warm welcome in Amman.

Najmaldim Karim gave his time graciously and let me study at the

Washington Kurdish Institute, where Tara Welat worked in the summer of 2006. Michelle Lunato, Rich Greene, and William Walsh helped me survive the embed system; and on the Kurdish side thanks to Leslyanne Robson, Kamran Karadaghi, and Hiwa Osman.

Matt McAllester, Eliza Griswold, and Peter Bergen all helped me get to the process of finding an agent and generously gave me advice on pitching. I'm lucky to call all three of them friends, and while I'm at it, there is no man on earth blessed with better friends than I: who put me up for weeks when I come through London, Washington, Bogotá, Istanbul, Boston, and New York; who took time out to make pancakes, play chess or water polo, or dance salsa in the middle of a war; who picked me up from helipads at four A.M.; who dropped everything to help when I needed it. No less to the folks who help to shine away the cloud I cast when I come back home in rough shape—thank you.

Ayub Nuri and Hard J. Lawrence read this book very early on and provided excellent advice and corrections. Thanks to Annie Manuel and Billie Mascioli, Norm Thurston, Karen Hanrahan and Dean Wagner, Zeynep Erdim, Richard Sanders, Brian Morrison, Mike Amitay, Anderson Allen, Jo Floto, and my brother, Tim, for reading the drafts and sharing their comments.

Robert Guinsler at Sterling Lord took a chance on this book and gave me great encouragement. George Gibson at Walker & Company also believed in this project and was a pleasure to craft it with.

My mother and father can take credit for everything I've managed to do right with this book (the errors are mine), and they also made possible a splendid winter up in Maine, writing. Lastly, mil gracias a Señorita Sarah Han.

Index

NOTE: An *n* after the page number indicates an endnote or footnote.

A Note on the Author

DAVID AQUILA "QUIL" LAWRENCE is Middle East correspondent for BBC/PRI's *The World*. He has reported for NPR, the *Los Angeles Times*, and the *Christian Science Monitor*. He has won awards for his work on Colombia, Sudan, and Iraq. This is his first book.